HITLER'S ENFORCERS

HITLER'S ENFORCERS

The Gestapo and the SS Security Service in the Nazi Revolution

GEORGE C. BROWDER

New York   Oxford
Oxford University Press
1996

Oxford University Press

Oxford   New York

Athens   Auckland   Bangkok   Bombay   Bogota   Buenos Aires
Calcutta   Cape Town   Dar es Salaam   Delhi
Florence   Hong Kong   Istanbul   Karachi
Kuala Lumpur   Madras   Madrid   Melbourne
Mexico City   Nairobi   Paris   Singapore
Taipei   Tokyo   Toronto

and associated companies in

Berlin   Ibadan

Published by Oxford University Press, Inc.
198 Madison Avenue, New York, New York 10016

Oxford is a registered trademark of Oxford University Press

Library of Congress Cataloging-in-Publication Data
Browder, George C., 1939–
Hitler's enforcers : the Gestapo and the SS security service in the
Nazi revolution / George C. Browder.
p.   cm.
Includes bibliographical references and index.
ISBN 0-19-510479-X
1. Germany.   Geheime Staatspolizei—History.
2. Nationalsozialistische Deutsche Arbeiter-Partei. Schutzstaffel—
History.   3. Germany—Politics and government—1933–1945.
I. Title.
DD256.5.B67984   1996
363.2'83'094309043—dc20   95-37252

1   3   5   7   9   8   6   4   2

Printed in the United States of America
on acid-free paper

In Memoriam
Marcus W. Orr, mentor
Elma Clark Browder, mother

Terminology and Style

Both the Nazis and the German bureaucracy employed long titles and designations. Whenever possible, I have translated them into a foreshortened English. For brevity, I employ standardized German abbreviations in the notes. The reader will find a list of such abbreviations on pages 282–285.

Critics have rightly complained that the use of standard German abbreviations results in a confusing alphabet soup. So in the text I limit them to a few inescapable terms that are central to the story. Surely everyone will recognize SS and Gestapo, and those who do not know SD will learn it quickly. NS or NSDAP frequently are desirable alternatives to Nazi and Nazi Party. It is my goal to add Sipo (Sicherheitspolizei) and Kripo (Kriminalpolizei) to the language of scholarly and popular awareness of the Third Reich and the Holocaust. The generic-sounding English words "security police" and "criminal or detective police" will never carry the appropriate force. Consider what would be lost if one had to say political police or secret police instead of *Gestapo*. Sipo should be as familiar as KGB or FBI.

Sipo and SD formed an amalgam, so I refer to "it" in the singular whenever that sense is intended. Throughout, I capitalize words like Party and Movement when they stand for the Nazi Party or Movement. Thus, they can be distinguished from other parties or movements and from the generic terms without repetitive use of longer titles. Likewise, proper nouns like Party Leadership are translations of titles like Partei Reichsleitung, a branch of the Party structure, and are not generic references.

I employ "ironic quotation marks" to set off certain words and phrases. These are not necessarily specific quotations, but rather terms and phrases commonly used by the subjects under study. I hope to emphasize the different normative framework in which thought and speech increasingly occurred in Nazi Germany and especially inside Sipo and SD. It seems necessary to remind the reader that this was an all-pervasive imagery or that these words often had different meaning than in our own normative contexts. I make no cheap shots at NS newspeak. This language constituted a normative reality unfortunately no more ridiculous to the immersed than similar norms in our perceptions of reality.

Acknowledgments

When one accumulates material for a book over a twenty-seven-year period, the obligations to acknowledge assistance become insurmountable. Thirty-three archives and a half-dozen libraries and consortia from around the world provided the necessary support staff for such research. I can only acknowledge these many people in the collective and hope that they will not be offended by my failure to name them individually.

Work began on the American Historical Association's microfilm of the captured German documents, carried over to the National Archives, and then the Bundesarchiv and the Geheime Staatsarchiv, Berlin-Dahlem. The most long-standing support came from the former U.S. Document Center at Berlin under the direction of Richard Bauer, Daniel Simon and David Marwell, consecutively. The Baden-Württemberges Hauptstaatsarchiv Stuttgart; Generallandesarchiv Karlsruhe and Staatsarchive, Freiburg and Ludwigsburg; the Bayerischen Staatsarchive, Bamberg, München, Nürnberg, and Würzburg; the Staatsarchiv Bremen; the Hessisches Hauptstaatsarchiv Wiesbaden and Staatsarchiv Darmstadt; the Niedersächsischen Staatsarchive, Aurich, Bückeburg, Hannover, Oldenburg, Stade, and Wolfenbüttel; the Nordrhein-Westfälischen Staatsarchive, Detmold, Düsseldorf, and Münster; the Rheinland-Pfalz Landeshauptarchiv Koblenz; and the Russian Center for the Preservation of Historical Documentary Collections, Moscow, all provided invaluable support. Most recently, Brewster Chamberlin and Carl Modig of the U.S. Holocaust Memorial Museum's Research Institute Archive chose me as consultant for microfilming at the former Osoby Archive, Moscow, and have facilitated access to their growing collection of microfilm.

Shlomo Aronson, Peter Black, David Kahn, and Robert Koehl all provided generous access to their own research sources. Financial assistance and other support have come from the National Endowment for the Humanities, the Research Foundation of the State University of New York, the Committee on Research and Creativity, Dean Sharon Zablotney, and the interlibrary loan staff of Reed Library, SUNY Fredonia. Charlotte Morse compiled the two maps of Germany.

William S. Allen, MindaRae Amiran, Robert Gellately, Harold Gordon, George Iggers, Michael Kater, Robert Koehl, Donald McKale, and Charles Sydnor, Jr. made suggestions for the improvement of the manuscript at various stages of its development. Their suggestions proved invaluable, but of course they bear no responsibility for any remaining shortcomings.

Contents

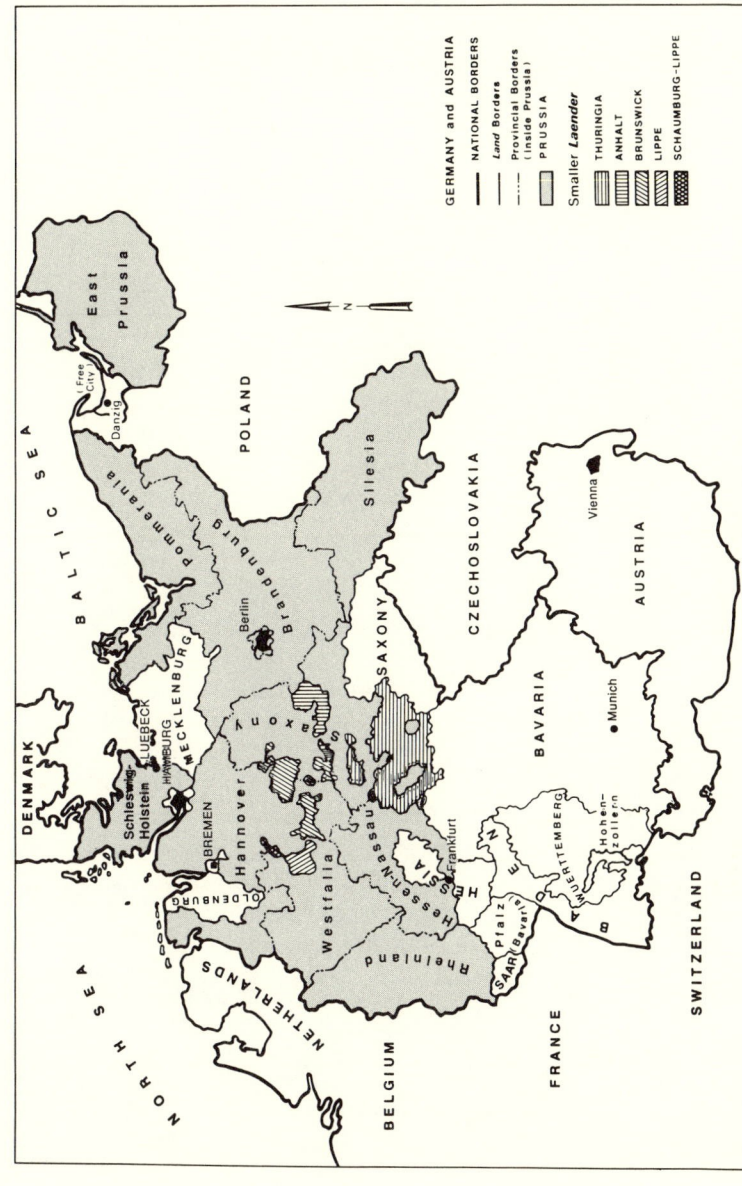

Map 1 Germany and Austria. Reprinted from George C. Browder, *Foundations of the Nazi Police State*, copyright © 1990 by the University Press of Kentucky, by permission of the publisher.

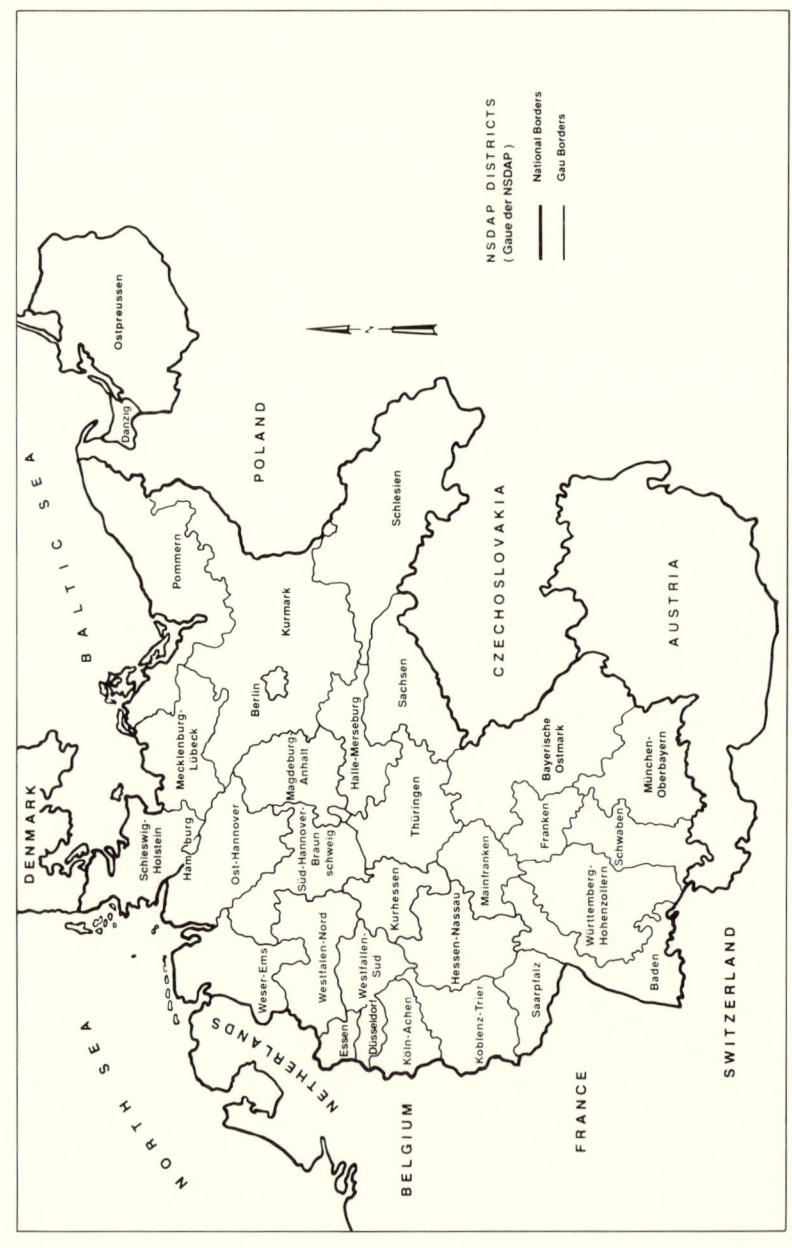

Map 2 NSDAP Districts.

HITLER'S ENFORCERS

Introduction

In 1936, when Heinrich Himmler, already Reichsführer of the SS, became chief of all German police, he created a special branch for the detective police which he designated Security Police—Sicherheitspolizei, or Sipo. Sipo reunited the political police, or Gestapo (Geheime Staatspolizei), with the regular detectives, or Kripo (Kriminalpolizei). As their chief, Himmler appointed SS General Reinhard Heydrich, who was also head of the SS Security Service, or SD (Sicherheitsdienst). Heydrich's joint command then became known as Sipo and SD, but that was much more than a logical alignment of complementary Nazi and state agencies (chart A).

In 1990, I published *Foundations of the Nazi Police State: The Formation of SIPO and SD* as the first part of a study of the creation of that organization and its place in the Nazi police state.[1] I hoped to bring more serious attention to Sipo and SD—more significant in its totality than the Gestapo, a component that has overshadowed it in popular and scholarly attention. This volume completes that study, and I hope that it will contribute to our understanding of both the Nazi experience and the emerging field of police history.

The previous book focused on the political power struggle in which the Nazi police state was created and on the goals of those who created it. Here I shall pursue, in contrast to that "history from above," an internal history, or "history from below." I concluded the first book by suggesting that "the membership of the separate agencies in Sipo and SD were bound together in an uneasy union, but in such a way as to drive them not only to fulfill their missions but also to contribute to the further growth of police-state terrorism and ultimately genocide."[2] The peculiar relationship among the members helped draw them into their future roles. I shall pursue that theme in this volume.

Robert Gellately has noted that all studies of the Nazi police-terror system from the top down have failed to show how the terror actually

Chart A   Ad Hoc Union of SIPO and SD as It Was
Originally Created in 1936

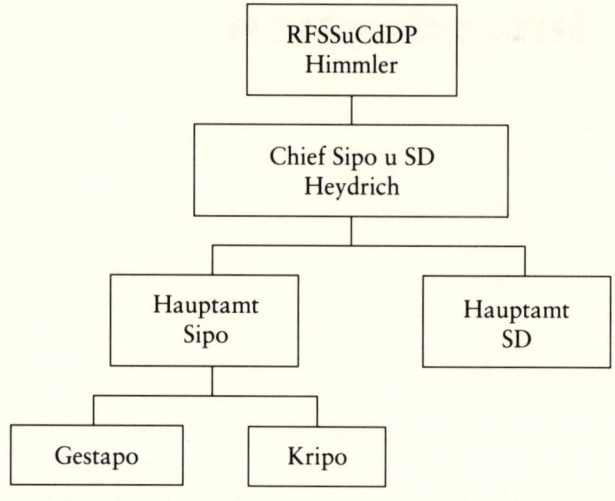

Semi-Legal Organization of SIPO and SD as It Was Finally
Created in 1939

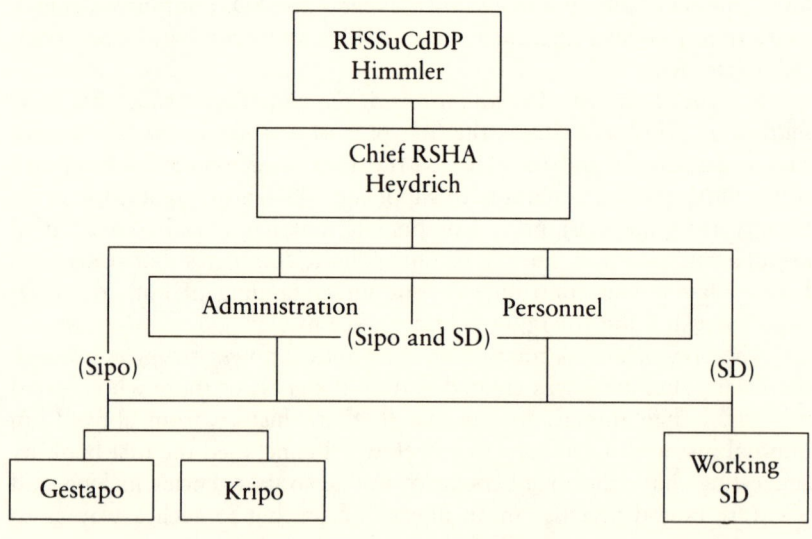

operated. To correct this failure, he and a few German scholars have
been revealing the disturbing extent to which the Gestapo operated successfully only because of public support or consent.[3] Although this
should come as no surprise to any student of law enforcement, historical analysis has generally overlooked this reality.

Along similar lines, I seek to unravel "the mediations between policy makers, policy enforcers, and ordinary citizens."[4] I shall focus primarily on the enforcers—not only their mediations between policy makers and the public, but also their roles as de facto policy makers that resulted from that mediation. It is at this level that one must test one major vector in the thrusts of functional interpretations of police-state terrorism and Nazi racial programs.

The popularly held image of everything the Nazis did as simply a product of Hitler's demonic intentions, executed by blindly obedient Nazi fanatics, was the primary target of functionalist revision. Functionalists believed that they revealed better those complex processes at work in all societies that might recreate any component of the Nazi horror. The current debate centers on a synthesis of functionalist and intentionalist interpretations that at least agrees on the evolutionary nature of most Nazi organizations and plans. Although the better analyses on both sides are now more sophisticated and contain syntheses of a higher order, disagreement remains over the role of "intentions" and when they were formed. Most progress has come, however, when scholars rise above the false dichotomies (Hitlercentric vs. polycratic, or intentionalist vs. functionalist) or monocausal focuses like antisemitism.[5] Rather than being bound to a particular school, scholars should employ these perspectives consciously as paradigms—tools of analysis to be used as the situation warrants. I use the functionalist approach as the most promising for an underside perspective on Sipo and SD, although one must never lose sight of the roles played by intentions and ideological consensus.

The Nazis in general and Hitler in particular came to power fully intending to create a police state—a widely held goal not only among Nazis but also among many of their nationalist allies. The distinction I make is between a police state in general and the SS-police state as it was ultimately created. It was Himmler's SS-police system that I refer to as "the Nazi police state." That, I argue, was not the intention of the Nazis' allies or even of most Nazis outside Himmler's circle. It is unclear exactly how much of the ultimate SS-police state was intended by Himmler or any of his subordinates. Hitler was inclined toward something on that order, and his sentiments inspired its creation. Consequently, Hitler did not have to be persuaded to adopt a police-state system like the one Himmler offered. The problem was that Hitler had to violate his principle of divide and rule and to concentrate enormous power in Himmler's hands in order to get Himmler's police state. Thus, his decision to do so required a special juncture of concrete needs created by his own dreams with persuasive arguments from Himmler and his supporters.

Although I argue that the Nazi police state was only nascent by 1934, a terroristic police state clearly came into being quickly in 1933. The relatively uncontrolled terror of 1933–1934 could be neither maintained nor used effectively for Nazi imperialism or genocide. These required the SS-police state.

The significance of these distinctions is central to many important questions about the Third Reich, not least of which are the evolution of Nazi war aims and the origins of the Final Solution. If, as I argue, Hitler did not simply call on Himmler to establish the SS-police state, which was essential to achieving his intentions, how could he have conceived of pursuing them without such a police state? Was not the emergence of such an instrument of power necessary for Hitler to move from inclinations to intentions? What role then did its availability play in such a move?

In neither of my books has it been possible to carry the analysis to the level of Hitler. In *The Foundations of the Nazi Police State*, by analyzing developments at the level of Himmler, Heydrich, immediate lieutenants, and leading rivals, I concluded that before 1936 Himmler built the SS-police state with only intermittent support from Hitler.[6] It grew from Himmler's personal interpretations of Hitler's goals and needs. Only in 1936 did Hitler recognize Himmler's version of the police state as so essential to his goals that he was willing to reward Himmler with a veritable monopoly of police power. Based on this conclusion, I argue that Hitler had not yet formulated clear lines of action that required the existence of the SS-police system for execution. Only after the potentials of the SS-police system became apparent could he realistically formulate such lines of action. Furthermore, in 1936 it was his anticipation of foreign policy brinkmanship and war in the next decade that necessitated the SS-police machinery for domestic control. It was only after the emergence of that machinery that the potential for radical solutions to "racial problems" came into view as a correlated result.

This seems to contradict the conventional wisdom that well before 1933 Hitler was possessed by such a pathological hate for Jews that he conceived and occasionally alluded to the destruction of the entire "race." There is no need to deny this image in order to pursue an evolutionary analysis of the development of Nazi horrors. Conventional psychological theory requires an evolutionary analysis of developments in the human mind as it moves from unconscious preoccupations to conscious intentions, then to goals, to plans, and finally to their execution. One will not feel any "action tension" to deal with a problem until one has perceived that the problem can be attacked effectively.[7] To arrive at the Final Solution, the machinery for its achievement had to be at least perceptible and already moving in that direction. There had to be many steps in the process before final plans achieved the full extreme of the subconscious drives.

Central to my position is the premise that Hitler's extreme hates and fears of Jews operated at an unconscious level, and were clothed at the conscious level in "rational" theories of social-Darwinistic racism, eugenics, and Judeobolshevism. Unrealistic fantasies of genocide lurked below, along with more rabid expressions of hate and fear, and they all bubbled up occasionally, especially in moments of emotional fury or exultation. But such fantasies could not emerge regularly into the conscious mind; other realities prevailed and required too much "rationality" to permit "plans" to execute the unimaginable. Talk of merely expelling the Jews was realistic enough. Only after the means were in place and the many details worked out through practical, limited steps at problem solving could the unimaginable become imaginable. Only then could the conscious mind formulate "intentions" and move toward planning their fulfillment.

The major breakthrough in that direction was the unification of SS and police. Although Hitler embraced this arrangement for rational, political-power reasons, he may also have moved "like a sleepwalker" toward his more unimaginable fantasies. Meanwhile, the structures and methods of the SS and police state evolved from below functionally, and it took several years after 1936 for that machinery to evolve in such detail that the Final Solution could become rationally and consciously a plan. Well before that, however, as the new consensus reality of radical anti-Semitism prevailed, many others would be drawn along with their Führer, like sleepwalkers, toward that end.[8] The planners, whether working toward conscious or unconscious goals, and the functionaries below, solving particular problems to achieve more limited goals, were symbiotic culprits in the crimes of a complex human system. The better the functionaries were at solving incremental problems, the more extreme the planners could become in setting goals.

This particular model for the evolution of Nazi intentions is central to my overall interpretation. Unfortunately, it is not directly testable at any level of research. It is, however, the most consistent, comprehensive interpretation that I can find for integrating the convincing scholarship and available evidence from all sides.

One main component of intentionalist interpretation centers on the obedient execution of the Führer's will. Intentionalists do not deny that most Nazis failed to share all his preoccupations—most resisted executing "unnecessary" inhumanities, and only some contributed to them spontaneously. Rather, they hold that the Nazis shared an ideological consensus that allowed them to be drawn along with him to the same extremes. I argue that the ideological "consensus" among Nazis that is generally offered as the bond that tied all to Hitler's will is better characterized as an ideological "conjunction."[9] It could thus reach well beyond a relatively few radically racist Nazis to suck in vast numbers of allies. No one has argued that there was a consensus to pursue a Final Solution to the Jewish "problem" like the one ultimately employed. There was also no consensus to build the actual police state that Himmler built. Rather, a broader cultural conjunction of assumptions, values, and beliefs characterized the antiliberal, anti-Marxist, nationalist, xenophobic, social-Darwinistic, culturally reactionary mentality that created a favorable climate for some type of police state and for extreme reactions to perceived racial, genetic, cultural, and ideological threats.

The fanatic "Nazi consensus" of which many speak existed among a minority. An anti-Semitic consensus of sorts was indeed created by Hitler with the support of other extremely anti-Semitic Nazis. This had not been a major preoccupation for most, however, until they had been drawn into the newly created consensus reality that emerged gradually after 1934. Before that, the ideological conjunction that did exist among the broad base of Nazis and those in its controlled agencies like the police contained many points of general agreement, including a tradition of "judeophobia." But it did not even approach the sort of preoccupation that called for a "solution to the Jewish problem." [10]

A similar area of conjunction was the need for more police authority to preserve society from a wide range of perceived threats. This conjunction included almost unlimited police powers for dealing with the enemies of society. It sloughed off the problem of distinguishing between the good citizen and the threat. Since the good citizen should have nothing to fear, any demand to protect his rights against the police state were misguided, liberal obstacles to a healthy society. Within this conjunction, the totalitarian extremes of this police-state logic were not usually perceived as something to be imposed on the general population. Rather, it was a totalitarianism of consensus that all right-minded Germans would accept. Coercion would be needed only against un-German elements. Most Nazis below Hitler did not willingly embrace the ultimate reality of Himmler's variant. Even Himmler preferred idealized versions of its ugly reality. That reality was created as much from below by functional pressures as it was from above by intentions and shared values. A significant part of that evolution from below occurred within Sipo and SD.

Although Himmler and Heydrich created Sipo and SD in an image that they evolved during the early years, no organization can be shaped and molded from above like an inanimate object. No totalitarian state, not even Stalin's often-purged system, has successfully eliminated either the human component of its machinery or its objects (the public). No matter how disciplined, the humans who make up instruments of power must interpret and apply the blueprints received from above to specific, everchanging contexts. Furthermore, the formulators on high must depend largely on those below them for interpretations of the changing contexts to which they must respond (i.e., the public: supportive, compliant or resistant). This book will detail how the members of the emerging Sipo and SD, at higher, middle, and lower levels, shaped their organizations at least as decisively as did their chiefs.

The first phase of the police state occurred between 1931 and 1934, when the SD emerged and Himmler and Heydrich staked out their claims for its future mission. During that same period, the police had to cope with the growing reality that they were coming under Nazi control. From 1934 through 1937, SD members suffered from crises of identity, resulting partly from their increasing ties to the police. Simultaneously, the police detectives found their professional status, image, and mission threatened by real NS control in the virulent form of SS command and penetration.

To unravel these internal developments and their significance, this book focuses on the emerging structures and the men of the three components of Sipo and SD; their organizational environments; how missions and institutional images influenced recruitment and development; the sort of men involved; how they perceived themselves; and how they justified or coped with their involvement in the emerging SS–police–concentration-camp system.

After establishing the ethos of each component, one can explore the impact of their fusion. The unique mixture of competition and cooperation and the complex interplay between different institutional images produced internal dynamics that may explain much of the historical role of Sipo and SD. When these internal dynamics are understood in the context of the external pressures created by Nazi radicals, then one of the alleged failures of functionalist arguments can be overcome. The connection between the role of pressures created by radicals to solve the Jewish problem and the ad hoc improvisations of the functionaries that made the Holocaust possible becomes more clear.[11]

Unraveling the nature of the personnel requires separating the professional policeman, whether he became Nazi or SS or not, from the SD members who entered Sipo and SD from other channels. Different pressures worked on each, and different appeals drew each into Sipo and SD. Within each group, further subdivisions provide greater insight into what drew diverse individuals into their involvements. Most important, one must test the widely held assumptions about these men and the several theories commonly offered to explain their availability for atrocities. One must also call on a wider range of social and psychological theories that argue that many Nazi experiences could be duplicated in more "normative" modern societies than Germany.[12] Such theories must be tested against the complex reality of "the policemen" and the "SS men" who actually made up Sipo and SD.

Before we can reasonably argue about whether the decisions made between 1939 and 1942 that led to unbelievable, organized mass murder were driven more by intentions than by functional developments, we need to know more about the time and the institutions in which both the intentions and functional pressures had their genesis. Toward that end, I continue to focus this analysis on the foundations of the Nazi police state and the formative period of Sipo and SD, 1931–1937.

ONE

Inside the Gestapo

In 1936, when Hitler appointed Reichsführer SS Heinrich Himmler as Chief of the German Police, Himmler assumed command of Germany's first unified Reich police force. Himmler proceeded to fuse his SS with those police to create the Nazi police state—which became more than simply a police state. The fusion of the Reich police force with the SS gave the Himmlerian police state a special edge that enabled it to fulfill Hitler's dreams of unlimited power to such a degree that he could pursue his ideological conclusions to heretofore unimaginable extremes.

Himmler immediately divided his police into two branches, the uniformed or Order Police (Ordnungspolizei, or Orpo) and the plainclothes detectives or Security Police (Sipo). Since 1933, these detectives had been divided into two branches that became the two divisions of Sipo, the Gestapo and the Kripo. The Gestapo, formerly the political police of the various German states, were now united into a Reich-wide force for ferreting out and eliminating all opposition to the Nazi regime. The regular detective police, Kripo, were also united for the first time as a Reich-wide force for controlling and eliminating all other threats to "social order."

Combined in the Sipo, they came under the command of SS-General Reinhard Heydrich, who was also chief of the Security Service of the SS, the SD. Thus Sipo became fused with the SS through its special intelligence branch, the SD. The effects of the marriage of Sipo and SD on all of its members is the focus of this book. That special combination of agencies became the linchpin of the Nazi horror. Its members became Hitler's executive enforcers and social engineers. Without them, it is hard to imagine the inhumane extremes of the Third Reich.

Yet close examination will reveal that most of these men would probably have served similar agencies among the western allied powers just as well as their counterparts actually did, and without any infamy. Some would have been our heroes rather than the villains they became. This study is a search for the organizational and functional forces in Sipo and SD that not only turned these men into Hitler's enforcers but involved them creatively in the worst horrors of the Third Reich.

The Weimar Police

Most of the police in Himmler's SS empire came from the professional police of pre-Nazi Germany. Even though many joined the NS Movement, and even became SS-SD members, the vast majority identified themselves primarily as policemen. Toward an analysis of these men, one should evaluate and apply as appropriate the sociopsychological theories that have developed from the study of modern police. When applied to the German experience between 1918 and 1945, some of these theories provide likely explanations for police behavior in the Weimar and Nazi eras. Yet one must be cautious when applying theories derived in one time and place to another. The body of theory in question developed largely from research on American police and then expanded, with appropriate modifications, to other societies within the Anglo-Saxon legal tradition. Although many German and Austrian sociologists have few qualms about applying much of this theory to their own contemporary police,[1] applying it to Weimar-era police requires caution.

Much of this theory revolved around two assumptions: that a certain type of personality is drawn to careers in policing; and that the roles the police play and the environment in which they operate have predictable effects on their personalities or behavior. Subsequent research has indicated little or no significant difference between police and the general population, and has revealed great heterogeneity among policemen.[2] Likewise, research focusing on the socialization of policemen does not clearly support arguments for increased authoritarianism resulting from police service.[3] The structure of police work itself deserves more of our attention. With that in mind, a focus on the social-psychological pressures of police work in general and the specific police-work environments of Weimar and early Nazi Germany should have more immediate value for this study.

One body of theory about police subcultures originally argued that role conflicts produce in the police a sense of alienation or isolation from the public at large. The resulting police subculture manifests elements of a "pariah subculture."[4] The role conflicts in question are complex. To begin with, the police simply cannot enforce all laws or official directives; besides, society never intends for all its laws to be applied literally to every situation. Therefore, the police must apply the law selectively, leading to role conflicts. For instance, they must comply reasonably with the interests of both the political and social power structures in which they work. Furthermore, the public displays ambivalence about both the police and law enforcement.

Friction between any society and its "out-groups" also creates severe role conflicts for the police. Ethnic minorities or the lowest strata may not identify with or benefit sufficiently from society and, therefore, may have less commitment to living by its rules. Society expects the police to control such out-groups. Although society usually prefers to remain oblivious to how this is done, the police can find themselves caught in a severe clash of expectations.[5]

As a policeman becomes aware of hostility and the inconsistent standards by which he is judged, he can feel sharply any contrasts between the level of esteem he receives and his perception of the important role he plays. When he receives inadequate external recognition, he may develop other standards by which to evaluate himself.[6] The police may develop a "code" different from that of their society. Specifically, their subculture can encourage mechanisms that protect the police from criticism.

The weakness of such theory is that it minimizes the forces that integrate rather than isolate the police, and it predicts uniform responses. The exact nature of the social pressures on the police, especially the extent of their alienation from society varies greatly in time and place.[7]

Any occupational group like the police should develop a subculture: they undergo a common program of training emphasizing teamwork, work together closely, socialize frequently among themselves, and are easily identifiable as a special group. In turning one's attention to the police of Weimar Germany, the question is whether their subculture was merely a strong occupational group identity, or whether it acquired any of the pariah-like qualities of the model.

Cross-cultural studies have shown significant differences that should affect police subcultures, perhaps preventing anything like that observed in the U.S.[8] Yet conclusions that high levels of professionalism, self-regulation, and public respect would mitigate against police responses in Germany that resemble American models would be unfounded. As with other aspects of conventional generalizations about German society and culture, the purported submissiveness to police authority does not hold up to scrutiny.[9] Although the Weimar-era police may have achieved admirable levels of professionalism, they were subject to many public pressures and confrontations that would turn them inward against a perceived "hostile public." Recorded behavior resembling that predicted by the model argues persuasively for its existence in Weimar Germany.

Innumerable variables must affect application of such theory to a historical situation. Among American police forces, attitudes and behavior vary greatly, depending on the nature of the department, its organization, relation to local authority, discipline, training, and the like.[10] The continental legal tradition, based on law codes, created a law-enforcement environment different from Anglo-Saxon society with its common law tradition.[11] As an institution, the police had significantly different history and traditions. Finally, the police of the Weimar period were unionized, thus creating other variables that could affect subculture formation.[12]

To adapt this theory to Weimar Germany, one must look to the historical specifics. The most obvious variable that should have been at work was the high level of social and political turmoil. The less homogeneous a society, the more inconsistent its values, and the sharper its social and political crises, the more the police should experience role conflicts. Not only was German society still markedly stratified, but the social and political disorder and the economic crises created significant, often openly subversive, out-groups and a radically polarized society. Polarization existed not only between classes but also among the political and ideological factions that would alternately control the police.[13] Consequently, a number of specific conflicts should have generated police-subculture responses, and there is evidence of the specific form they took.

Any police subculture must provide the policeman with a positive self-image, internal rewards and recognition, and mechanisms that project a positive police image and protect the police from external criticism. In the model, one key mechanism is secrecy. To the extent that role conflicts dictate police behavior that might produce criticism, policemen come under pressure to keep such behavior secret. From the day he enters the force, the policeman encounters overt and covert indoctrination into the secrecy mechanisms of the subculture. This sense of unity against the outside can go so far as to conceal corruption and brutality to defend the honor of the corps.[14]

Most contemporary comparisons of Weimar German and American police noted a marked lack of corruption and brutality in the German forces. If true, the professional self-image held by the German police apparently created subculture pressures, a self-enforcing professional image, that mitigated against corruption and brutality that would discredit the force. During the 1920s and 1930s, envious American reformers attributed these differences to the training and command of the respective forces. The American police traditionally belonged to the local political system. This, along with lack of professional training and civil service regulation, meant that American police became easily enmeshed in local corruption. The German police had few such disadvantages, and benefited from a professional command.[15]

Studies of the German police reveal that a key element of their self-image was that of a professional force beyond political influence. Even obvious ideological biases, like those in Bavarian political police offices, did not necessarily deny them a sense of being above "political"—that is, party—influence. Unfortunately, efforts to reform the police into a force suitable for a democratic republic inevitably required "political interference." Consequently, regardless of where the policeman stood ideologically in his perception of his professional image, pressure for changes could appear as "political" interference threatening his professionalism.[16]

Since conservative politics demanded little "democratic reform" in public institutions, the "political interference" that the police experienced inevitably came from prorepublican circles. Whether in Prussia, where the Socialistische Partei Deutschland (SPD) dominated, or in conservative Bavaria, efforts to move the police to the center required movement to the "left." This image-reform conflict helps explain why police could see left-wing political orientations as contaminating their professionalism, while the right was less threatening. Predictably, as enforcers of order and the status quo, police should have less empathy for the left, but when it threatens their own internal order, it becomes an overt "enemy of order."

If the image of apolitical, professional autonomy was central to their police subculture, the psychological need to preserve that image would have been great—even more so when image conflicted with reality. In his case study of Berlin, Hsi-Huey Liang concluded that the Police Presidium made little effort to detect undesirable political affiliation in its police. Rather, it relied on denunciations by fellow policemen. Not only were denunciations generally not forthcoming, but commanding officers usually preferred to deal personally with such problems. Denunciations coming from outside the police were readily disbelieved, investigative teams were understaffed, and internal disciplinary courts were generally lenient. The standard procedure was transfer to less sensitive positions. Files on the political activity of policemen in the south German city of Stuttgart indicate similar responses.[17] These are the predictable responses of a police subculture with pariah-like undertones.

If the comparative studies were accurate in observing that, unlike American police, the German police reported and openly disciplined cases of corruption and brutality, then we may have a significant scale for analyzing the character of a "Weimar" police subculture. Such violations that could be openly reported and disciplined reveal the existence of well established or "real" professional internal controls. Where the secrecy mechanisms operated extensively (as for political involvement), they revealed both real problems against which the subculture had to protect its image, and a social-psychological weak spot.

Despite significant cause, the Prussian police did not have a special force to investigate subversion and political deviance within the police until January 1932. Once created, it became a coordinating center for the entire Reich, but with a ludicrously small staff. As a measure of attitudes elsewhere, this office complained of lack of cooperation from the other states, and one can interpret the official response to its complaint as "don't make waves." [18]

Returning to the issue of police brutality: contrary to the ostensible immunity of the German police, the theory argues for a tendency toward violence in a police subculture. Society requires a policeman to tread the fine line between legal and illegal violence daily. Role conflicts can make the police regard "force as a necessary and justifiable means of instilling 'respect' for the police among those who would not otherwise be likely to display it." Since there is evidence of such attitudes among many German policemen,[19] their alleged resistance to unnecessary violence requires careful reexamination.

Brutality is obviously an issue for this study. Even if the Weimar police were relatively immune to abuses, some advocated (and practiced) third degree techniques and summary justice. In Bavaria, during the early crisis period (1919–1921), the political police indulged freely in such "preventive action." Under NS rule, the police became notoriously involved with the physical abuse of arrestees. Since police professionalism could not prevent these abuses, especially when committed by Nazi auxiliaries, the mechanisms of secrecy and subculture indoctrination came into play to protect the police image—facilitating the conversion of the police to NS practices. The professionals covered up and denied Nazi excesses.[20]

Before that and despite their professionalism about controlled violence, or perhaps because of it, the German police of the 1920s and 1930s experienced more role conflicts that generated alienation. For instance, the allegedly lower level of police brutality in the Weimar period conflicts with the uniformed police reputation for toughness in dealing with demonstrations. The Weimar police were born amid the use of deadly force to protect the Republic against its enemies, and throughout their short history were regularly reimmersed in such confrontations.[21] This brought them severe external criticism, especially in the liberal, socialist, and Communist presses, and even from the radical right when police toughness was "misdirected" against "good citizens." Police failures to maintain order brought rebuke, but so did the application of "inappropriate" force to the "wrong" people. No matter what the police do in an unstable society, controlling its numerous out-groups will bring rebuke from some quarter. In a police subculture, this friction should produce two effects that help explain the German experience.

The first effect is police hostility toward those groups who threaten order and create the crisis situations most conducive to role conflicts for the police. Police hostility toward the Kommunistische Partei

Deutschland (KPD) is well known, and police-subculture theory adds to our understanding of why. In contrast, police attitudes toward the NS Movement were more complex, and this theory also contributes to analysis of those attitudes.

The second effect introduces another mechanism of police subcultures. In any isolated group, authority tends to become more personal than it is supposed to in a legal, bureaucratic command structure. Authority gravitates to leaders who identify with the values of the group rather than with those of society. Examples of this are obvious in the problems of reformers like Albert Grzesinski and Bernhard Weiss in Berlin, but they can also be read into Harold Gordon's analysis of power relations in the Bavarian police.[22] Furthermore, external appeals directed at the police should gain more favorable responses when oriented toward police subcultural rather than toward societal values. This provided a lever that the Nazis pushed most effectively.

These two effects help clarify the crises in the police and their susceptibility to NS penetration, control and use. Subculture theory facilitates evaluation of more traditional explanations of the police role in the Third Reich. An overview of their organization, the nature of their personnel, and their career conditions provide a further test of the applicability of such theory and may suggest some suitable modifications.

The Professional Police Establishment and Its Problems

Under the Weimar constitution, the federal states retained police authority, while many municipalities retained independent forces. There were no federal police. Each state force was divided into several components, the most central of which was the uniformed force most commonly called Schutzpolizei (Schupo). The Schupo in turn consisted of two forces. Part were heavily armed and housed in barracks, to be employed in force for crowd control (especially strikes and demonstrations) and the suppression of revolutionary uprisings. The remainder were assigned to urban precincts for routine patrol and police work. In the countryside, each state maintained a uniformed Gendarmerie or Landjägerei separate from the Schupo. The remainder of the state police served in plainclothes. Units of detectives, Kriminalpolizei, were assigned to the cities, and administrative police (Verwaltungspolizei) performed regulatory roles (housing, sanitation, etc.) and did administrative work for the other police.

Since the Reich supplemented state police budgets, the Reich minister of the interior could encourage uniformity among state forces. Each state minister of the interior regulated organizational and personnel policies throughout his state, but each unit was commanded by regional or local authorities. Thus, policy was centrally regulated while command was decentralized. The central authority of the states and the Reich Interior Ministry's influence over training and personnel created a uniform police career system that varied only slightly from state to state.[23] Even municipal forces generally followed the pattern.

The system divided careerists into two groups, those with higher education, who began at officer ranks, and the rest, who worked their way up from below. For the latter, entry began in the uniformed Schupo as a police candidate in the Basic Police School. With police training also came access to general education, through which one could achieve the equivalent of the Abitur. Entry into officer career lines required such a diploma. Meanwhile, after one year, graduates from police school became police corporals (Wachtmeister) and were assigned to a tactical unit for several years. Housed in barracks and employed as teams against hostile citizens in strikes, demonstrations, and riots, the young policeman experienced an environment highly conducive to subculture formation, but also providing strong group support for those who fit in. Some training programs deliberately inculcated a sense of closed-group identity and alienation from society,[24] but pending more case studies, one can argue only that evidence implies strong police enculturation at the entry level.

After completing tactical unit service, policemen served in precinct stations. They took courses to qualify for sergeant (Oberwachtmeister) to become eligible for transfer to other branches of the police. They could soon retire with entitlement to preference in a middle civil service career. Meanwhile, those who aspired to officer rank, the equivalent of higher civil service, attended police officer schools.

Men who sought detective careers could transfer after eight years of Schupo service as detective assistant candidates (Kriminal-assistant Anwärter), or after twelve years directly as detective assistant. Promotion depended on successful completion of training courses and examinations through which one could rise to detective (Kriminalsekretär), the top of the middle detective career ladder. To advance to the higher, or officer, levels, one became a detective inspector candidate (Kriminalkommissar Anwärter) and negotiated more schools and examinations.

Direct access to higher detective ranks was open to police officers and university graduates, who after passing state qualification exams (usually in jurisprudence) entered as detective inspector candidates. From detective inspector, one could rise ultimately to government counselor (Regierungsrat), the equivalent of police major. At this command level, higher civil servants transferred freely throughout government administration, so that one could command police detective offices without having risen through the detective ranks. It was at this level that qualified NS civil servants without police backgrounds would make their entry into Kripo and Gestapo.

The reformed police career system of the Weimar era gave secure employment, good working conditions, educational opportunities, good pay, regular leave, insurance and pensions. In the early years, promotion came rapidly, but the ranks soon filled with many men in the same retirement age groups so that advancement stagnated. Younger policemen especially faced many years frozen in lower ranks. Thus, at precisely the time when the police experienced heightened role conflicts through violence and politicization, they also experienced reduced recognition.

Unfortunately, we have no reliable studies of who filled the ranks of the professional police, not even the most basic official statistics. One anonymous publication gave a statistical profile of the Prussian police in 1929 which was probably based on official statistics. In terms of rural-urban origins, the police closely matched the general population. The largest group (40 percent) had originally trained for careers in the crafts; the next largest group (22 percent) came from white-collar jobs; about 12 percent came from agricultural backgrounds. Educationally, 77 percent had completed only primary school, while only 10 percent had the eleventh-year high-school-leaving certificate and 2 percent the Abitur.[25]

Nothing that one can deduce about a hypothetical German police subculture suggests any special vulnerability to NS appeals; on the contrary, the relative security of their positions should have provided some immunity. Manipulation of that subculture would be as important as the ideology of the manipulators. Frustrations over limited promotional opportunities and mandated retirement peaked just when the Republic's last trial had begun, when the depression closed all other opportunities, and when the police confronted the full brunt of Nazi and Communist assault. As role conflicts increased and recognition decreased, the mechanisms of a police subculture should have created levers that could be used to "turn" the police.

The ultimate crisis of the Weimar police grew from several problems: their prerepublican traditions; the origins of the new police as a force created to restore order and guarantee the safety of existing governments; the transition from an authoritarian police tradition to a force appropriate to a liberal-democratic republic; the complication of that transition by a lack of consensus in the broadest terms over the proper form and mission for this new police; and the renewed assault on the republic and its police before the new society and its police could find accommodation. Such problems not only generated role conflicts but threatened the police establishment itself.

The changes from old to new order produced powerful stresses.[26] Usually, the royal state police forces had aspirations to the image and prestige of the military. Almost all policemen had been soldiers. With the military model came an image of the police as aloof agents of the state rather than servants of the people. After 1919, the combat environment in which the new police emerged required an equally militarized force. The resultant preference for veterans as policemen preserved a military ethos that would have taken several generations to wear away.[27]

Pressures counterbalancing military and authoritarian traditions came from many quarters that wanted a police image of servants of the public interest. The arrogant and authoritarian imperial police prototype had to give way to the friendly cop on the beat or, better still, the Social Democrat's ideal of a "people's police." Unfortunately, there was not enough time to effect these changes. Although considerable agreement existed over the need for law and order, there was no agreement over the proper role and relation of the police in society. The anti-republican forces exploited this weakness effectively in their efforts to undermine the Republic.

Perhaps the major transitional problem facing all modern police has been the curbing of police powers in favor of guarantees for individual rights. In this respect, Germany had to make a greater than average transition under revolutionary conditions. During the Weimar period, the process of restricting police power advanced considerably through a system of administrative courts that protected the individual from police excesses.[28]

While the forces of liberalism and socialism tried to curb police power, right-wing movements argued that the restrictions of the liberal, constitutional state had "chained the police" and paralyzed the authority of the state. Again the police were caught in the middle. Modern developments constantly put stumbling blocks between them and the performance of their duty, while seemingly encouraging a popular view of the police as oppressors against whom the people needed protection. Yet, simultaneously they were taunted with the image of an emasculated force and chided for their failure to protect society.[29]

In this respect, the paramilitary units of the police—the training ground for rookies—became the center of conflicts. When used to control strikes and demonstrations, they encountered the working class, the unemployed masses, or the politically active and public-spirited citizen. Both the Communists and Nazis made the most of that conflict in their propaganda. They portrayed the police as agents of an evil regime directed against the people.[30]

The preceding description paints an image of a police force torn by contradictory tendencies and pressures, both internal and external. Although the fate of this police force is known, the relation between these pressures and that fate is more problematical; however, the potential for such conflicts to generate predictable responses from a police subculture seems readily apparent.

The tug-of-war over militarism and authoritarianism versus a "people's police" image produced a decisive split within the police subculture itself. In Prussia, the policemen's unions represented the split. From early on, the Schrader Verband (Allgemeine Preussischer Polizeibeamten Verband), which claimed to represent 70 percent of the rank and file, supported and encouraged government reforms to "democratize" the police. This movement generated a counterpart, the Verein der Polizeibeamten Preussens, which claimed to represent 90 percent of the officers, and which fought for the military and authoritarian traditions. After 1928 it conducted a veritable feud with Severing's regime, and in Berlin from 1930, it stood in an almost open state of war with Grzesinski, the SPD police president.[31]

From such tension many policemen, especially officers, grew isolated from the government and hostile toward liberal and socialist politicians whose reform efforts associated them with hostile critics of the police. Considering such great potential for a rift in the police, one wonders that Liang detected no lack of discipline or insubordination among the lower ranks in his study of the Berlin police. Perhaps the "fundamental solidarity in the police" that he describes attests to the power of a police subculture to bond its diverse components despite such internal disagreement.[32] The police career system apparently produced tremendous cohesiveness and in-group support.

The Detective Police

In light of such complexities, it seems appropriate to focus specifically on the detective police who would form the bulk of Sipo. Their uniqueness and its possible effects on how they related to the rest of the police, to society, and to the above conflicts should indicate whether they remained part of the general police subculture and whether they had any special susceptibility to NS subversion.[33]

The detectives with their laboratory technicians are universally distinct from the uniformed police. Their more specialized, technical, and mental work and their academic promotion process ensured that this field drew the better educated or the more determined from among police recruits. Advancement into the middle and higher levels depended on qualifying examinations, and continued promotion depended, among other things, on academic course work. Among detectives, intellectual ability rated high in peer evaluation at all levels, and the higher one rose the more important became signs of social status. The high civil service commonly based personal evaluations on bearing, dress, cleanliness, manners, speech, and cultural polish.[34]

Nevertheless, the detective ranks were filled mostly by men who had risen from Schupo service. The majority had entered Schupo with grade-school educations and finished their formal schooling within the police. Generationally, they were divided between older holdovers from the imperial era, who were often frustrated by their personal limitations or bad luck, and the younger Weimar era-recruits, some better educated, who were blocked by the "bottleneck" of seniors ahead of them.

Among detective officers, even greater divisions existed. Men with university educations had become officers directly. They served side by side with older detectives who had risen through the ranks and younger recruits with the Abitur who had become candidates after only two years of Schupo service. The older men had often experienced a rush forward in the early years, but had to share their status with the better educated newcomers. Despite their privileged status, these newcomers also felt they had good cause for resentment. In the old days, their social standing would have meant more prestigious careers. Under the Republic, careers were more open to talent, but advantages derived from social origin remained. Thus when anyone failed to achieve a status commensurate with either his origins or his supposed talents, "the system" could always be to blame.

Among detectives, competition for potentially rewarding cases created a ready-made environment for charges of favoritism. Younger men blocked by more established professionals became active in concerns that promised to change things. For some, this meant greater involvement in police unions or in politics.[35] They might seek reforms within the system, or they might join the ranks of those antirepublicans who favored more radical programs of national rejuvenation.

Despite such frustrations, detectives usually had the most positive public image among police, especially in a society fascinated with sensational crime stories. In Prussia, the detectives claimed a phenomenal record of success to bolster their image: in 1925–1926 solving 86 percent of all murders, 95 percent of all homicides, and 51 percent of robberies; even in massive urban centers like Berlin, 97 percent of murders, 94 percent of homicides, and 38 percent of robberies. But such status did not accrue uniformly, and state funding was cut during the depression despite mounting case loads. Furthermore, public response to the detective force was mixed and transitory. Acclaim for individuals mixed with criticism of the force for unsolved, sensational cases, while worsening social conditions produced ambivalence about many aspects of law enforcement.[36]

There are problems in assuming a uniform subculture shared by detectives and other police. The detectives who had risen from the ranks should have brought a police subculture with them, but among the officers there must have been less unity. Nevertheless, those with educational advantages eventually experienced the same frustrations and had to work as members of the same team. All shared the self-image of the "detective." Perhaps their subculture was less cohesive and supportive, perhaps their frustrations and sense of alienation were greater. Although there is not yet any empirical base, the impression emerging from the literature and from the personnel files of Sipo men is that the detectives, like the uniformed officers, were attracted in disproportionate numbers to right-wing causes and ultimately the NS Movement.

This seems like a contradiction, for despite possible differences, one element stood out as clearly among the detectives as the regular police: the self-image of apolitical professionalism.[37] In the late Republic, politics and police frustrations became so mixed as to challenge that cherished image, which helps explain the contradiction.

Undermining the Police

Dissatisfaction over promotions and professional police attitudes that run counter to liberal beliefs about law and order tend to be mutually escalating. In the police, frustrations over promotion intensify tendencies toward an alienated subculture.[38] In an alienated subculture, such frustrations tend to find the "real" cause in external sources. The German police, like the general population, increasingly shared the conviction that the problem lay with "the system" and Germany's humiliated position.

For instance, the identification, apprehension, and conviction of a lawbreaker and the published crime rate provide major measures of success for the police. Under the influence of an alienated subculture, such measures can become all-important, a symbol to the police of real "law and order" and their self-esteem. Anything that interferes with the ease and success of convicting criminals becomes an unnecessary encumbrance.[39]

In nationalist circles, the liberal restrictions of the Weimar Constitution that "handcuffed" the police appeared as foreign concepts, undermining Germany's institutions of order. By trying to enforce these restrictions, the Weimar system seemed responsible for the perceived decline in law and order. Given a press much preoccupied with the sensational crimes of the era, an individual detective could become a public hero, finding a forum from which to enter public debate on the state of law and order. As a "man in the know," he could advocate more severe sentences, sterilization of social degenerates and habitual criminals, and a more free hand for the police.[40] When a policeman took such public positions, the right frequently proclaimed him as an ally. In return, their promises to bring the laws, the judiciary, and the legal profession into line with a stern Germanic tradition of law and order must have had the desired effect on many policemen.

Yet despite all these reasons why policemen might have been drawn away from support of the Republic, scholars until recently generally agreed that in fact the police served the Republic dutifully to the end. Scholars also agreed, however, that powerful traditions hindered the successful introduction of liberal democratic principles into the police professional self-image and concept of mission. This seems a paradox worth explaining, for it meant that the police would be less resistant to right-wing arguments and more resistant to a government that would "democratize" them. It could not have been the liberal constitutional Republic to which they remained loyal. Furthermore, the negative effect on the police of the efforts of the left (both the SPD and KPD) undermined their resistance to Nazi appeals. It added to dissension among the police and intensified the traditions and attitudes upon which the Nazis could capitalize.

The German police were hostile to Communism and to working-class and other elements that joined the Communists in protests and demonstrations. For the police, no real distinction existed between such disruptions and any other criminal activity. Furthermore, most policemen, like other people, saw Communism as subversive of all the values they held dear, because of its internationalist, Comintern alignment; its attacks on property and profit; and its atheism. The KPD enhanced its association with lawlessness and anarchy by its call to smash the police as the state's tool of oppression. Most extremely, the KPD drove the police deeper into hostility by acts of violence and murder directed specifically at policemen.[41] Police training manuals and other publications further inflamed their hostility. They described Communist Red Front fighters as "the most worthless, criminal elements in society," and "rabble of the meanest sort, interested only in selfish gain."[42] Anti-KPD indoctrination and physical confrontations with the KPD undermined police resistance to right-radical appeals. Although lowered resistance would not necessarily make the police pro-Nazi, it enhanced NS appeals for some.

An anti-Communist sentiment had been firmly established among German police everywhere after 1919. The German "police-armies" had emerged specifically as the counterrevolutionary arm of the Republic. Consequently, they viewed Communism with open, extreme hostility, while perceiving the right more ambivalently. Rightists represented a rowdy and dangerous element, but at least their national loyalty was beyond question. From the beginning, the prevalent attitude of the police was anti-Communist, strongly nationalistic, but otherwise indifferent to "partisan politics." They generally disapproved of right radicals, but did not consider them too serious a threat.[43] Meanwhile, police hostility toward the Reds had developed into a preventive-attack mentality that, in the long run, may have produced more trouble than it prevented.[44]

Although time might have worn away the anti-Communist fixation and tightened the bonds with the Republic and its principles, events did not allow it. The KPD strategy became more radical just as the depression began to exaggerate tensions. Pressures escalated between 1928 and 1933. One sees clues of a significant breakdown within the police before 1932. For "breakdown," however, one should not read "collapse," for that did not happen. Instead, there was a subtle shift from a police force that tried to serve a republic to one increasingly alienated from that role, imposing its own definition of law and order. The shift paralleled the general move of Germany into a right-radical phase after 1929.[45]

By 1927, increasing clashes between the Sturmabteilung (SA) and the Red Front led the police to use a heavy hand in managing political demonstrations. Their lack of restraint often ended in shootings that sometimes killed and wounded bystanders. The police perceived an apparent decline in their public image, for they certainly got bad press. Tensions came to a head on May Day 1929, when working-class districts of Berlin erupted into near civil war. Thirty-one people died; more than a hundred were injured. Innocents along with insurgents became victims of police gunfire. The press also accused the police of beating up reporters who filed derogatory reports. For months thereafter, part of the press attacked the police for bloodthirsty and callous behavior. Whatever the real public response was, it was irrelevant: the critical press and Communist propaganda told police that respectable citizens feared and hated them.[46] The police responded with blind self-justification, even pride in their display of technical proficiency. Their sense of growing public hostility had turned them inward. They felt betrayed by the people and the government.

The Berlin experience may have been extreme, but the general effect all over Germany was the same. Despite efforts by leaders who saw threats from the right, most attention focused on the Red danger. While policemen readily reported Communist subversion among themselves, they apparently did not see the Nazis as subversive.[47] For a growing number of policemen, what the Nazis said about the link between crime and disorder, International Communism, and the weakness of the Republic made sense. From this point on, individual policemen drew increasingly closer to the Nazis, some joining the Movement.[48]

In addition to violent confrontations, Communist propaganda intended to subvert the police created an additional psychological confrontation. Although the Communists directed extensive efforts at the police, they won few policemen to their side. If anything, their efforts backfired and drove policemen into the Nazi camp. Communists saw the police as a major instrument of the capitalist establishment. They represented an enemy force to be attacked and destroyed, if the revolution were to succeed. The Communists had two objectives: penetration for intelligence purposes and subversive activities designed to undermine the force and to win individual policemen to the revolution. Efforts to win policemen generally failed. The Communists compounded this failure by trying to give the impression of greater success, and by openly flaunting police authority in distributing their propaganda in barracks. Worst of all, KPD propaganda attacked the police as an institution and a profession.[49] It increased their sense of alienation, drew them inward, and made them ever more ready for radical reforms in "the system."

In contrast, the Nazis did not usually attack the police as an institution nor try to destroy them from within. To be sure, many Nazi activities left policemen with hostile impressions. They intimidated individual anti-Nazi policemen, but they made no centralized effort to destroy the police. Nazi intelligence agencies penetrated the police, but without a Party policy for undermining and destroying them. For most of the NS Movement, the police represented an essential institution to be maintained and strengthened after their power seizure. For this purpose, policemen could be recruited in advance into the Movement.[50] With the Nazis, the police encountered less psychological confrontation, and more sympathy.

The Nazis would take over the police when they took over the reins of government. Before Hitler became chancellor, they already controlled the governments of Anhalt, Mecklenburg, Oldenburg, Thuringia, and Braunschweig. But the real blow came in Prussia. Until the spring of 1932, the Prussian government, firmly in the hands of prorepublican parties, notably the Social Democrats, influenced the police strongly enough to counterbalance the swing to the right. Then "von Papen's Coup" so thoroughly purged the Prussian police of SPD men and elements friendly to them that the Nazis had no problems directing the police to their own ends.

In July 1932, Reich Chancellor von Papen, declaring that the Prussian government had failed to maintain public order, declared martial law and relieved SPD government and police officials and their prorepublican allies of all authority. In a complete about-face, the SPD now appeared on the political police list of potentially subversive organizations. The purge of the administration and police was so efficient that when Hermann Göring took charge in Prussia, much of his work was already done.[51] If the backbone of the German police was not broken, it was at least twisted to the right. All over Germany, pro-Nazi elements could emerge more openly, and those who had disdained Hitler's followers must have had second thoughts.

From the beginning, the political "meddling" of left-wing politicians had caused tension in the police. Open confrontation with Communists, hostile criticism from the left, right-wing taunts of ineffectiveness, and the conflicts of police work in an unstable society produced a growing, hopeless frustration. The relative economic security of the policeman kept him tightly identified with his service, though not necessarily with the Republic. On the other hand, his social and professional frustrations appeared to be the result of a weak, corrupt government. Ambivalence toward the Republic grew and in many cases turned into disdain and hostility.[52] The right, especially the Nazis, recognized this discontent and took full advantage of it in propaganda directed at the police.

Nevertheless, the continued presence of prorepublican elements in the police until at least the summer of 1932, and the relatively small number of policemen openly favoring NS, clearly show that Nazi hegemony in the police was never inevitable until they had won political victory. In that process, within both the state and the police, the forces of the conservative counterrevolution paved the way. Once the Nazis were the legal government, however, they had in the police a susceptible agency, if they appealed to them through the channels of their subculture and stroked their professional image.

The police corps generated a powerful institutional identity that rejected alignment with specific political parties. Yet the pressures of the Weimar environment made its members susceptible to NS appeals. There were enough conjunctions with the values of the NS world view to facilitate an incremental transformation of police values.

Early Transformations

Well before the "power seizure," important elements in the Movement had paved the way. Although the Nazis had no uniform approach, the main thrust of NS propaganda, especially the line that Himmler pushed, appealed to the values of a police subculture. It smothered any sense of hostility and opposition. If the policeman felt alienated, the Nazis offered a warm and loving embrace. They portrayed the policeman as a man who served out of a sense of duty to society. He was no more the willing agent of the Republic than any other good German; instead, he was also its victim.[53] They exonerated the police and their profession from responsibility for existing evils and promised them "that the police in the Third Reich will be conceded a more esteemed and respected place than at present." Nazi service chiefs would support their police unlike "the superiors in the present system, where indeed the police, especially the Schutzpolizei, are viewed and treated only as a necessary evil."[54]

They projected respect for the image of apolitical aloofness by promising that under the new regime the police would stand above politics and become truly the police of the entire people rather than of just one ideological interest group (the left implied).[55] Although this "respect" seems grossly cynical, such a promise was hardly incompatible with the perceptions of NS leaders like Wilhelm Frick or Himmler. They meant it in the sense that the Movement was "above" partisan politics (it intended to end it) and represented the interests of the "true Volk."

Regardless of how strong the Nazi appeal should have been for policemen, we have little knowledge of how well it worked. A 1935 report to Hitler claimed that before 1933, 700 uniformed policemen (only about 0.7 percent) became Party members. This figure excluded administrative police and detectives, and apparently did not include policemen who had only joined NS-affiliated organizations.[56] Beyond that lies the question of NS sympathizers with no official affiliations.

The issue is clouded because, before the summer of 1932, the law prohibited membership for most policemen in NS organizations. Also, subsequent claims of a pro-Nazi stance before 1933 are impossible to substantiate. Liang estimated that since many Nazi policemen were officers, they had a disproportionate influence in Berlin, eventually wrenching control of more precincts from the SPD than the socialists retained. In Hamburg by 1932, 27 out of 240 officers joined the Nazi Police Officers' Group, and a similar ratio existed in Lübeck. In Rüstringen, Oldenburg, where the Party dominated the government, a local NS official claimed that by 1932 60 percent of the police had joined his NS policemen's group. All over Germany success from within the police went hand in hand with influence from above through electoral victories.[57]

Among the detective forces, a few specific cases of NS penetration reveal the diversity of links with the Movement. An example of the earlier recruits, Erich Vogel of the Saxon Criminal Police had begun an officer's career in the army, but after suffering a disability, was released in 1916 to begin a detective career. He quickly revealed his political inclinations, establishing connections with the German Peoples' Freedom Movement, and by 1926 he was working for NS intelligence operations. At the request of the Party, he did not join until 1933, so he could work clandestinely, keeping the Party informed of police and government plans. By 1932, he had a working relationship with the SS, and in November 1933, he became a member of the SS-SD. He had been a member of the Saxon Gestapo since March 1933, and would become the center of a sensational proceeding in 1935 against Gestapo and concentration camp officials for brutality.[58]

In Thüringia, where the Nazis participated in the government as early as 1930, detectives Hellmuth Gommlich and Max Rausch could openly join the Party in 1931 and 1930, respectively, Rausch serving with the Nazi district intelligence service. Both had fought during the war and entered police service from the military. Gommlich, a police lieutenant, became a detective inspector in 1926; Rausch, rising from the ranks, became a detective sergeant in 1920. Both joined SS-SD in 1933.[59]

Berlin had a fair share of prominent detectives who turned Nazi.[60] Erich Liebermann von Sonnenberg became a detective officer candidate in 1912. By 1915, he was frozen in rank. As an outspoken advocate of forced sterilization to prevent crime and reduce burdens on society, he put himself at odds with the regime. In January 1932, he became the unofficial representative of the higher criminal police officials in the NS Fellowship of Civil Servants, where his theories found approval, and he joined the Party. He had allegedly served for "a long time" as an especially esteemed V-man (Vertranensmann—trusted agent) of the SA and SS. With the NS takeover, he became head of the Berlin Criminal Police, quickly rising in rank to assistant commissioner. There he would "lead the fight against crime using methods which I always thought proper, but which could never have been applied but for . . . the National

Resurrection." After 1936, Sonnenberg's status declined; he served obscurely in the Gestapo and died of illness in 1941.[61]

Philip Greiner became a detective officer candidate in 1920, but was frozen in rank by 1923. Failure to complete university may have hurt him. He became involved in a long-standing personal and political feud with Deputy Police President Weiss, providing a point of contact with the Nazis. In August 1932, his NS affiliations became open when he became head of the NS civil servants' organization and joined the Party. With the "power seizure," he would insure NS interests in the criminal police as head of personnel affairs for the detective division of the Berlin Presidium. Like many of his colleagues, he entered the SS-SD only in 1938 with the official fusion of SS and police ranks.[62]

Among the less "apolitical," Dr. Rudolf Braschwitz turned from dentistry to become detective inspector in 1927. From 1928 he served as a political police expert on the Communist Movement. "To please his superiors," he joined first the Union of Democratic Officials, then the Democratic Party, and finally, in 1930, the SPD. His nose for politics led him out, however, in 1932, and somewhat belatedly, on January 1, 1933, he became a contributing member of the SS, an honorary affiliation open to almost any German. Soon his expertness and the performance of "special assignments" against KPD and SPD for Göring gave him early entry into the Party and guaranteed his career.[63]

One element stands out among these and other detectives. By 1931, either NS appeals won them, or they sought to guarantee themselves in that camp. After the Papen coup in 1932, they could proclaim NS loyalty and openly recruit others, or they rushed to establish their first link with the Movement. Obviously, they remained a minority, but that did not make them insignificant. One cannot judge which of them were simply opportunists, and which embraced National Socialism because it spoke to their values or needs.

Regardless, in 1933, all policemen found themselves in the service of NS regimes. In Prussia that came suddenly when Herman Göring became provisional Minister of the Interior. According to Rudolf Diels, first head of the Gestapo, the police responded positively to Göring. The Nazis called for "Law, Order, and Authority," and Göring demanded that the police be freed of encumbrances that prevented them from achieving these goals. He also seemed to protect their integrity from the sort of sweeping purges, or worse still, replacement by a Nazi militia that radical elements threatened. One gets the impression that the police generally shared the sense of national rejuvenation that the new regime brought. Less than 2 percent of the ranks and 7 percent of the officers fell victim to the NS purge. As a result, the police turned diligently to the job of cleaning up the Reich, and they gave an image of legitimacy and propriety to the extralegal acts that ensued.[64]

The NS purge hardly touched the detectives and administrative staff of the Prussian criminal police. By the end of the year, the Nazis purged only 103 or (1.5 percent) in all of Prussia. Detectives like Liebermann von Sonnenberg replaced the liberal policymakers. Liebermann became chief of the Berlin office, and by March had risen three ranks. To be sure, Nazis or, most commonly, nationalist sympathizers filled the key positions under him, but most important, they all came from the detective-trained staff. Like all police, these detectives had an appreciation for order and authority which, reinforced by the values of their professional subculture, made them willing participants in the first steps toward the police state.[65]

Encouragement to use their new protective-custody arrest powers went hand in hand with constant reminders against too much caution in using firearms. Through the so-called "Shooting Order" of February 17 and numerous speeches, Göring left no doubt that he would consider caution in the use of force and firearms as dereliction of duty. In contrast, he would exonerate policeman from any repercussions from free use of arrest powers and weapons. Göring, as their superior, would assume the blame and shield them from criticism.[66] He reinforced such authorization with appeals to professional and patriotic duty.

With this pressure to do their duty against the enemies of society, the police must have been keyed up psychologically for the outburst of anti-Communist action that followed the Reichstag fire of February 28. As long as their SA auxiliaries only went after the Communists, beating them up, killing a few, and destroying their party facilities and homes, the police felt little concern at seeing their old enemies put down. But as the SA wrath spilled over onto individual Jews, the SPD, the labor unions, and even the would-be allies of the Nazis, they could not deny the lawlessness of it all. Worse yet, they had to include these thugs in regular patrols and police routine. The SA's lack of professional know-how, its swaggering and brutality belied the policeman's self-image of legitimized authority and force.[67] All told, the collective police response to the new regime had to have been as mixed as everyone else's.

Until some empirical base can be established, the impression stands that the police were not overly inclined in NS directions. Nothing indicates that they led rather than followed the general public in embracing the NS cause. As elsewhere in German society, a few well-placed Nazis worked disproportionately well in establishing NS influence until the local government turned. Once the Nazis became the government, the police not only continued to serve, but like most Germans embraced the Movement as Germany's hope. Once that happened, their police subculture may have made them more vulnerable to becoming Hitler's enforcers.

From Political Detectives to Gestapo, 1933–1934

Under the Weimar system, most German states had a central office that coordinated the investigation of political crimes. In the field, detectives working in the political branches of regional police offices supported this central office. Though political detectives were usually specialists, the overlap with other crimes was so great and political specialists so few in number, that some detectives did double duty, supported as usual by the uniformed police.[1]

As the Nazis acquired control in each state, their preoccupations led to enlarged, often independent, centrally commanded political police forces. In several states, a conventional title from the age of absolutist monarchs, Geheime Staatspolizei (secret or privy state police), came back into use, soon abbreviated as Gestapo. Usually a Geheime Staatspolizeiamt (Gestapo office) commanded a system of Staatspolizei regional posts. Some states used other nomenclature: for instance, the Bavarian or the Braunschweig Political Police. Until 1936 and the creation of a Reich Gestapo under Himmler, there was no national political police.[2]

Nevertheless, by the spring of 1934, Himmler succeeded in coordinating all the separate political police under Heydrich, who headed Himmler's Central Office of the Commander of the Political Police of the German States and Inspector of the Prussian Gestapo. After the Nazi seizure of Bavaria in March 1933, Himmler had become commander of the Bavarian Political Police. Then, in the fall/winter of 1933/34, he convinced the Reichsstatthalter (extraordinary governors appointed by Hitler) of most smaller states to appoint him commander of their political police. This uniform "command" created Reich-wide coordination, but it was limited because each Reichsstatthalter maintained primary influence over the actual chief of his political police, who was usually both the Reichsstaathalter's man as well as an SS officer. Nevertheless, by April 1934, Himmler's status had led Göring to appoint him inspector of the Prussian Gestapo. Thereafter, Himmler increasingly tightened his hold over the separate state political police forces until they were fused into the Reich Gestapo in 1936.[3]

After Himmler acquired de jure command and made Heydrich their chief, the political detectives had to work increasingly with the SD. With the creation of Sipo in 1936, the inclusion of Kripo made that marriage even more complex. Since this involved a transfusion of personnel rather than mere administrative coordination, Sipo and SD became a complex network of interlocking, multiple identities, as each branch had its own heterogeneous ethos. Before one can explore this mix fully, the transformations that the detective police underwent during the initial stages of fusion require elaboration. In the process one can also unravel some of the early mechanisms of "legitimization," the process by which they came to accept sanctioned violence as their duty.

Social psychologists argue that it is "ordinary people" who participate in sanctioned violence.[4] A brief summary of such theories provides a model against which to compare the experiences of the men of the Gestapo. Several interrelated processes help weaken moral restraints against sanctioned violence: authorization, bolstering, routinization, and dehumanization.

Authorizations are the official sanctions that encourage participants to feel that their moral principles do not apply. Authority may explicitly order, implicitly encourage, tacitly approve, or merely permit the inhumanity, but by doing so, it ostensibly assumes the responsibility.

Bolstering enables one to cope with any moral or ethical dissonance through group support. The conformity of the group reinforces certainty in the rightness of the choice. Bolstering can be enhanced by an "elite" organization, or by any group that is central to one's identity, and may be in proportion to the sacrifices one has made to belong.

While bolstering helps smother moral dissonance, and repeated authorization eases coping, *routinization* obscures any moral crisis. Highly routine processes greatly reduce the likelihood that one must confront one's scruples, if the routine reduces the need to make decisions and allows one to focus on the job rather than on larger consequences. Responsible neither for starting nor for finishing the process, each individual finds comfort in the knowledge that if he does not do his job, someone else will. The more automatic a process, the fewer the decisions one must make, and these are generally restricted to decisions about how to proceed, rather than whether to proceed.

Routinization works best when one has distance, as at a bureaucrat's desk. When one has direct contact with the victims, the key process involves dehumanization. Abstraction, *dehumanization,* and brutalization taken together best describe what happens.[5] This process is a double-edged sword: in denying the humanity of the victim and, therefore, his right to moral consideration, the victimizer brutalizes himself as well, weakening his moral restraints. In war we abstract and dehumanize our enemy, projecting on him our fears, for he represents a real threat.[6] Participants become brutalized to the point that they commit atrocities. The same forces work in severe domestic, political, social, and economic conflict—for instance, in a crusade against Communism, especially if the public media are controlled or cooperative.

Defining "appropriate" action against "the enemy" involves a tension between traditional moral restraints and authorization. The extent to which the victimizers will refrain from violence against helpless victims ceases to be a function of whether the victim poses an objective threat and revolves instead around the extent to which the victim has become an object and the victimizer has undergone brutalization. The fully abstracted enemy collectively poses all the threats of a monster, while individually, at the mercy of the victimizer, he has the status of vermin. His totally degraded position proves his subhumanity. The categorization of enemies prescribed by Nazi ideology and sanctioned through fully controlled media created the psychological environment to generate such processes. As we shall see, both police and SD created their own evidence and convinced themselves that the NS-designated enemies were indeed threats to society.

The following social history of the Sipo detectives shows how authorization, bolstering, routinization, and dehumanization contributed to their evolution. Throughout the process, professional detectives and civil servants experienced an uneven, sometimes jarring, sometimes gradual transformation from apolitical professionals to "Gestapo men."

The Political Police of Prussia: Early Transformations

Nowhere has this transformation been better documented than for the Prussian Gestapo.[7] Even so, we have uneven knowledge of its early organization, character, and activities. Göring ordered the creation of the Gestapo office (Geheime Staatspolizeiamt, or Gestapa) in Berlin in spring 1933 under Rudolf Diels, a political detective who had established ties with Göring before the Nazis came to power. By no means an NS stronghold, the Gestapo office had proper civil service, police, and administrative personnel. Long careers in the future Sipo and SD lay ahead for many, while others were merely passing through. All were bureaucrats and policemen whom Diels thought suitable. Few pro-republicans or anti-Nazis were left after the Papen coup; most were conservative nationalists, and many had become outwardly pro-NS, but only two were already NS members.

Aside from purely administrative sections, the office consisted of nine "desks" (Dezernat) dealing with subjects under political police scrutiny. All organizations on the left dominated Gestapo attention. In addition, the parties of the center and allies on the right became proper subjects for suspicion, before they became illegal. Beyond the political movements, the Gestapo viewed emigrants, Jews, and Freemasons as potential criminals in accordance with the Nazi world view. Not yet major targets, they had low priority compared with political organizations. For instance, as late as October, although Diels had stressed the importance of building files on Jewish and emigré circles, little had been done at the field level because of inadequate staffing.[8]

Although the organization of the new office resembled outwardly that of its predecessor, Department IA of the Berlin Police Presidium, it revealed significant differences.[9] The shift of focus from the NSDAP to the SPD as a threat to the state had been a product of the Papen coup and was an easy transition for conservative and nationalist detectives. Monitoring the Nationalist and Center parties as threats, abolishing the right of free speech, and freely using protective custody to deal with all such threats were major transformations that must have produced mixed reactions among the detectives. The new focus on Jews and Freemasons must have seemed ridiculous to some, even if it was an extension of popular prejudices.

A strange mix of jurisdictions assigned to the desks gives the impression of ad hoc organization. Over the next year, Diels tightened the structure and built an ever larger and more far-reaching Gestapo office (see Appendix B.1). By late summer, it had expanded to five departments and undergone further transformations toward service to the Nazi regime. Formal links with those agencies of the Movement that supported the Gestapo had emerged: the Intelligence Service (Nachrichtendienst, ND) of the Party, the SA, and the SS—most notably, the SS-Commando at Columbia Haus, the SS-run detention facility. The military's increased concern over adequate police support for counterespionage (Abwehr) had brought the Abwehr-police (Department IV) into their own, and both there and in Department II the Gestapo was nosing increasingly into foreign countries. By the end of the year, further transformations reflecting Nazi preoccupations added religious organizations as objects of scrutiny.[10]

As for size, accurate figures for 1933 are problematic, because official budgets and allotments were frequently circumvented. According to Diels, he began the Gestapo office in April by enlarging Department IA to about 250 detectives and detective employees. In addition, there would have been administrative civil servants (41 by June) and office employees, plus numerous SA and SS auxiliaries. By the beginning of 1934, the Gestapo office had grown to 645 personnel total: 88 administrative civil servants, 94 office employees, 179 detectives, and 284 detective employees (Kriminalangestellten, i.e., below civil service status), most of whom were former auxiliaries. Despite the dissolution of the auxiliary police, the SS-Commando Gestapa still supplemented these numbers with 60–70 SS guards. By this time, the fully formed Gestapo included 34 regional posts with 1,025 personnel, of whom 793 were detectives and 73 detective employees. This gave the Gestapo a total of 1,329 executive personnel: 972 detectives and 357 helpers. By the end of Diels's reign in April, he reported the Gestapo office at a peak of 680 personnel.[11] Although Diels had doubled the size of the central headquarters, he may not have changed the number of political detectives. However, most had been separated from other police agencies and were available full time for Gestapo work.

One can make only a few safe generalizations about the regional Gestapo posts. Despite Nazi bombast about a Marxist-dominated political police, district governors did not need to purge except minimally, and they created regional offices staffed mostly by professionals.[12] Many of them took NS affiliations now that it was safe or expedient; less-qualified Nazis only gradually joined, usually as employees. The head of a Gestapo post was usually an appointee of the governor, which often interfered with control by the Gestapo office until after the Röhm purge. Support from uncontrolled SA and SS auxiliary police also added to confusion throughout much of 1933.

The Gestapo post at Dortmund for the department of Arnsberg in the province of Westphalia is a good case study, for it was a middle-sized office. Like all regional posts, it came into being in April 1933, formed from the political departments of the local police presidium and the state detective posts (Landeskriminalpolizeistellen) at Dortmund and Bochum. It had a staff of 4 administrative police and 33 detectives, supplemented by 69 employees, mostly SA auxiliaries.[13]

It was not until fall, however, that such Gestapo posts could be fully shaped. The problem was compounded by overlapping jurisdictions and a rapidly expanding mission. The post commander estimated that three-tenths of their time was devoted to "local work," which seems to have referred to political police actions ordered by local officials. He needed a larger administrative staff to handle the greatly expanded paperwork, especially the new card files to be created for Jews, Freemasons, and SPD members, and the registry of all political leaflets.[14]

During this transition, the main problems for Gestapo workers in the field were a combination of (1) confusion over distinguishing between state (Gestapo) work and purely local interests; (2) closely related bureaucratic competition at the local level; and (3) the intrusion of Nazi Party, SA, and SS. Originally created as field offices under the local governments, the Gestapo posts were entangled in local politics. Although this might have provided more uniform coordination of state and local investigation, in fact local police rivalries impeded the coordination on which the Gestapo depended for political work in the rural areas. Local officials also failed to coordinate with the intelligence agencies of the Party (ND), SA (Ic), and SS (SD), and had to be ordered to maintain liaison. Finally, the independent actions of SA and SS resulted in a loss of evidence. The relatively better-controlled SA auxiliaries of the Gestapo posts caused fewer problems. In Dortmund, 32 SA men worked under the supervision of 8 uniformed policemen; in the outpost at Bochum, 19 SA men worked under 7 detectives. All this competition undermined the collective effort in which each could have benefited from the knowledge of the other.[15]

Between fall 1933 and spring 1934, the struggle over the Gestapo had temporarily resolved itself, with the posts placed directly under Gestapo office control and merely coordinated with and nominally subordinate to the governors. As a result, the Gestapo posts assumed full responsibility for all political work including that of purely local interest. This allegedly gave them improved authority over local police as support for the Gestapo. Although Gestapo posts usually remained in regular police office buildings, their equipment and facilities became separately managed. Nevertheless, they continued to draw on regular police and detective offices for material support. Göring and Diels had interfered increasingly in the assignment of post leaders, previously the creatures of local governors and Party, SA, or SS chiefs. Finally, the independent actions of both SA and SS were terminated by Himmler's appointment as head of Gestapo and by the Röhm purge. Thus, Himmler inherited a fully formed Gestapo that needed only fine tuning and some reappointments to make Gestapo post leaders his own men. His Gestapo would command 34 posts with 56 outposts under them, and border police outposts in those provinces that adjoined foreign countries.[16]

Once again, using Dortmund as a case study, one can measure growth and activity at the working level. There a government counselor now had a staff of 15 police administrators and 12 office employees, while 5 detective officers supervised 36 sergeants and 7 employees in field work. Under this Gestapo post were four outposts: the main one at Bochum, with 1 detective officer, 12 sergeants, and 2 employees; and three smaller ones at Hagen, Hamm, and Siegen with 2–3 detective sergeants each. In March 1934, the post reported that 40 detective sergeants were handling 980 criminal cases per month (500 in Dortmund, 360 in Bochum, and 60 each in Hagen and Hamm), an average of 25 each. In addition, his staff processed 1,300 to 1,525 requests for reports from the Gestapo office and other agencies and 410 character reports per month. Finally, surveillance for counterespionage had increased so much that all other surveillance was in arrears.[17]

To facilitate this work, they established a fourth outpost at Siegen. Unlike the middle cities of Bochum, Hagen, and Hamm, clustered around Dortmund in the north-west corner of the department, Siegen was a small city at the southernmost tip, 125 km from Dortmund. It possessed the best transportation connections with the rest of its district (Landkreis), the rural hinterland of the department. Bochum was the most important of the outposts because it and adjacent industrial communities were the heart of the Polish Movement in the Rhineland and

Westphalia. Hagen and Hamm also centered on troublesome industrial districts with local KPD headquarters.[18]

To cover such a diverse department, the detectives found their traditional means of travel, the railroads, inadequate. Yet they had the use of only two small, four-passenger cars. Even after they became independently budgeted in 1934, they acquired replacements only for the two cars plus a third six-passenger vehicle ("for larger actions") and four motorcycles, confiscated property of "enemies of the state."[19] Working-level detectives were clearly overextended and minimally supported for the ambitious mission of the Gestapo.

Equally "typical" in their own way were the tiny Gestapo posts that covered the backwaters. The post for the department of Aurich in the province of Hannover was set up in the only politically significant location, the small port city of Wilhelmshaven (actually inside the adjacent state of Oldenburg). The department itself is a quiet rural area, known mostly for its fishing ports and North Sea resort communities. Previously, the area had no political state detective post. One detective officer and 2 sergeants had done double duty as regular detectives and political officers under the police chief in Wilhelmshaven. They became the Gestapo post in April 1933, while continuing to do double duty. When the separate organization was established for 1934, although the commander had called for a fivefold expansion, all he got was administrative help, 2 additional detectives, and 3 employees. The sole detective officer continued to command both the Gestapo post and the local Kripo staff.[20]

There is little reliable evidence for describing the actual behavior of early Gestapo men aside from the obvious—collecting information (from informants and from material they seized on raids), assembling it into dossiers on enemies and enemy organizations, arresting or ordering the arrest of suspects, and interrogating them. The terrorist brutality we associate with the Gestapo may have been more excessive and random before Himmler gained full control, and one cannot determine how much of it originated with the professional detectives. Considering the constant admonition to get tough with antisocial elements, all policemen probably resorted more freely to third degree interrogations, and incidents of "shot or injured while resisting arrest" greatly increased, but professional restraints survived.

Over an especially violent two-day period in August 1933, eight cases of police shooting suspects or arrestees involved mostly SA and SS auxiliaries: four prisoners trying to escape from internment; one trying to flee arrest by an SA man; two bold Communists who had forced armed SS men to defend themselves; and one automobile driver shot by uniformed police when he failed to heed a command to stop. On the same days, there had been two drive-by shootings at the SA; an SS man had wounded two gendarmerie; and a shoot-out had occurred between uniformed police and SA men, in which they wounded a bystander. In contrast, other surviving Gestapo reports from that month were incident-free.[21]

In the same period, arrests for "political offenses" in Prussia ranged from 50 to 80 per day, of which only about 15 were ordered by the Gestapo. Ten to 20 of the others were for besmirching the government or Nazis.[22] SA and SS auxiliaries clearly reigned with a free hand.

In May 1933, Göring's ministry had chided the detectives for not being as successful as the SA and SS at interrogating political suspects. It was noted that they should therefore have no reservations about turning suspects over temporarily for interrogation.[23] Such a procedure represented for the professionals a loss of control over their work that paralleled other intrusions by Nazi auxiliaries, but at the same time it promised a freer reign to accomplish their mission. Furthermore it authorized that freer reign in a way that left their hands clean.

Victims and witnesses usually could not distinguish among the SA, the SS, the auxiliary police, the regular police, and the Gestapo, much less tell the difference between Gestapo-ordered action and that ordered by a local Nazi official. Their accounts of atrocities by "uniformed" Gestapo men must have referred to SA or SS employees. Most murders and fatal beatings were the acts of SA and SS men, though their victims may have been arrested on Gestapo orders. A few victims do speak of being hit by plainclothes Gestapo detectives. Apparently the common pattern was for a detective to conduct an interrogation using standard psychological techniques until a suspect failed to provide important information they believed he had. Then a team of SA or SS employees would work him over until the detective decided he had gotten all the information he would get. Further abuses occurred in SA or SS holding facilities such as the Columbia Haus in Berlin, even to victims whom the detectives had not singled out for such attention. Here the SA Ic and the SD pursued their own ends, or the guards simply vented their spleens without the victim knowing the difference.[24]

Inside sources of information contradict hopelessly. Diels's memoirs contrast with those of Hans B. Gisevius, who began work in the Gestapo in August. Reality probably lies somewhere between their extremes. On the one hand, Diels claimed he cared only about prosecuting Marxist enemies and spent most of his time guarding both guilty and innocent from the excesses of the SA and SS. He attributed all Gestapo excesses to Arthur Nebe, head of the "executive" section, whose SS auxiliaries Diels could disassociate from "members of the Gestapo." In contrast, Gisevius tells us that Diels and his ilk already took victims "for a ride Chicago-style," and joked crudely about it. He could hear screams of agony within the halls of the Gestapo office.[25] Gisevius freely painted SA, SS, and Diels's people with the same brush, and exonerated Nebe. Both Diels and Gisevius agreed, however, that the Gestapo office became a rat's nest of intrigue as various elements aligned with competing forces among the Nazis.

At this early stage, the detectives undoubtedly responded more as individuals than as an organization about which one can make safe generalizations. Some victims felt that the Gestapo professionals they encountered disapproved of the brutality. Frequent and extensive transfers of personnel, complete reorganizations, complete shifts in officially and publicly expressed demands on the police, the elimination of many external restraints, and the general insecurity of career policemen in the face of revolution made chaos of the professional's orderly world. Although the professional value system apparently survived, authorization, bolstering, and dehumanization were at work. Each individual probably responded erratically, depending on his experiences.

For every breakdown of integrity that the professional encountered, a force for stability and order countered it. Despite their radical rhetoric, chiefs like Göring, Diels, and Nebe tried to keep a lid on things and saw a continuation of police professionalism as the only viable route. Diels and Nebe represent the range of transition through which the Prussian political detective went, seeing the Nazis as Germany's last hope and expecting them to become normalized. Nebe was one of the relatively few who made the transition to full NS membership before 1933, embracing the Movement and its ideology insofar as they did not impinge on his professional autonomy.

One can understand Diels' behavior only as the mixed responses of a professional policeman, an empire-building bureaucrat, and a cold-blooded realist limited by some convictions. He tried sincerely to protect society from what he saw as the Communist threat on one side and radical-Nazi extremism on the other. As a professional policeman, he worked for freedom for his men to perform their mission unhampered, yet there were limits to how far he would go. Although these limits did not prohibit getting rough with those who presented obvious threats to national security, he worried over "unjustifiable" excesses. He helped cover up some Nazi murders, but wanted to prosecute others.[26] He and his kind would gladly take the first steps toward a police state and obediently legitimize Nazi illegalities. Nevertheless, they would also impede the next stages of development that Himmler and Heydrich ultimately brought. Meanwhile in Bavaria, those two supervised the induction of the political detectives into the new order.

Himmler and the Other Länder

As Himmler acquired his offices, Heydrich finally became Director of the Bavarian Political Police (BPP). Heydrich knew that, compared with the police professionals, he and his SD were amateurs, dependent totally on the professionals for effective political police work. Consequently, the BPP remained no less professional a force than the Gestapo.

Before March 1933, the political police in Bavaria had shared the professional's general disdain for Nazi riffraff. Although penetrated by Nazis, they may not have been as extensively in liaison with the Movement as political police in other states. Although the conservative Bavarian government doubted their support, the political police continued surveillance of the Nazi threat until March 1933. Allegedly, men like Heinrich Müller, Franz Huber, and their associates spoke openly of defending police offices against any Brown coup.[27]

When Heydrich took over the Munich Political Section, he began a screening process. Much to the surprise of that group, nothing like a thorough purge resulted. Instead, Heydrich kept men like Huber, who had worked against right-wing movements, including the Nazis. Huber had great value against enemies on the right like Strasser and Stennes, but also against "unreliable" elements still within the Movement.[28] Most significantly, however, he was an experienced political detective and an established member of a tightly knit team. Less disrupted than the Gestapo office, this team became the core of the BPP, beholden to Heydrich for their survival. They served loyally in the SS, which had recognized their value, seemingly preserved their professional integrity, and maintained their continued service.

Among these men, the most important was to be Heinrich Müller, the final head of the Gestapo. This thirty-three-year-old police detective began his career in 1919 following distinguished military service. The records of his life belie many of the derogatory descriptions so common in histories of the Gestapo. Although he worked mostly from behind a desk, he was no "cowardly bully." As an aviator he had earned the Iron Cross First Class, among other decorations, for such daring exploits as a solo raid on Paris. Later he and Huber found relaxation in the less-than-safe sport of mountain climbing. Although his thick build and Bavarian accent may have given some the impression of dull coarseness, he had enough intelligence to receive highest honors on exams for middle-grade detective. He was an intelligent and especially diligent professional detective with a reputation as a compulsive worker. For this cool, withdrawn man with few intimate relations, even among his circle of friends, his work was his life.[29]

All sources agree that even Müller's membership in the SS and Party grew not from ideological conviction, but rather from common interest. He never had a party allegiance until he belatedly joined the NSDAP. As an ardent nationalist, he saw the left, especially Communism, as an extreme evil to be combated by every means. When Heydrich took over, he turned almost instantly to Müller as an expert on the Communist movement, and the two developed a close working relationship. In Bavaria, Müller served as a less independent, more cooperative counterpart of Diels. Expertise and his ardent hate for Communism guaranteed his future.

Even during the Weimar period, Müller had a reputation for exceeding legal norms in work against leftist movements.[30] Never adverse to strong-arm tactics when "necessary," he soon emerged as an open, if laconic, advocate of whatever means were necessary to get police work done. From such beginnings, he went on to become a chief executive of genocide and every extreme of inhumanity, without displaying any pleasure or lust for blood.[31]

Victims of Nazi terror who confronted him personally often contradict popular images without reducing his terrible significance. When Helmuth von Molke was arrested in 1944 as a leader of the Kreisau resistance circle, his wife sought in vain for Müller's intervention on her husband's behalf. Nevertheless, in their interview she found him courteous and sympathetic, even persistently offering to help the future widow and her children. Despite her vulnerability, he used no intimidations to get further information, only the psychological ploys of the "good cop" to win her trust. Finally, he explained why there could be no reprieve for her husband. "After the first world war all our enemies had survived and came out to take over. We shall see to it that this will not happen this time."[32] In Müller's mind, von Molke had to die. Even in the face of ultimate defeat, it was the policeman's job to ferret out and *eliminate* the sources of all "threats to society," no matter how otherwise respected or ineffective they might be.

As the son of a police family, he must have been tightly enmeshed in his police subculture, which clearly could allow illegal violence for "righteous action." One should not, however, describe Müller and other Gestapo types with police origins as typical products of a police subculture. They represented an extreme type that might be labeled "radical enforcers." Such policemen and their "civilian" counterparts want an absolutely free hand to strike at the root of crime by eliminating all antisocial elements, usually defined abstractly. They argue that such "enemies" should have no rights and deserve no consideration, and they always slough off problems of distinguishing enemies from good citizens. They willingly assume the duties of judge, jury, prosecutor, and even executioner. Under Himmler and Heydrich, radical enforcers found encouragement and reward, but they still had to function as disciplined "political soldiers" rather than spontaneous killers.

To build their new central office for the BPP, Himmler and Heydrich drafted trained personnel. The bulk of the original force, fifty-two officials, eighty-one detectives and uniformed policemen, and nineteen temporary employees (152 total), came directly from the Munich Metropolitan Police. To these they added civil servants from other sources and an undetermined number of SS men placed in official police service, giving an early total of 181 officials and 14 temporary employees. Of course, SS auxiliaries augmented this force, while political police attached to regional and local offices as well as regular policemen provided field support.[33] In composition, the BPP and its central office resembled the Prussian Gestapo and its Gestapo office.

The BPP also performed typical political work: surveillance of individuals and organizations, control of the news media, collection of intelligence for police files, and ordering or execution of arrests. Massive arrests of Communists began March 9, even before the embryonic BPP could start to work. Then came the center and right parties and the non-Nazi trade unions and workers' organizations, whom the BPP often harassed, making raids and arrests well before these organizations became illegal. The Nazi leaders hardly hesitated to employ the BPP and their SS-run concentration camp at Dachau as tools of persuasion to accomplish any end they considered political, even the control of price gougers.[34] Here, Himmler used his legal powers extralegally in contrast to the more spontaneous excesses of the SA revolution.

Under Himmler's personal command, the BPP quickly carried its concept of political suspects well beyond norms. Freemasons and Jehovah's Witnesses, suspect by Nazi definition, were joined quietly by homosexuals, a special concern of both Himmler and Heydrich. Of special significance in Catholic Bavaria was the attention paid to priests. Since the regime officially tolerated the Church, it could not define priests as suspect, unless their political activities made them so. Then, of course, there were the Jews. At this stage only certain Jewish organizations and otherwise suspect individuals suffered official harassment and arrests.[35]

Such early expansions beyond the purely political realm did not necessarily represent a radical transition for the men of the BPP. One of the major problems in controlling any police force is that police subcultures reflect native prejudices and attitudes. Minority groups, organizations associated with the forces of change, and groups with nonconformist attitudes and values are easily confused with "antisocial elements" as causes of trouble and, therefore, challenges to authority. As such, they can become targets of suspicion and hostility within police ranks. It is harder to keep the police from being suspicious of such groups than it is to encourage them to be so. Radical enforcers like Müller actually led the way in prosecuting people for their relationships rather than their acts.

Even among devout Catholics, priests can become targets of suspicion and hostility, especially the priest who is too outspoken about socially sensitive issues, who "meddles in politics" or other matters "which don't concern him." Thus, Catholic policemen would often work well against the incautious priest. Even if devout Catholics among the police became stumbling blocks in the SS campaign against the Church, they might be more severe on the priest who made the Church vulnerable to attack. Such harassment made the issue of the Church so touchy that Himmler had to restrain SS and police hostility toward individual priests lest they create crises that would disrupt his anti-

Church program. So, in early July, he limited grounds for action and required his personal approval for the arrest of priests.[36]

Delving into the actual behavior of the BPP, one confronts the same problems as with the Gestapo. Clearly, however, there was an increase in police excesses.[37] Himmler's joint command over both the BPP and Bavaria's concentration camp escalated the detectives' involvement in sanctioned violence.

In Dachau, a small branch of the BPP, the Political Department, provided the sole official link to the SS-run camp. The excesses there were not performed by men of the BPP. This convenient separation always allowed the professional policemen the excuse that they and their organization had no part in SS crimes. As transparent as it may seem, such an excuse grows so naturally from authorization and routinization that it allows the individual "to do his job" and escape concern for what happens thereafter, leaving that to the responsibility of superiors.[38]

Those superiors were SS commanders, but inclusion under SS command marked merely a second step for Bavarian detectives in a process Aronson has aptly labeled a "transvaluation of values." From a police subculture with its own value system balanced against the demands of society, they entered the more-extreme SS subculture. Here, the radical enforcers blossomed, and the more-conventional detectives felt pressures contrary to the restraints of former years.[39] Well before that, however, during the crisis years of 1919–1921, the political detectives under Ernst Pöhner had introduced brutal interrogations, "preventive" murder and political terrorism, and even prototype concentration camps.[40] In Bavaria, the transvaluation for political policemen began with the Republic that never escaped its birth pains.

With the advantage of well-prepared ground in Bavaria, Himmler created a radical departure from normal law enforcement with his synthesis of political police, SS, and concentration camp. By the time he arrived in Prussia, the groundwork already existed there as well, and the Bavarian professionals he and Heydrich brought with them spread the infection within the police subculture to facilitate further transvaluation.

Not all professionals, even those drawn early into SS and SD, succumbed readily to the transvaluation. Dr. Karl Schäfer of the Frankfurt am Main political police attempted in his memoirs to show how, through it all, he retained his professional and ethical standards.[41] Although one might doubt the depth of his self-criticism, he was convinced in his own mind of his relative success. He claimed that under the Republic he had served to maintain order with equal vigilance against left and right (NS included). Under the Nazis, specialization in training and counterespionage made it easier to keep his hands clean.

In spring 1934, as the official responsible for training SS detective employees, he was offered SS-SD membership. He accepted as part of the new rules of the game. He claimed he indoctrinated SS recruits in proper police procedure, to which they responded well, heading off excesses.[42]

The maintenance of such professional integrity in no way undermined Himmler's progress. On the contrary, as long as professionals like Schäfer did their jobs, they would serve well until Himmler could replace them with a new generation of SS policemen. They not only provided the image of legitimately maintained law and order, but their very professionalism ensured control of the police during the transition period.

In the smaller states, especially where Himmler was only nominal commander of political police until 1936, professional policemen experienced radically different transitions.[43] On the one extreme, they lost almost completely their professional autonomy to wild Nazi actions, without any restoration of apparent normality. In other states, the transition was gradual, and early Nazi excesses were seemingly replaced by a restoration of professional norms that lasted several years.

In Braunschweig, the system became so dominated by Nazi radicals that the political detectives were almost completely displaced. Prime Minister Dietrich Klagges had unleashed the SS auxiliaries, and their brutal regime had been so successful that he apparently felt no need to reorganize the small political police under SS-General Herbert Jeckln as head of the state police. Such excesses led to friction with Himmler who, with Reichsleitung intervention, got himself appointed titular commander in Braunschweig. Thereafter, a Braunschweig Political Police under Jeckeln's command was created to normalize political police action.[44]

Unlike most political police chiefs, Jeckeln did not build his force from professionals. The few political detectives available were so thoroughly outnumbered by SS coworkers that no sense of restored professionalism could have ensued. In the central office, with an initial staff of 14, only Jeckeln's deputy (an administrative civil servant soon replaced by a qualified SS man) and 3 detective sergeants were qualified. Seven other detective positions were filled extralegally with SS men. They and subsequent additions were later legitimized through tests that were watered down so they could pass. The eight outposts were also staffed by SS men regardless of qualifications.[45]

By the time the Braunschweig Political Police were absorbed into the Reich Gestapo at the end of 1936, 77 percent of the detectives and administrative staff were SS men, and all but one were Party members.[46] The Braunschweig Political Police were clearly an NS-SS police first and a paraprofessional force second.

Elsewhere, the ostensible preservation of professional autonomy enabled some policemen to defer transvaluation. In Bremen, a Gestapo was created in June 1933 from the P-Post (former Nachrichtenstelle) of the Bremen police chief.[47] Only two detectives were Nazis at the time, but five more joined the Party in May 1933. SS penetration was slow: the captain joined SS-SD in 1935, as did two other detectives in 1936; other SS members mostly rose from the auxiliaries through the ranks. By the end of 1936, as the men of Gestapo Bremen were screened for transfer into the Reich Gestapo, the force had grown to 81. Of these, only 31 were Party members, 4 of whom were office personnel. Of the 13 SS members (16 percent of the total staff), 3 were still only candidate members.[48]

Police Lieutenant Erwin Schulz had aided NS penetration, cooperating clandestinely since 1931 as a confidential agent of the local SS and the Party district leader. In 1932, he more openly joined the NS Civil Servants, then joined the Party in May 1933, along with several of his detectives. By then he was the captain commanding the Bremen Gestapo. His ties were to local Nazis who trusted him, and he was not drawn into the SS-SD until 1935, when Himmler began to tighten his hold.[49]

Numerous colleagues testified that Schulz kept his NS ties so separate from his professional role that they were unaware of his NS connections. He never pressed his men into NS affiliations or church withdrawal. He regularized and humanized protective custody affairs and prosecuted excesses by SS and police. As late as November 1938, he spoke strongly against anti-Semitic excesses and prosecuted NS men and police for illegal persecutions and plundering.[50] Although such a righteous image is hard to swallow whole, he was better positioned for an alliance with Nazis against the "enemies of German society" that allowed him to retain professional autonomy and postpone transvaluation. Indeed, the Nazi Police Senator for Bremen issued a shooting order like Göring's, but that hardly undermined the authority of police officials. Furthermore, the senator strongly admonished Nazis in police service to submit themselves to the discipline of their officers.[51] For Schulz the transvaluation could be postponed.

Even though he served in the proto-Einsatzgruppen establishing Gestapo posts in Austria, the Sudetenland and the Protectorate, Schulz maintained a sense of moral limits. For instance, in 1941, he was head of the Sipo officers' school in Berlin when its candidates were suddenly detailed to Einsatzgruppen staffs in Russia. After a few months, they returned to the school. According to one student, Schulz objected to the shooting of Jews and threatened that if they had been involved, he would have them expelled for unsuitable character. Although he knew this was done on orders, he considered it an abominable act. If this story is true, he apparently did not yet understand the extent of the authorization. Unfortunately, he left no insight into his own transvaluation, which must have occurred fairly rapidly, for shortly thereafter he personally led an Einsatzkommando in Russia. He must have succumbed to authorization in order to maintain that transcendent mission of professional police service with which he had deluded himself for so long.

One should not condemn too easily those detectives who continued their careers into the Nazi era. They continued to serve the legitimate government, which struck at its enemies with police force that remained within the law. Extralegal excesses came from "uncontrolled" elements which the regime gradually brought into line and which could be justified during the emergency period of alleged Communist threats to the state. Erosions of their professionalism and integrity seemed realistic necessities and, one could hope, were temporary. Amid the depression, few could give up secure careers and subject their families to uncertainty and hardship. Most professionals rightly felt that it would be irresponsible to relinquish control of police work totally to the uncontrolled NS rabble. To stay on the job was to serve one's society and country; to leave was to desert it. Such were the lures that drew the professional detectives into the continued authorization, routinization, and brutalization that would blind them to the reality of their moral dilemma after the true nature of their role should have become clear. There is, therefore, some point after which one can judge moral failure, but it must have varied greatly among individual experiences.

The relationship of such policemen to the Nazis never became one of complete support. The partnership into which the police were drawn between 1933 and 1937 was not with the practitioners of unlimited imperialism and genocide, but with a right-radical party that many conservatives expected to be moderated by the responsibilities of office— the party of "legal political power." Although they bear full responsibility for the role they played, one must remember how they were drawn by stages into a system whose ultimate conclusion was not visible.

As with the military, the industrialists, and many other professional groups, the police remained uneasy in their partnership with the Nazis. Yet to a greater degree than the others, the police more directly developed the worst aspects of the Third Reich. Many policemen who joined SS and SD men in the SS-police directly earned their brutal reputations. They were not only escalated into what they did, they also contributed to the escalation.

Further Transformations under Himmler

Like Göring, Himmler promised to advance careers, increase rewards, and free police from confusing liberal constitutional limitations. Furthermore, after the summer of 1934, Himmler's command ended more than a year of instability and disorder in Prussia.

Within a month of taking over the Prussian Gestapo, Heydrich had reorganized its Berlin office.[52] A careful study of personnel changes shows that he inflated neither numbers nor ranks. The growth of the staff merely matched that of the entire organization and the increased responsibilities of the office, which now served as a coordinating center for the political police of all states. A sizable number of the new men had already come in under Diels between January and April, and Heydrich's additions after April merely conformed to the accelerating growth of the previous months. He even reduced that growth rate.[53] Considering the comprehensiveness of its mission, the Gestapo did not have an overblown bureaucracy, and Diels and Heydrich claimed with justice that their people were overworked.

Despite increased size, the new organizational structure had a simpler, more consistent distribution of responsibilities. Three major departments (Hauptabteilungen) with more-uniform responsibilities replaced Diels's five departments (Abteilungen). For instance, the old Department II had mixed desks for legal affairs with those responsible for handling enemies. Under the new organization, Major Department I handled most legal and administrative matters, Department II dealt with enemies, suspects, and the press, and Department III, the Abwehrpolice, combated high treason, espionage, and sabotage.

The new organization also reveals the work of the Gestapo and changes resulting from Himmlerian ideology. The objects of Gestapo concern remained a list of NS enemies: Marxists, reactionaries, foreigners, Jews, and a wide variety of societies and orders. The number of desks devoted to Marxist, specifically Communist, activities shows that the Gestapo's major concerns remained the same. Those also "suspected" still included reactionary nationalists, monarchists, and former members of all outlawed organizations (including former allies, free corps, and veterans' groups), and, of course, all foreigners. From their previous place on the suspect list, however, the religious organizations had joined the distinct enemy category of Jews, Freemasons, and Emigrants. Of course, the NS Movement and its organizations did not escape surveillance. The press police still monitored both domestic and foreign publications, suppressing the undesirable. Finally, the Abwehrpolice still concerned themselves with attacks on the nation's defenses and armament.

The new organization also reflected SS militarization. SS General Heydrich replaced Ministerial Counselor Diels, and the more traditional Prussian bureaucratic superstructure gave way to a "staff" organization for managing support functions under an "adjutant," who replaced a civil servant.

Despite this militarization, the new organization also gave the impression of a return to preemergency status, for what it was worth. The SS-Commando disappeared into the concentration camp system, and liaison with Party paramilitary organizations to support police actions was no longer needed. The SS had taken over the police, but, more important, it had taken command "only," and all NS formations terminated their direct, uncontrolled participation in police actions. The "regular" police would do their jobs while things got back to normal. Although this image of propriety was conjured to please Nazi moderates, the conservative allies, and perhaps large segments of the public, it had to be balanced carefully with an image of a properly Nazified police, to mollify more radical elements. Simultaneously, the capacity for extraordinary police measures to crush opposition had to be retained. Himmler and Heydrich's efforts to balance such conflicting concerns provide a central theme for the history of Sipo and SD.

As part of the militarization of the Gestapo office came a typical NS assault on the bureaucratic mentality. For instance, although civil service ranks increased along with growth, advancement came mostly at the intermediate and lower or working levels. The number of superior civil servants declined while their responsibilities expanded. For instance, the departments under Diels (a Ministerialrat) had been run by four government counselors. Heydrich used only two, each responsible for a major department; he ran the other one through two SS lieutenants who supervised working-level police officials, usually of detective lieutenant rank.

Throughout 1935, although the Gestapo continued to grow, the Berlin office remained more streamlined than under Diels. In June, the Gestapo office had only 618 male personnel of all types, marking a significant reduction from Diels's high of 680.[54] In fact, civil service and budgetary constraints required that Heydrich keep his machine lean. The budget for 1934, to which he had gained supplements in July, allotted only 2,658 positions all told (1,854 civil servants). A sizable part of the thousand-man increase over 1933 had been gained by Diels. By June 1935, only about 2,602 positions were actually filled (1,972 civil servants, but fewer employees). By the spring of 1936, Himmler reported that the Prussian Gestapo had 2,050 civil servants, with a total of 2,650 in the entire Reich, to be incorporated in the new Reich Gestapo.[55]

Streamlining and militarization conformed with NS and SS ideological objectives: to impress the policemen with an "NS equality" that would close the gap between the old elite and the little man; to create the impression that under the new leadership the hardworking policeman would win recognition and reward; and to replace the machinery of bureaucracy with a military system of command and compliance in tune with the führer principle and "SS elitism."

Such was the mood that Himmler and Heydrich sought to purvey in their pep talks to Gestapo officials. In October, Himmler defined the sort of personal relations and behavior he wanted. He demanded that the Gestapo handle its business with soldierly speed rather than through bureaucratic red tape. The staff should also be immune to rumors that cause dissension, and he wanted none of the anonymous informing that "characterized the management of offices under Jewish chiefs." He and Heydrich would create a sense of soldierly camaraderie. "I look on you all only as associates and comrades, not as higher, middle, and lower civil servants." He wanted all to see him as a fatherly chief and to feel free to come to him with their problems. Furthermore, he assured them that he knew how poorly they were paid, especially the lower ranks, and he would do everything in his power to correct that.[56] Himmler sought to infuse an NS and SS ethos, while appealing intuitively to them through their existing police subculture.

He especially wanted to establish a proper image with the public. When "the little man among the people" reported something suspicious, or when a wife waited anxiously to learn the fate of her husband taken into custody, they were not to receive routine paper work.

> The Volk must hold the conviction that the most just authority, which works the most exactly in the new state, is the dreaded Gestapo. The Volk must come to the view that, if someone has been seized, he had been seized with right; it must have the view that, in all things that are not to the detriment of the state, the members of the Gestapo are men with human kindness, with human hearts and absolute rightness. . . .
>
> I also wish that everyone who comes to you will be handled courteously and sociably. I wish that you will use on the phone a courteous and proper tone. I wish further that no man will growl in any way. Please, see yourself as helpers and not as dictators.[57]

On the other hand, Himmler and Heydrich increasingly emphasized the necessity for an extraordinary, unrestricted political police that could take whatever measures were needed to eliminate all threats. A proper totalitarian society was an "organically indivisible national community" that could not tolerate "any political ideas at variance with the will of the majority." They depicted Germany as a nation under siege, surrounded by hostile enemies and permeated with their camouflaged agents. Since all open opposition was illegal, formerly open domestic enemies had become the "camouflaged enemy." Undetected enemies had penetrated every institution and worked to weaken the new order. With the help of the SD, the Gestapo would be able to separate the good from the bad, and had to be free to round them up without any interference. Everyone had to trust the properly guided Gestapo to strike well and to correct on its own initiative whatever mistakes it might make. Its power had to be completely open ended.[58]

Meanwhile, the contradictory demands that Himmler's beliefs placed upon the real-life Gestapo official must have produced frustrations ironically similar to those felt by the policeman under a liberal constitution that limits his freedom of action. His police superior called for sharp, decisive actions that could bring him under attack from more conservative authorities and make him hated and feared by the public who were supposed to admire and respect him. Then, if his police subculture functioned according to theory, it generated greater loyalty to the police superior and a desire to carry out his orders as secretively as necessary. Toward interfering officials and disapproving elements in the public he would direct a hostility grown of the frustrations he experienced in the process.

Theoretically, the results should have been the innumerable violations of due process that actually occurred. In some cases Himmler or Heydrich might be forced to discipline the offender, but to do so too often would undermine the loyalty of their subordinates. For the subculture to work to their advantage, they had to protect the policeman who did his "duty." They seemed to sense this, for they usually disciplined lightly, treating the offender as an overzealous, but basically good boy.[59] Reward often followed discipline, with discipline so disrupted and restraints so undermined that the Gestapo, like the concentration camps, remained a peculiar mixture of spontaneous, cruel excesses with cool action and propriety.

In the transformation of the political police, Werner Best formed a unique bridge between the conservative and radical-right forces, and, therefore, must have contributed greatly to the split personality of the emerging Gestapo. An Old Fighter with a juridical civil service background, Best had played a key role in the Nazification of the Hessian police until he ran afoul of local NS politics. Himmler then drew him into the SD where his political and administrative talents and his legitimate credentials made him ideal as Heydrich's lieutenant for shaping the Gestapo office. He staunchly advocated a powerful SS-police force that could stand above the law when necessary. In contrast to the true radical enforcer, he appreciated the need for some limitations. He conceived them as something akin to professional self-discipline, imposed from within by leaders like himself and based on training programs that balanced a legal education with a solid foundation in the NS world view.[60] This open-ended dichotomy helped shape the character of the Gestapo into something like a vacuum cleaner with several mouths, sucking in susceptible idealists among conservatives and right radicals, as well as radical enforcers and opportunists. Each could see in the Gestapo an opportunity for what he considered desirable.

Efforts to weigh authority and organizational rectitude against revolutionary flexibility gave the Gestapo a unique balance between a professional police organization and one amateurish enough to allow a strong element of gangsterism. Although the Gestapo undeniably perpetrated cruel excesses, Best's job involved curbing their spontaneous manifestations and replacing them with more "legitimate" repression.

In conjunction with concerns about public image and tighter control over their political police, Heydrich and Best also had to sharpen police awareness of the ideological enemy and to heighten their men's determination to strike with cold-blooded efficiency. Of course, their real enemy was the left, but they had successfully reduced it to a tolerable level. At the moment, the conservative and reactionary allies, who would limit or reduce NS power if they could, represented the major problem. To thwart a coup against the regime, one needed a reliable police, and SS penetration was directed toward that end. Heydrich intended his indoctrination about the camouflaged internal enemy to heighten police suspicion of this opposition.

By and large, the police retained its traditional repressive-defensive role. Himmler, Heydrich, and Best conceived the role as more positive, however, for they wanted to create a force to serve as the cutting edge of the new order, leading the people in a silent revolution by showing the way and by being available for whatever action the Führer might deem necessary. To be prepared for such a role, the police had to see society and the enemy through the perspective of the NS world view so they could sweep away any obstacle with cold-blooded self-righteousness. In this way, Himmler, Heydrich, Best, and Müller, each in his own way, worked toward a transformation of professional police personnel.

Transformations, 1934–1937

Indoctrination probably contributed to the transformation of the professional police. The next chapter deals with those indoctrination programs designed for all detectives. What will be said there applies to the Gestapo detectives discussed here. This chapter focuses on an analysis of Gestapo operations and personnel. From that will come insights into the more significant, functional forces at work in their transformation.

Personnel

The personnel changes that Himmler and Heydrich made contributed to transformations. Although historians usually assert that they purged the Gestapo, that is a half-truth.[1] Extensive changes did occur in those sections responsible for administrative and legal affairs. New people, mostly from the Bavarian police, now formed Heydrich's staff. In Main Department I, however, one Prussian high civil servant replaced two, consolidating work from former Departments I and II. Perhaps only a stopgap, he lasted less than a year—to be replaced when Werner Best arrived in Berlin.

A number of persons left the administrative offices, especially department heads; however, their replacements usually came from other branches of the Prussian police, often Gestapo posts. They were not Himmler's outsiders. One major exception, SS Lieutenant Trinkle, took over administrative-financial affairs. A finance officer in the Bavarian State Police, he had enough contacts in the Movement to be known as reliable, so when Himmler and Heydrich moved to Berlin, they drafted him from the SA. They had a special interest in control of Gestapo funds.[2]

Of all the changes, only ten clearly stand out as purges. Furthermore, with few exceptions, one set of Prussian bureaucrats merely replaced another. An analysis of the changes under the new Main Department II raises further questions about purges. Its director had been Arthur Nebe, whom Frick and Daluege transferred to the Berlin Kripo. Heydrich allegedly wanted to keep him, and he gladly retained many of Nebe's former department heads. Most of them found secure careers in the later Gestapo. Reinhold Heller, who had worked closely with Diels, an expert on Marxist movements, stayed on as Müller's deputy. Even the expert on Jews and Freemasons, Dr. Hasselbacker, was retained and brought into the SD rather than replaced by an SD expert.[3]

Among the detectives who did leave, a large number turned up in the Prussian Kripo.[4] That raises the possibility that, like Nebe, they moved by choice rather than by purge. According to Gisevius, Nebe did not want to serve under Himmler and Heydrich.[5, 6] Both purge and flight probably explain the personnel changes in the spring of 1934.

Christof Graf has analyzed the men in Diels's Gestapo headquarters who held civil service status.[7] Because of educational requirements, about one-half had passed the second exam for full juridical status, while another tenth had concluded with "only" a doctorate in jurisprudence. One-sixth had failed to complete higher education; those without full juridical status were detectives rather than administrative or juridical civil servants. Presumably, the remaining 25 percent or so were also detectives who had completed only the Abitur plus detective officers school.

Only two were Party members before 1933, but from one-fifth to two-fifths had been members of NS ancillary organizations. About one-fifth had been members of the Center party. A good four-fifths would eventually join the Party, and about one-half joined the SA, but only one-third joined the SS (presumably most of those who remained in Sipo). About one-fifth joined the SD, mostly after 1934.

By September 1939, about one-third were still in the Gestapo, while more than half remained in some branch of Sipo and SD. The other half, however, had left the Gestapo before the end of 1934. The detectives tended to hang on more than other civil servants. Most of those who departed, either by purge or choice, were the conventional bureaucrats whom Diels had relied upon to staff his headquarters, as opposed to the detectives with the expertise that Heydrich could less easily replace.

Furthermore, the purge/departure was not "political." Of those whom Diels had drafted from outside the political police, one-third had been affiliated with the NS before 1933, and one-quarter joined the Party in 1933. The juridical civil servants on whom Diels relied had been earlier joiners than the detectives.[8] Apparently, it was the expertise of the detectives and the personal ties of the administrators that determined who remained and who departed. Nazi status was less significant. Himmler and Heydrich found their own administrators among SS jurists or those who had less-objectionable NS connections.

Such SS-SD penetration helps explain the transformation of professional policemen, but penetration of the Gestapo was much slower and more limited than generally believed. Himmler and Heydrich's arrival with a number of Bavarian policemen in train marked the first group absorption of policemen into the SD. Heydrich absorbed these Bavarians at this time to solve the problems of the move. They had no authority or standing in Prussia. He could not solve that problem by official transfers into Prussian service, because their police ranks were too low. The easy answer lay in SS-SD membership. This also gave Heydrich more complete command over them beyond any police authority, and, in turn, it gave them greater rank and status than their lower Bavarian police ranks would have provided. In this way, the team of Reinhard Flesch, Heinrich Müller, Franz-Josef Huber, and Joseph Meisinger could run Subdepartment Enemies and Suspects. Other members of the Bavarian Political Police and Gestapo remained in the regular SS. An exclusive role for the SD in penetrating the political police had yet to emerge.

A similar pattern occurred in the field posts, with even less SS penetration and little SD presence. In most cases the rate of SS infiltration remained what it had been under Diels. Even into 1935, the Gestapo was not dominated by the SS; it was commanded from above with heavy reliance on policemen and bureaucrats for execution. Together, Party members (21 percent with only Party membership) and SA men (19 percent) exceeded SS-SD men (21 percent) in the Nazification of the Gestapo.[9]

In most cases, one or two SD men commanded the Gestapo posts, which also had a few scattered regular SS men, usually in the lowest ranks where they had entered from the auxiliary police. At one extreme, the Bielefeld post had only one SS member. As late as summer 1935, this office still had no SS chief and no SD members. Posts like that at Breslau, within the fiefs of powerful opponents like SA leader Heines, remained under limited control by Heydrich until the Röhm purge. At the other extreme were exceptions like Kiel, Königsberg, Liegnitz, and Schneidemühl, where SS men constituted one-quarter to one-third of the personnel, but two of these were established by Himmler and Heydrich. Even in these posts, aside from one or two officials, most SS men served as employees and temporary help.[10]

Practical considerations retarded SS penetration. Budgeted Gestapo positions remained limited. The more significant positions also required qualifications for professional-police or legal work, and few SS men had such qualifications. Even at the lowest levels, the limited number of openings could not be given exclusively to SS men. Propriety and camaraderie required that other deserving Nazis also get employment.

Himmler's limited authority as Inspector of the Gestapo also retarded penetration. As Aronson put it, in Prussia he faced a threefold problem. He remained subordinate to Göring. He had to avow subordination to Frick as both Reich and Prussian Minister of the Interior, for their momentary alliance required such pretenses. The provincial and district governors formed the third obstacle, for their partial authority over the field posts still limited Himmler's freedom.[11]

Ironically, the relative slowness of SS penetration probably facilitated the transformation of the professionals. They resented that penetration and distrusted the penetrators. But as long as the SS had to observe civil service and professional limitations, there was always hope that the police would absorb them rather than vice versa. The professional was encouraged to stay on and absorb the interlopers.

Of course, to shape the police, Himmler's plan was to fuse them with the SS. Not until the summer of 1935, however, did the logic of SD preeminence in that penetration finally emerge. We may never know to whom it first occurred, or what calculations produced it. Since at least May, Heydrich had begun transferring SS members of his Berlin Gestapo office into the SD, where they constituted a special detachment, SD-Dienststelle Gestapa. As of June 25, out of slightly more than 600 officials and employees, there were 180 SD members (29 percent), plus an additional 65 SS men (10.5 percent) who had not yet transferred.[12]

In June 1935, Himmler ordered all Prussian Gestapo posts to submit complete rosters indicating membership in NS organizations. This was apparently the first time anyone tried to determine where and how well the SS had penetrated, and indicates that penetration was haphazard. Himmler needed an accurate assessment upon which to base future plans. The results offer a rare source of data on Prussian Gestapo personnel.[13]

In the field posts, the extent of SS-SD penetration remained considerably below that of the Gestapo Office. Only 13 percent of 1,984 field personnel had SS membership, and they included only 52 SD members (2.6 percent). For the entire Gestapo of about 2,600, 232 SD members provided less than 9 percent penetration. An additional 325 SS members might be transferred into the SD to raise the total above 21 percent. Almost half of these, however, were merely employees. Aside from a few key officials, the SS-SD did not dominate the Gestapo, although the interpenetration was significant. Conditions in Bavaria may have been comparable, but elsewhere, such as Bremen and Hessia, penetration was minimal. Braunschweig must have been an exception with its heavy SS presence.

As for other aspects of Gestapo personnel, 74 percent had been recruited from Prussian police professionals, with an additional 2 percent from Bavaria. Another 2.4 percent were drawn from other Prussian civil service, of whom 25 percent were Party members only, 18 percent SA, and 8.3 percent SS or SD members. Although more than half the professionals had affiliated with the Movement, few had yet joined the SS-SD. Among the 21.6 percent of Gestapo personnel who had been recruited from outside the civil service, 9.3 percent were only Party members, 20.7 percent were SA, 37.6 percent SS, and 30 percent SS-SD members. Thus, 69.3 percent of the SS presence was SS men joining the Gestapo, usually at the lowest ranks, while 30.7 percent was professional police and other civil servants who joined the SS-SD.

The majority of SS penetrators at the lower ranks, who would have had lower educational and social status, were not drawn into the SD until 1935 or 1936. But together these SS-SD members of the Gestapo would form the Sipo-SD; that is, they were those members of the SD whose affiliation served primarily to facilitate fusion of SS and police. The earliest members of the Sipo-SD were of three types. More than one-third were pre-NS professional police suited for early SD membership. A few had qualified to become policemen during the interim before Himmler's takeover. The rest were SD men with qualifications for police service who transferred into the police, mostly after 1934. More than 20 percent came from other branches of the civil service.

The most outstanding characteristic of this early Sipo-SD component was its expression of prejudice in autobiographical statements written for SS records.[14] Although the validity of these tabulated expressions as scientific data is questionable, the degree of difference in attitudes about Jews and Communists is too marked to ignore. While about 4 percent of the regular SD recorded mild to strong anti-Semitism, the Sipo-SD men expressed *none*. In contrast, 29 percent of Sipo-SD men expressed hostility to Communism, 5 percent to SPD, and 18 percent against the Republic—as opposed to 9 percent, 2 percent, and 12 percent, respectively, among other SD men. This markedly stronger preoccupation with purging society of left-wing threats, as opposed to NS racial-ideological concerns, contrasts equally sharply with their subsequently greater involvement in NS racial programs. Of those for whom Einsatzgruppen involvement is clear, 69 percent of the Sipo-SD versus only 49 percent of the regular SD saw action. Thus political-ideological conjunctions may have held or drawn them into Gestapo service, but Nazification added the fillip of racial ideology. Himmler's fusion of SS and police was central to that process.

Fifty percent of the SS penetration in Gestapo headquarters had occurred under Diels. By far the largest single group (94) came into the Gestapo in October 1933, when the SS auxiliary police became employees. As Christof Graf has correctly argued, the pattern for SS penetration was set well before Himmler took over. This was because Diels felt compelled to use SS men to legitimize the Gestapo among Nazis and gain their cooperation with his otherwise professional political police.[15] There is no reason to argue, however, that either Diels or Göring pursued a union of SS and Gestapo as a plan for the police state they envisioned.

All involved had agreed that additions to the police should come from persons who had proven themselves in the fight for NS victory. Göring, Daluege, and Diels had also agreed that SS men were best for the Gestapo, but to maintain some modicum of quality, they had instituted an indoctrination course at the Police Institute. At least four classes had graduated by the end of 1933. Toward the end of his reign, Diels became sufficiently concerned about professional quality to issue more stringent recruitment guidelines. Even so, he continued to support Daluege's requests that Göring waive civil service requirements that blocked SA and SS men. Thus, an SS infusion had occurred on which Himmler and Heydrich could build. Even so, they remained dependent on Göring's approval of personnel policies that violated state regulations.[16]

To formalize Heydrich's consolidation of SS Gestapo men into the SD, on July 4, 1935, Himmler ordered their transfer. It is not known when he applied this order to the other states' political police. The action involved no mass transfer, however, for they executed it on an individual basis at a rate the SD personnel office could manage. Consequently, many of the transfers remained unprocessed well into 1936, and during the process, the SD rejected many.[17]

By 1935, the Prussian Gestapo had assumed the composition that the Reich Gestapo would retain until the uncontrolled growth of the war years. Basically, the professionals represented the vast majority (approximately 76 percent). Among them, slightly more than half had become Nazis by 1935. Of new recruits from the Movement, some were qualified civil servants, and most had SA or Party membership; the rest were SS. One has no basis for determining how many NS infiltrators became policemen simply to find a secure job, and how many felt some commitment to creating an NS police.

Once Himmler acquired command over all the German police in 1936, Göring lost control over personnel, and only the Reich ministries remained as barriers to an arbitrary policy for the Gestapo. Nevertheless, the realities of detective work and the need to show some deference for the professional's image kept Himmler and Heydrich from deviating radically from civil service guidelines.[18] For better control, however, they employed a more closed application process. In 1936, Sipo avoided public recruiting through official channels such as unemployment offices, alleging that it already had a full contingent of civil service candidates for all Kripo and Gestapo positions.[19] Here the intention was to prevent an influx of older, unemployed Nazis at the expense of more suitable candidates. The SS old-boy network and increasingly a Hitler Youth young-boy network were to provide routes of entry.

Although guidelines for induction into the Gestapo took on an image of normality, it could not obscure the Nazification and "SS-ification" that prevailed. For instance, at officer entry levels the minimal educational requirement of Abitur or equivalent remained in force. However, in addition to the three traditional sources (nonpolice or "free" occupations, nondetective police officers, and detective sergeants), candidates for detective officers' ranks could also come from officers of the armed SS detachments. Also, men from "free" occupations had to be members of an NS organization, and of pure German blood traceable back to all grandparents. Most interesting, however, was that application could not come through ministry or Party offices, but only through Gestapo headquarters or posts. The leader of the Gestapo had final approval.[20]

Officer training was more rigorous than before. Lasting two and one-half years total, it included a practical introduction to all relevant police work: twenty-one months in police administrative, uniformed police, Kripo, and Gestapo interior and Abwehr offices. A seven-month course at the Police Institute followed, culminating in the usual detective lieutenant's exam. Then came six months of probational service before full detective-lieutenant status was awarded.[21]

In contrast, the back door into the Gestapo remained open for suitable NS members as employees and workers. After acquiring the patina of police experience and with a little help on the tests, they could win civil service status as detective or administrative sergeant candidates. Even here, however, SS penetration encountered problems. The SA and SS men who had taken these positions in 1933 and 1934 caused one. They were frequently older than the conventional entrants, often with families to support. Pay was too low for them to stay on for as long as it took to get full civil service status. In question were 675 SA and SS men: 40 administrative and 70 detective candidates, 500 detective employees, and 65 workers designated as "drivers," all slated to assume civil service candidate status as soon as budgeted positions became available.[22] In short, the Gestapo was not a fully open door for NS-SS penetration.

A few examples provide an impression of the full range of Gestapo personnel in Heydrich's SD by 1936. Most favored was the pool of NS civil servants with the education and credentials for immediate qualification as high officials. They came from branches of the Prussian juridical and administrative services. As early as December 1934, Best charged the SD with identifying such suitable men for Gestapo recruitment.[23] These they simply transferred into Gestapo, SS, and SD.

One example of this favored source was Dr. Hans Fischer, who had been involved with NS since 1923 in various affiliations; he took Party and SS membership in 1932 while still a legal intern (Referendar). After completing the state exam in 1933, he served in the juridical service, from which he entered the Gestapo to serve as a field post leader. As an active member of the SS, in June 1934, he became commander of a local unit. By March 1935, he found both his full-time Gestapo responsibilities as post leader and his part-time SS command too demanding, and requested release from SS duties. Such practical problems must have contributed to the absorption of all SS-Gestapo men into the SD to rationalize SS demands on their time. In September, the SS personnel office began arranging for Fischer's transfer into the SD.[24]

By this time, the Gestapo had also become alluring to respectable, young middle-class aspirants to higher government service careers. From here on, a pool of young, qualified functionaries became available. The new atmosphere of normality and the campaign to sell the Gestapo's image of propriety succeeded in giving the organization the appearance of a respectable career for ambitious young men. One such, Hans Blomberg, had no apparent NS affiliations until he joined the Party and SA in 1933. He completed his state exam in November 1934, and in September 1935 transferred from juridical service into the Gestapo and served as deputy leader of several field posts. In 1936, he gained SS-SD membership.[25]

Professional policemen with NS connections also provided a major source of qualified Gestapo personnel. Dr. Emanuel Schäfer had pursued a law degree for a government career. Politically, he represented the young war veterans who gravitated gradually through free corps (1919–1921) and Stahlhelm (1925–1928) to the NS orbit. While in the Prussian Criminal Police since 1926, he could not have open membership. Yet he could work actively for the cause during the early 1930s, becoming a contributing member of the SS in 1931. In February 1933, he became head of the new Gestapo post at Breslau. Given the political realities in Silesia, where Edmund Heines reigned, he took up SA membership. Nevertheless, he retained his SS connections and worked closely with the SD. Despite the extension of Himmler's control over the Silesian posts following the purge of Heines, Schäfer retained his SA membership until September 1936. Perhaps this membership still served well in Silesia, since SA membership predominated among local police professionals. By late 1936, the open move to closer Gestapo-SD affiliation negated such necessities, and Schäfer transferred into SS-SD.[26]

Other professional policemen gravitated into the Movement more gradually, without detriment to their careers. Although some Gestapo men may have believed opportunistically that proper membership brought more rapid promotion, until we have some quantitative testing of this belief, we must consider the many examples to the contrary.[27] Individuals apparently felt varying degrees of pressure to join.

By and large, the bulk of professional policemen did not really feel that pressure until 1938, when Himmler decided that all suitable policemen should become SS members. One of Heydrich's adjutants, Police Captain Kurt Pomme, is a prime example, but he at least had secure NS standing. Far less secure, Reinhold Heller had been one of Diels's first Gestapo men, transferred from Section IA with prorepublican political affiliations to overcome. He joined the Party in 1933, while Diels advanced his claim that his suspicious political membership had merely provided defense against political discrimination. Despite what should have been a weak basis, Heller advanced to the highest ranks under Himmler and Heydrich without joining the SS-SD until 1938. Younger professionals like Hans Gippert and Kurt Riedel, civil servants only since 1931, had no apparent NS ties until they finally joined the Party in 1937. Neither joined the SS until 1937 and 1938, respectively.[28]

The bulk of SS men in the Gestapo, who had won only simple employment or civil service status at the lowest levels, formed a sharp contrast to the qualified officials. Most notably, their lives lacked stability and, therefore, social respectability. Usually, they had found their way into völkisch politics through either the war veteran–free corps channel or the youth movements, but a decisive factor in their NS affiliation had been depression unemployment. Most became affiliated between 1930 and 1932. As SS members in the spring of 1933, still unemployed, they became auxiliary police or SS-Commandos. Most became state employees in October 1933, but some as late as 1935. They could then become civil service candidates if they passed qualifying examinations. Although many would become SS officers by 1936, few would rise high in either the SS or police. Becoming SS officers often corresponded to transfer into the SD, perhaps to give them more influence in the Gestapo than they had as employees.[29]

A younger and more successful member of this group earned his high-school-leaving certificate in 1928. After a three-year business apprenticeship with a Berlin firm, he remained employed until released for lack of work in 1932. For a year he helped in his father's business. Meanwhile, he had joined the Party in 1930, the SA in 1931, and in 1933 shifted into the SS, perhaps to find employment. In March, through his SS unit, he joined an SS-commando, employed as auxiliary help, and was finally attached to the SS-Commando Gestapa. Along with many others, he became a Gestapo employee in October. In 1936, he became a civil service candidate, and in 1939 began entry into the detective officer ranks. He passed his qualifying test in 1940, and began training school in February 1941, completing the course in January 1942. By 1943, he was an SS first lieutenant and detective inspector.[30]

For the contrasting experience of an older candidate: after demobilization in 1918, a war veteran found a job as a railroad machinist. In 1925, his problems began with a layoff. He worked for his father for three years, then found another job, only to be laid off again in 1930 at the age of thirty-six. He remained unemployed and without political commitment until he joined the Party and SS in 1932. There he rose rapidly to SS second lieutenant. In January 1934, he became a Gestapo employee, serving as the head of Outpost Hanau and rising to the terminal rank of SS captain by April 1935.[31]

His career is interesting on several counts. Without strong NS attachments or other qualifications, he won early employment in the SS and police. In the Gestapo he had command of small field posts from almost the beginning. Then, in April 1936, the SS personnel office began work on his transfer into the SD. He apparently conflicted with the SD image of propriety, however, for full membership was deferred for two years and he remained frozen in rank until he was expelled back into the regular SS in December 1943, as "fully unsuitable for SD work."[32]

Thus, in contrast to the "respectable citizens"—qualified civil servants and police officials—the Gestapo had a significant influx of victims of the depression or of other personal-social problems, many of whom found newly respectable, relatively stable positions in the Gestapo. There must have been a sizable gap between the two groups. In fact, there may have been a three-way split: (1) the basically "apolitical" (though conservative-nationalist) professionals, (2) the NS professionals with some ideological commitment, (3) and the NS employees, some potentially qualified, some not, some ideologically committed, some not, but all without secure positions unless they served obediently.

In addition to creating internal tensions among personnel, this composition gave the Gestapo a split personality—disparate organizational identities involving diverse personalities in processes legitimizing violence. For some, the Gestapo offered a respectable career. At first, they performed relatively legal functions, often at an intellectual-detective level culminating only in reports. The action taken on such reports usually fell to another type, while responsibility lay with their superiors. Within the value system of the police subculture, even those professionals involved in increasingly excessive executive actions could rationalize them as necessary and, therefore, proper up to a certain point. If, beyond that point, they began to have qualms, there were less-restrained SS and SA men to do the "necessary" dirty work. Although disdained by the professionals, such men became increasingly indispensable. Thus, the professionals must have developed a relationship with the "paraprofessionals" that resembled that between military and SS—one sought to preserve his old status and simultaneously retain his self-image by tapping the energy and lack of restrained respectability in the other. But given the growing momentum toward the radical-enforcer approach, even the most restrained professionals must have succumbed to authorization, bolstering, routinization, and dehumanization.

The political police of the other states evolved along the same lines as the Prussian Gestapo. Key figures in SS penetration, such as Dr. Wilhelm Harster in Württemberg and Police Captain Erwin Schulz in Bremen, were coordinated into SD membership about the same time as their Prussian counterparts.[33]

By the summer of 1934, any illusions of apolitical aloofness that the professionals might have held should have eroded. The source of Nazification was not just SS infiltration. Even "moderates" like Minister of the Interior Frick called for a thorough infusion of NS thought into all ranks of the police so they could serve the new state properly and execute the Führer's will. Indoctrination courses intensified, and officers were instructed to model NS behavior and attitudes for their men. All were expected to immerse themselves in NS publications.[34] Although overt pressure to join the Party and SS-SD was several years away, the cherished apolitical posture of the professional required a considerable denial of reality.

But then, postures and reality are slippery things. Who believes that level-headed fellows like himself will be seriously affected by obvious propaganda? And of course, nationalistic fervor is not really "political"; it can even be a valuable leaven, especially for an endangered society. Also not "political" are those things that "everyone knows" about racial differences, even when they are pushed to questionable extremes. Besides, a few such extremes might bring some divisive and destructive elements into line.

Based on the size of the Prussian Gestapo, historian Elisabeth Kohlhass estimates the total political police force in Germany in June 1935 at about 3800 men—4200 counting female clerical support. A more conservative estimate would put the male personnel at 3450, giving a complete staff of 3800. By March 1937, she estimates the total to have risen to 6500 men—about 7000 counting women. Whatever improvements this might have brought in the capacity of the Gestapo to accomplish its missions would vanish in the rapid expansion of the Reich and its occupied territories beginning in 1938.[35]

Efficiency, Routines, Identities, and Further Transformations

Despite the growing transfusion of personnel, as organizations whose missions overlapped, the Gestapo and SD generated friction and competition. Gestapo officials required continual reminders of their duty to keep the SD informed. By 1935, they had proven so resistant to this violation of police secrecy that Best had to order the routine filing of reports with a coordinating desk at Gestapo headquarters responsible for liaison with the SD.[36] Toward the SD, Gestapo personnel wanted the cover of secrecy that police subcultures generate against all outsiders.

Professional policemen generally saw SD policemen among themselves as spies and NS subverters of professional relationships. Actually, the Gestapo and SD served as mutual checks. The Gestapo also watched and occasionally arrested SD men. Such arrests caused friction and required intervention to curb police highhandedness and to cool tempers on both sides.[37]

This double-cross was, of course, ideal for a model totalitarian system, and Himmler and Heydrich could exploit this rivalry to manipulate and goad personnel to compete for proof of reliability. To see this as calculated or even desired, however, is to interpret from results back into intentions. Actually, all the leaders involved devoted much time and energy to deflecting the competition, and were obviously uneasy about handling the energy their dynamo generated so spontaneously.

They really preferred a smooth-running team in which overlap merely guaranteed thoroughness and the satisfaction of both ideological (SD) and police-technical (Gestapo) needs in security work. Mutual surveillance offered perhaps a desirable side effect as insurance against the camouflaged enemy, but not as "spying." Spying would impede cooperation, reduce efficiency, and damage morale.

To develop such teamwork, by 1936 Heydrich began joint meetings of all Gestapo and SD field and main office leaders for mutual briefings on their work.[38] The rivalry must have turned these meetings into self-escalating mutual-indoctrination sessions in which each vied to show how his knowledgeable application of ideological insights facilitated security work, but that was merely incidental. Heydrich intended these meetings to create the desired unity of Sipo and SD.

Meanwhile, the Gestapo had assumed an intermediate position—not a thoroughly Nazi police, but also not a true component of the more traditional state machinery. Often distrusted by both the Movement and its allies, the Gestapo hardly lived up to Himmler and Heydrich's ideals. Depending on one's perspective, its image shifts radically. When one analyzes Nazi Germany as a model of totalitarianism, the Gestapo spy system, the SD intelligence net, and the command and reporting system of the Party based on the local block leaders usually add up to an all-pervasive police control. Indeed, this was one aspect of reality, but studies that explore the details of this coordination always emphasize the internal rivalries, the extensive duplication of effort, and even the sabotage of competitors. Also, since a heavy ideological perspective guided security work, one must raise the question of the true efficiency of the Gestapo.

Evaluating Gestapo work enmeshes one in a three-sided perspective. On one side are the conflicting testimonies of victims and participants. All are based on individual perspectives, limited and frequently mixed with second-hand information whose origin the memoirist never questioned. All go well beyond what the source could know, but the scholar is hard pressed to tell when. Official directives and guidelines provide the second perspective. These represent the official self-image of the organization, often embraced by members as reality—that is, their personal institutional identity. The third perspective comes from surviving records of activities. Since these records are fragmentary and also served purposes other than objective communication, they are equally problematic.

Recently, a few scholars have sought to extract what should be more-reliable evidence. This more thorough examination of the evidence has led to controversial conclusions about the efficiency of the Gestapo. These conclusions, in turn, have become the focus of heated debate among German historians.[39] The following evaluation of Gestapo work is based on a combination of traditional perspectives, evaluated against the results of this new work and some additional exploitation of reasonably reliable quantitative reports of Gestapo agencies. The results challenge some of our assumptions and confirm others.

According to official guidelines, the Gestapo handled six types of offenses: (1) high treason (espionage and sabotage), (2) political assassination, (3) political "excesses" (propaganda dissemination, riots, and demonstrations), (4) violations of arms and explosives control regulations, (5) insulting the Reich government and its members, and (6) malicious attacks on state and Party.[40] For the sake of analysis, one might regroup them into two categories. The first would include offenses of types 1 through 4—that is, action related to (political) crimes and the suppression of illegal organizations. These might be called normative police functions, repressive measures of the sort that modern states consider essential to their survival. The second category would include types 5 and 6 and less-threatening "excesses" under type 3. These might be called extreme, petty or totalitarian repression of the sort usually avoided by most states.

Official directives emphasized the normative nature of Gestapo work, insisting that all their actions were based on laws. But this legality included enforcement far beyond normal conceptions of political crime. For instance, in common with many Western security forces, they perceived homosexuals in sensitive positions as security threats. But they went farther, including anyone's homosexual inclinations, abortions, and, of course, miscegenation as threats to national security. Thus, all laws dealing with such threats came within their purview. This and more was implied in official directives, with the usual aside that the full mission of the police could not be limited to particulars, for they had to guard national security against all dangers. Thus, directives emphasizing legality only seem to contrast with the open-ended mission proclaimed by their leaders. Written for the working police detective, they had to be compatible with the professional's self-image, while putting professionalizing limits on the zeal of the Nazi recruit who was not meant to exercise unlimited freedom in "law enforcement."

For a comparison with actual practice, one can turn to Reinhard Mann's study of Gestapo Düsseldorf. Unfortunately, he did not include cases dealing with racially related offenses, emigrants, foreign workers, prisoners of war, separatism, or espionage—significant parts of Gestapo work.[41] Of the cases covered, Mann concluded that (approximately) 30 percent dealt with forbidden organizations (political, religious, and youth), 12 percent concerned conventional crimes, 13 percent were administrative control measures, and 46 percent were suppressions of non-conformist activities. Among the illegal organizations, only 46 percent were political groups that have been prosecuted in most modern states. Of the remaining, 37 percent were "moderate" political groups, and 17 percent religious and youth organizations.[42] Thus, more than half of all this work was "extreme."

Conventional crimes included (approximately) 33 percent economic (hoarding, price gouging, etc.), 6 percent sabotage, 12 percent espionage, 4 percent excessive leave from work, 13 percent misrepresenting one's self as an official, 4 percent giving false information to authorities, 13 percent homosexuality, 3 percent other moral offenses, and 13 percent miscellaneous.[43] Though normally not considered political crimes, most such offenses are prosecuted through the police in modern western states, especially in war-time, and so were "normative."

Nonconformism constituted the most clearly excessive category. Fully 53 percent were utterances, including jokes about the regime or sympathetic to the opposition, and during the war, defeatist remarks. Thirty percent included a wide range of usually petty, occupational, public and private activities that raised someone's suspicions. Only 10 percent dealt with producing or distributing forbidden printed matter, and 5 percent with listening to foreign broadcasts. Two percent were charged with "political passivity."[44]

For his comparative study of Gestapo Würzburg, Robert Gellately reported that although there was great similarity, local preoccupations varied according to local circumstances. Largely agrarian Lower Franconia had fewer Communists and Socialists but at least as many "politically active" priests. With fewer Marxist enemies, the Würzburg Gestapo could devote more time and energy to petty prosecutions. Clearly, "petty-extreme" repression consumed a considerable portion of Gestapo work.[45]

Both case studies also indicate significant changes in that work over time. For the "foundation" years, 1933–1936, rapidly growing case loads prevailed in most categories of Gestapo work. The "normative" years of 1937–1939, the victorious years of 1939–1941, and the years of total war and disillusionment, 1942–1945, each produced different patterns of Gestapo work and public support. For 1933–1936 (only one-third of its existence), the Düsseldorf Gestapo did over half the work it would do against illegal organizations. These years involved the successful breaking of organized opposition. The prosecution of conventional criminality also mounted, but only 13.5 percent of such cases were handled in the formative years. Aside from "moral" offenses and impersonating an official, most of these would be war–related crimes. Less than 21 percent of the post's work against nonconformist utterances would be done in the first four years.[46]

Such changes show that as real threats declined, petty repression increased. One suspects that this shift was driven by a need to justify the organization and its growth. But evidence indicates that external, public pressures also kept the personnel overworked and overextended. Finally, that "need to justify" was more than conscious self-aggrandizement. By 1937, some SD reports on KPD activity argued that, even in areas where the apparatus was still active, "oral propaganda" revealed the "true vitality of the Marxist threat." Other reports, however, made it clear that this "oral propaganda" was basically the grumbling of impotent, frustrated, former Marxist workers grousing among their coworkers. At the same time, the Gestapo was reduced to conducting a roundup of "former KPD members who had not mended their ways since release from the camps." [47] The need to be effective and forceful against an allegedly vital threat drove the Gestapo to increasingly totalitarian and petty action against mere grumblers.

For more-normative functions, Gestapo work closely resembled that of any detective force. They handled political crimes like sabotage, assassination, or possession of illegal weapons like any other crime. Even the surveillance and suppression of illegal organizations involved basically the same techniques as those employed against organized crime. [48] This explains why Himmler and Heydrich and most other Nazis felt dependent upon professionally trained policemen to staff their political police.

Given the rate of growth of the Gestapo, however, they could not staff it with fully qualified men except at the expense of regular detective forces. For a "law and order" state, they had already plundered those ranks excessively. Therefore, the Gestapo had to accept large numbers of marginally qualified recruits for its more routine work. The need to hire unemployed Nazis and to win the respect of the Movement by including "reliable" types also dictated such recruitment. Some could be trained for essential functions; however, many must have remained limited if not detrimental in professional quality. Despite inadequate staffing, men from these lower levels were constantly weeded out as unsuitable.

Although Gestapo headquarters and some of the major field posts had highly qualified staffs, the average Gestapo man may have been less well prepared for detective work than the average regular policeman. He could handle routine matters, but whenever there was a serious crime, his superiors could trust him only to preserve the site of the crime until the arrival of experts. Often, for such experts, the Gestapo relied upon the regular criminal police. [49] Nevertheless, the size of the Gestapo, with field posts for every department and outposts in many districts and small cities, guaranteed the presence of local "specialists" who devoted themselves only to political problems and, therefore, guaranteed a level of attention that other police would not provide. These specialists also provided the machinery for reporting more political information to central police intelligence.

As for its methods, the Gestapo prided itself on having as scientific a methodology as any other modern detective force. Of course, such pride was self-delusional, because political police work is, by definition, predetermined by the political ideology that guides it. Modern police work relies on some theory or theories of criminology to identify likely criminals and to understand their behavior. In contrast, the racist element of the Nazi world view gave Gestapo work a bent that was of little value for real detective work. Occasionally it must have been detrimental, but, of course, it served other purposes.

The process hinges on the concept of *a crime:* a combination of official definition and public perception. Police action begins as a result of either their own work, or an external report. In his study of Düsseldorf, Mann reported that, of those cases that could be determined, fully 33 percent were initiated by the public, 34 percent by other official agencies, and 33 percent by the Gestapo (15 percent from surveillance, including V-persons, and 13 percent from interrogations).[50]

Since Mann did not include racially related "offenses" in his study—that is, cases of a more-private nature that are difficult for official agencies to detect—Robert Gellately believes Mann's results underestimated the degree of public involvement. Gellately reported that for Gestapo Würzburg, 64 percent of the cases of "race defilement" and "friendship to Jews" that could be determined were reported by the public, and only 15 percent by other official agencies, mostly Party. Gellately now believes that most of the undetermined sources were private denunciations, thus raising their percentage even more. Gestapo surveillance accounted for less than 1 percent, while its work on political evaluations added 4 percent, and its interrogations another 17 percent.[51]

Clearly the all-pervasive "spy net" that covered Germany played a significant role in repression. The Party system of observation based on the block warden (Blockwart), who was to know and report every enemy and nonconformist in his neighborhood,[52] generated 7 to 10 percent of the Gestapo's cases—significant, but certainly not as all-pervasive as often supposed. The SD, with its "army of spies," did not devote much of its energy to reporting offenders to the Gestapo,[53] for they along with all the rest of the police initiated only 5 to 19 percent. Altogether, however, 15 to 34 percent of Gestapo cases grew from its cooperation with other official agencies. Building and maintaining that cooperation always required a major effort, because the infighting of the Third Reich compounded normal bureaucratic rivalry.[54] One cannot measure the effect of these conflicts on real versus perceived Gestapo efficiency, but clearly the high percentage of cases based on this cooperation shows its significance.

Finally, one can get a false impression of the relative significance of public denunciations versus those from official agencies by simply comparing the percentages of each. Reports from the network of Party and state agencies supporting Gestapo work were frequently screened both to eliminate false reports and to insure ideological or political propriety. The uncontrolled nature of public denunciations probably inflated their numbers, as the subsequent analysis will show. Screened Party and state agency reports represented external influences on Gestpo work, making it more sensitive to the ideological consensus being created by the Nazis.[55]

In contrast, public denunciations provided both a major source of Gestapo efficiency and an unmanaged, more "spontaneous" driving force in initiating its actions. In Düsseldorf, they mounted steadily until the war went bad, after which they declined rapidly. Only 15 percent of them came in during 1933–1936, however, indicating that public acceptance of the Gestapo and its work accrued later during the "normative" peace and victorious war years (66 percent in five of the twelve years). A major increase did come in 1935, however, marking a first wave of acceptance following stabilization of the regime.[56]

Mann judged 24 percent of these reports to be based on pronounced loyalty to the regime. In 39 percent, motive could not be determined; presumably these included those who informed out of a nonpolitical sense of propriety. The remaining 37 percent derived from personal, nonpolitical motives such as revenge or personal gain. Political motives exceeded personal only in 1935 and 1942, but during 1933–1936, the overall ratio was 13 to 16, political versus personal.[57] Apparently, the more real everyone perceived the enemies to be, the more sincere their motivations.

For Würzburg, Gellately reports steady increases in denunciations of Jews, with a major burst in 1936, following the Nuremberg laws. This probably speaks to the success of Nazi propaganda and role modeling. Of these denunciations, almost 41 percent proved baseless according to Gestapo conclusions,[58] which may reflect sincere versus venal motives. Such high levels of unreliability apparently characterized all public and Party-member denunciations, for Nazi officials and professional police alike originally looked askance at them and did not want their institutional identities tainted by denunciations.[59] Nevertheless, they proved increasingly essential to repression of nonconformity in those private realms into which the state could reach only with great difficulty. Also, according to Himmler's previously quoted admonitions, the confidence of the Movement in his SS-police system required it to demonstrate responsiveness to Party-generated complaints. Public acceptance and support had to be cultivated by a similar responsiveness. Thus, the Gestapo found itself devoting increased time to pursuing petty complaints and involving itself in petty repressions that it did not generate. Ironically, much of its success as an all-seeing instrument of police terror derived from functional pressures the leadership never intended. Denunciations also created functional pressures that transformed police perceptions, defining the "threats" that "society" wanted controlled or removed.

In other words, the Gestapo, like police anywhere, could not do its work without public support. In that respect, it was effective. This effectiveness was greater in the more excessive or trivial repression, however, for that was the area where the public had its only significant contact with "criminals." As Gellately has concluded, one must question the degree to which the Gestapo should be seen as an instrument of terror imposed on German society. The Nazi police state represents not so much an aberration of modern policing as the police powers of the modern state, carried to a logical extreme based on the dominant world view. This is a perspective through which it must be studied.

As for prescribed Gestapo procedures, aside from ideological diversions, one must admit that they were good, basic police procedures. They even preferred solid investigative work to heavy-handed or "intensified" interrogation. They did indeed place heavy emphasis on interrogation as a component of investigation, as indicated by the 15–17 percent rate of interrogation-based cases in the two studies just discussed. But interrogation technique relied generally on an understanding of the limits of its value, of the psychology involved in extracting information, and of the problem of distinguishing what was reliable. The Gestapo did include forceful interrogation in its repertoire, subject to periodic limitations from above; however, it officially preferred more subtle means of persuasion. Although it seems insensitive to the victims who actually suffered through it, one must say that the popular image of ubiquitous sadistic Gestapo torture is quantitatively exaggerated for the period between late 1934 and 1938. Gestapo officials considered brutal force "justified" in "extraordinary cases"—for instance, to prevent an imminent act of sabotage or to penetrate a dangerous organization. Clearly, KPD leaders frequently experienced brutal beatings, even during these more-normative years.[60] If one eliminates such "justified" cases, and the more or less spontaneous excesses of 1933–1934 (mostly at the hands of "wild" NS "police"), what remains of Gestapo brutality before 1938 were the excesses of the sort that plague many police forces. Himmler was probably justified in comparing the excesses of his police to those of other states, including the contemporary United States and Britain. Nazi rates of occurrence must have been higher, given the radical enforcer philosophy dispensed from above. No one can yet say how much higher. Predictably, the Gestapo, from Himmler down, insisted on dealing internally with reported violations and investigated them perfunctorily. But violations were reviewed with an effort to uncover sadistic and undisciplined personnel.[61]

Although the Gestapo interrogator has often been described as "schooled in the arts of torture," nothing relating to such alleged training survives. Instead, all training materials focus on the psychology of interrogation. All credible descriptions of torture involve crude techniques, easily learned at levels below official training. Case studies for Gestapo post Saarbrücken lead to the conclusion that such methods probably did lead to extended arrests in KPD ranks, but they did not always produce reliable results, especially when evidence was needed for court. Brutality could not compensate for inadequate technique. It might have reinforced psychologically the myth of an all-knowing

Gestapo, but it did not produce real efficiency. Increased reliance on interrogation through torture during the war years reflects the declining professionalism of an overextended staff much watered down with neo-phytes.[62]

Since Gellately determined that more than 41 percent of denuncia-tions in the racially related cases he studied were judged by the Gestapo as unfounded, the popular idea that the Gestapo always beat a confes-sion out of its suspects becomes questionable. The abuse and humilia-tion of Jews, seen increasingly by Gestapo personnel as enemies by definition, probably resulted more from overflowing hostility than from Gestapo technique. None of this minimizes the significance of Gestapo brutality, but rather places that brutality in the context of modern po-lice problems, especially those involving minority out-groups and racism.

Much of the alleged efficiency of the Gestapo was supposedly based on its extraordinarily thorough system of card files. Many descriptions of them exist, focusing usually on one or two file sets, and describing their cross-referencing. In fact, there were numerous file systems used for diverse purposes, and no single description seems to account for all of them. None explains adequately how they allegedly operated so efficiently, despite elaborate descriptions of fantastic mechanical ar-rangements.[63] Before computers, systems of tabs and punch cards al-lowed for mechanical extractions from a massive file. But as with com-puters, the system was no better than the program's design, and could be nowhere nearly as complex in cross-referencing as modern comput-ers allow. There were physical limits to such a system, and the human limitations were even greater. All cross-referencing requires a complex sequence of decisions, and the more complex the system, the fewer the people who can be trained to work it effectively.

Although early punch-card tabulation machinery had been in use in Germany for decades, it was the Nazis who initiated their use to tabu-late census and other data sources that could be used for population control. Nazi statisticians foresaw a future of efficient population man-agement and control through such techniques, and probably contrib-uted to the execution of Nazi population policy—that is, genocide.[64] It is not clear yet when and to what extent the Gestapo possessed or em-ployed such machines for its files, although the above-mentioned de-scriptions indicate that they played some role. Such primitive computer technology would have contributed minimally, however, to the ongoing file access that was needed.

Unsatisfied with the system under Diels, in July 1934 Himmler or-dered the establishment of a centralized file system for all of Prussia, later extended to the entire Reich. It was based on uniform local files maintained by the Gestapo posts, which would forward copies to head-quarters. There were two main human subjects files, each cross-referenced to other special subject or informational files. Because the two main branches of the Gestapo were separated by the Abwehr-police's veil of secrecy, Department III had its main file (blue cards), and Department IV, Abwehr-police, had its separate file (orange cards) on persons of interest. Only as late as 1940–1941 did they initiate a cross-reference of these two files to eliminate duplicate searches. Each Gestapo post had local files, and all were allegedly coordinated with the central file system at headquarters.[65] Increased complexity usually comes with more thoroughness, and this system may have consumed more man-hours than most Gestapo posts and outposts could generate. The Gestapo main file ultimately required 250 clerks to maintain it.[66]

Throughout the early years, Gestapo headquarters or the commander of the political police frequently called on the field posts to compile special files, such as the Judenkartei. This usually signaled intensified Gestapo attention to such a group and defined them for the detectives as "proper suspects." For instance in the fall of 1934, all suspected homosexuals became the target of such an exercise. They (males only) were to be divided into convicted, charged but not convicted, and suspected homosexuals.[67] Thereafter, in 1935, the punishments for homosexual offenses were increased, and the Gestapo began raiding homosexual gathering places.[68]

Another special file was initiated in February 1936, as Himmler pushed to expand his command over all police. He hoped to appeal to Hitler's growing anticipation of war and his belief in the need for a force to prevent "another stab in the back."[69] Toward that end, Himmler and Heydrich initiated a project that would show that their police would be ready to prevent such a threat. Out of this grew the A-Kartei. Heydrich ordered all political police posts to create this special file for all residents who should be interred in concentration camps in the event of an extraordinary occurrence. He gave this top priority and called for a report by the first of May.[70]

Gestapo post leaders were not consistent in tackling this project, but given its priority, many erred in overzealousness. For instance, the leader at Köln specifically included all dismissed civil servants, separatists, foreign legionnaires, unsuitable priests and pastors, and Jews.[71] Heydrich may not have received the final results until January 1937, over seven months behind schedule. They did not please him.

Since Prussian posts had reported less than half the suspects per capita than posts in other states, he concluded that there was no consistent definition of "enemies of state." Characteristically, without providing such a definition, he ordered a careful reevaluation of the lists, which he apparently considered excessive.[72] Since both the original lists and the revised lists would have resulted in far more internees than the camps could hold, Heydrich's reaction probably had a purely practical base.[73] Nevertheless, the political moment had passed and Himmler was now chief of all German police, so Heydrich could let the files stand until tensions resumed in 1938, when he had to devise a truly workable system.

Given all of this, one suspects that Himmler and Heydrich were preoccupied with card files as icons of efficiency. That preoccupation may well have created both work and information overloads for Gestapo personnel.

Other facilities available to the Gestapo were among the best criminological-technical resources in the world. Germany had generally kept abreast, even pioneering in some areas. Undoubtedly, however, the racial-biological trend that increasingly prevailed eroded this position as time wore on. For monitoring wireless communications, the Gestapo relied on Göring's Forschungsamt.[74] It had its own telephone monitoring facilities. For the mail, it had liaison with the Post Überwachungs Amt (ÜWA), which could open any individual or organization's mail. The ÜWA is reputed to have steamed open and resealed a suspect's mail so well it was undetectable. It delivered the mail to a Gestapo office for study. Allegedly, the teamwork was so efficient that the mail was delayed less than half a day. Despite the technology, all such techniques required the availability of adequate human resources to collect and exploit useful information. No amount of technology could overcome the bureaucratic red tape and jurisdictional warfare that occasionally derailed these processes.[75]

The spy net of the Gestapo also added to its efficiency, but the Gestapo depended on its agents less than it relied on private denunciations, at least until late in the war. Public belief in the "ever-present" Gestapo spies was probably more effective than their real presence, and even that belief grew from the private denunciations. Much has been written about Gestapo agents and their classification, but its accuracy is questionable. Case studies for Gestapo post Saarbrücken indicate that the value of its agents, especially against illegal organizations, was largely a matter of chance. Overall, the use of agents, their evaluation, and their classification changed constantly.[76]

All police use agents or informants, in Germany traditionally called Vertrauensleute, V-persons or confidential agents. In the Third Reich, the practice differed little from other police practice.[77] The Gestapo's agents paralleled closely those who inform on organized crime. Unlike undercover detectives who actually penetrate an organization, agents are persons with some contact with suspects. Roughly they fall into two classes: (1) "good citizens" whose contact is incidental, and who serve for a variety of reasons not unlike denunciators; (2) implicated persons induced to betray their colleagues for either personal gain or promises of immunity. Agents differ from occasional informants in that their cooperation is ongoing and might involve some remuneration.[78]

For the formative years, surviving records do not indicate any elaborate system of classification; all seem to have been referred to generically as either agents or V-persons, with no clear distinction. Initially, the use of agents was typically informal, based mostly on the personal contacts of individual detectives. What, if any, central coordination came over from the Weimar-era political police is not known. Diels's offices seem to have done little more than issue a very few directives to minimize the compromising of secrets and embarrassing incidents with agents overseas.[79] Shortly after his arrival, Heydrich tried to gain some control over potentially embarrassing agents in foreign countries. But only at the end of 1935 did Werner Best establish a Reich-wide system for warning political police against unreliable agents.[80] Clearly in these early years, agents provided the Gestapo with no uniquely efficient base.

At some point, the Nachrichten or Intelligence Departments of Gestapo headquarters and each field post maintained a file of all their official agents, both those who were used as informants, and the more officially affiliated Auskunfts-Personen, A-persons, who provided regular intelligence reports for an area of personal expertise. These furnished much of the basis for the Gestapo situation reports. Intelligence Department files never included all agents, however, for individual detectives still maintained their own personal sources.[81] The organization of intelligence agents into files must have improved the Reich-wide coordination of political police intelligence. Nevertheless, one must wonder about an information overload where it all came together. Typically much information is lost in police files around the world because of such overloads.[82]

In this respect, another essential perspective for evaluating an organization's effectiveness is the workload that fell on the personnel at the cutting edge. From all appearances, this was excessive. According to official guidelines, the Gestapo had a workable, bureaucratically regulated routine that guaranteed that nothing should go astray. Furthermore, the personnel had an official workweek that compared favorably with other police agencies. Except for Wednesday and Saturday, their workday began at 8:00 A.M. and ended at 7:00 P.M., with a two-hour break from 1:00 to 3:00 P.M.. Wednesdays and Saturdays were half days from 8:00 A.M. to 2:00 P.M.. Sundays and holidays were free, and standard sick leave and vacations were provided. The leading detective officers at a post rotated a week-long duty service (Bereitschaftsdienst) during which one of them had to be on call at all times. The rest of the staff performed a rotating daily standby service (Dauerdienst) for twenty-four hours to receive priority calls and take emergency action.[83]

Gestapo reports indicate that Heydrich did not greatly exaggerate when he claimed that his personnel did extensive overtime, rarely got allotted vacations, and still could not keep up with the workload. Sick leave resulting from predictable fatigue and normal patterns of illness could totally disrupt badly understaffed posts. For instance, while still an independent state force, the Braunschweig Political Police reported in November 1934, six months after its creation, that it was understaffed, sorely overworked, and inadequately housed.[84]

With only fifteen men, they had assumed in the first six months extensive new responsibilities. These included monitoring all military facilities and their civilian employees, all persons released from civil service under the new laws, all licensed peddlers, foreigners, deserters, and returned foreign legionnaires; evaluating all entrants into military and voluntary work service and all applicants for travel passes; monitoring all presses and publications; and maintaining a standby service for the teletype link with Berlin established for sensitive matters relating to the Röhm purge. In its first five months this agency processed 1,800 documents, 500 informational requests from Reich and Abwehr posts, about 500 administrative-technical proceedings, about 1,400 reports on entrants into military and work service and evaluations of officers for government and Party agencies, about 400 postal investigations, and about 4,000 new entries into the main card file. In addition, they made seventy-five arrests, of which sixty-two had been ordered by justice authorities.[85] For fifteen men, this was clearly an impossible load, but until a fully centralized Reich-wide Gestapo was established, any ministry or high Party office, any regional governor could contribute assignments.

Until 1935, these fifteen men worked in nine rooms in a closed section of an old ministry building. By spring 1936, a thirty-six-man force had expanded into twenty-one rooms spread across two floors. Many months after this agency had become the Gestapo post Braunschweig in the new Reich Gestapo, it remained below its budgeted allotment for personnel and from 36 to 60 percent behind in its case loads and paperwork. Such problems were described as typical of other posts.[86]

The outpost at Bückeburg under Gestapo post Bielefeld covered the little state, Schaumburg-Lippe, whose "political police" had been incorporated into the Prussian Gestapo in 1934. As late as March 1936, this outpost consisted of one detective responsible for political work, assisted by a Gendarmerie candidate, and working in conjunction with a detective responsible for regular work. The political detective reported that during the first three months, he and his assistant had received 486 orders from various Gestapo and other state agencies. The majority of them were not simple enquiries, but required numerous procedures, interrogations of witnesses and suspects, inquiries, seizures, and arrests. Between 1930 and 1933, he and his fellow detective alone had handled an average of 850 cases and inquiries a year. In 1934, they handled 1,037 Kripo and 254 Gestapo affairs. Working alone in 1935 he had 1,446 Gestapo assignments. His share of the load was no longer bearable.[87] Even if one assumes that everyone exaggerates his problems, these examples reveal a force dangerously overextended, if it had indeed been doing work truly crucial to national security. The officer at Bückeburg was so preoccupied by external directives that he could not have had time to uncover local threats.

Clearly a post leader had to make judgments of priority in handling cases or directives that were not already prioritized by headquarters. Thus, when Gestapo post Frankfurt used inadequate staffing as excuse to defer action on an order from Diels to create a Judenkartei, while the Kassel post acted promptly, it was no unique violation of orders. Where no clear priority was established, Gestapo directives could stay on hold indefinitely. Although Heydrich, Best, and Müller would try to minimize such problems of control, they probably never had adequate resources to do so. Certainly during the war years worse situations accrued. For instance, in 1943, when Gestapo headquarters (RSHA IV) ordered the fusion of the political (blue) and Abwehr (orange) files, most posts allegedly deferred action.[88]

Apparently, overload perennially undermined Gestapo efficiency. This is basically the conclusion drawn by Mallmann and Paul from their case study of Gestapo post Saarbrücken. They depict a staff so overworked by reports and filing that they could do little real detective work. They relied heavily on preliminary work by uniformed police and denunciations to build their cases. Outsiders assigned by a national bureaucracy, they never got to know their territory. They wrote reports that depicted extensive knowledge and contact, but their real work was spotty. For good reasons, Gestapo headquarters did not always trust the evaluations of its field posts. The goal of all-seeing eyes created an unrealistic workload that produced a Gestapo whose efficiency was simply hit or miss.[89]

Of course, the major instruments for the efficient repression of opposition were the combination of protective custody and concentration camp. Throughout the early years, local SA leaders, Frick, Göring, and Himmler had waged among themselves a running battle over control of these two weapons. After Himmler's appointment as inspector of the Gestapo in April 1934, for all practical purposes he controlled both, and all remaining maneuvers proved futile.

Legally, Gestapo headquarters had to approve all protective custody actions. At headquarters, the Schutzhaft desk processed proposals from the Gestapo posts or a headquarters specialist and forwarded them to Müller, who allegedly decided which were processed through the courts and which simply went directly to a camp. If the proposal was not approved, the arrestee had to be released after eight days. Every three months the case was supposed to be reviewed to determine if national security still warranted detention. In each case this required the Schutzhaft desk to collect and review the recommendations of the relevant camp commandant, the appropriate expert at headquarters, and the field post that had initiated the arrest. No matter how perfunctorily they performed the actual process, such regulations generated much time-consuming paperwork at all levels. Shortly after Heydrich's arrival at the Gestapo, the Röhm purge had generated massive arrests, and the control system broke down so badly that he could not get an accurate count of internees for several months. He had to order yet another card file into existence, the Schutzhaftkartei.[90]

In contrast with the image of the camps as a black hole into which internees disappeared forever, most cases of protective custody were apparently short-term, "educational" experiences. At least this was true during the period of "normality" between 1934 and 1939. For instance, during the spring of 1934, the Bavarian Political Police reported an average of 169 arrests and 247 releases per two-week period—they were reducing internees after the initial terror. Between late 1935 and mid-1936, they incarcerated 504 persons and released 417. During several weeks in the fall of 1936, after becoming Gestapo posts, they incarcerated 184 and released 103.[91] With arrest requests and quarterly reports on each accumulated case, even with hardened cases handled perfunctorily, these five posts generated a mountain of paper for protective custody arrests alone.

Contrary to the regulations, they used protective custody freely to remove permanently all serious threats to society. Any accused whom the courts released on technicalities or who got "too light sentences" was rearrested on release and spirited to a camp. Communist leaders and second offenders faced long, often permanent stays, and they along with Jews were slated for more severe treatment.[92] If such terror did not avert determined resistance, it reduced the resisters in number.

Protective custody also served the purpose of "public education." Most political internees were successfully portrayed as enemies of social and national security. When a price gouger or an exploitative or irresponsible employer disappeared into the camps for a short stay,[93] that encouraged the public to associate the Gestapo-camp system with righteous justice. That in turn encouraged denunciations based on all motives. The detectives responded to such denunciations righteously whenever they proved well founded, and they could feel good about it.

Furthermore, the detective and the administrative bureaucrats involved could tell themselves that this was all done according to law. The detective's arrest had to be approved by a higher authority who decided the fate of the internee. When they turned the internee over to the separately administered camps, conditions there were somebody else's responsibility. If an internee got lost in the system and never came out, if someone suffered unjustly or inhumanely, no one person was to blame. No *one* felt responsibility, for no *one* had responsibility in such a bureaucratic maze. Like so many other aspects of Sipo and SD, the link with the camps enabled one to "do his job" without threats to his institutional identity. The dirty work was somebody else's responsibility.[94]

Preliminary Conclusions

From the short-range perspective, the Gestapo was efficient and successful—at least the political purge of German society succeeded. The initial blast of 1933–1934 that broke the spirit of much opposition derived, however, from the revolutionary terrorism that the police were hard pressed to control. Initial success against the KPD came essentially from exploitation of political police work done before 1933 and from the local Nazis' intimate knowledge of their enemies. Himmler's political police elaborated on this success to the point of destroying the KPD as a centralized German organization by 1935. Walter Ulbricht had to move what remained to Prague, and the KPD operated primarily from foreign soil. By 1936, it could only smuggle propaganda and work through small, scattered cells; the Third Reich was secure.[95] Himmler's claims to the contrary were exaggerations to justify his organization.

If the destruction of the Communist threat and even the Socialists came naturally to conservative-nationalist detectives, their transformation into the persecutors of Jews and many other victims requires more explanation. For the conventionally anti-Semitic, Jews were merely disdained. The Nazi world view required that they learn to see the Jews at the root of almost every problem. This is not to say that as early as 1933 or 1935 the NS leaders prepared the Gestapo for the Final Solution. They did, however, need police to execute any solutions that might be ordered, including a cleansing of the Reich.

From 1933 to 1938, the political police had a limited role in Jewish persecution. Of course they enforced laws that became increasingly detrimental to the Jews, who were disproportionately subjected to police surveillance, raids, and arrests as assumed enemies of the Volk. Most such action was precipitated by zealous informants and frequently resulted in dismissal of charges after what the victims must have seen as calculated police harassment, especially when they fell to the mercy of over-zealous employees. Ironically, some cases of Schutzhaft were indeed protective custody of several days because of "popular" threats to the person's security.[96] Regardless of the motive for that "protection," the victim would have perceived calculated harassment. In such ways the detectives became involved in the early persecution and increasingly perceived Jews as the appropriate target of suspicion and a growing popular hostility that "must have been earned."

Generalizations about early Gestapo involvement have to be made with caution, for the extent of attention devoted to Jews varied greatly among field posts in 1933 and 1934, if not later. Prime determinants were the post leader and regional police authorities. For instance, comparing two posts for which records from early 1933 survive, Hannover and Kassel, one sees distinct differences up to the summer of 1934. Thereafter, under Himmler and Heydrich, more uniformity ensued.[97]

The police president of Hannover until 1936 was Johann Habbens, former head of the political police department and a secret collaborator with the Nazis before 1933. The first two heads of his Gestapo post were administrative civil servants and nationalists. Only under the leadership of Dr. Ewald Hasstert, who arrived in October 1934, did post Hannover report on the Jewish problem in ways more appropriate to a proper Gestapo stance. The first SS officer to command the post, Paul Kanstein, did not arrive until 1935.[98]

The reports of both the police president and the post paid no attention to Jews throughout 1933. Thereafter, a couple of reports indicated no illegal activities in the Jewish community and spoke positively of the Reichsbund Jüdische Frontsoldaten. Throughout 1934 and 1935, reports on incidents directed against Jews increased, with Hasstert participating in the coverup of NS crimes for which "the culprits could not be identified." He also reported with more appropriate approval on Zionists advocating emigration and disapproval of the assimilationists like the Reichsbund. Eventually, Kanstein displayed increasing concern over the proper education of the Volk to the Jewish threat and frequently described the victimization of Jews as well earned.[99] Thus, the detectives of Hannover experienced a gradual evolution in official interpretations of the "Jewish problem" as expressed by their superiors.

In contrast, post Kassel was continually under SA General Pfeffer von Salomon as police president and after July 1933 also head of the post.[100] He asserted his personal influence over the post and provided a proper NS stance on Jews. As soon as he took over, Pfeffer's reports frequently contained whole sections on Jewry.[101] The guidelines for reports under which all Gestapo posts operated referred simply to "enemies of the state," specifically conventional political parties and movements. Professional civil servants like those at Hannover would not include Jewish or religious organizations, except for overtly political exceptions. For a Nazi like Pfeffer, however, Jews automatically came along with Communists, Socialists, and Liberals.

His behavior was certainly encouraged from headquarters, for Diels repeatedly ordered the posts to create files on Jewish associations and all politically active Jews as threats to national security. Unlike those posts that continued to read this as low priority and deferred action, Pfeffer put his people promptly to work and soon bragged of his progress.[102] His detectives got an early and proper NS orientation on Jews as appropriate targets of Gestapo suspicion. Under Heydrich guidelines for reports mandated routine coverage of Jews,[103] creating a more uniform emphasis across the Gestapo.

As soon as Himmler had settled the more real threat from Röhm, he turned to the Jewish threat in talks to policemen. He clearly expressed the racist ideology that should shape all future criminological theory and detective work. As the lieutenants primarily responsible for the political police, both Heydrich and Best embraced this theme and almost exceeded their boss in a drive to pass on that vision to their police charges.

Among Best's early acts in office was to issue a general directive on the role of the Gestapo in developing attitudes toward Jews. Specifically, he ordered Gestapo personnel to adhere rigidly to Party guidelines against patronizing Jewish businesses and professionals.[104] This order served a double purpose in transforming detectives. It established anti-Semitism and racial prejudice as social norms worthy of propagation. It also created a depersonalizing barrier between the executor of police action and his potential target. Eliminating his personal contact with Jews helped dehumanize them into abstract enemies.

The surviving records of Desk II 1B2, the section responsible for Jews, Freemasons, and immigrants, reveal an escalation of interest in the Jews during 1935. Until August, records cover only specific actions such as bans on individual Jewish professors, or the abolition or surveillance of particular Jewish organizations. Then, however, Heydrich, unsatisfied with the haphazard work under Diels, reinstated orders for the creation of a Judenkartei that gradually expanded from Diels's proposed coverage to include every Jew, even the "camouflaged Jew." [105]

During the summer and fall of 1935, field reports depicted steadily mounting numbers of "popular" actions against Jews, ostensibly based on the success of NS propaganda in educating the public to "Jewish chicanery." Then the actions decreased dramatically after the Nuremberg Laws, and reports monitored increased emigration with approval. Meanwhile, during the escalation of "popular" anti-Semitic actions, the police had found themselves typically in the middle. Gestapo posts reported regularly that they were required to protect Jews and their property from both "righteous" public outbursts and Nazi excesses. They complained of mixed signals from Party and state: the Party agitating and educating against Jews; the state agencies showing more concern over repercussions and expecting the police to maintain law and order. Apparently the Hannover post at least outwardly tried to enforce the law, while Pfeffer bent the law more freely. After the Nuremberg Laws, both worked with local Nazis to restore order.[106] Heydrich ordered the posts to cooperate with state agencies to expedite emigration and to deter the return of such emigrants by sending any to a concentration camp.[107]

Although the Nuremberg Laws may have decreased "popular" excesses against Jews, they increased Gestapo involvement in persecution. Whereas before most cases of alleged race defilement were precipitated and extralegally handled by local Party and SA, with the Gestapo intervening to "protect the victims," the now illegal act was reported to the Gestapo for prosecution. Gellately's study of the Gestapo post at Würtzburg (Bavarian Political Police up to 1936) shows major escalations of cases of both race defilement and friendship with Jews during 1936. Fifty-six percent of its race defilement cases were handled between 1936 and 1938. Sixty-two percent of such cases for which the source of information is known were based on reports from the general population. Another 27 percent grew out of the interrogations that ensued. Thirty-six percent were found to be baseless. In other words, the Gestapo increasingly devoted its limited resources to the pursuit of "race-defiling" Jews, arresting and interrogating those brought to their attention by the "righteous indignation" of the public.[108]

The Jewish question added progressively to the pressures at work on the future executioners. Increasingly aroused against "the enemy," they were denied action except within the parameters of official orders, rarely severe and decisive. Thus any opportunity for sharp action must have unleashed considerable tension in a burst of barely restrained hostility. By the time conditions had ripened for decisive action against "the Jewish enemy," many of the Gestapo should have been well prepared for each new step. Then the pogrom of 1938 provided a major step, but no significant Gestapo leadership, except the arrest of thousands of Jews to restore order.[109]

The upshot of this process from 1933 through 1938 was that anti-Semitic propaganda, role-modeling by Nazi extremists, and illegal Nazi excesses justified or required legislation to define Jews and limit their rights. Then the police and courts assumed the burden of "legally" managing the Jewish Problem. For the police, that defined the Jews as public enemies.

If a Jew pursued a profit with the same zeal as an Aryan, he was a price gouger or labor abuser. If he courted an Aryan like any other man, he violated the laws of nature and subverted the genetic strength of the nation. Once the police were required to act on all such reports and prosecutors pursued them more seriously, the statistical evidence of such "misbehavior" mounted precipitously. All involved in law enforcement confronted "concrete evidence" of what the Nazis propagated as reality. Once in power, the Nazis naturally made their world view a reality. In this respect, they were no different than any other establishment. What was revolutionary was the rapidity with which they relegitimized prejudices made suspect by two centuries of Enlightenment and Liberal ideology.

The police role in all this was not extraordinary. It was simply police work taken to whatever conclusions the state developed. The men of the Gestapo participated in this process because of their roles. As policemen, they saw themselves as the servant-shapers of their society: an active, constructive role that requires one to respond to problems correctively. One corrective involved educating the good citizens whose whole-hearted cooperation is essential to combating crime and other affronts to public order. Meanwhile, bombarded with evidence of the threat both from above, through indoctrination, and from below, in the form of public complaints, old prejudices against Jews, Gypsies, homosexuals, or whatever became "reality" for the policeman. Ultimately, attacking the source of "crime" involved eliminating its evil "subhuman" source. Such can be the psychosocial consequences of police work; they are functional processes that, if unchecked, can move a society to directing police terror at out-groups.

One record of a resistant professional policeman caught in this transformation has survived. A war veteran, Polizeirat, and former DNP activist joined the Nazi Party in 1931 and entered SS and Gestapo service in 1933. As senior SD member in Gestapo post Berlin, he lead its Sipo-SD post. Although Sipo and SD colleagues respected him for his character and NS commitments, in November 1935 the SD Main Office recommended that the Gestapo release him as politically unsuitable. He did not accept the solution of the Jewish problem as essential to the NS world view. He had even spoken against the *Stürmer* for its crude anti-Semitic propaganda.[110] This case shows the growing pressure on police professionals by 1935. They accepted the definition of the Jew as an enemy of society and the proper target for special police attention, or they lost their position in police service.

Returning to Gestapo efficiency at extreme or petty repression, one finds in Martin Broszat's study of protective custody arrestees in 1935 and 1936 that approximately 20 percent were for "subversive remarks," spreading rumors, insulting leaders, and so forth. Even among the remainder of cases, the majority were for propagandizing or other activities on behalf of enemy organizations or for suspicion of enemy affiliations.[111] In other words, the political police, while making fewer arrests, directed them increasingly at petty offenders and an overblown enemy.

The image emerges of a Gestapo overwhelmed by informing, over-zealous, "good citizens." Although they had to ignore many complaints as insignificant or based on questionable motives, the Gestapo had to act on most of them to preserve public and Party faith in their "efficiency" and "reliability." Consequently, the greatest testament to the efficiency of the Gestapo was the necessity to devote increasing energy to campaigns against helpless "enemies" like gossips, grumblers, Gypsies, and Jews as a raison d'etre. For the short term, real internal problems had been sufficiently eliminated.

The resultant police state was indeed an efficient "instrument of terror." But it was not the terror of an efficient bureaucratic and technological machine that knew all. Its energy worked in ways few if any understood, and it frequently drove in directions no one planned. Though it could be thorough when focused by priority directives from above, it more frequently ground up its victims randomly. Most of its work was a mindless, normative routine of processing endless mountains of paper. Few had time to think about what they did, much less its social or ethical consequences. One merely rushed to keep up with endless, mundane requests and assignments. A relatively small part of the organization's energy was available to discover on its own initiative true problems of national security. Reality diverged greatly from the intentions of the creators, while they were rarely forced to see that reality behind the facade they had created. The Gestapo responded to their highest priority commands with reasonable efficiency, and it ground away mindlessly at "ideological enemies" otherwise.

Nevertheless, a combination of bravado about an all-seeing Gestapo and a paranoid exaggeration of an all-pervasive enemy provided both the general public and Gestapo personnel with justification for actions that most considered necessary evils. If Gestapo personnel were so socially and psychologically diverse that they defy most previous analyses to explain their roles, then that justification of necessary evil may provide a key to their transformation. It certainly provided a transcending mission that could justify otherwise unacceptable acts. Here routinization and the complexity of membership provided special branches or less respectable functionaries to perform the "dirty work" without tainting "the organization" that provided ego identity. If one could not justify an action as necessary, one still could deny personal responsibility for any unacceptable "side effects" to which he did not directly contribute. Though the leadership bore the burden of responsibility for such consequences, it could remain worthy of obedience because it had to put national interests first at any price.

Gestapo personnel divided sharply between the socially and educationally privileged or professionally established, and those who lacked any hope of status or security outside their Gestapo careers. The majority of the latter came in from below as employees, and almost always with some NS affiliation. Many were dedicated NS enforcers, committed to cleansing and strengthening the nation—"idealists" of sorts. Although many would have taken any job of comparable salary and status, one should use the label "opportunists" with caution. A few files reveal clearly amoral persons who feathered their nests at every opportunity. Most, however, derived some fulfillment from a career of service to the nation and to some NS cause that they embraced. Their lower functionary status and their formative environments probably did condemn them to roles of blindly obedient factotums. Yet even they needed immersion in the complex legitimizing processes to prepare them for their later roles.

Among the other extreme—those with status to qualify for middle or upper ranks—widely differing dispositions created diverse but no less binding identities with the Gestapo. This group ranged from middle-rank professional detectives to law-trained civil servants: some with established careers, others just out of university and looking for promising starts. Again, one should not apply the label "opportunist" too easily.

Although the detective may have seen the Gestapo or SS as a route for personal advancement, service in these organizations also enhanced his ability to serve society effectively. In any profession, self and service become inseparable enough to provide ethical traps in even the most mundane circumstances. In this case, the common denominators of nationalism, anti-Communism, and a general combativeness toward anything that weakened national strength created powerful personal linkages that carried over from traditional detective to Gestapo and finally

SS work. The professional wedded to "apolitical" scientific methodology may have had a few more defenses than the radical enforcer, but once those defenses were weakened, the linkages between ego and institution that professional images provided may have blinded him even more effectively.

Much the same applies to those with juridical qualifications for immediate, high status. The social analysis of this group performed by Gunner Boehnert demonstrated that the largest number rushed to join the cause during the fourteen months between Hitler's appointment and the Röhm purge. The flow thereafter grew in proportion to the establishment of the SS and police system as a legitimate state agency of public service and prestigious careers. Among these men, recent college graduates predominated. Gestapo-SS-SD offered them the best hope of achievement.[112]

Here again, the delicate balance between opportunism and professional service baited the trap. As Boehnert demonstrated, men of status served Himmler by "ennobling" the SS. Their membership lent social prestige while simultaneously giving him leverage to ensure their loyalty to the regime. Yet to include them, Himmler had to compromise SS standards and doctrine. These men adhered to values formed in the Wilhelmine and Weimar eras, and the system had to remain normative enough to involve them. Although this slowed the "revolution," that seeming normalization drew them on. They then contributed to the system that would produce their successors, more fully imbued with SS values.[113] Many such men undoubtedly sought to hold the SS and police system on a more proper course, but their success brought ironic twists—not least of which were the ensnaring organizational identities they themselves spun.

4

From Kripo
to Sipo

The 1936 inclusion of the regular Kripo detectives in Sipo adds a larger, allegedly more professional and less ideological group of detectives to this already complex analysis. Though the avowed political aloofness of these detectives requires skeptical analysis, its half-truth enhances the argument that processes rather than predisposition provide better explanations for their involvement in NS inhumanity. With that in mind, one must turn to Kripo—to its organization, mission, image, and personnel, and their transformation into members of Sipo.

Although no modern society ever seems to have enough detectives, Germany was comparatively well off when the Nazis came to power. Approximately 12,000 detectives were in the service of the states. All were stationed in cities, for the Gendarmerie did the spade work on criminal cases in the countryside. Berlin, at about one detective per 1,800 inhabitants, had more than twice as many detectives per capita as comparable capitals like London and Paris. Major non-Prussian cities averaged one detective per 2,600 inhabitants.[1]

During their first year, the Nazis in Prussia purged only 103 detectives or about 1.5 percent. In the entire Reich, more than 11,500 detectives remained in service.[2] The most significant cause of attrition from regular crime fighting was transfer into the political police. Out of the original 10,000 detectives in Prussia, 1,400 went quickly to the Gestapo. By October 1935, only about 8,000 remained, and an additional 50 were on call to create the new Gestapo post for the Saar. The Kripo department at Wilhelmshaven lost one-third (three) of its detective sergeants and had to share its one officer with the local Gestapo. The men lost were apparently the younger, for most of the remainder (four of six) were between the ages of 57 and 59, approaching retirement, and one was chronically ill. In June 1934, the department reported that it could bear no more plundering of its ranks.[3]

Kripo officials sorely resented the high-handed use of Kripo as a personnel pool for the Gestapo. The Gestapo continually drew its detectives from Kripo ranks without regard for the effect. What was worse, they allegedly sought to replace these draftees with detectives dumped from the Gestapo as unsuitable—for instance, men who had been drunk on duty, or poorly qualified and inadequately trained recruits from Old Fighter ranks. Kripo considered Gestapo-trained detectives so poor that they refused to accept them with equal Kripo rank. They wanted to accept only men expelled from the Gestapo as "politically unsuitable." They argued that not only should the Gestapo have to rely on its own recruitment and training, but that it should return to Kripo standards.[4]

In 1935, to supplement Kripo forces, the Reich minister of the interior ordered the expansion of detective forces in the municipal police—a way of shifting the tax burden. He set a uniform ratio that provided coverage for cities without a Kripo department. Of course, Nazis also wanted to rebuild the Kripo, but as late as 1939, the Reich Kripo still numbered only about 12,200. It had not kept up with population growth.[5]

Nevertheless, Kripo may not have been overworked, for Reich centralization may have rationalized the distribution of staff, and conventional crime rates continued to decline. As a base scale, we have a worktime study of the detective force of the small state of Lippe, done in 1931. The little force of eleven detectives worked with an average population ratio of about 1:4,000 urban inhabitants. They handled 47 felonies and 384 misdemeanors during a three-month period. The men averaged between 59 and 65 hours per week when not on vacation or sick leave.[6] Obviously they put in much overtime. Compared with this 1931 norm, the reduced forces of the Nazi era ostensibly benefited from greater standardization. The official office hours posted for the Prussian Kripo Post at Hannover in 1935 were from 8:00 A.M. to 1:00 P.M. and 4:00 P.M. to 7:00 P.M. daily. During 1939–1940, Lippe fell under the supervision of the central Kripo post at Dortmund, which had for its area a total of 164 working detectives who handled 613 felonies, claiming a 95 percent success rate. Reich-wide, 12,682 working detectives handled 20,561 felonies, claiming an 82 percent success rate. Of course, such cases are a small part of the working detective's load, but it seems to have been considerably reduced.[7]

Until June 1936, the transformation of the detectives into Nazi police moved slowly. Both reorganization and the extent of NS control had developed as a product of the power struggle over the police. Until 1936 Himmler had wisely concentrated his energies on the political police, while his competitors dispersed theirs among all the different police. Reich Interior Minister Frick came closest to consolidating control over a Reich-wide Kripo. He planned to use it as justification for eliminating a separate political police, thereby breaking Himmler's power base in the police. Thus, most Kripo forces remained relatively free of SS influence and penetration until after 1936.

As early as February 1933, Frick's ministry sponsored a study of the Kripo of the states. They repeated the process again in September 1934 as the ministry began to work openly toward centralization. Meanwhile, Himmler had pulled the political detectives out from under Frick's encroaching net and brought them under his own order as commander of the Political Police of the States and inspector of the Gestapo. To counter, Frick's people had removed Arthur Nebe from Gestapo headquarters and set him up as head to the Prussian State Kripo Office (LKPA). Long before the Nazis, the LKPA had served as the de facto Reich-central for coordinating intelligence on most crimes. Though it remained technically subordinate to the Berlin police president, they gave it special direct advisory status in the Reich Interior Ministry. They intended to develop it as a Reich Kripo headquarters that would eventually reabsorb the political police.[8]

When Himmler became chief of all German police in June 1936, he turned the tables. Building on Frick and Nebe's work, he rapidly consolidated the LKPA into a Reich Kripo Office, included it with Gestapo headquarters under the Sipo Main Office, and consolidated all the Kripo departments of the states into posts under its authority.[9] Then SS command and penetration began, along with infusion of a Himmlerian variant of the NS world view that had already begun to permeate Kripo.

Well before 1936, the Nazis had already affected Kripo work. Outwardly, it remained normative detective work. Kripo had to control the same elements and behavior that concern all modern societies, and they devoted modern criminological methods to that work. From all appearances, changes in regime had not significantly affected their professional service. The transformations that had occurred by 1935 related to "legal" improvements in the control of crime.

Nevertheless, Nazi efforts to build a unified and more efficient Kripo involved a transformation of ideas about crime fighting and the role of the police.[10] Like the unification of Kripo, that transformation was as much a product of ongoing trends in Germany as it was of NS ideas. But because it did not figure significantly in the power struggles over the police, it developed smoothly from an ideological conjunction among Nazis, their allies, and policemen. The transformation evolved from initiatives taken in Prussia by Göring, Frick, Daluege, and Nebe before 1936, then escalated under Himmler's uniform, Reich-wide command.[11]

This transformation was twofold. On the one hand, police crime fighting shifted from its primarily reactive posture to preventive intervention against professional criminals and habitual offenders. On the other, it involved a shift in the ideological underpinnings of criminological theory. Although ideas about the roots of crime differed as much among Germans as elsewhere, a general balance between environmental and biological determinism prevailed. Since Hitler had embraced this balance, the general Party line agreed that some criminals become involved incidentally and could be reformed by education, or scared straight: hence, short stays in concentration camps for most—what one might call "severe-shock incarceration." Others, however, were inherently deviants, and the only cure was their removal in one way or another. Among Nazis, racist ideology blended with crimino-biological theories that supported a belief in hereditary criminality.[12] The successful shift to racial perspectives in crimino-biological theory was basically a Nazi contribution, but the overall shift to preventive crime fighting grew from a broadly based consensus.

As champions of law and order, the Nazis had promised to restore effective crime prevention and the moral fiber of society. During the early 1930s, Germans suffered from hysteria over an allegedly growing crime wave and moral decay. Actually, by 1928, the general crime index in Germany had dropped about 50 percent from a high in 1923, rebounding only about 10 percent during 1929 and 1930. Thereafter, the general decline resumed, dropping below the 1928 level by 1933. The depression figured more strongly in the short upswing than did any breakdown of morality. Nevertheless, sensational press coverage, demagoguery, a public fixation on a true increase in theft, robbery, and organized crime (as opposed to overall crime), along with the general pessimism of the era, produced the hysteria. Stung by public criticism of their alleged ineffectiveness, detectives found a concordance with right-wing politicians in a call to end liberal constitutional restrictions that tied their hands and soft-hearted penal theories that coddled criminals. Thus, from 1933, Nazis and their conservative allies among the jurists and policemen worked together well in mounting a campaign for an effective, cost-efficient assault on crime and immoral behavior by striking at its alleged roots—professional criminals and habitual sexual offenders. In this endeavor, they won great popular support through well-publicized claims of success, which in turn justified the concentration camps, their harsh regimen, and almost unlimited authority for police intervention.[13]

The assault on professional criminals (third-time offenders), vagrants, prostitutes, and repeat sex offenders began in Prussia with legislation and decrees that went into effect at the beginning of 1934. Repeat offenders got more severe sentences, vagrants and prostitutes could be committed to work houses and labor camps, and courts could impose up to three years of "security custody" on persons deemed an imminent threat to society. Kripo was also empowered to impose "preventive police custody" on those known as professional criminals, habitual sexual offenders, and imminent threats to the community, even if they had not committed a new offense since the new legislation. This conspicuously paralleled protective custody used against political criminals, whom preventive custody internees joined in the concentration camps. Subsequent decrees in 1934 and 1935 expanded the targeted population and added the power of police "preventive surveillance," which allowed Kripo posts to impose curfews and limit the activity of people they considered redeemable if allowed to work in society.[14]

All these actions depended largely on Kripo's distinguishing the irredeemable criminal and degenerate from the redeemable. Increasingly, crimino-biological theory provided the basis for this judgment, which under Himmler would boil down to Nazi racial theory. Not only did racial prejudices affect Kripo decisions, but so could other social and cultural assumptions. Meanwhile, they mixed sociopaths indiscriminately with all who had problems conforming, and police terror was the only prescribed treatment. The only protection one had against such police powers lay in the sense of professional restraint of the police and juridical civil servants. To understand fully the involvement of the detectives as active agents in their own transformation, we badly need a comparative study of their profession's social and criminological perceptions from the Wilhelmine to the Nazi era.

As a measure of the extent of this early transformation, by the end of 1935, the LKPA reported that 492 persons (3 women) were in preventive police custody. An additional 139 had left police custody: some by release, some by death, some by transfer to security (court-imposed) custody. Under preventive surveillance were 801 persons (32 women), 38 of whom had been released from concentration camps. For an additional 228, preventive surveillance had been lifted, and for 12 security custody had been imposed by the courts. Of course, the Nazis and Kripo took credit for the decline in thefts and robbery, attributing it to their new, decisive powers of intervention. Undoubtedly their activities had destroyed criminal organizations, but improved economy and political stability also accounted for the falling rate of crimes against property.[15]

Most other states adopted Prussia's preventive crime fighting, with encouragement from Frick's Ministry of Interior. Likewise, the Reich and Prussian Ministries of Justice set no obstacles in the way of this "progress,"[16] for these developments did not involve uncontrolled Party radicals or the threat of Himmler's growing power. All such procedures were conducted by professional civil servants in the administration, judiciary, and police "within the law" and with "proper" internal controls that allegedly guarded against abuse. Riding on Nazi and conservative rejection of liberal guarantees to individual rights, Kripo detectives had risen above the laws of restraint without seeing themselves as in any way corrupted by Nazi excesses or ideology. They were now free to do what was necessary to protect society. For this they were duly thankful to the new national regime, and embraced those of its ideas which overlapped their own. The way was paved for further transformations.[17]

Despite strong parallels with the Gestapo's unrestrained power, Kripo detectives increased their sense of self-righteous separation from unprofessional Gestapo detectives and the NS/SS thugs. Regular professional detectives had generally disdained political police work for its taint of partisan political enforcement and spying on the political underdog. Furthermore, the youth of the majority of detectives drawn into the Gestapo added to the disdain felt by the older professionals who remained behind. It is not clear whether this youth was a result of the selection process or the opportunism of the younger men. Regardless, Kripo men embraced an image of the Gestapo as comprising the more amorally opportunistic and less qualified detectives. This image was compounded further by the influx of truly less-qualified Nazis, ultimately elevated to full detective status.

Even young recruits into Kripo were inoculated with this attitude as part of their new institutional identity. When a detective trainee at the police academy encountered Gestapo trainees, his disdain was inevitably reinforced. The Gestapo recruits' élan was perceived as arrogance—totally unjustified compared with Kripo. They swaggered and lorded it over fellow students, while of course, they were unsuitable and their accelerated training course was obviously inferior. Even their instructors were inferior.[18]

As is often the case, the ego-institutional identity of Kripo detectives could embrace contradictions without cognitive dissonance. On the one hand they could complain that the Gestapo raided Kripo ranks for the best specialists, while at the same time labeling Gestapo detectives as unqualified, inferior, and opportunistic. A detective released from the Gestapo for most reasons was automatically unqualified for Kripo service, but a detective expelled for "political" reasons could be embraced.[19]

It made no difference that after the initial influx of Old Fighters into Gestapo ranks, professional standards for detective rank were gradually restored, and after 1936, official standards for detective rank and training became identical in the two organizations. Kripo detectives continued to disdain the Gestapo for lack of professionalism.[20] The men of Gestapo and Kripo had formed self-fulfilling images of each other and entered into a "team" rivalry that became part of each side's organizational image.

There were, of course, real differences in the ethos of the two organizations. But one is hard-pressed to know what the real functional differences were[21] aside from the presence of greater numbers of SS "infiltrators" in Gestapo ranks. Kripo prided itself on greater technical and procedural professionalism, but the only concrete point ever put forward for this claim was their official refusal to employ "intensified interrogation." Beating suspects was below their dignity and counter to all professional procedures. From Nebe down, Kripo superiors allegedly enforced such prohibitions and never succumbed to Heydrich and Müller's admonitions to employ the technique.[22]

So intense was the hostile rivalry, that once Kripo and Gestapo were united in Sipo, Heydrich and Best repeatedly had to admonish against mutual acts of discrimination. Best warned against discrimination directed at detectives transferred between the two organizations. Heydrich ordered them to work together as a team, openly referring to their former "discord and misunderstanding."[23]

At the bottom of all this was undoubtedly the Kripo detectives' sense of apolitical professionalism. Such an aloofness from the "corruptions" of partisan politics was a form of naïveté. In conjunction with their staunch nationalism, it left them vulnerable. One of them recalled how oblivious the professional detective had been to the sequence of political transformations that went on around them. From the advent of the NS regime to their inclusion in Sipo under Himmler, they remained insulated inside their professional envelope, unaware of what the changes meant for them.[24]

Despite their self-image of apolitical professionalism, the plain-clothes police proved more acceptable to the Nazis than any other branch of police. Far fewer needed purging during 1933.[25] Apparently, they all took up NS affiliations with about the same alacrity as the political detectives, but there was little reason for them to pursue SS membership until after 1936. Unlike the political detectives, however, NS membership for Kripo was largely a one-way process. Many detectives became "Nazis," but since they had few detective employees, there was no open back door for Nazi infiltration like that into the Gestapo. Nazis who became Kripo detectives had to be qualified.

Unfortunately, for testing these conclusions, I have found personnel files containing political information only for Kripo detectives in Baden. A 1938 list for the Kripo post Karlsruhe included 130 men. Only 2 (1.5 percent) had NS affiliation before 1933. Another 20 (15 percent) had rushed to join the Party in the spring of 1933, and 2 more (1.5 percent) would gain entry before the end of 1936. Thereafter, 45 more (35 percent) would join, especially when the Party reopened its doors in 1937 and policemen were strongly encouraged to join. Fifty-five men (42 percent) who never joined a major branch of the Movement joined some NS civil service association, usually the NS police union when it was formed in 1933. Only 7 (5 percent) had abstained completely from any NS affiliation as late as 1938.[26] In regard to Party membership, these men do not seem significantly different from their Gestapo colleagues.

They did differ, however, in their tendencies toward the Movement's paramilitary organizations. Only 5 (4 percent) joined the SA, 2 before 1933. Only 2 (1.5 percent) had joined the SS by 1938, 1 of whom was already a member of SS-SD when he joined Kripo as a detective lieutenant candidate in 1936. Almost all of these men had served in the police before 1933. Of the 3 Nazi-era entrants, 2 had no NS affiliation before 1937. The SS-SD member represented the first of Himmler's new SS-police officers, the future he intended for Sipo. An additional 8 men (6 percent) had acquired contributing-member status in the SS or some similar titular affiliation, 6 before 1936 and 2 thereafter. For the rank and file in the field posts, SS infiltration apparently did not come until the 1938 drive for joint membership, whereas in the Prussian Gestapo field posts it had already reached 21 percent by mid-1936.

Only 25 of the detectives (19 percent) had non-NS-Party affiliations. Two had been in the German Volks Party and 1 in the German State Party; 22 more had been members of the SPD, though most severed ties when Germany began moving to the right, and half of them turned to the NSDAP, 5 in 1933. The vast majority had, however, been members of police unions, mostly the Schrader Verband or its affiliates. Since union politics, especially in the local branches, was ephemeral, too much should not be made of these "republican" loyalties. Nevertheless, one might assume that at one time most of these men had accepted the politics of the Republic, just as they would that of the Third Reich. Establishing the degrees of relative enthusiasm is another matter.

At the leadership level, one sees similar differences and similarities between Kripo and Gestapo in 1935, before the incorporation of Kripo under Himmler. A comparison of the heads of the field posts yields interesting details.[27] In contrast with the heads of criminal police posts, who were all professional police detectives, less than half of the Gestapo post leaders were professional detectives (13, or 42 percent), of whom only six came up through the ranks (less than 20 percent). Nevertheless, most of the remainder were qualified administrative officials (15, or 48 percent), some from police administration. Of course, the difference derived simply from the role of the political police as a political instrument. Not only did this mean that the Nazis paid more attention to the "reliability" of the leaders, it also meant that a detective career provided no advantages over an administrative or juridical background for the head of a Gestapo post.

There were other differences, however. Kripo leaders were decisively older: average age of 53, with an age spread of 36–60, as opposed to the Gestapo leader's average age of 37 and a spread of 28–59. NS distrust of civil servants (therefore, the younger the better) may account for the comparative youth of Gestapo leaders. Perhaps it relates to a higher degree of politicization, for Party members were younger on the average, especially in civil service. It may also indicate that the younger, more ambitious men were drawn to Gestapo service, as is often contended. Most likely, all these factors contributed to the age difference.

The greater degree of Nazification among Gestapo leaders comes as no surprise. Among the Kripo leaders, fifteen (about 39 percent) never joined the Party, only one had joined before 1933, and fifteen joined quickly in 1933. In contrast, among Gestapo leaders, twenty-seven (almost 87 percent) definitely joined the Party: 6 before 1933 (over 19 percent), seventeen by 1935 (55 percent). The greatest difference came in SS membership. Twenty-eight (72 percent) of the Kripo leaders never joined the SS, and two others were not allowed to join, although they won permission to wear the uniform. Only 3 (less than 1 percent) joined in 1933, and 7 (18 percent) trickled in after 1935. Among Gestapo leaders, 1 had joined as early as 1932, 15 (almost 49 percent) by 1935, and 4 (almost 13 percent) thereafter. It is less clear how many never joined, although 3 (less than 1 percent) definitely never became members.

Even if one limits the comparison to the professional detectives among Kripo and Gestapo leaders, the differences remain marked. The average age of detectives among the Gestapo leaders was less than thirty-nine, and only two could have entered police service during the Wilhelmine Reich. In contrast, among the much older Kripo leaders, at least thirty (77 percent) served as police professionals before the Republic. Most of the remainder came in through the military and free corps. Their backgrounds predict not only a strong inclination toward nationalist conservatism, but also many ideological conjunctions with the Nazis. Of course, this comparison of the leadership cannot be applied to the rank and file of Gestapo or Kripo.

Returning to a more general comparison, one must note two major differences. A more sizable percentage of civil servants in the Gestapo came in through administrative and legal rather than detective career lines. The ratio of administrators to detectives was about 1:35.[28] So many more law-trained, higher civil servants should have made Gestapo civil servants a more elite group in terms of education and probably also family social status. On the other hand, more than 20 percent of the Gestapo were employees without civil service status,[29] while Kripo had few support personnel. As already described, the sizable body of employees provided the prime avenue for SS penetration of the Gestapo and thus represented a more "unprofessional" element. Thus the Gestapo had a greater social split and was less homogeneous than Kripo.

Beyond these distinctions, the most interesting comparison would be between the professional detectives of the two services. The literature has traditionally described Kripo men as less political, and implicitly less opportunistic and more professionally dedicated than the Gestapo. Kripo supposedly had fewer Nazis and SS men. Except for SS membership, such alleged differences require careful scrutiny. Kripo's relatively lower SS membership derived largely from circumstances—up to 1936, the Gestapo had been the primary target for penetration, and Nebe and Frick partially shielded the Kripo from it. This proves nothing about the professional detectives themselves nor about their political or ideological inclinations. Whatever they were, integration into the SS-SD would have been inevitable. As in Gestapo headquarters, the men in the Reich Kripo Office felt and responded sooner to the call for SS-SD membership. Although we do not know the degree of penetration there by 1939, during that year 3 percent of the civil servants joined. New men, SS-SD members like the new man in Baden, now constituted 14 percent of the total. More significantly, 35 percent of the existing staff were candidates for SS-SD membership. Kripo headquarters seemed to be running about three years behind Gestapo in this process.[30]

The later entry of Kripo men into the SD meant that fewer show up in membership samples for recruits of 1936 and earlier, and, consequently, they escape careful analysis in this work. Personnel records of those studied to date provide few clues as to how they might have differed from the professionals in the Gestapo except for age. A few examples must suffice.

Johannes Thiele had advanced to detective counselor and head of the criminal police in Wesermunde by 1928. Although not a member of a political party or organization before 1933, in October 1931, he was disciplined for some form of political activity and transferred to Berlin. In August 1932, he joined the NS civil servants; in April 1933, the Party; and in July, the SA Reserve; followed in September by promotion to government and detective counselor. Thiele handled criminal police affairs in the Prussian Ministry of the Interior before he was absorbed into the Sipo Main Office in 1936 to manage Kripo personnel affairs. He had openly expressed Kripo-like disdain for the Gestapo and had worked closely with Nebe and Frick in building Kripo. Nevertheless, in 1936, the SS-SD admitted him as a member. He rose rapidly to become head of Superior Post Hamburg and then inspector of Sipo and SD, Hamburg.[31] Like Nebe, this key Kripo leader had to embrace an outward identity with the SS in order to preserve the position from which he could maintain influence over Kripo professionalism. He thereby legitimized Kripo-SS identity.

Dr. Werner Kattolinsky had become a detective inspector in Prussian service in 1930. He also had an NS political affiliation, but its exact origins remain undefined. By July 1932, he served as acting deputy leader of the detective branch of the NS civil service division, Party district Berlin. He became an official Party member a few months later, but did not join the SS until the coordination process of SS and police membership began in 1938.[32]

Dr. Rudolf Braschwitz joined the SS even later. A detective inspector in Prussia by 1927, he entered political work and was subsequently absorbed into the Gestapo. In May 1934, he returned to the Kripo, perhaps fleeing SS control. One could describe his political behavior as opportunistic, because during the Weimar era, he had joined first the Democratic Party and then the SPD "to please his superiors." Before Hitler's victory, however, he revealed NS sympathies, became a contributing member of the SS (like Nebe) and joined the Party "at the earliest opportunity in 1933." He did not enter the SS-SD until 1943, but rose rapidly to major while doing Einsatz service at Kiev.[33]

These three men appear indistinct from their Gestapo counterparts. Even if they were not "typical" of Kripo professionals, they belie an apolitical Kripo image. The Kripo men who never acquired Party or SS affiliation also had their counterparts in the Gestapo. Apparently, a sizable percentage of Kripo Party members had joined the Party during the first months of 1933, revealing either an affinity for the NS or political opportunism. Most of the remainder joined after 1936, when the significance of membership to professional advancement became increasingly obvious. The number who joined the SS, especially after 1938, seems to have been significant. Even many who never joined applied and were denied. Subsequently, some of them won permission to wear the uniform only.[34]

The differences between those admitted and those merely allowed to wear the uniform may be seen in two cases.[35] The first was born in Berlin in 1897. After studying law, he became a detective lieutenant candidate in police administration. In 1933, he entered the Prussian Ministry of Interior and rose shortly thereafter to detective counselor. From 1936, he served in the Sipo Main Office, ultimately as a group leader in the Reichssicherheitshauptamt (RSHA). He had no political affiliations before joining the Party in 1940.

Josef Menke was born in 1905. He studied law, entered the juridical civil service, and received his doctorate in 1933. He entered Kripo service in 1934. Meanwhile, he had joined the Party and the SA in 1933. He terminated SA membership on entering Kripo, and had risen to the same rank as the other man by 1939, government and police counselor. As part of SS-police coordination, he became an SS candidate in 1939.

In contrast, when the first man applied for SS status, he was denied membership and merely allowed status as a "uniform bearer," wearing the SS uniform with appropriate rank of major. Menke had embraced the Party at the earliest safe date. The more "apolitical" man had delayed excessively long in doing so. Each seems to have represented different degrees of the "SS-ification" of Sipo. While the first could only outwardly represent SS-police unity, Menke could be brought one step further into the fusion—undoubtedly never fully converted, but enough to facilitate the greater fusion that would occur in the next generation. These two represented degrees 3 and 4, respectively, on a scale in which 1 equaled total unsuitability even to wear the uniform, 2 equaled refusal to apply for SS status though technically qualified, and at the other extreme, 5 was a more full personal identification with the SS-SD.

From all indications, many who served in Kripo did not differ significantly from the professionals of the Gestapo. Their careers and backgrounds compared closely. Many had an affinity for NS, but before 1933, professional restrictions retarded open acknowledgment. The affiliation dates of Kripo detectives resemble those of Gestapo officials. Branded opportunists by Old Fighters, many served diligently under the Nazis to overcome this stigma, but afterward fell back on their late affiliation to claim separateness from true-believer status. As respectably stationed, securely positioned middle-class men, they had embraced the new order, but undoubtedly retained a sense of aloofness from Nazi rabble. They had served to preserve in the new order what they cherished from the old, especially their own status and their concept of their role in society. Their avowed disdain for NS did not constitute a rejection of all the most basic principles of NS, but rather of particular elements in the Movement.

NS affiliation was one thing, and more research should be able to measure it better, but the degree of true Nazification among the Kripo detectives represents a more complicated question. Most studies of Nazification in the German bureaucracy conclude that purge and infiltration achieved only limited gains, and that indoctrination foundered on polycratic struggles, a lack of clear direction among the Nazis, and resistance by the civil service. In regard to indoctrination, the police, especially both detective branches, appear to have been a special case.[36] From all appearances, Nazification may have been more successful there, even among Kripo detectives.

Unlike all other aspects of the development of Sipo and SD, polycraty and infighting may have had little negative effect on Kripo Nazification. Granted, until their inclusion in Sipo in 1936, Kripo detectives experienced uncoordinated efforts at Nazification. The only uniform guidance came from Frick's Ministry of Interior, which did, however, have a traditionally strong voice in matters of police training. In apparent contrast to Frick's general failure in all other branches of administration under his authority, his ministry's guidance may have supported a more uniform and effective appeal directed at the police until Himmler was able to take an even firmer hand. Unfortunately, these tentative conclusions derive from random impressions given by the available evidence, and a more thorough, comparative study is needed to test them.

Only a relatively few Nazi radicals hoped to displace the professional police with Nazi amateurs, and their cause was totally lost by the summer of 1934. Thereafter, the SS increasingly provided an effective organizational vehicle for the simultaneous infiltration and conversion of the police. During the interim, Frick paved the way.

The Nazis never had an ideological consensus that governed the establishment of a police state beyond the necessity to do so. Nevertheless, they benefited from an ideological conjunction to the effect that the police had to be thoroughly imbued with NS values. Although Frick represented the relatively moderate wing in this conjunction and may have been ambivalent about the need to "Partify" or "SS-ify" the police, he had no doubts about the need to Nazify them. Thus, in his mind, there was no contradiction between the promises he made before 1933 to respect the apolitical professionalism of the police and his strong call for their conversion to the NS world view thereafter. He rejected partisan/party politics, especially party influences in a professional bureaucracy, which should be above politics. This exclusion of politicians extended to the politicians of the NS Party as well. He may eventually have accepted SS influence as essential to the ideological conversion of the police, but only insofar as he saw SS men as political soldiers, as opposed to politicians in black uniforms. For Frick, all civil servants, but especially the police, should be imbued with the NS spirit. But as professionals, they should not be political organization men; membership could only be incidental and part of one's private life.[37]

Unions had played a significant role among Weimar police, but they had been sharply divided along political and ideological lines. In August 1933, they were dissolved, and all policemen felt pressure to join the Nazi union, Kameradschaftsbund Deutscher Polizeibeamten, at the head of which Göring and Frick had placed Old Fighter and police Sergeant Major Luckner. Like Himmler, they relied on Nazis who had been immersed in the police subculture for guidance on how to approach police professionals, which helped to ensure an NS indoctrination that might ring true for policemen. The Nazi union's monopoly offered the possibility for a uniform indoctrination of policemen. In September, it initiated a newspaper for Reich-wide distribution among policemen, and an inaugural article by Frick set the tone.[38]

Frick began with a line aimed at the policeman's sense of professional service and designed to tie it to NS arguments. He criticized the previous regime and its unions for propagating partisan interests. They had disseminated negative ideology and created dissension among the ranks. Since the NS state should serve the well-being of the total community, there was no place for such partisan interests and disruption of discipline. The NS State needed a police built on comradeship and discipline to serve the nation as the Army did, a parallel most policemen could readily embrace.[39]

Soon the well-established professional journals for policemen, *Die Polizei* and *Kriminalistische Monatshefte,* were converted to Nazification purposes. In their pages one can see the evolution of a line identifying the police with the NS regime. Everything emphasized the Nazis' contributions to the improvement of the police mission and image in parallel with their success in overcoming unemployment and the international humiliation of the nation. Nevertheless, indoctrination was well integrated and did not displace the predominantly technical-professional character of the journals. Their reputations were such that some ministries provided sufficient copies to police posts for the personnel to keep abreast of professional developments.[40] Of course, the annual Day of the German Police employed typical NS pageantry and ritual to impress upon them their new positive image and identity with the Third Reich.

Meanwhile, in November 1933, Frick's ministry had decreed a regular program of indoctrination for "the deepening and broadening of the NS ideology within the police." Every police post was charged with conducting regular instruction sessions. Kripo posts responded dutifully. For instance, in Wesermünde, Kripo and Gestapo personnel assembled jointly, once a week for an hour, beginning promptly on December 4,

1933. Despite the mounting pressure of work overload, by March 1934, only one weekly session had been canceled for "pressing service business."[41]

It would be naive to suggest that such an obvious program could make good Nazis out of the detectives. But fragments of material related to such indoctrination indicate that (1) it was not always heavy-handed and off-putting; (2) some of it was well chosen to fuse effectively with a police subculture; and (3) it gradually succeeded in inserting key elements of the NS world view into the consensus reality of the detectives.

For example, during the first four months of the program at Wesermünde, there were indeed such flagrant themes as "Race and Destiny," "Adolf Hitler our Führer," "Nationalism and Population Politics," "Horst Wesel," and "From the History of the S.A. and the Party." But unlike other such programs where Party agencies were counterproductively in control,[42] most presentations were made by local detective officers. Out of fourteen, only two were made by gymnasium professors who may have been provided by a Party agency. Equally important, many of the themes commingled indoctrination with concerns of the detectives: "National Socialism and Criminal Law," "The Law for the Combating of Sexual Diseases, Implementation and Consequence in Marxist States," "The Success of the National Government in the Realm of Crime Fighting," and matters pertaining to their civil service status.[43]

By 1936, such a presentation prepared by an anonymous detective lieutenant displayed an almost natural integration of NS rhetoric with technical exposition. Titled "Police and Wehrmacht," it addressed the relations with the military recently returned after the remilitarization of the Rhineland. Although it began with an almost perfunctory bow to standard NS rhetoric about the police as the domestic counterpart of the Army, other NS ideological themes integrated themselves almost naturally with the technical discourse. Nationalist xenophobia emerged when the author described the return of the troops as a triumph of the regime over the Diktat and national humiliation. His analysis of the detectives' role in the racial and character review of military inductees accepted matter-of-factly racial characteristics as equal to criminal and political records. NS legal and judicial reforms that reestablished the autonomy of the military implicitly paralleled other legal and police procedural reforms that were restoring propriety in German society. A typical detective may have disdained the stereotypical Nazi and SS man and crude ideological spoutings. But wherever themes from the NS world view overlapped with those of the police subculture or with deeply rooted cultural themes and prejudices, the conjunction provided powerful reinforcement.[44] Endless repetition turned other themes into part of the detective's consensus reality. Even the most resistant could not escape significant internalization of some NS ideas, especially since most of them were hardly unique.

We fortunately have a sketch of one of those late-joining professionals who achieved the "fourth degree," SS membership, with limited internalization of SS ethos or ideology. Milton Mayer's pseudonymous, "Willy Hofmeister" was the criminal inspector of a small town in Hesse. Only a few years from retirement and hoping to stick it out, he did his job right through the 1938 pogrom and forced "resettlement." As he described it, he despised the SA riffraff and had no use for NS opportunists and upstart officials. But he asked no embarrassing questions of them or of himself. He kept his nose clean and obediently joined the Party in 1937, when his superior explained that he "had to." His political aloofness, which may have been real, did not preserve him from contamination. Survival required an acceptance of established values, and the police subculture reinforced this by generating hostility toward people "who made trouble." For instance, he saw nothing wrong with sending the Jews off to farms where they could learn honest work, and he resented the local pastor who read forbidden letters from the pulpit.[45] Yet whatever NS/SS indoctrination he may have internalized, he conveniently forgot it after 1945. What remained, however, was the ideological conjunction that made him SS-eligible in 1938. This seems a clear example of how a role orientation that began in Kripo could be stretched to inclusion into Sipo and ultimately the SS-police corps, and then be retracted thereafter to pre-Nazi norms.

To return to analysis of pre-Himmlerian indoctrination: in July 1934, Frick ordered all police authorities to assume responsibility for reinforcing the formal indoctrination program. They had to extend NS influences into the most ordinary aspects of the policeman's daily lives. They should call on policemen to use some of their free time to educate themselves by reading, not just professional journals but also the NS press. The officers had to be role models, exhibiting proper NS values and demeanor in everyday life. Meanwhile, the ministry circulated articles by NS leaders who spouted lines designed to make the police feel like a respected and responsible part of the new order.[46]

If Nazification produced serious morale problems, disruptions of discipline, and a decline in professional quality in other agencies,[47] the effects seem to have been minimal in Kripo. Minimal purging and infiltration and the maintenance of standards in recruitment and training preserved quality and effectiveness. Kripo was one of the few bureaucracies the Nazis respected precisely because they did not see it as such.

Of course, indoctrination became part of all formal training programs. To ensure this, the most heavily purged component of the Prussian police (42.1 percent) had been the staff of their schools. Daluege bragged that the Police Institute for detective training had especially been reorganized according to NS viewpoints. At the same time, he emphasized that recruits received training in the latest scientific criminology,[48] a juxtaposition that alluded to a heavy overlap between ideological and technical training. Eventually, any and all advancement hinged upon one's ability to display at least an apparent internalization of NS themes.

Since the training and certification was in the hands of the professional staff and proctors appointed by the Ministries of Justice and Interior,[49] we really need a thorough study of the Nazification of the police schools. In fact, we badly need comparative, longitudinal studies of all ideological elements in police training for both Germany and other modern societies.

Until the "SS-ification" of these schools after 1936, NS indoctrination may merely have replaced former liberalizing emphases at a comparable level of intensity.[50] Such a transition by stages might have been more effective than a sudden burst of Himmlerian claptrap, especially with relatively mature professionals. Whereas, under the Weimar regime, up to 15 percent of "non-practical" instruction might have been clearly devoted to liberalization (in the form of civics instruction, for example), all nonpractical instruction in the 1933 curricula could have been heavily laced with ideological perspectives. Still, only 27 percent of that would have been overtly so; the rest could have been woven more seductively into instruction on law, ordinances, and criminal theory, as it had been before.[51] Most significantly, for German police trainees during the first half of this century, "alien" liberal and socialist ideas about law, human rights, and criminality might have been seen as more conspicuous and jarring than those coming from a conservative, nationalist, NS conjunction.

Several significant points derive from these observations. Precisely because the Nazification of the nonpolitical detectives involved a minimum of purging and of interference in professional training and certification until after 1936, the relatively gradual transition brought along most of the professionals already going through career development programs. Only during the oral component of certification tests and in the student's daily practical performance were the candidate's ideological perspectives and his "character" evaluated by the examiners—police and administrative civil servants,[52] usually not in Nazi uniforms. Probably they did not emphasize NS "character" evaluation over more objective professional criteria until after the "SS-ificiation" of the schools, and even then the transition may have been gradual. In fact, as late as 1938, most evaluations by police superiors of Kripo detectives, unlike those of the Gestapo, contained no political evaluation.[53] That was left to the SD and other Party agencies.

Before 1938, guidelines governing entry into Kripo officer rank paralleled those of the Gestapo, including racial qualifications, except for the preferences the Gestapo gave to Party members and SS officers. Application processes remained through normal civil service channels rather than through SS-dominated offices, as in the Gestapo.[54] In other words, Kripo professional standards remained intact, except for the insertion of racial barriers—a "subtle" infusion most detectives could easily tolerate.

As Nazification accelerated, both branches of Sipo had their training programs fused in the Führer School of Sipo, which replaced the Police Institute in Berlin in 1937.[55] Later Sipo and SD training would increasingly overlap as a de facto union emerged. Only the intervention of wartime pressures saved the professional police from full "SS-ification."

None of this adds up to a failed Nazification of Kripo. The very success of the process derived from its gradualness and the seeming preservation of Kripo's professional separateness. This gradualness resulted from polyarchic power struggles, and not from any grand Nazi design. The gradual transformation of Kripo detectives better enabled them to preserve their ego identity with an apolitical aloofness from Nazi corruption. Thus, they could be called upon to do criminological-technical work or even to make arrests for the Gestapo as unfortunate side effects of their highly professional status. As the logic of preventive crime fighting drew them in, they could justify responsibility for the permanent preventive custody of very broadly defined "asocials" and finally euthanasia for the "incurable." The extraordinary threats of war brought Einsatz duty, but only as a temporary "detachment" from Kripo. As with Gestapo and SD, perhaps even more so, a separate, strong organization identity enmeshed Kripo detectives in the dirty work of Sipo and SD, while allowing them to deny their corruption, at least until it was too late.

Their professional autonomy had been most important to the detectives; the Weimar experience had entrenched this, and the NS takeover hardly swept it away. Since the Gestapo professional also retained this sense of separateness, and insisted at Nuremberg that SS penetration had not succeeded in destroying it,[56] one can imagine how much more strongly the "nonpolitical" detectives would have insisted upon it had they been forced to defend themselves. Its constant assertion in post-Nazi literature speaks clearly of its significance to their self-image. As late as 1936, regulations governing advancement into the higher ranks of detective service still favored those who worked their way up in the police, and, therefore, would have minimized NS infiltration for a few more years. Such career guidelines soon came under attack from the new SS police chiefs because they limited development toward the Corps for the Defense of the State.[57] Kripo's defenses against "SS-ification" would not have survived long.

TWO

Inside the SD

The preceding examination of the police detectives, other civil servants, and employees drawn into the Gestapo and the Kripo has revealed the complexity of the Security Police, Sipo. A few were indeed the sadistic sociopaths of popular imagery. The vast majority, however, were not. After several years of transformations, however, these more or less "normal" men would manifest behavior that made it difficult for their victims to distinguish them from that stereotype. Furthermore, all contributed in some way significantly to the horrors of the Third Reich.

So far I have argued that these men drew into this transformation process for different reasons. Many were opportunists, but the opportunities they sought were hardly as simple or purely self-serving as the term denotes. Some were neither socially prepared nor intellectually equipped to escape becoming the tools of Nazi leaders. Others, however, entered the partnership capable of understanding their personal, moral responsibilities, at least at some time before it was too late. I also argue that most of these men probably had positive, in some ways admirable, perceptions of what they had set out to do. In Sipo, they built for themselves a lure of different institutional images that could hold them together until they played out their roles.

Yet this argument remains incomplete, because Sipo, Gestapo, and Kripo cannot be understood as if they were discrete entities. They were part of a conglomerate in which each was wedded to each other and the SS through its Security Service, the SD. It was this fusion which rounded out the package of appealing institutional identities and seductive lures that drew an even more heterogeneous mix of men. Once the larger picture is established, the entire network upon which my argument is based becomes visible.

The Emerging SD, 1931–1934

As head of the SS, Heinrich Himmler was responsible for the security of Party speakers and of the Führer himself. The SS had emerged after the 1925 reorganization of the NSDAP to serve initially as an elite bodyguard. Since it soon came to serve as a police force within the Party, it had to keep tabs on infiltrators from enemy movements and the police, and on Party members who might hurt the Movement. Since such responsibilities required knowledge of all potential threats, as early as 1927 Himmler (then second in command) had ordered all SS men to report on the enemy and on problems within the Movement as part of their daily duties. In spring 1931, he formalized this intelligence network by creating "Ic" (intelligence) staff positions in each SS unit to collect and forward reports.[1]

On June 15, 1931, when Himmler interviewed Reinhard Heydrich for the position of Ic officer on his personal staff, he allegedly instructed him to draw up a brief outline of an "intelligence service for the Party," suggesting the breadth of mission he imparted to Heydrich. Himmler concurred with Heydrich's draft and appointed him to the position.[2] Unfortunately, we do not know on what they agreed, which would be useful information. There has been much speculation about how much of the Nazi police state was a product of Heydrich's genius as opposed to Himmler's. Also open to question is how much the final product resulted from their original ideas as opposed to functional pressures and the initiatives of their subordinates.

We do know that well before Heydrich's arrival, both Hitler and Himmler admired the British intelligence service for its ability to attract well-placed, public-spirited citizens rather than paid agents with questionable commitments. All NS intelligence services, including the SS Ic, had already built networks of contacts with sympathetic and knowledgeable persons (V-men). Scouring newspapers and collecting clippings on friends and foes alike was also standard procedure. Collating such information into a cross-indexed card file designed to reveal connections among enemies was no new idea. Producing regular reports summarizing this information and the general political climate was regular routine in police, government, and Party agencies. There is no reason to credit such aspects of SD operations to any one person.

Early on, Himmler had acquired the idea that Germany needed a central, politically directed service to give domestic, military, and diplomatic intelligence the proper political (i.e., ideological) perspective. He also adopted Hitler's fixation on the need for a domestic police force capable of preventing another "stab in the back" during times of crisis. Gradually, these roles coalesced in his mind as the mission of the SS. Although all this extended logically from the mission of the SS as Party police and security agency, such a concentration of power ran counter to Hitler's instincts. While Hitler would only gradually adopt Himmler's dreams, Himmler was constantly expanding their scope. By the time of Heydrich's appearance, Himmler had already conceived a fusion of SS and police, later called the Corps for the Defense of the State (Staatsschutzkorps)—an agency that would encompass all aspects of national security and be both the model and engine for shaping German society. For several years, Heydrich apparently lagged behind Himmler in conceiving the full scope of this idea, but soon he was adding details of his own. For instance, the role of the SD vis-à-vis the police had developed only vaguely as late as 1934, and took several years to define itself precisely. Heydrich was not as aggressive in this process as previously assumed, for organizational and functional relationships had a way of defining themselves.

Himmler's and Heydrich's personalities and their variants of Hitler's ideology set the stage on which the men of Sipo and SD would perform, but not as puppets. That ideology depicted Germany as undermined by numerous enemies and alien ideas, many of which ultimately sprang from the machinations of "international Jewry." Such threats required a combination of preventive policing and public education. Thus, the NS list of enemies and racist reductionism would define all Sipo and SD work. Even so, Heydrich, most SD intellectuals, and most professional policemen would express disdain for one or more elements of Nazi, especially Himmlerian, ideology. As a group they were probably as intellectually autonomous as any other diverse group, perhaps more than the average. But institutions define the goals toward which one works; only the details can be rejected, never the whole, if one is to survive for long in the institution. Things like the "Jewish problem" became consensus realities, and one had to think in such terms. Almost all members of Sipo and SD were sufficiently prepared to do so by judeophobic elements in contemporary Western culture. Finally, Himmler's tendency to perceive all enemies in terms of complexly interrelated conspiracy networks would demand that all information be presented in such a context, until it became second nature—something not entirely new to political police anyway.[3]

Meanwhile, Himmler's Ic and the other intelligence agencies of the Movement had problems of control. Their amateur functionaries got carried away with conspiracies and usually operated too spontaneously. Well before Heydrich's interview, the SA's larger Ic service had seriously compromised itself. Then, shortly after the interview, some elements in the Berlin SS triggered the ire of Josef Goebbels and Hermann Göring. Goebbels assembled materials on this "SS Spy Department" and on July 3, confronted Himmler and Hitler. Hitler allegedly ordered its dissolution.[4] Himmler was already concerned over both discipline and local political influences within his apparatus. So when Heydrich arrived for his interview, he was looking for someone who could not only expand the Ic but bring it under control.

After their meeting, Heydrich returned to Hamburg, where he would soon join the SS. As SS lieutenant, Heydrich would move to Himmler's staff with the grand monthly income of 80 RM, fortunately still supplemented by his naval severance pay of 200 RM. To this, Himmler was able to add supplements, but initially only 40 RM. Heydrich was expected to support himself and finance his operations on this 120 RM and his personal resources.[5]

Meanwhile, Heydrich began work in Hamburg. There he probably met Hans Kobelinski, a thirty-one-year-old, apparently unemployed jurist (Referendar) who had participated in the Munich Putsch as a member of Oberland, but who had just joined the Party in 1930 and the SS in June. Kobelinski would become Heydrich's first right-hand man. In September, after Heydrich had moved to Munich, he engineered Koblenski's appointment to the Ic position with the 4th SS Regiment at Altona. By February, Heydrich had made him Ic officer for SS Region (Abschnitt) III (East), headquartered at Berlin, but Kobelinski stationed himself temporarily in Braunschweig, from where he seems to have monitored the growing Ic structure for all north Germany.[6]

In August, when Heydrich assumed the Ic position on Himmler's Munich staff, he had no command authority. Although he made inspection tours, the Ic men were the adjutants of each unit, and, therefore, the personal agents of each SS unit commander.[7] At his desk in a shared office in the Brown House, Heydrich merely assembled reports on enemy infiltration and problems in the Movement.[8] Within two weeks, however, he was briefing commanders on these threats, already adopting the characteristic posture of expert in charge of an efficient service.[9] From the beginning, Heydrich's posturing set the style for both Gestapo and SD and helped to build their overblown images.

On September 4, Himmler outlined a reformation of the Ic service. New Ic specialists were to be appointed at each division by October, replacing the adjutants. Regimental appointments were to follow.

Himmler also ordered that the Ic was not to be a secret service; instead, it would operate legally, keeping its nose out of state agencies.[10] This was obviously to avoid embarrassments like those of the SA Ic.

By December, Heydrich, now an SS major with a little more pay, still had no budget for his operations, but received special appropriations. He rented a dwelling for his new bride, and shifted his Ic office from the Brown House to his former apartment several blocks away in Türkenstrasse 23. Although he merely sought to remove his operations from prying eyes in the Brown House, he could not have picked a better time. The move protected his Ic staff from the exposés and embarrassments that befell other NS intelligence operations in early 1932, culminating in raids on Party headquarters. As he observed his competitors' embarrassment and wrestled with the problems of the Ic staff system, he allegedly studied other national intelligence operations, and evolved plans for his own.[11]

By the end of the year, there should have been forty-nine Ic officers, one for each of the forty-one regiments and eight divisions/regions into which they were divided, covering Germany, Austria, and Danzig. Each should have been receiving reports from all 14,964 SS members plus his own information network.[12] Furthermore, the SS Ic service was a partner in a larger NS intelligence network dominated by the SA Ic and the ND, the Intelligence Service (Nachrichtendienst) of the Propaganda Headquarters. Each was supposed to share information appropriate to the others' missions.[13] Of course, the SS Ic system was not fully formed, most SS men paid little attention to shuffling paperwork, cooperation among Nazi agencies was always problematic, and everyone involved was an amateur. In short, Heydrich's organization developed haphazardly in a confusing environment.

Then, in February 1932, Kobelinski's operations were compromised when the Oldenburg police uncovered one of his regimental Ic men, Herbert Weichardt, involved in military espionage. This incident revealed problems that Heydrich had to overcome. Weichardt's agent nosing into the military implies that either the Ic regularly violated its directives, or that those directives were phony. Weichardt insisted that he had not solicited military information, but that his agent had provided it spontaneously. He contended that his mission merely involved probing political attitudes among civil servants and military personnel. Of course, the police did not believe this.[14] Nevertheless, Weichardt had openly admitted that his mission included monitoring police and military attitudes, contrary to the written directives for the Ic service, and elsewhere other Ic men were also reporting on the political leanings of policemen.[15] Perhaps the Ic had secret orders that exceeded its written directives. But certainly Ic officers were poorly controlled, ordinary SS men like Weichardt, who often did whatever they thought they should.

To gain control, Heydrich required direct command, including the authority to appoint, discipline, and dismiss his own personnel. If direct command of an independent intelligence service had not already been part of his plan, a second, more devastating compromise of the SA Ic, including police raids on headquarters followed by the banning of the SA and SS in the spring of 1932, determined the outcome. During the ban, Heydrich's Munich office dropped its Ic designation and hid behind the cover of Press and Information (PI) Service of Reichstag deputy Himmler. After the ban was lifted in June, the Sicherheitsdienst SS emerged with Heydrich in command.

The SD Emerges

Heydrich set about recruiting his personnel directly and established a network that gradually replaced the locally appointed Ic-PI Service. Since spring 1932, he had traveled to recruit local leaders, who in turn built their staffs and established a network of agents.[16] After its official creation in July 1932, the SD began to take shape.

By October, Heydrich had acquired a two-story house for SD Central, his Munich headquarters. It served as both SD office and home for the Heydrich family. Located adjacent to the Nymphenburg Palace grounds in a pleasant residential neighborhood and screened by trees and bushes, it provided an ideal cover. He thus established seclusion in residential neighborhoods as the preferred pattern for SD offices at all levels.

The staff of Central included about a half-dozen men.[17] The poorly paid staff workers merely made clippings from newspapers and filed materials. Their equipment remained makeshift, for the SD still had no operational budget.[18]

Similar problems plagued the field posts. In its origin, the SD field structure paralleled that of the SS, which during 1932 consisted of four to five groups (Gruppen) subdivided into 18 regions/divisions, and 59 regiments.[19] From existing records one cannot describe the new SD field structure in detail, partially because both SS and SD organization were in constant flux. Geographically, five SD groups roughly equaled those of the SS by the end of 1932, but never conformed exactly; for instance, headquarters were not necessarily in the same cities. Comparable to the SS regiments, SD districts (Bezirke) emerged covering several Party circuits (Kreis) or an entire district (Gau). Below this level, SD subdistricts (Unterbezirke) slowly developed. They were originally to cover a single Kreis, and, in turn, to be composed of wards (Revier), but such an ambitious network never emerged. Eventually, the SD-subdistricts acquired the simple designation of "outposts" (Aussenstellen) as the lowest-level-office in the field structure. No counterpart to independent SS Region VIII existed for Austria, for the SD had no formal organization there until after the Anschluss. Similarly the SD apparently could not penetrate East Prussia-Danzig, also an independent region, until late 1933.[20]

Sometimes, the old Ic officers merely assumed comparable SD positions. For instance, Group West developed under SS Captain Dr. August Simon. This thirty-three-year-old physician had served as an SS doctor until January 1932, when his group leader asked him to take the Ic position from which Heydrich recruited him. Simon drew no salary for his SD work, because he preferred to remain full-time at his profession, doing SS work part-time. He remained unsalaried as head of SD-Group West until September 1933. Then he stepped down to command a district and continue unsalaried.[21] Heydrich allowed such key men as group leaders to work only part-time until as late as fall 1933 because of the small-scale, amateurish, low-budget nature of the SD.

A group leader like Simon played a highly independent role. Aside from responding to queries, and limited only by a general understanding of the mission of the SD, he remained free to determine what work his group did and whom he recruited. He immediately began the work of recruiting the district leaders who would, in turn, build their own field structure, and by 1933 his group consisted of ten districts. Simon often relied on old Ic staff personnel, but not exclusively. Among those chosen, SS Sergeant Erich Rasner remained unsalaried until the fall of 1933 and remained an SS Ic man until 1934 before becoming an SD member. Others never became members, and would be replaced by externally recruited SD district leaders.[22]

For the area of SS Group South-East, Heydrich had SS Lieutenant Lothar Beutel, a twenty-eight-year-old pharmacist. Unlike Simon, Beutel drew a salary as group leader. His district leader for Dresden and two subdistrict leaders for Chemnitz and Upper Silesia remained unsalaried from their entries in March 1933 until 1934.[23]

In Beutel's group, Ic men did not automatically form the new SD posts. The Ic officer for SS Regiment 46 was not called into SD service until late in 1933, after he had proven useful to Beutel's penetration of the Saxon political police. In contrast, one district leader came from the Party district intelligence office (ND).[24] Heydrich and his group leaders weeded through the available human resources based on some unknowable criteria.

For the South Hannover-Braunschweig district in SD Group North, we have a glimpse into operations in late 1932. By the summer of 1932, Hans Kobelinski and Heydrich had established the local field structure, for which Heydrich recruited SS Lieutenant Paul Leffler as district leader. From Kobelinski, he inherited several interesting "associates" (Mitarbeiter), the most important of whom was Police Lieutenant Colonel Herbert Selle, who had been working with the Ic for an indefinite period. Heydrich introduced Leffler to Selle immediately, and for the rest of the year this man at the top of the Braunschweig police provided the SD with information on the police.[25] Heydrich encouraged this illegal activity, but by this time, NS nosing into the police had become a less sensitive offense, especially in Braunschweig, where the Party was in the coalition government.

Another, less desirable, associate was careless about secrecy. He kept his SD papers in the same place where he stored materials for illegal work, even explosives. Realizing such carelessness could compromise the SD, Leffler limited this man's involvement to the elaboration of KPD affairs,[26] where he could not expose anything that would embarrass the SD.

The rapid expansion of Leffler's responsibilities further illustrates the makeshift nature of the early SD. For an indefinite period, he served as both district leader and a member of Heydrich's staff in Munich, which must have involved considerable logistical problems.[27]

Lack of information precludes any picture of early SD Group South, centered on Munich. Perhaps Heydrich ran this group personally out of SD Central. In any case, for some reason it seems to have evolved more slowly than others.

The most important group, SD Group East, centered on the Reich capital, Berlin. In August, Heydrich had transferred SS Captain Kobelinski there to directly assume his duties as Ic officer for SS Group East. There he created the new SD group, which became official on September 15. As a measure of the significance of his Group East, Kobelinski, unlike the other group leaders, had some salaried staff as early as September 1932.[28]

When Kobelinski was transferred to Berlin, he entered the domain of highly independent SS General Kurt Daluege, who had built his own intelligence operation before the Ic. Daluege exercised considerable influence over the local SD as well. For instance, he got one of his own men assigned as head of SD District Berlin. This SS corporal had served with Daluege's intelligence service since November 1931. Since Kobelinski and Daluege appear to have had smooth relations until well into 1933, the corporal apparently thought his Daluege connection would be helpful. In later years he had problems and eventually resigned from the SD.[29]

In this emerging field structure, an ill-defined distinction existed between the new SD and the old Ic service until well into 1934. Ic men served as an interim net of field staff, reporting to the SD but not considered members. Most SD information gathering and field network construction fell to these men (even some SA Ic men) and other people, loosely called associates (Mitarbeiter), yet few held official SD membership. At this early stage, Heydrich apparently preferred to build his organization slowly.

This, then, was the SD that, according to legend, was so all-pervasive by January 1933 that it frightened many Nazi leaders, maintained extensive files on thousands of friends and foes, and prepared to penetrate and take over the political police forces in Germany. In fact, the most liberal estimate of its size by the end of 1932 cannot exceed thirty to forty official members, only a handful of whom were salaried.[30] Even counting associates, such as Ic men, the SD had little more than 100 people, assuming all Ic positions had been filled, which does not seem to have been the case.

The little SD nearly collapsed under the financial pressures that threatened the Party in late 1932. No serious intelligence operation could run entirely on voluntarism, and the lack of any regular budget meant no reliable work force or equipment. Since SS funds were so limited, Himmler had to wheedle a supplement out of Ernst Röhm, head of the SA, and Rudolf Hess, Party Secretary. After a tour of SD Central, they had promised 1,000 RM, of which only 500 accrued. By December, salaried workers received only a few marks each, and Frau Heydrich ran a soup kitchen to keep them going. At Christmas, they were furloughed home without enough money for return tickets. Leffler resumed his unsalaried Braunschweig office and looked for some means to support himself and his family, which had been living off relatives.[31]

Even worse than its patchwork development, the SD suffered from an almost deliberate vagueness about its mission. As Heydrich recruited his people, he briefed them on the nature of the SD in grand but elusive terms. Paul Leffler recalled a meeting held on September 11, 1932, in the office flat on Türkenstrasse. The newly appointed field officers and central office staff came together for a briefing by Himmler and Heydrich. Then and on many other occasions, both asserted that the SD was patterned after the British Intelligence Service and the Deuxieme Bureau.

> Both repeatedly stressed that they intended that the service should not be an organization of paid agents and informers; they firmly intended that it employ only men of unimpeachable and unobjectionable character. Aside from the lowest possible number of salaried staff in the offices, the SD would depend on unsalaried trusted people who were involved only out of ideal motives and who had to enjoy respect in the population based on their life's performance, their technical ability and their objective, sober judgment. At that time, those of us present got the impression that they were both fully earnest about this declaration.[32]

Such pronouncements in no way delimited the mission. They resembled the sort of pep talks leaders always give to lend their organization a sense of pride and dedication. Most significant, however, was that the ideals expressed contradicted the implicit work of spying and informing. Such contradictions led to many conflicts and later to the disillusionment of many members, as Leffler's last sentence indicated.

The contradictions became apparent in the real work. According to Leffler, the SD work on " 'political enemies' dealt preponderantly with the marxist parties, especially the KPD . . . [but] also . . . reactionary currents in the economy. . . [and] the political currents in the then badly splintered organization of the Work Service. . . . Furthermore, I already had to occupy myself predominantly with Party affairs."[33] His "predominant preoccupation" grew from the unlimited idea of potential enemies, especially where it directed suspicion into the ranks of the Party. Within a year, that would lead to conflicts with Party leaders that threatened the very existence of the SD.

In June 1933, in both Hamburg and Braunschweig, the SD clashed with local Party leaders. In both cases, SD men became involved in Party rivalries, in opposition to powerful bosses. The worst case was in Braunschweig, where Leffler and his lieutenant were eventually called before the High Party Court. They had been overzealous in their mission to report on elements in the Party that endangered its position. When local bosses uncovered the SD network, they saw intriguers conspiring against Party comrades to overthrow them. It took several months for Himmler, with the help of Party Secretary Hess, to settle the case, and meanwhile the future of the SD hung in the balance while several Party magnates called for its dissolution.

During that crisis, Heydrich described for the court the official mission of the SD as objective intelligence gathering in the service of the NS revolution. The SD was "a post that is bound by the Party leadership to an objective, official enquiry, and its subordination under the Reichsführer SS offers, in his person, sufficiently guarantees that troublemaking and animosity have no place here."[34] Nevertheless, SD functions included informing on one's NS comrades, a reality that could not be obscured by such idealistic rhetoric.

In Nazi circles, a more acceptable image for the SD was that of cloak-and-dagger squad, a romantic role that attracted many members. They would penetrate and disrupt the enemy, foiling his espionage activities. But "the enemy" was everywhere. Before 1933, penetrating the state bureaucracy, the military, and the police was illegal and could bring undesirable attention from the police. After the NS acquisition of power, these agencies came under NS command, expanding the problem of spying and informing on comrades. Thus, the SD could only proclaim openly its mission as an information service that watched "the enemy" and kept the leadership informed on the mood of the nation. So, to avoid addressing unpleasant contradictions inherent in the SD mission, Himmler and Heydrich preferred to leave it in vague and idealistic terms.

The SD had to be the kind of national institution that all respectable citizens could aid and support out of a sense of patriotism. Toward that end, Heydrich recruited men of education, professionals, civil servants, and well-placed businessmen, further enhancing contradictions between mission, image, and personnel. This information service of public-spirited citizens who sought to help guide the leadership bespoke an idealism incompatible with the semi-gangsterism of NS cloak-and-dagger work or with totalitarian police-state terrorism.

Passing the Crisis, 1933

Endless organizational readjustment and a perpetual groping for more satisfactory missions would plague the SD to the end, but its embryonic state contributed greatly to its problems during the first year of the Third Reich. Until he got his first police responsibilities in March, Heydrich should have been able to focus on building the SD, but before Hitler became Chancellor, resources remained too sparse either to do anything significant or to allow him to focus his attention.

During the January maneuvers to win Hitler's appointment as chancellor, Heydrich's responsibilities were spread thin when Himmler assigned him as staff officer for special duties (Führer z.b.V.), serving as liaison in Berlin. For the next two months, he forwarded his SD reports from Berlin, where he moved SD Central. Then came Hitler's appointment and with it just enough funds to pay SD salaries. Now, Heydrich had a better prospect of building his organization, but less time to give to it. He settled SD Central in a rented villa facing Branitzer Platz in a quiet residential neighborhood in Charlottenburg. Its size revealed more regular funding. As in Munich, this would be his home and SD headquarters. He returned to Munich in March to fetch his wife, just in time to take part in the seizure of power in Bavaria. There Himmler rose rapidly to commander of the Bavarian Political Police, which Heydrich assumed the responsibility of running.

In the same month, the SD began to grow, just as Heydrich's added responsibilities overextended him. Besides commuting regularly between Munich and Berlin, he had special assignments such as touring SS field offices with Himmler and serving as observer at the Geneva disarmament conference. Since the growing SD required full-time management, his plans included a salaried administrative staff. For staff leader (Stabsleiter), he recalled Paul Leffler.

Leffler was a thirty-two-year-old engineer, war veteran, and Free Corps officer whose own business venture had recently folded. He became staff leader, Heydrich's deputy in charge of the Berlin Central until its return to Munich, and thereafter Heydrich's adjutant. His rapid rise to SS lieutenant colonel by June 1934 mirrored the development of the SD, as did his transfer out in early 1936,[35] a time when many early members temporarily parted ways with an organization that had outgrown them.

Two other early members of SD Central round out an image of a soldiers-of-fortune operation. Arthur Bork and Karl Oberg joined the staff as early as May. In their early forties, both men were senior in age to Heydrich, but his contemporaries in the NS Movement. Both had served in the war and pursued active Free Corps careers. Bork, a former sergeant and finance clerk, became administrative officer, handling finances, and Oberg, a former officer, gradually replaced Leffler as Heydrich's right-hand man. Like Leffler, they rose rapidly in rank, then found themselves estranged from the established SD that had emerged by 1936.[36]

A band of adventurers penetrating the establishment was neither the image nor the reality that Heydrich wished to cultivate. Nevertheless, any security service inevitably exceeds intelligence work and performs "special actions." For instance, SD involvement in excesses against their enemies during the spring months resembled that of their fellow SS men. Also, former members of the SD alleged that Heydrich had a special team (Rollkommando) in SD Central for conducting special investigations (Ermittlungsaktionen). Its alleged commander was Walter Sohst, who indeed served as liaison for Himmler and Heydrich in Berlin from November 1932 until their arrival in April 1934. After Göring created the Gestapo, Sohst served as its official liaison to the Reichsführer SS. There he allegedly made photocopies of documents that were not supposed to go to the SD.[37] One source who described Sohst's background with great accuracy went on to claim that his "SD Alarm Command" conducted Feme murders for Heydrich, eliminating embarrassing accomplices and personal enemies. Sohst was in fact a mechanical and electrical engineer (without diploma), and a veteran of the war and Free Corps combat who never found a settled place for himself after the war and began doing photographic and communications technical work for the NS Movement.[38] Conceivably, he could have done everything attributed to him, but the sources of these allegations are notorious for mixing accurate detail with sensational accounts.

Often, however, the legendary dirty work of Heydrich's SD fell to men outside the membership. For instance, in April 1933, Heydrich allegedly dispatched a murder squad to Austria to eliminate an NS renegade.[39] The availability to the Movement of murderers was not new, but this may have been Heydrich's first contact. From then on, however, he would employ such elements, who considered themselves SD members. When they were exposed, of course, the SD denied them. As we shall see, they did not have official SD membership, were not typical of the SD, and were not in tune with Heydrich's desired image of propriety.

Regardless of what Heydrich intended, "available for special dirty work" became an element of the SD's growing reputation. Even while the organization remained little more than an embryo, it earned its reputation for spying on colleagues. The overly conspiratorial atmosphere of the Party and the power seizure combined with the SD's open-ended mission and independent, unregulated behavior to create the previously described crisis in June 1933, in which several Party District Leaders accused the SD of conspiring against them and undermining their new NS governments. But the High Party Court hearing that ultimately quashed the case and saved the SD revealed a poorly coordinated, untrained, amateurish operation. As the High Party Court later concluded, "the mission of the SD was not yet laid out unmistakably clearly and its organization not yet entirely accomplished."[40]

Leffler testified that because Himmler and Heydrich had been so overextended, the SD got no particular instructions. The independent field officers and their loose network of associates was on its own just when the power seizure created so many new situations. Leffler could not provide his subordinates with any clear definition of their mission or its limits. Undoubtedly with some admonition from the embarrassed Himmler, Heydrich reined in his SD, resumed more direct control, and began reconsolidating SD headquarters in Munich where his police responsibilities demanded his presence.[41] He abandoned his premature move to Berlin.

Once its takeoff began, however, the SD acquired priority in SS personnel policy. Himmler considered building the SD so important that he let Heydrich have free rein to plunder the SS for recruits. Regular SS commanders occasionally resented such high-handedness and tried to block some commandeering.[42]

The need for knowledgeable persons from all walks of life lay behind the pirating of men from SS units. Many SD men were recruited for the contacts they provided. For instance, when one Old Fighter began work for the Reich Ministry of Propaganda, his potential attracted the SD. His SD position was apparently no secret in the ministry, but others were. Another SS man who had been a Referent in the ministry became a secret SD member.[43] The SD recruited a Party district office leader of the NS Welfare Organization for Greater Berlin to provide contact both in Party circles and later in city government. Leo Hausleiter, who had a wide circle of foreign and domestic contacts, was another ideal recruit. He had a reputation as an expert on world economy, which he enhanced in 1936, when he joined the Hamburg World Trade Archive and subsequently became its director and head of the Hamburg World Trade Institute. The SD also recruited an employee in the Saxon Ministry for Popular Education as soon as he became head of the Division for Professional Training and Teaching Appointments in the Chemnitz Labor Office. When a longtime SS member acquired local leadership in the German Textile Workers Union and the German Labor Front, the SD acquired him as member, but apparently also in secret.[44]

The SD drew in other men to serve on its staff because of their expertise. Retired Major Walter Ilges was a right-wing playwright. Since 1931, he had made himself an expert on separatist movements in the Rhineland. Bringing his own "archives," he began work at SD Central on separatist enemies. Himmler's cousin, Dr. Wilhelm Patin, was a Catholic priest and the author of many scholarly works on Catholicism. He became the staff expert for "Observation of the Catholic Action."[45]

The SD also sought another type of contact. Herbert Mehlhorn, a member of the Brown Shirts and a confidential agent for the budding

SD since April 1932, was a lawyer in Saxony. In short order, he gravitated into the SS and SD, soon playing a key role in their penetration of the Saxon political police as deputy to the president of the Gestapo Office Saxony.[46] Cases like Mehlhorn and the 19 percent of the early members who were or became political policemen lend credence to the tradition that Himmler and Heydrich always intended for the SD to fuse with them. For instance, almost all versions contend that as soon as Heydrich took over the Bavarian Political Police, his SD screened their members and penetrated their ranks in large numbers. Yet the early SD had neither the capacity nor the numbers for such a job. The facts belie the tradition.

Among the known 1933 members, no SD men entered the Bavarian Political Police—many Nazis and SS men, but no members of the SD. Most SD-police links formed the other way around, with policemen joining the SD. Some, like Dr. Georg Hagen and Richard Wendler, had legitimate credentials for police positions. Both entered the political police in March, and Wendler must have been among the first SD links when he became an SS-SD member effective April 1. Dr. Hagen, who served as a police link to the post office, joined in September. Other SD-police links defy explanation. For instance, one man with no apparent NS background came from a judicial civil-service job in Kiel to join the political police, SS, and SD, all effective August 1. Similarly, a non-NS, naval civil servant drawn into the political police in September and into the SS-SD in October must have been an acquaintance of Heydrich, for there is no other likely reason he would have been personally called to service. Two obvious examples of SS penetration into the political police joined the SD only in June and October.[47]

Walter Potzelt may have served as Heydrich's chief adjutant responsible for monitoring SD-police personnel connections, but Heydrich called him to Munich only in 1934, on the eve of the move to the Berlin Gestapo office. There he probably played a key role in watching the police bureaucrats and regulating their entry into SS and SD, but by then the SD–political-police link was becoming less haphazard.[48]

In the fall, winter, and spring of 1933–1934, while Himmler became commander of the political police in the other states, more links between these police and the SD developed. Except for a few SD cells in the Prussian Gestapo and Beutal's work in Saxony, however, regular SS men achieved most of the penetration, and the SD did not draw them in until later. Cases like Bruno Streckenbach in Hamburg, who was drawn immediately into the SD, were exceptions, for he was a trusted local political police chief whose affiliation made him into a Trojan horse for the SD. His connections won for the SD acceptance by local Nazis who had previously distrusted it.[49]

Although SD infiltration of the political police may have evolved casually, as early as 1933, the SD developed an additional secret mission: penetrating significant institutions of society, not just to acquire intelligence, but also to exercise influence in them. The most open and significant example of this mission was the SD's role in shaping Sipo.

Meanwhile, as Himmler began his move to net the little state political police forces, the future of the SD seemed more secure. In November, Himmler elevated it to an independent SS office (Amt). The new Security Office (Sicherheitsamt or SHA) developed a more impressive organizational structure—one that provides insight into SD work. (see Appendix B.3)[50]

Heydrich, now titled Chief of the Security Office, commanded a staff of five departments (Abteilungen) and two independent desks (Referenten). The operational components of the Security Office were charged with coordinating comprehensive-sounding intelligence and counterespionage work—too comprehensive for such an embryonic organization.

Department III, Information (Internal-Political), was to compile intelligence on enemy movements and important spheres of life in German society. Its first desk dealt with the illegal right-wing opposition ranging from the Strasser Movement, through völkisch organizations, the former Free Corps, and the Stahlhelm, to organized monarchists. Desk 2 focused on "religion and ideology," which included Catholicism, Protestantism, and all Christian sects. Its charge was to report on the personal and public activities of clerics, lay leaders, and their organizations, especially on foreign-mission connections and the movement of church funds. Since Nazis suspected Catholics of sponsoring separation, reporting on separatist enemies fell to this desk as well. The third desk, Marxists, reported on both the KPD and the SPD. Desks four through six reported on spheres of life: respectively, science and education, government and law, and the "strengthening of ideological thought in public opinion." This revealed the extent to which the SD saw itself as shaping as well as monitoring German society. Similarly, the desk dealing with science and education called on the field offices to begin compiling files on "intellectual currents," specifically the men of the universities.[51] This went well beyond spying, for they would establish their influence in higher education, garnering confidential agents in intellectual circles who could also recruit for the SD.

Department IV involved counterespionage and "foreign questions." That only one desk was devoted to foreign intelligence shows how little the SD had done in this direction. The second desk had a wide-ranging charge: Jews, pacifists, hate propaganda, and emigrants in foreign countries. It was to report on Jewish community life and their organizations, economic activities, connections, and migrations. To do this, it monitored Jewish publications. In line with Himmler's idea of ideological intelligence, the SD had to put together all the links in the "elaborate web of the international Jewish conspiracy." Work on hate propaganda sought to establish how and why anti-German feeling developed abroad and whether it affected Germany's position in the world market. Desk three worked on Soviet intelligence, treason cases, and immigrants in Germany, while desk four handled "counterespionage," both military and economic, and desk five reported on "armaments." Desk six reported on general economic conditions and the mood in business and industry. It devoted special attention to such things as the improvement of unemployment, commercial espionage, and Jewish involvement.

From the very creation of the Security Office, work on Freemasonry occupied a major position, as indicated by the assignment of an entire department (V) to it. By November 1934, with a grand staff of fifteen men,[52] this department maintained its own separate files, library, archive, and museum, built from the materials captured in police raids. The man who apparently developed this office was Gregor Schwartz-Bostunitsch, Russian emigré and self-styled expert on Freemasonry, "political culture," Jewry, secret societies, and Bolshevism. When Eichmann arrived in fall 1934, Bostunitsch already cut an "outlandish" figure and had to be retired for diminished capacities in 1936.[53]

There is no reason to suspect that the lack of a special office for Jewry reflected any lesser interest. It revealed rather a more typical NS attitude. All SD research into other enemies always sought the Jewish ties among them, which was all that required clarification from an NS point of view. Until 1935, the SD, like other Nazi agencies, felt no need to study Jewry as an ideological enemy, for its character and methods were a matter of dogma. At some point, perhaps as early as 1933, the SD's expert on Jewry was apparently one Julius Blaichinger, who seems to have become a SS lieutenant in 1933, served into 1935, and then like Bostunitsch disappeared from rosters.[54]

Finally, two independent desks in the SD Office dealt with the press and with technical support and radio. The press desk not only monitored and evaluated publications, but also disseminated ideas, perhaps in the form of planted articles. The technical support desk maintained the enemies file for the entire SD, provided photographic and communications services, and maintained statistics and a library.

Although this organization looks impressive on paper, it was neither fully staffed nor evenly developed. Extensive guidelines outlined the research, but their ambitious scope stands in sharp contrast to the small number of experts who divided their time among multiple responsibilities or only worked in their free time. Furthermore, these guidelines included an extensive list of publications that were to be read regularly by the central staff,[55] suggesting that the Security Office relied more heavily on analysis of publications than on any covert sources. The seemingly impressive central structure with its ambitious guidelines for gathering intelligence contrasted even more sharply with the field network that had to support it.

For instance, during 1933, most group offices acquired their first salaried staff personnel. Only some district and subdistrict offices had salaried commanders. It still seemed a matter of indifference whether such leaders were full-time salaried or part-time unsalaried, workers. The primary concern seems to have been whether the men needed a job.[56]

The memoirs of Alfred Naujocks, who joined the staff of Group East at the end of the year, provide a picture of the daily work. Group headquarters occupied the old Berlin villa that Heydrich had abandoned. Naujocks and his colleagues all spent their days poring over the files. They cross-referenced news clippings and SD reports by all names mentioned in them and established files on each individual. They sought the personal and business connections of all enemies, to expose their net of contacts and to reveal potential spies and agents.[57]

Naujocks' version of Kobelinski's introductory briefing warrants quoting. It gives credence to Heydrich's frequent claims that his personnel suffered hardships and worked at great personal sacrifice.

> I warn you . . . that no one can work here for the money. Our funds do not run to salaries of the kind you would find in a business house; in fact, all you get is ninety marks a month, and fifteen would be deducted for your food and so on here. From the rest, you would have to buy your uniform, and make a very small contribution to Party funds.

> Finally, I will say this: if you now have second thoughts about joining us, you had better leave right away. You must realize—once you are engaged on work of this kind, you cannot just decide to leave when it suits you; you are in it for good, committed completely. Understand?[58]

Regardless of how accurate this rendition may be, it corresponds with other sources. The only incongruity is the overly dramatic conclusion about no one leaving the SD. That simply was not true. However, Kobelinski may have said it, for such posturing is consistent, and a romantic air of intrigue prevailed throughout the history of the SD.

Much of this intrigue was little more than petty personal scheming. For instance, Kobelinski allegedly demoted and punished Naujocks for disobedience. Naujocks claimed that he had a chance for revenge when Heydrich arrived for a visit. Naujocks accused Kobelinski of homosexuality and of conspiracy with Rudolf Diels, head of the Prussian Gestapo and Himmler's chief rival. Regardless of whether this contributed to Kobelinski's dismissal, Naujocks prospered. Within the year he became top sergeant in the Berlin office, and went on to become one of Heydrich's favorite agents for special, extralegal work.[59]

Of course, some of the cloak-and-dagger trappings were more than posturings; SD work did require secrecy. For instance, all SD workers and members received a code number (Chriffre-Nummer). To the informed, it revealed the exact regional office for which the person worked, and may even have identified his position. For instance, during 1933, Group West used the numbers 30001 through 35000, subdivided among the group office and its ten districts. Group East apparently had the numbers in the 10000 range, with Kobelinski designated as 10001. Of course, when one addressed a report to Heydrich, it went to number 1.[60]

Turning to developments in the rest of the field structure, during 1933, the number of SD groups increased along with the growing SS structure. By November 1933, new groups included South-West, North-East, and Middle, (a short-lived Elbe soon fused with Middle), but records are too fragmentary and the alterations were too frequent to allow a reliable listing.[61] For example, in autumn, the geographically large Group South split, creating South-West, responsible for Baden and Württemberg. This became the first SD command for Werner Best, whom Himmler and Heydrich adopted into the SD in October. After Best had lost his police command in Hesse, his experience and talents became available to them. Heydrich gave Best the key post at Stuttgart, where he proved his merit and quickly became the number-two man in the future Gestapo-SD system.[62]

Best established his headquarters in Stuttgart with command over only an adjutant and three district leaders for Baden, Württemberg, and Rheinpfalz. In the whole area he had only a handful of affiliates, and little real information gathering could be done. He operated with great independence and got little in the way of guidance. Of most value were his skills in personal politics. Although he denied involvement in Himmler's acquisition of the Baden and Württemberg political police, he developed SD contacts in those forces and allegedly extended Himmler's Bavarian police authority over the Pfalz, where Party District Leader Buerkel had previously blocked it. He also developed espionage and counterespionage facilities that allegedly gained the SD some respect from the Abwehr.[63]

For Saxony and the area of group leader Lothar Beutel, the surviving evidence discloses still more about the haphazard growth of the early SD. SD field offices were not just created where they were needed, they also appeared where there was an available, trusted man. If he changed his residence to another area, a new subdistrict would appear at his new address.[64]

In Group West, the part-time group leader Simon surrendered his post. The new salaried, full-time head, SS Lieutenant Wilhelm Albert, set up headquarters in Frankfurt. His work there revealed the expanding horizons of the SD, for he began building an espionage system directed into France. Of more immediate importance was the extension of his network into the very crucial Saar.[65] Not only did Albert's arrival mark the beginning of salaried command in all groups, but he also acquired salaried staff personnel with responsibilities that paralleled the organizational structure of SD Central.[66] September 1933 marked the beginning of a professional, uniform field office system, but that did not extend much below the group level until 1934.

Group West provides a picture of one of the best-developed groups. Even after its reduction with the creation of SD Group North-West, Albert's group still did not conform exactly to SS Group West. SD field structure corresponded only roughly to that of the SS, with the political elements of SD work and personal connections taking precedence.[67]

Below the group level, evidence of the field structure evolution is fragmentary and confusing. The SD district remained the basic field unit until well into 1934, gradually giving way to the larger region (Abschnitt), often covering more than one Party district. The SS Ic continued to provide part of the field structure until April 1934. For instance, a roster of intelligence personnel for Superior Region West lists intelligence officers (Ic ND-Führer) for two regions, but lists SD leaders for another. Although in SD service, such "intelligence officers" still did not have SD membership.[68]

For spring 1934, a clearer picture emerges of the size of the SD and the full scope of its network. Under Albert's command, besides himself and his group staff of eight full SD members, there were two regions and five districts, each of which had at least one intelligence officer or SD leader. Region XI, centered on Frankfurt, was a special case. The region intelligence officer was SS Private Wilhelm Günther. For his significant territory, he had twenty associates, three of whom headed subdistricts within the city, the rest being "experts" on various subjects of interest to the SD. Among the twenty, fourteen were SS members, but only one an SD member. Outside Frankfurt, Günther had three other subdistricts, Wiesbaden, Hanau, and Wetzler, staffed by two intelligence officers and a "former" SD man.[69]

For the subdistrict of Wiesbaden, a list of confidential agents (V-men) survives. Fourteen of them lived in thirteen towns scattered irregularly over the district. Thirteen were SS members, one a former Ic man. One was the mayor of his town, another active with the police. Most important, the intelligence officer who compiled this list could not evaluate the reliability of ten of his fourteen agents, and he did not even know three of them—undoubtedly a product of the part-time nature of everyone's work. Among those he could evaluate was a "newcomer" who made "an entirely good impression."[70] This report instills little confidence in the early SD intelligence network.

Thus, the SD membership of Albert's superior region was probably ten, few of whom were salaried. They were supported by at least seven Ic intelligence officers and several other associates. If each of these had about fourteen agents, as in Wiesbaden, there could have been a network of between 100 and 150.

Unfortunately for our picture of the SD, Albert's command was not typical, for it was one of the oldest and better established. Only 250 members is a good estimate of the size the entire SD had achieved by the early months of 1934. If the Ic officer in every SS unit supported the ten SD groups, nonmember associates on staffs and in field posts could have exceeded 400, plus the agent or V-man network, which should theoretically have numbered in the thousands.

To cover the entire Reich, these were small numbers. Furthermore, one must remember that most still worked part time, most were amateurs playing detective, and some were Party hacks who needed a job. For instance, in the well-developed superior region West, the "specialists" could have three or more diverse areas of responsibility. To do their jobs, they had to review all relevant publications in their region, build their own personal net of agents for each of their areas of responsibility, collate their own research with reports from lower field offices and agents, and participate in police raids from which they might gather materials. Finally, the agent or V-man net that fed these staff officers their information offered marginal reliability at best. None of the reports from the field seem to have survived, but one must doubt that they came close to fulfilling the goals set by the Security Office.

With the growth of the field structure came a reorganization that would remain basic for the SD until 1939. As part of a major organizational change for the SS during the fall and winter months of 1933–1934, SS groups became superior regions (Oberabschnitte) to conform more closely to the military districts (Wehrkreise) of Germany. Made in accord with the SA and as part of plans for more efficient mobilization, these changes brought parallel developments in the SD, including a new terminology to conform to that of the SS. The old groups became superior regions (SD-Oberabschnitte), regions became the basic field unit replacing districts, and the subdistricts became field posts (Aussenstellen). But simultaneously, the changes in the geographic organization of the SS increased the differences from SD organization. Contrary to all published studies, SD boundaries remained coordinated with the Party districts and state borders until 1939.[71]

Unfortunately, the surviving records tell almost nothing about the work of SD men in the field in 1933. During the first chaotic months of power, like other SS men, they dove enthusiastically into the work of rounding up enemies, sometimes cooperating and sometimes competing with the local political police and other NS intelligence agencies. Until Himmler gained his political police commands at the end of the year, work with the police was usually indirect and depended on the positions and attitudes of local SS men who got police appointments.[72]

A flagrant case of SD involvement in early police-state terrorism was the Columbia Haus in Berlin, run by SS auxiliaries of the Gestapo and used to house Gestapo arrestees. During the wild early months, it became notorious for brutal treatment of internees. Even after the end of early excesses, the SS guards continued to indulge themselves in forceful, occasionally deadly interrogations. The Berlin SD maintained its own interrogation team (Vernehmungskommando) at the Columbia

Haus beginning some time in 1933.[73] Whether their techniques differed from other SS men is not a matter of record, but obviously, the early SD deviated in its special actions far from the ideal images that its leaders projected and to which more idealistic members aspired.

The SD as Supplement, 1934

By 1934, the SD had come of age; however, remnants of its amateurishness would survive until at least 1939. Improved control over organization and personnel seems related to the March 1934 arrival of Werner Best at the Security Office, still in Munich. At the same time, he became commander of Superior Regions South and South-West, while in the SD Office he assumed responsibility for Department I, Organization. Best devoted much effort to developing guidelines and traveling to supervise the development of the field structure.[74] His overextension shows how thinly spread the SD remained. Best's arrival also involved him in the problem of defining the SD mission.

Until the war, defining that mission remained a major concern. One reason may have been morale, for the SD apparently suffered from a growing sense of insecurity in the ranks: a product of relative neglect by Himmler and Heydrich, attack by Party leaders, and rumors of dissolution. As opposition in the Party continued, so did the rumors. This insecurity apparently drove SD members to expand and clarify their missions. In contrast, Himmler's primary concern with the SD mission was to set limits that would keep his critics quiet.

Before Himmler acquired command of all political police forces, no one questioned the need for a Party security service. Ironically, with the acquisition of the SD's monopoly position and its partnership with the political police, it suddenly found itself without an independent function of its own. The political police had responsibility for collecting information, conducting investigations, and taking action against all enemies. The growing demand for a return to normal policing led Himmler to forbid the SD any further executive actions, which now had to be referred to the police.[75] To redefine the SD's new status and mission, Himmler and Heydrich proclaimed it an essential supplement to the Gestapo, capable of providing ideological insights that the detectives could not have.

This new status as "essential supplement" to the political police had the appearance of a step backward. While the police combated the enemies of the NS state, the SD observed the enemies of the NS idea. Although this corresponded with Himmler's idea of ideological intelligence, the distinction undoubtedly did not provide many SD members or their critics with a justification for the SD. Meanwhile, Himmler, Heydrich, and their policemen would continually expand the horizons of police work. For instance, the "Jewish problem," a formerly ideological issue, would eventually become the Gestapo's mission, not the SD's. The SD always seemed vulnerable to replacement by a more fully empowered and better financed police force.[76]

Regardless of how such worries may have troubled some SD leaders, nothing suggests that Himmler or Heydrich expected the SD to become superfluous. The SD as a vehicle for transforming the political police and developing their intended character had recently acquired greater significance. Finally, Himmler's perception of an "ideological intelligence service" differed from police work,[77] as did Heydrich's image of an information service to guide the leadership. These elements of the SD mission found expression in a reorganization of the SD Office.

After his move to Berlin in April to take over the Gestapo, Heydrich again relocated the SD Office to the Reich capital. He could maintain his preference for residential buildings, for the Prinz Albrecht Palace was conveniently located in the same block as the Gestapo Office, and it became the new SD Office at Wilhelmstrasse 102. The Gestapo building on Prinz Albrechtstrasse abutted the spacious gardens behind the palace, providing an ironically pleasant campus for the allied Gestapo and SD. The splendidly refitted palace denoted the arrival of the SD at the seat of power.[78]

Under the 1934 reorganization of the SD Office, Best had consolidated personnel and finance under Department II and focused the work of his own Department I on SD organization and all surveillance of and liaison with NS organizations, the Arbeitsdienst, the military, police and civil service, and other intelligence agencies.[79] Thus, he put all potential sources for conflict with other official agencies under his direct supervision, and also minimized the impression that the SD spied on these agencies. They were now "administrative" relationships rather than the responsibility of intelligence and analysis departments. In fact, SD concerns went well beyond monitoring these agencies; they sought to influence the appointment of right-minded persons to key positions, beginning especially with those they could directly affect—the political police.[80]

Departments III (domestic political), V (Freemasonry), and VI (foreign) worked as the ideological intelligence service against "enemies." To achieve Himmler's goal of revealing the international conspiracy against Germany, they maintained the SD card files. They cross-referenced these files to relate individuals to one another, to organizations, to places, and to abstract enemy groups, specifically Jewry. In these files, leaders' cards were blue, ordinary members' yellow, but Jews stood out on white cards to reveal their key roles in all enemy efforts— a self-fulfilling prophesy, since Jews covered the full cultural, social, economic, and political spectrum.[81] Such ideological research exceeded normal political police work, even of the NS variant.

Aside from providing the police with information on enemies and screening appointees to police and other key offices, the major product of SD work was its situation reports (Lageberichte). This was no SD innovation. Such reports were standard procedure in the state administration, the police, and all intelligence agencies. Nazi agency reports differed from those of state agencies only in their ideological focus, and that difference rapidly eroded. Before the SD, the SS field structure had forwarded such reports and continued to do so until the SD became fully established. At some unknown date, the SD began its mission of informing the leadership through its reports, at first focused exclusively on enemy threats. For May/June 1934, it issued report "Nr. 123," the oldest surviving issue.[82]

Guidelines and reports show better than the organizational structure the actual emphases of SD work. The Catholic Church had emerged as the prime focus in 1934. Its outspoken opposition to both the racist-eugenic and nationalist-state elements in the NS Weltanschauung combined with its international organization and influence made it a major threat, and one that Himmler felt should be brought to ground next. Though of greater popular force in Germany, the Protestant churches were more cooperative and less hostile to nationalism. Marxists and other illegal organizations, the former major preoccupation, were for all practical purposes broken, and, moreover, the proper focus for the political police. Although the SD would always monitor them, and take credit for much of the police success against them, they no longer dominated its attention. Freemasonry retained its second position in the lexicon of enemies, proclaimed as the only other power on earth that could rival the Catholic Church, but more threatening because it operated in secrecy. The seemingly lesser attention devoted directly to Jewry still stands in strange contrast to constant official reminders that they were the ultimate threat.[83] Nevertheless, the transfer of the desk dealing with Jews, pacifism, and hate propaganda from the foreign to the domestic intelligence departments signaled a shift in focus.

Whenever the police had a pretext to ban a Jewish organization or bust up a Masonic lodge, the SD could go along to collect intelligence. Gradually, they accumulated extensive archives, and with a little conspiratorial imagination assembled impressive proofs of evil schemes and elaborate charts showing international connections. Such ideological intelligence was to "educate" the public and especially the police. This indoctrination of the police became part of the SD's ideological and supplemental role.

Although ideological intelligence involved collecting information on some bizarre topics rooted in Himmler's mysticism, the information service role would eventually provide the most satisfactory mission for most SD intellectuals. This role fell to Department IV, which monitored foreign and domestic presses, all aspects of the national economy, and the intellectual, educational, governmental, and legal spheres of public life.[84] From this work, situation reports would develop to inform the NS leadership on the mood of the nation and the effects of policy decisions.

During 1934, the intellectual component of the SD began to coalesce. Before 1933, the Party had limited appeal to intellectuals. But once it became apparent that National Socialism would infect all aspects of German life, intellectuals could no longer ignore it. Some of those who could identify with one or more elements of NS ideology were alienated by the circles of NS intellectuals around Rosenberg or Goebbels, and almost all felt threatened by the antiintellectualism of Robert Ley's educational reforms. The SD's image as the sole source of information to the leadership and the intellectual shaper of the new nation drew these intellectuals as their great hope for influencing the future Reich.[85]

Contacts between such intellectuals and the SD grew rapidly from a few SD affiliates in academic and journalist circles. These men recruited among their established colleagues, who would serve as sources, contacts, and unsalaried staff experts. Among young academics, they recruited full-time, salaried members. In May 1934, the field posts got orders to begin files on intellectuals so they could expand their contacts with them. The key person in these developments, however, was Dr. Reinhard Höhn, recruited by his old friend Kobelinski as early as 1932. By 1934, he was a Dozent with connections at the Universities of Jena and Munich, from which his recruitment network spread. After the SD moved to Berlin, he became established at the University of Berlin. Höhn, with his staff of young intellectuals, began building the network that would produce reports on the mood in influential circles and the general public, focusing especially on criticisms of policies and practices that they wanted the leadership to reconsider.[86]

In all the SD's diverse responsibilities one perceives an almost deliberate attempt by Himmler and Heydrich to leave its mission open-ended and vaguely defined. It had to remain a flexible instrument for all eventualities. Thus, there would always remain certain cross-purposes between the two chief commanders and the more-directly involved SD leaders who sought more satisfactory self-images. The conflict would intensify as opposition in the Party and state mounted against the SD in 1935 and 1936.

Before pursuing this crucial issue of mission and image, other measures of the growth of the SD warrant mention. In terms of actual size, the SD grew from about 250 members to about 850 during 1934. Many of these men, however, merely assumed positions formerly filled by the Ic associates and represented only a modest increase in organizational control. A good estimate of the numbers of associates still working in SD offices would be about 10 percent of the membership, most of them being probational members.

A picture of growth in the field offices comes again from Main Region Rhine, the new name for Albert's group. Headquarters in Frankfurt was a three-room apartment at Kronprinzen Strasse 25. In contrast with the nine-man staff of early 1934, SS Major Albert still ran his operation without benefit of an adjutant, but now had eight sergeants as research specialists, with six assistants, six workers, and four trainees. Most covered one to three specialties each, but one still worked eight. Under them in Region XXX, there was one lieutenant and a sergeant with one assistant and three trainees. Another sergeant ran the special post for Fulda. In Region XI, one lieutenant and a trainee did everything. These regional staffs had replaced the former Ic affiliates,[87] but there was still no true working force below the main region level.

Another perspective on the expansion of the SD can be had through its finances. During 1932, the SD had no budget, surviving on the ad hoc contributions of Hess and Röhm. For the period between January and July 1933, no financial records have surfaced. Apparently, sources included extortion and fund-raising activities. For example, according to one inside source, beginning in 1932, SD Group East had blackmailed the firm of Eduard Winter AG, the distributor for General Motors and Opel in Greater Berlin. If this seems fantastic, in July, an SD agent reported that Daluege was soliciting 900,000 RM from industries like Siemens, partially to finance the SD.[88]

Regardless of how much money the SD actually realized from such sources, any amount would have been significant in the summer of 1933, when the official budget from the Party amounted to only 4,000 RM per month.[89] In June, Hess curbed Daluege's sources with the creation of the Hitler Fund. Henceforth, Hess monopolized all such lucrative solicitations, but they were now limited. How much the SD continued to collect clandestinely is unknown; however, it could not have been consistent or significant. Even if the story of the Eduard Winter Firm can be believed, it must represent an exceptional case, for it is the only specific example ever cited.

A July 1933 allotment of 4,000 RM from Party Treasurer Franz X. Schwarz apparently marks the beginning of a regular budget. This tiny monthly sum remained the only known regular income until May 1934, when Schwarz increased it to 20,000 RM. Immediately, however, he began having trouble meeting the growing demands of the SD, including a lump sum of 68,000 RM to defray the initial costs of absorbing the Party's other internal intelligence agencies. By October, the Deputy of the Führer had temporarily assumed financing of the SD, drawing between 250,000 and 270,000 RM from the industrialists' Hitler Fund for this purpose.[90] In November, Heydrich requested a budget of 700,590 RM per month.[91] Perhaps this represents an accurate measure of the growth of SD operations, or Heydrich may have been playing a clever game to eliminate Schwarz's supervision of SD finances. Heydrich had asked for the bulk of Party funds. Schwarz stated that he could give the SD only 80,000 RM per month and asked Bormann to see if the remainder could be covered by the Hitler Fund.[92]

Bormann responded that 270,000 RM was the absolute maximum they could raise from that source.[93] Thus, if Schwarz added no more than he estimated, Heydrich got slightly less than half of his request. If he had played a shrewd game, grossly inflating his estimate to force the matter out of Schwarz's hands, then he won a victory. Of course, this is only conjecture, but it conforms with his and Himmler's objectives.

Considering all these possibilities, external budgets cannot reveal accurately the growth of SD operations. Nevertheless, one can see that official funding multiplied two to two and one-half times as fast as official membership—undoubtedly reflecting the transition from part-time amateurs to full-time, salaried workers.

Regardless of whether Heydrich had played a game with Schwarz and won it, the SD would remain pressed for funds until at least 1939.[94] So, no matter how big the organization became, it could not accomplish everything that Himmler or Heydrich might have wished during these formative years. It remained a limited tool under constant assault by rivals and opponents in Party and state who sought to limit it even more.

Early SD Membership, 1932-1934

The most elusive aspect of any organization is its human component. To capture that component, this chapter offers several perspectives on the early members of the SD. Specifically, one must consider in what ways they and their experiences were typical of other Germans, Nazis, or SS men, and in what ways they were special. Of course, the question that drives such enquiry is how could they have contributed to the creation of a totalitarian police state and then become executioners of genocide? Regardless, a thorough analysis of the personnel is essential to any serious study of an organization.

First, the relationship between the SS and the SD requires explanation. From the beginning the SD was semiautonomous in its personnel. Although SS men could be transferred into and out of the SD, SS membership did not automatically qualify one for SD membership or vice versa. Although a slim majority of early recruits came from the SS, originally one could become an SD member and remain one for some time without becoming an SS member. By the same token, for the period under study, SS rank often had little to do with one's position in the SD, but was rather a function of one's SS status. Only by 1936 were serious efforts afoot to correlate rank and position in the SD. Thus, the SD was the most autonomous of the SS special units (Sondereinheiten). In terms of "membership" definitions, it was more autonomous and unique than the Camp Guards (Totenkopfverbände or TV), or even the later Waffen-SS. Consequently, the SD always had its own ethos. Nevertheless, most SD men thought of themselves as SS "political soldiers," just differently elite. Most wore the SS uniform with pride and assumed all the responsibilities that entailed. Yet, because of the distinctions, many SD members had or took more leeway than is traditionally attributed to the "asphalt soldiers" in interpreting what SS status meant and required of them.[1]

One unique aspect of the SD was the complex nature of "membership" and how one achieved it. Several major categories existed, and each requires different approaches for analysis. For instance, the most important distinction among SD men was service in a police branch of Sipo—the Gestapo or Kripo. Heydrich would eventually pursue a personnel union among all branches of Sipo and SD with the goal of having all these men hold SS membership through the SD. For a variety of reasons, by 1945, only about 18 percent of Sipo men were caught in this union as members of the SD.[2] On the other hand, within the SD as early as the end of 1934, more than 20 percent worked or would soon work in some detective police force.[3]

Thus, by the end of its third year, the SD already had a major subdivision within its ranks. To describe such complexity, one must coin some labels. The "total SD" will refer to all persons who had any official affiliation. It consisted of the "working SD," anyone who worked in or for an office of the SD, and what was later called the "Sipo-SD," or those SD members who worked in a branch of Sipo. They were those administrators, detective policemen, and employees of the Gestapo or Kripo who were members of the SS, organized and commanded by the SD. Although the term Sipo-SD instead of Gestapo-SD is anachronistic for the period before June 1936, I will often use it for the sake of simplicity. By 1944, more than 55 percent of SD members would be Sipo-SD.[4] The police work involved in Sipo membership adds different perspectives for an analysis of these men, for instance, the effects of a possible police subculture.

Beyond the example of Sipo-SD, other aspects further complicated the total SD. Since one ideal was to have as few paid personnel as possible, they were divided between unsalaried (ehrenamtlich or alternatively nebenamtlich) and salaried (hauptamtlich). As previously described, this distinction had little to do with the office one held, or even how many hours he worked at it, but whether one earned his living at SD work or merely served the SD in his "free time."

A second distinction was between full members (Mitglieder) and "associates" (Mitarbeiter). This distinction began with the SS Ic "intelligence officers" who worked with the SD but without membership during the early years. It soon spread to include a wide range of persons with semiofficial affiliations but without full membership, including the salaried clerical staff, especially female typists, who appeared in increasing numbers from 1934. The largest number of associates were the trusted agents or V-persons (Vertrauensleute).

Between members and associates lay the probationary members. At least by 1933, a probationary period became part of SD membership. During probation, a candidate had to work for several months under the supervision of his nominating officer as a V-man, an expert in an SD office, or even as a field post leader. The SD could draw its probationary members either from among associates or from entirely outside the SD. A member who knew enough about them to think them suitable nominated them, but they had to be approved by SD Central.[5]

Thus, the total SD was divided by a two dimensional set of distinctions as illustrated in chart B. The greatest number were always the associates (Mitarbeiter), who could be either salaried or unsalaried. The salaried were clerical staff and a few experts working full-time in a field office or the SD Office. The probational members could be either salaried or unsalaried, working in any capacity. The vast majority were the V-persons who drew no pay for their services. Women could be associates, but never members.

Salaried members (hauptamtlich Mitglieder) usually served in command, staff, expert, or helper positions in the field or central offices. Most members were always unsalaried, however, serving in the same kinds of positions in SD offices or working as liaison with some other organization where they earned their living, but openly providing a link with the SD and representing its interests. Some such SD connections with other organizations were secret, however, with the SD member representing a more potent SD presence than the more typical V-man. The largest concentration of such members were, of course, the Sipo-SD. In the early years, their membership in the detective forces of some of the states might have been clandestine, but with the creation of Sipo in June 1936, SD members constituted open, special Sipo-SD units within each Gestapo and Kripo office.

Finally, a small percentage of unsalaried members who worked in some other agency or held an important position in government or society were truly "honorary," the conventional translation for the label ehrenamtlich. Himmler bestowed honorary SS membership and elevated SS rank in the hope of winning support and influence. Those honorary SS men who also held actual SD membership garnered some prestige and legitimacy for the SD. Since few honorary SS appointments involved actual SD membership, it must have reflected some commitment to SD goals by the recipient.

All these people together constituted the "total SD." Unfortunately, the SD did not use labels for such categories with any consistency. Variations in both official and common usage occurred over time. At first, Mitarbeiter referred to members (Mitglieder) who did not hold a position in an SD office, but served only as its contacts in the field. By 1936, such men were called "observers" (Beobachter).[6] To add to the confusion, Mitarbeiter also became the term for all personnel of the total SD, whether members (Mitglieder) or associates (Mitarbeiter). Since they finally used the term Mitarbeiter both in this generic sense for anyone officially affiliated with the SD, and as a specific for nonmember associates, I will use the term "affiliates" for the generic, that is anyone in the total SD. I will use "associates" for the nonmember affiliates.

Of course, all this complexity, especially the ill-defined terminology, caused much confusion both then and since. A further element of confusion resulted from the range of agents used by the SD. For instance, there were the occasional informants (Zuträger) who might bring in

Chart B The Total SD: All SD Affiliates (Mitarbeiter)

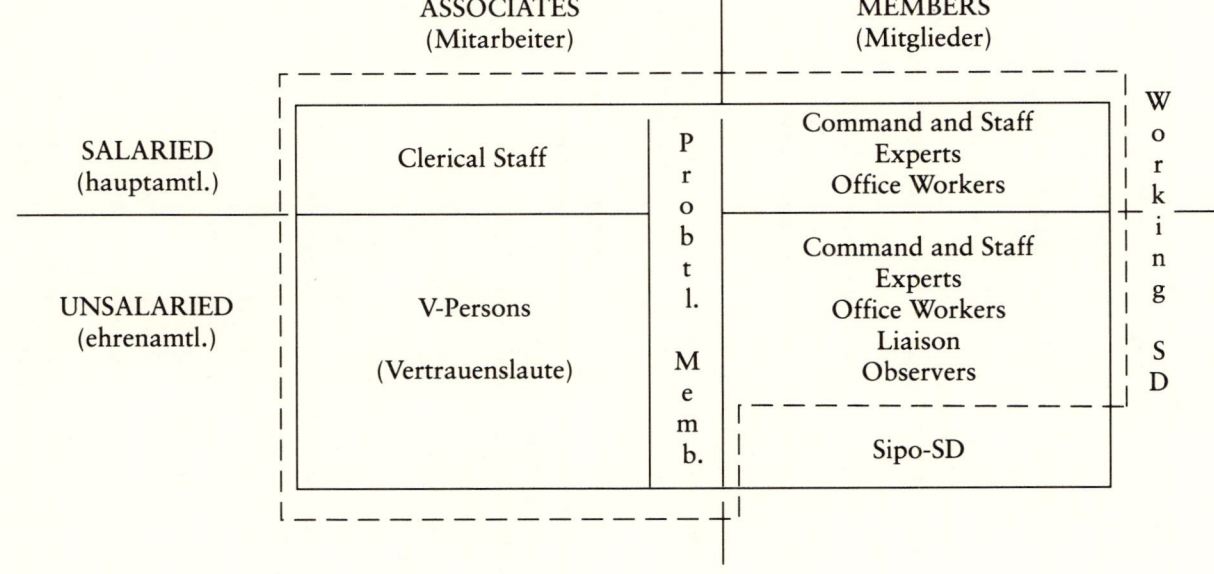

odd pieces of information or who might be used for a special enquiry; such people were not considered associates. Even lower on the scale were "agents," a term limited to paid informants. The preferred informational sources were the V-persons, ostensibly respectable members of their community, knowledgeable and so situated as to be reliable sources. They were considered associates.

All associates and members had SD code numbers (Chiffre Nummer). All associates also took an oath of secrecy and, apparently above the level of V-person, carried an SD identification card.[7] Such paraphernalia led many associates to believe themselves members, for they were apparently unaware of the distinctions. Such confusing distinctions allowed the SD to deny the "membership" of a compromised V-man with no fear of contradiction. More importantly, unless he was indiscreet, no one could uncover his affiliation.

Unfortunately, hardly any guidelines governing the selection and screening of members for this period have survived. The few that have suggest that formal guidelines existed as early as 1933; however, many cases cast doubt on the thoroughness of actual procedures. Nevertheless, by fall 1933, not only did the usual criteria for SS membership apply, such as physical condition, but an affiliate had to exercise "discretion." Associates had to be suitable for both SS and SD membership. Presumably, the SD judged female associates on all SS criteria other than gender.

When they decided to elevate an associate to membership, and he had successfully completed probation, his superior region office assembled the paperwork required for review by the SD Office. The superior region commander had to testify to his suitability and aptitude. The candidate had to reaffirm the SD oath of loyalty and secrecy, write an autobiographical statement, and complete two questionnaires. One was the standard Reich Ministry of Interior form for testing the racial background of civil servants, for which he had to provide genealogy through all eight great-grandparents. The ministry apparently confirmed this information. The second questionnaire provided the necessary information for a background check, including military or police service, record of convictions, history of NS memberships, and outstanding debts. To establish his possible usefulness, they also wanted to know in what enemy circles he was known as a Nazi, and what contacts he had in industry, the economy, or the press.[8] Apparently, when an applicant was not yet an SS member, the SD simultaneously pursued joint membership. If that was not appropriate for some reason, the SS process could be postponed, but unfortunately no surviving guidelines clarify this.

During July and August 1932, Heydrich recruited about a dozen men as the first members of the SD, men who staffed field offices for at least four groups and a few districts. From this kernel, the SD grew slowly, like a chain letter, with field officers recruiting their subordinates. By January 1933, 40 members would be a reliable estimate of size; by the end of 1933, 240 members; and by the end of 1934, 820 members.[9] Until April 1934, the old SS Ic provided many of the active field workers, while full SD members gradually replaced them. Thus, for the first two years in the field posts, the nonmember associates outnumbered members, but the ratio slowly reversed itself.

Quantitative Analysis of the Membership: 1932–1934

Since no lists of SD associates have survived and there can be no random sample of them for analysis, one must restrict this study to members. In any case, there is no reason to expect significant differences between associates and members after 1934 and the end of the Ic affiliation of more ordinary SS men.

The personnel files of 526 men who joined SD between 1932 and the end of 1934 provides a sample of identified early members that includes at least 99 percent of the officers and about 62 percent of the total membership. This sample provides a total population for analysis of the early officer corps. Although biased in favor of those who became officers early, it also offers the best available picture of the entire early membership, especially those who would shape the future SD as its leaders. (For discussion of the sample and its analysis, refer to Appendix C.)

Date of birth determines which events of German history could have affected one's development through personal involvement. For instance, one generally had to have been born by 1900 to have served in the First World War or to have experienced related events as an adult. Those born after 1900 experienced them as adolescents or children and matured during the Weimar era.[10] Most early SD members were young, only 32 percent of those identified being born in 1900 or before. Naturally, the officers were older, 51 percent being born by 1900. The average SD member was about two years younger then the average Party member, but both SD members and officers were slightly older than their regular SS counterparts. Within the Party, the SD drew disproportionately well from the under-30 cohorts, proportionately from the 31-40 cohort, and poorly from the older men.[11] Whether these differences have any significance is hard to surmise, but the SD fit the general NS and SS patterns of appealing more to youth.[12]

About 4 percent of the known members came from outside the borders of the old Reich, and an additional 3 percent from territories lost by Germany in postwar settlements. Among the German born, 63 percent came from north of the Main-Rhein-Mosel line and 37 percent from south Germany. In regional origins, the early SD reflected the general composition of the SS, but here the parallel ends.

The sample of SD members disproportionately represented the urban sector of the German population. Only 39 percent were born in rural environs or towns that had not exceeded 20,000 by 1925, as opposed to more than 59 percent of the German population at large. More significantly, 45 percent of the SD members came from large cities of over 100,000 people, as opposed to only about 27 percent of the general population.[13] This disproportionate distribution of urban versus rural origins also marks a first symptom of major dichotomies among SD members—45 percent "urban" versus 39 percent "provincial."

SD members professed their religion disproportionately in favor of Protestant backgrounds: 73 percent Protestant and 25 percent Catholic, as opposed to the national ratio of 63:33. Again, known SD members closely resembled SS officers during the same period (71:29), undoubtedly reflecting the lesser appeal to Catholics by the SS, with its harsh anti-Catholic line. Contrary to what one would expect from anti-Catholic bias, however, the early SD officers more closely approximated the national norm at 67:30 than the rank-and-file members at 76:22. One might propose that the difference of 9 percent between officers and other ranks resulted partly from the greater number of southerners among these officers, a difference of 12 percent. However, that begs the question of why there should be either regional or religious differences between officers and other ranks only for this short period of SD history. Regardless, their presence argues against any bias within the early SD against recruiting Catholics. Why early officers of Catholic background were drawn disproportionately to the SD between 1932 and 1934 is an enigma.

As for social status, 26 percent of the members came from families that could be classed as secure upper-middle class or even elite. Sixty-two percent belonged to lower-middle-class families, including white-collar workers. Only 12 percent came from working-class origins. Both in such a class-conscious society as Germany and in comparison with the general NS membership, the SD rank and file represented a socially elite group.[14] Men drawn to the early SD presaged the higher social class of officers drawn to the SS after it became part of the new establishment.

Predictably, the early SD membership also represented an educated elite. Forty-one percent of the known members had pursued higher education, with 14 percent earning doctorates, 17 percent completed secondary education with either the prestigious Abitur or the leaving certificate for grade eleven, and 42 percent had middle or primary educations supplemented usually with formal vocational schooling and apprenticeships. Only thirteen, or 3 percent, appear to have been educationally unprepared for a respectable occupation in a modern Germany. Early SD officers stood higher: 49 percent had attended university, 16 percent had doctorates, 17 percent had finished secondary school, and 34 percent had not. Such figures far exceeded the record of the pre-1933 SS officer corps.

From all appearances, as an educated elite, the SD rank and file stood quite high, considering that only about 2 percent of the population of comparable age had attended university.[15] The educational level of SD officers remained stable between 1932–1934 and 1939.[16] More significantly, education marked another sharp dichotomy among early members, with 42 percent below high school and 41 percent receiving higher education—a strange split, even for an intelligence organization.

Their educational status allowed many SD men to improve their social standing. Occupationally, 32 percent of known SD members began careers associated with the upper classes, with the largest group, 6 percent, in the higher civil service, 5 percent as professionals, 3 percent in executive-managerial positions with business or industry, and almost 3 percent as military officers. Fifty-two percent pursued lower-middle-class careers, of whom the largest single group, 36 percent, were white-collar employees. Only 16 percent began in the working class, 14 percent as skilled laborers. Officers, of course, stood higher: 42 percent upper class, 45 percent lower-middle class, and 13 percent working class. Thus, early SD officers had higher social status compared with SS officers at anytime, or compared with the Party in 1933.[17]

Although these men suffered from Germany's economic problems, they fared better than the general population. Thirty-two percent of the identified membership suffered unemployment at some time before 1933, for an average of twenty-two months. An additional 15 percent were suspiciously vague about their occupational record, suggesting a high probability of at least under-employment. Seventy-seven percent of these were victims of the great depression, while 5 percent got caught in the unemployment squeeze between 1925 and 1927, and 4 percent were caught by both. Only 14 percent suffered more chronic unemployment or vagueness about activities outside these two hardship periods. The early SD officers fared a little better, with 28 percent admitting unemployment and 18 percent suffering from "vagueness of record."[18] Considering that most segments of the population suffered comparable unemployment rates in any one year of the depression, SD members should have been considerably less traumatized than most Germans.[19] Equally significant, however, is the dichotomy between SD members who were and were not traumatized by loss of work—yet another split among them.

Despite the economic hardships of the age, the records of both officers and rank and file indicate what may have been an unusually large upwardly mobile segment among them compared with the rest of German society. The sons of lower-class and lower-middle-class families disproportionately pursued higher education.[20] Seventy-five percent pursued occupational areas different from their father's, 28 percent of whom had risen above their father's status. Even among those who stayed in their father's occupational area, 22 percent had risen above his status.[21] After an average of a little more than six and one-half years in their learned occupations, 66 percent of the men began second careers or underwent an advance in status within that occupation. The net change between father's status and that of mature son was 27 percent apparently increasing in status versus 28 percent perhaps declining.

At first blush, this seems like another sharp dichotomy. Application of the concept of "structural mobility" to these changes reveals a more complex picture, however. Persons moving from traditional, independent lower-middle-class families to salaried white-collar or skilled-labor careers (conventionally counted as a possible step down in status, 17 percent) could gain more opportunities, while probably maintaining or improving their standard of living under normal economic conditions. Even if they perceived this change as advancement, they would, nevertheless, constantly encounter persons who treated them with less respect in such a transitional society as Germany at that time. Thus, while they might have behaved economically as upwardly mobile (or more aggressively modern), psychosocially they may have resembled more closely downwardly mobile people, especially during the depression.[22] This theory is reinforced by the large number who readily abandoned their white-collar and skilled-labor jobs as soon as a salaried position opened for them in the Party, Sipo or SD. All this adds further to the general picture of heterogeneity and calls for more detailed analysis of subgroups. But a sizable set appear to have been aggressively modern, and the majority to have been relatively successful, while others experienced considerable social frustration.

SD members also had a high level of military involvement. Forty-one percent of the identified membership performed active service before entering the SD, with 30 percent involved in the war. Of these, 31 percent achieved officers' rank and 31 percent were sergeants. Eighty-nine percent of those who were of age had served in the war. Twenty-eight percent involved themselves later in paramilitary activities before joining the SA or SS, most being involved during the upheavals between 1919 and 1923, giving combat experience to some who had been too young for the war. NS paramilitary activities involved even more: 42 percent had joined the SA before January 1933, and 41 percent the SS, many of whom had transferred from the SA. In terms of both service to country and rank achieved, SD men could claim status in both the Movement and the nation.

Although the Old Fighters of the Movement may have considered that SD men were simply jumping on the band-wagon, the identified members were hardly late-joining opportunists. Although only 10 percent could claim senior Old Fighter status (joining before 1928), 74 percent had joined before Hitler's chancellorship. Beyond membership, 21 percent had NS affiliations before 1928, and 82 percent before 1933. The late joiners numbered only 18 to 26 percent, depending on whether one demanded full Party membership as the criterion. Only two would never join the Party. Notably, however, only 55 percent had belonged to the SS before joining the SD. Here is another sharp dichotomy—between those whose first identity had been with the SS and those drawn first to the SD.[23]

One outstanding characteristic, even among NS followers, who tended to have stood outside Weimar political activity before joining the Movement, was that almost 98 percent had no formal party affiliation before the Nazi Party. Twenty-three percent admitted other völkisch, bundisch, or right-wing political affiliations, but only about 2 percent had ties with rightist political parties. Only one man had Central Party (Catholic, BVP in Bavaria) membership, and one a short membership in a liberal party, which he claimed was pure occupational expediency. There were no SD members with former Marxist affiliations.[24] One cannot assess the significance of these data without comparable statistics on Party and SS members, but SD men seem to have been slightly more politically alienated than comparable NS and SS members, and more pure of liberal or left-wing taint.[25]

The problem with statistical analyses is that they usually depict either a homogeneous body or one spread along some continuum or statistical curve. Instead, the most significant data here are those that hint at sharp splits among the members. The rural-urban and high-low education splits were made even sharper by the gross overrepresentation of both the urban and university-educated segments of society sharply contrasted against the more provincial and the undereducated segments, with relatively small middles to balance each set of poles. This is especially puzzling in a paperwork agency in which one would expect mostly middle-educated workers and well-educated experts.

The other split between upwardly versus apparently downwardly mobile men becomes more important when one considers that it, like urban versus rural and grade school versus university education, relates strongly to one's ego identity. Furthermore, the 55 percent who joined the SS before the SD must have had some identity with an SS image, while those who joined the SD directly were more likely to have identified with some SD mission or ethos. Even those looking primarily for jobs cannot be entirely excluded from these categories. Clearly, what demands further examination is this apparent "multiple personality" of ego identities among early members. A consideration of recruitment practices in the early SD should cast more light on these divisions and other aspects of the organization and its personnel.

Recruitment

One should not necessarily take the apparent political "cleanness" of the early membership to mean that they represented a carefully screened, hard-core Nazi element, chosen for ideological dedication or any other such characteristics. In fact, the SD recruited many members because of some area of expertise or some needed skill, including proven leadership ability. Thirty-seven percent of identified members apparently attracted the SD's attention because of positions they occupied (10 percent police). Many of this group possessed no proven ideological reliability. More baffling, another 31 percent had no apparent appeal to the SD, not even membership in the Movement for more than a year or two.[26]

In contrast with those who could bring knowledge or valuable contacts to the SD, some recruits completely defy explanation. For instance, a twenty-three-year-old, unemployed, white-collar worker, who had established his first formal link with the Movement as late as November 1933, became an unsalaried member of the SD in January 1934, and won a salaried position by May.[27] Only personal contacts within the SD offer a likely explanation for such recruitment, as illustrated by a similar case. In May 1934, a twenty-one-year-old unemployed printer's helper won a salaried position in the SD after only two years' affiliation with the Movement. He openly admitted that his brother got him the position.[28] Few cases were as extreme as the first. Most, like the last, included young recruits to the Movement who were not old enough to have joined sooner.

The Movement took care of its own with jobs. Fifteen percent of the known 1932–1934 membership apparently used Old Fighter status to get their jobs in the SD. Many local offices of the Party and its affiliates, including SS, served as employment agencies for their members. They pursued jobs for their people in the Party, the salaried SS, or the state.[29] The SD was hardly immune to such pressure.

The cases of two SD "experts" offer good examples of how the SD provided jobs for needy members. Both men, born in Kiel, had earned only high school leaving certificates, followed by some business apprenticeship. One, a member of the Hitler Youth since 1931, joined the Party in 1933. After completing his apprenticeship with a publishing firm, he left his job, allegedly because of political differences with his employer. In short order he found a job with the SD in Berlin and became an SS-SD member and an expert in the Jewish department.[30]

Aside from his apprenticeship, the other young man was apparently never employed. As a member of the Party and SA since the spring of 1932, he got work in the auxiliary police in Kiel for a few months in 1933. Finally, in September, SD Group East employed him. He became an expert on Freemasonry.[31]

Both men illustrate one aspect of the "intellectual" character of the SD and indicate that expertise often meant nothing more than the ability to assimilate an NS line on the enemy. At least this was true of those experts who dealt with the "enemy."

Fortunately, the published memoirs of Alfred Naujocks, a 1933 recruit, again provide more insight into people like these two. Naujocks was also born in Kiel, in 1911, as the son of a grocer. He finished Oberrealschule in 1926 and passed a mechanics exam in 1930. During this phase of his life, he held odd jobs and had typical teenage adventures like a street fight. Through such activities and the influence of a friend, he became a Party and SS member in August 1931. By this time, the depression had cost him a job as chauffeur. After a period of unemployment, in 1932 he worked as a mechanic until his employer liquidated. In 1933 he got another job as a locomotive driver. Finding such an existence unfulfilling, he decided to move to Berlin where the same friend, now working for the SD, could get him a job.[32]

Naujocks became a salaried member of the SD, working for Kobelinski in the office of SD Group East. His entry through his friend, and the common origins of all four young men in Kiel, indicate that much of SD "recruitment" simply involved one man getting a friend a job. The careful screening process of legend seems to have been nothing more than one man's personal knowledge of another and SS comradeship. Group leaders like Kobelinski would take the word of one youth for the reliability of a friend, and the rest of the process was routine paper shuffling, with the SD Office balking only at some obvious oversight. A "young boy network" for recruiting workers paralleled the old boy network for finding credentialed experts.

Such amateurish personnel policies were dangerous for a security service, and the SD paid a price for them. For instance, the previously mentioned cloak-and-dagger posturing and romantic, secret-agent image drew some unstable personalities, of whom Kobelinski may have been a prime example.

One 1933 recruit was a comic prototype of the "secret-agent romantic." Riechers had received a technical school education in mechanical engineering. During the war, he had his first adventure as a sergeant in counterintelligence work. After the war, he could not hold a job for long because of his political adventuring. Between 1919 and 1922, he served with intelligence sections in the Free Corps, and in 1922, he joined the Party and the SA, going to work immediately in an intelligence section. From 1931 to 1933, he headed a Party district intelligence service. After transferring to the SS, he promptly took over intelligence (Ic) for his unit. He then transferred to the SD in September 1933, where his experience earned him immediate officer status. Becoming an SS major by 1935, he served well until 1937. By then, however, his cloak-and-dagger romanticism had become a detriment. He had been telling his girlfriend fantastic stories, and his "adventures" became a favorite topic for the women in the neighborhood. Most embarrassing, the Abwehr reported these rumors to the SD. Riechers was disciplined for endangering his real work and damaging SS and SD images.[33]

Riechers provides one more measure of the "careful screening" of SD personnel and the general amateurishness of the organization. Undoubtedly, his record impressed other amateurs, but a truly professional service would not have touched him. His adventures revealed potential security risks; for example, he had been imprisoned in 1927 for abducting his illegitimate son. Of course, his explanation that the mother was left-radical and provided a bad environment would have made him a hero rather than a suspect to those who "screened" him.

One case contradicts even careful political screening. In April 1933, at the age of thirty-two, he went to work for the SD. He professed activity with the Movement since 1923 as an SA and an SS officer. He had quit his job in 1931 "for active political participation" and remained unemployed until SD entry. In the SD he rose at least as high as captain by 1937.[34]

He became the subject of endless disciplinary actions. He had problems handling money and proved to be a habitual liar and faker—particularly about his political credentials. He evidently falsified so many records that his real political history could no longer be unraveled. He was apparently kicked out of the Party in 1930 and at some point was blacklisted against further entry. Much to the embarrassment of the SD personnel office, they did not become aware of this until as late as 1943. They did not believe such an entry could have gone undetected and reported that they were unable to determine when and why it got into his Party file.[35]

Nevertheless, applicants underwent screening of some sort, and the SD even rejected some who would otherwise seem perfect candidates.[36] Despite whatever screening criteria were used, cases of problematic recruits constituted discipline and security problems throughout SD history. Such men found a home in the early years, and despite his stated desires about the SD image, Heydrich appreciated and employed their "talents." It would be left to his more respectable recruits to purge such men, as the more respectable sought to achieve a more proper image for their SD.

The first small steps away from amateurish recruitment came when Werner Best took over personnel affairs for SD Central in 1934. In June, he issued the previously described guidelines for the adoption of members, but they clearly did not suffer from rigidity. More-stringent SS requirements than the civil service genealogical check would come later, but they had little to do with suitability for SD work.

In some aspects of recruitment, however, the SD was leaving its amateurish origins behind. Many young recruits, slated for leadership roles, underwent extensive training programs to acquire firsthand knowledge of the growing SD and the Gestapo. For instance, as part of his practical training period (Vorbereitungsdienst) one candidate for membership had a half-year informational training period as Referendar with the Gestapo Office at Berlin before being taken into SD service as a salaried member.[37]

Although the quality of many recruits stood high from an educational or administrative point of view, it left much to be desired for security and intelligence work. Aside from the few professional policemen, the early SD drew meagerly on any real investigative or counterespionage experience. Only 7 percent of the identified membership were professional policemen before 1933; an additional 3 percent added some police experience after that but before entering the SD. Less than 1 percent (3 men) had military backgrounds even peripheral to intelligence; one of them was Riechers and the other Heydrich, a communications officer. Those with relevant experience in the Movement included four from the SA Ic, nine from the Party Intelligence Service, and eight from miscellaneous agencies, totaling less than 5 percent. The vast majority had no experience to offer. The potential for professionalism that they did offer lay in the cadre with legal, administrative and political skills, and in a few knowledgeable individuals who could direct intelligence gathering in their area of expertise and attract more recruits like themselves.

Aside from the general amateurish cast of the early SD, two major insights into the membership emerge from this information on recruiting. First, a sizable percentage were simply Party and SS men who won a job or a better position through the SD. Their attraction to the SD had little to do with the organization's mission or image. Their initial ego identity with the SD would have been status. Later links between that status and a mission or ethos of the SD would have varied greatly among individuals.

The second insight into images is that of the romantic secret service. This seems to have cut across class and education lines, often supplementing other identities. It must have appealed to many of the above-mentioned unemployed, and clearly accounted for many who would be available for dirty work, relishing something like the "007 licence to kill." Many educated and urbane members were also susceptible to such romantic imagery, however.

Modal Profiles

In contrast with these flesh-and-blood examples, the previous quantitative analysis offered only cold generalization. Statistical means and modes obscure the reality of a collection of individuals. The data do reveal that collection as extremely heterogeneous, however. There was no "typical" SD man or SD officer. A better image of the membership emerges when one breaks it down from a few significant perspectives and fleshes out the data with some real-life examples. The sharp dichotomies should provide those perspectives.

Since education was a distinguishing feature, constituting a sharp split and a key element in ego identity, it provides the best perspective for breaking out some representative types. Forty-two percent of the sample did not receive a high school leaving certificate—at best, some got its equivalent through vocational schools. At the other extreme, 41 percent had a higher education. In between, a small middle of 17 percent left secondary school with either the Abitur (thirteenth year) or the lesser middle certificate (mittlere Reife) upon completion of the eleventh year. These three groups can form the bases for profiles of the membership in its full diversity.

Beginning with members with only lower education, one finds that they were younger on the average. The majority age group (55 percent) was born between 1901 and 1910; the 1891–1900 (20 percent) and 1911–1915 (19 percent) groups almost equally divided the remainder. Thus, one can easily generate three profiles: the mature one, who served in the war; the modal individual, who witnessed the war as an adolescent; and the youth, who had to assume adult responsibilities during the depression.

The modal representative was born in 1909 in northern Germany, in a city of between 100,000 and 500,000 population such as Altona or Bremen. The family belonged to the Evangelical Lutheran Church. Most likely, his father was either a lower civil servant or a white-collar employee. Otherwise, the father was a master craftsman with his own shop, or a skilled worker holding a valued position in some large manufacturing operation.

Regardless, his environment did not foster academic aspirations, so the boy went no further than the eighth year in Volksschule or the tenth year of Mittelschule. Thereafter, he either combined an apprenticeship with vocational school to become a white-collar employee, or he apprenticed into a skilled craft. In either case, he joined the labor force as the inflationary crisis peaked. Nevertheless, he worked steadily in his chosen occupation. He married either just before the depression, as he began to feel established, or he waited until his SD career offered security. When the depression hit, his first career foundered, and he (62 percent) suffered through a total of twenty-three months of unemployment, interspersed with short-lived or odd jobs. Usually, he tried to stick to his original occupation, but if he changed, he sought the security of a middle civil-service position, simultaneously developing an interest in the Movement.

If he had a political orientation before discovering NS, it was not toward the conventional parliamentary parties. He had no party affiliations, and if anything "political" drew him in, it was one of the völkisch leagues that many young people joined. As the Nazi Party rose to prominence, it attracted his attention. Invited by a friend, he attended an NS rally, and what he saw made him feel that this Movement had the answers to Germany's problems, with its call for a government of decisive authority that stood above petty partisan bickerings. He joined the Party in 1931 at age twenty-two. Amid the excitement of the "time of struggle," he joined the SS in June 1932, for reasons he never committed to paper, unfortunately. Perhaps its elite pretensions bolstered his sagging self-esteem. As a private in his local SS unit, he learned of various job opportunities with the Movement. Perhaps compared with his old occupation, or the unpromising position he now had, these jobs seemed more hopeful, especially since they offered participation in the making of the new Germany. But his calculations are lost to posterity. Regardless, in June of 1933, he took a salaried position as a sergeant on the staff of the SD Office in Munich. Why he stood out from so many others like him to be chosen for such a job remains the mystery of SD recruitment.

He was promoted to lieutenant in February of 1936. His next two promotions came regularly thereafter at one-and-one-half-year intervals until he achieved his highest rank, SS captain. He stayed with the SD to the end, unless he was one of the few who sought transfer to an active military unit, taking a role he had prepared for only in a few reserve exercises. Perhaps he also answered a short call to action for the Polish campaign.

For the older counterpart of this profile, a real-life figure will do as well as modal statistics. Franz Xavier Helldobler[38] was born into the home of a Catholic peasant family of Griesbach, Bavaria, on April 19, 1889. After completing the minimal seventh year of Volksschule, he apparently apprenticed as a tailor, his learned occupation and the only vocational information his records contain. In 1909, he began a three-year military service, which made him subject to mobilization in August 1914. He served throughout as a sergeant, and in the midst of it all, at age 28, married. Upon demobilization, he joined his wife in Munich, where the Movement attracted him. In January 1922, he joined Sturm Schlageter of the prototype-SA, and in April, the Party itself. Like Himmler, he carried a standard in the November Putsch of 1923, and quickly rejoined the Party when Hitler reformed it in 1925, receiving membership number 792. When the struggle resumed full force, he rejoined the SA in 1931.

As a senior Old Fighter, "personally praised by the Führer," Helldobler was entitled to a significant job in the new order, so in March 1933, he was transferred into the SS and given command of SD District I, Superior Region South (Munich), as a salaried lieutenant. The need to create a district office in Munich may have provided sufficient pretext to give him the status demanded, but he may not have been up to command responsibilities. Within a month, the SD recruited a certified economist to manage Helldobler's organizational and administrative affairs.[39] In less than a year, Helldobler found himself apprenticed to Werner Best's regional staff in Stuttgart, where he remained in various staff positions. Still, his recognitions continued at regular intervals until his final promotion to SS colonel, but always in staff work. His elevated rank is one achievement that distinguishes him from most of the lesser educated.

For the younger member of this educational group, one can do no better than Alfred Naujocks or any of his friends, born around 1911 in Kiel. No sooner had they finished their apprenticeships than they found themselves unemployed victims of the depression. The Movement offered answers—both exonerating explanations and employment. Through the SS, they found semiemployment in the auxiliary police cleaning up the Red quarter, and then they got jobs on Kobelinski's Berlin staff. They "reapprenticed" to become "experts" on some enemy of the Movement, rose a little more belatedly in rank than the average, but may also have finished as captains before the end.

Like all SS men, two to three times in his career an SD man had to write a short autobiographical statement, the only occasion on which most men of this educational level recorded their personal attitudes. Of course, he did so with an eye toward impressing his superiors, but he had guidelines that told him to be brief and focus on his origins, education, military and vocational record, and political activities, and not wax eloquent about ideology. In most cases he followed the guidelines, recording a sterile sketch of his past, but if he expressed any feelings or vented grievances, he mixed references to enemies who undermined Germany with self-pitying references to personal hardship. Those who did this seemed to identify totally with "national degradation." If he lost a parent, especially a father in the war, he not only recorded it but connected it with any educational disruption or frustrated career aspiration. If he failed to complete his educational goals, he gave economic hardships or family problems as the reason. He neither admitted failure, blamed persecutors, nor claimed commitment to a higher political calling as the reason.

If he mentioned an enemy, it was most likely the Republic, whose weakness allowed external enemies to keep Germany down. He might complain of how he lost one of those short-term depression jobs through political "discrimination." Marxists were his second hate. He may have witnessed the 1919 uprising, but more likely he participated in some later political combat. Jews were a distant third on his enemies list, and he worried not at all about pure blood. One must emphasize, however, that in the vast majority of cases, SD men rarely gave any insight into their attitudes or prejudices in their routine life histories.[40]

As a final insight, although these men were no more likely than the higher educated to have written about their involvement in Nazi violence, they more frequently claimed involvement in political crimes during the "struggle for power." Since they were not actually charged with such crimes at a higher rate, this may simply reflect a more macho posture in this class. Regardless, they would be the most involved in SS violence during the wild phase of the 1933 power seizure. Almost 19 percent would experience brutalization in the SS Special Commands or as auxiliary political police. This was another product of their availability as unemployed SS men.[41]

In summary, the "lower-education group" was still split into large-city (47 percent) versus rural (41 percent) backgrounds. In family backgrounds, the splits were between white-collar employees and lower civil servants on the one hand and craft masters or skilled workers on the other. Only 12 percent were from agricultural families. Socially, 50 percent came from traditional lower-middle-class families, while 27 percent were from the more modern white- (23 percent) or blue-collar (4 percent) families. Nine percent came from the secure middle class, presumably the ones who suffered from disrupted educations. This lower-education group seems to have lost traditional status, with a net loss of 26 percent from upper-middle-class and traditional lower-middle-class status. Net status gains were achieved by 25 percent who rose from white-collar employee and skilled worker families. Unskilled workers experienced mobility only from rural to urban. By and large, this group represented the traditional lower-middle echelons of society undergoing modernization. The sons were making the right moves, but suffered more from the depression than the better educated. Although comparable employment statistics for the general population are not available, this group seemed to have fared better than other people their age in comparable careers. They did not come primarily from the unemployed with the most damaged egos.[42] But they had at least experienced a temporary shock and frustration.

They must have harbored the same resentments, fears, and prejudices as their peers, but directed them most specifically at the systems of the Republic and at Marxists. They were the most likely to have seen themselves as the typical German "little man," honest, hard-working citizens who had little control over their world, and who were usually the recipients of whatever came down on the bad side. Among them, however, were also those most available for extreme physical violence or direct dirty work.

Because of unemployment and Party service, a greater percentage of them than the better educated found employment in SD offices. Predictably, fewer held command and most got office-work positions, but for them, this brought elevated status. Furthermore, their SD positions provided more-positive ego identities, both in status and role, though many like Naujocks were bored by the routine until they rose above simple worker status.

For the small middle group between the educational extremes, its modal representative was born in 1903 to a Lutheran family in Magdeburg in Prussian Saxony. His father, a middle civil servant, had a better appreciation of education as a key to secure middle-class status, so the boy at least earned the eleventh-year leaving certificate that entitled him to enter the middle civil service. Otherwise, with a little extra formal work in a vocational school, he became a bookkeeper, apprenticed in Frankfurt. Vocationally, he remained more secure, for when his employer folded in 1930, he suffered eleven months of unemployment, but then found civil-service security with district governments in Wiesbaden and Potsdam, where he weathered the depression quite well.

Though a staunch nationalist, he too had been apolitical until he joined the Party and the SS in 1932. Given his government position, he served as Ic. By 1933, as SS sergeant, he was district intelligence officer and an unsalaried SD associate. In spring 1934, he became an unsalaried SD member, serving on the staff of Region Brandenburg with responsibilities for five different specialties, reporting on such diverse subjects as the SPD, the press (domestic and foreign), and constitutional-legal affairs. By 1935, as SS lieutenant, he had assumed a salaried position and achieved the final rank of major by 1940.

If he vented personal insights when he wrote an SS autobiographical outline, the enemies he identified were those nations that had ganged up to keep Germany from her rightful place, and the republican system they had forced upon her to perpetuate her weakness. After the war, when he visited his parents now living in Cologne, French occupation officials had frequently harassed him and arrested him twice for carrying agitational literature. The Communists were a more-distant third concern, and Jews worried him even less than they did his associates from the other educational groups. His group contained the only men to express hostility toward the Old Guard elements of German society who had blocked them and hindered progressive trends. Again, one must emphasize that such expressions of personal feeling or grievance rarely surfaced, and men like this left few clues to the truly formative experiences of their lives.

Surprisingly, these men were the most likely of the three educational subsets to have recorded participation in Nazi violence during the "time of struggle," and the most likely to have been charged with a political crime. A greater percentage were involved in political fights, killings, and bombings. They were close behind their less-educated peers in additional brutalization through involvement in SS actions during the 1933 "power seizure." Of those so involved, most served as auxiliary political policemen—an escape from unemployment.

More solidly lower-middle class in origin, this group may have suffered the most status loss. Forty percent apparently declined from their father's social status (although much of this may have been structural mobility), while only 19 percent improved their status. Thirteen percent were unable to get the higher education they wanted, usually because of economic hardship. All this frustration may account for their greater political activism. Nevertheless, they were more aggressively modern in both their pursuit of education and their choice of careers. Although they suffered slightly less from unemployment than the less-well-educated, they may have suffered more underemployment. And although perhaps more aggressively modern, they seem to have had another internal split between those who found reward in their efforts, and those who were frustrated, at least until SD careers offered a more appropriate status.[43]

Because of greater Party activism and availability due to underemployment, they also tended to find salaried SD positions more readily than the highest-educated group. Probably because of their better training for office management, there were more command and higher staff positions for them than the less educated.

The other large group, those who experienced higher education, require two subsets to profile them properly. Representing by and large the older membership, they consist of the modal profile, the younger member born between 1901 and 1910, and a member of the war generation, born before 1900.

The modal profile was born in 1902, son of a Lutheran, middle-rank civil servant in a small town in Saxony. After the proper preparatory education, he attended the universities of Freiburg, Halle, Bonn, and Leipzig, studying law. In 1926 he passed the first state exam, and passed the assessor exam in 1929. Typically, he married only after achieving his full professional status in the higher civil service.

He joined the Party in summer 1932, after membership had become safe for civil servants, but the Movement had attracted his interest and sympathy earlier. It certainly did not hurt his civil service career when he joined the SS-SD in summer 1933. The SD needed qualified civil servants and offered more leverage for advancement. This was not entirely opportunism, however, for he had been serving the SD as V-man since he had joined the Party, and worked as an unsalaried associate in the regional staff office for his probational period of seven months. He continued as an unsalaried member on the regional staff for three years. Then, in November 1936, he became an SS second lieutenant and a staff officer for SD Superior Region Dresden and began his rise through the officer ranks, still unsalaried. During the early war years, as a salaried major, he commanded an SD Superior Region in the territories reincorporated from Poland. Before the end he was serving on the staff of the Reich Security Main Office, perhaps as a lieutenant colonel and superior government counselor. He never saw military service.

Dr. Hermann Müller can serve as his older counterpart. He was born Catholic on May 30, 1891, in a small town in the Pfalz. As the son of a gymnasium teacher, he naturally pursued higher education. After completing the Abitur in 1909 and the minimal one year of military service, he attended the universities of Munich, Heidelberg, and Würzburg, studying medicine until 1914. For the duration of the war he served as military physician, passing his state exam in 1916. After the war, he turned to private practice.[44]

The Party became Müller's first political involvement in 1922, when in his early thirties he assumed local leadership and served on his town council. After a lapse, he rejoined the new Party in 1925 and the resurrected SA. He led a small SA unit, and became a Party speaker and a local leader. Like most doctors, he was not unemployed during the depression, but probably suffered significant declines in his income and standard of living. He claimed, however, that it was his involvement in the political struggle that caused him professional injury. After the victory came his rewards: he became mayor of his town. His troubles were only beginning, however, for he had difficulties with the SA and "incapable people" maligned him, pursuing their self-serving goals while he tried to combat the harmful elements within the Party, so he had to surrender his Party office. In July 1934, he transferred to the SS-SD, which had just emerged as the cleansing agent of the Movement. Müller defined Germany's enemies as those within the Movement who prevented it from being what it should be, and he pledged himself to keeping the local leadership clean, simple, and suitable.

SD Superior Region South took him in as an SS lieutenant and unsalaried member assigned to field post Freising. Beginning his SD career at age foury-three, he rose at regular intervals, reaching the rank of major by 1940. From all indications, he remained active in his profession, serving continually as an unsalaried member. Müller did not marry until after 1936, at age forty-five. Perhaps the political struggle had to abate before he could turn his attention to a family.

Unemployment was not characteristic of this group; only 13 percent of them recorded it, for an average of about nineteen months. Underemployment, loss of income, and with it a decline in their all-important status was, nevertheless, possibly more traumatic for such men than for blue-collar workers inured to the cycle of joblessness.[45]

If these educated members expressed their feelings and grievances in their SS autobiographical sketches, first Marxism and then the republican system emerged as the key enemies. Hostile nations were third in rank. The Catholic Church and Jewry ranked lower at fourth and fifth respectively, although these members expressed more anti-Semitism than any other group. The educated shared slightly less than the least formally schooled associates the sense of having suffered personally. More of them, however, blamed Catholics or Jews ensconced in the Republican system. They included the only person who expressed concern with moral decay. They talked about being involved in violence about as much as the lower educated and claimed more involvement in political crimes than their high-school counterparts, but they were by far the least likely to be charged with such crimes.

Among the educated, there was another sharp dichotomy, because they were not all typical of their class. Among the families that usually provided university students, the upper and middle civil service and the landowners and farmers were all grossly underrepresented. Representatives of military officer, business and industrial elite, and middle- and lower-class white-collar families were at par. Sons of professional families (20 percent of the sample) far exceed the norm (6 to 9 percent). More important, the usually underrepresented lower civil service, Army sergeants, and peasant and blue-collar families (6 to 8 percent all told, normally) provided 29 percent. If one adds to these "outsiders" the sons of middle and lower white-collar, old lower-middle-class, and perhaps also farmer families, 45 percent of the higher educated represented aggressively modernizing young men, likely to encounter the most obstacles to career entry, and most likely to have experienced social snubbing. Nazi calls for the removal of social barriers would have drawn them, and the "open-careers" ideal of the SS and SD must have been as compelling as their own "opportunism." Their opposites, the sons of the educated elite, would more likely have seen NS and SD as vehicles for preserving the threatened values they pursued in their educations and careers.[46]

At least 16 percent of this group failed to complete their program of higher education, while 63 percent earned a university degree (35 percent doctorates). Only one admitted having "failed" academically; the majority who did not complete claimed some economic or other hardship. In contrast with any other group, 24 percent claimed to have abandoned their education for political activity. One can only guess whether this represented real NS commitment or merely a rationalization they expected to go down well with SS superiors. Much of their political activity was as students, some fighting "Black" (Catholic) or Jewish influences in their schools. Those who felt themselves victims of discrimination usually encountered it either there or in their early professional careers.

Although there may have been another dichotomy here—a cleavage between those who earned lesser Hochschule degrees (37 percent) and university graduates (63 percent), especially those who earned doctorates (35 percent)—it is not likely that this was a split between nonintellectuals and intellectuals. The majority (58 percent) pursued government careers, with free professions and business management sharing second place (22 percent each), and technical degrees in third (18 percent). Only if one combines academics (20 percent), journalists (9 percent), and artists (7 percent) was the second-largest group in "intellectual" careers. None of this speaks clearly, however, to intellectual ego identities. If there was another split here, it was probably in status identity between the educated elite and those with no credentials or with nonuniversity credentials.

The strongest single identity likely among this group would be that of professional status (Berufstand), which among Germans entailed more of a sense of premodern status and calling than in contemporary America. Both the Weimar and Nazi eras were periods of great stress for German professionals, and many were drawn to Nazism. Due to Nazi hostility toward most professions, however, the relationship remained stressful to the end.[47] Within Sipo and SD, the conflicts experienced by lawyers, bureaucrats, and intellectuals became increasingly acute after 1936. As the educated sought to professionalize their branches commensurate with their ego images, they ran afoul of "SS-ification."

Perhaps this tension best explains why the higher-educated group more commonly severed its ties with the SD, with almost equal frequency during the period after 1936 and again after the invasion of Russia and the beginning of full-scale genocide. There seems to have been a direct correlation between level of education and a tendency to move from or break with the SD: 21 percent lower education; 27 percent high school; 32 percent higher education. For the less educated, there was simply a fairly steady, low rate of withdrawal. High-school graduates displayed a more steadily increasing rate of withdrawal over the years. However, the rate doubled after 1936. They were most likely to leave the SD temporarily for military service during the war, but returned before it was over. With the higher educated, the rate of withdrawal rose most rapidly after June 30, 1934, peaking in the period after 1936. It dropped radically during the early war years, bursting forth again after the invasion of Russia. It is as though they, more than the other groups, encountered conflicts of some sort with either the reality of the SD as it actually developed or between the ideals or missions of the SD and the new establishment of the Third Reich. Again, such crises of identity increased as Sipo and SD assumed its wartime missions related to genocide. Of course, during peacetime, it was easier for the higher educated to return to esteemed professions, especially after the resumption of economic prosperity. That option does not preclude, however, crises of idealistic identity. It merely facilitated the separation without loss of status.

Overall, among the entire early membership, the social diversity, especially several stark dichotomies, is more striking than any signs of predispositions to their future roles. Rarely did these men express any grievance, fears, prejudices, or hostilities in autobiographical statements: collectively, 13 percent were hostile to the republican system; 13.5 percent were anti-Marxist (11 percent anti-Communist), 8 percent were hostile to foreign powers, 3 percent were anti-Semitic, and 2.5 percent were hostile to Catholicism. No one expressed concern about Himmler's other major bogeyman, Freemasonry, and only one or two had preoccupations with society's "morality" problems, like homosexuality or "filth and smut." Only three or four expressed resentments against capitalists or the old guard. This group hardly seems outstanding for its hates and prejudices, given its environment. They had the proper Nazi concern for their real major enemy, the Communists,[48] and directed appropriate hostility toward the Republic.

Once Hitler's regime held power, albeit tenuously, they focused rapidly and naturally on those within the Movement who could discredit it or pervert its "idealistic" course. The socially and educationally elitist element inevitably manifested its disdain for the riffraff and opportunists in the Movement and even in its own SD ranks. Indoctrination and time in a redefined consensus reality would be required for them to focus on Masons, Jews, and Catholics as the major enemies.

Equally heterogeneous are the several, often overlapping ego identities that could have drawn men to the SD or could have developed after entry. They raise the question of analysis from a psychological perspective.

Toward a Theoretical Perspective

The clues to the significance of self-images or ego identities in some of the modal subsets in chapter 6 encourage one to look for links between them and the different missions and images within Sipo and SD. The analysis of SD membership also suggests the relevance of theories about "sanctioned violence" developed by Herbert Kelman, a social psychologist. He rejects all explanations based on any abnormality among the perpetrators, arguing instead that most participants are "ordinary men" drawn into committing such acts.[1] His theories cast light on how such a heterogeneous group involved themselves in sanctioned violence.

Theories About "Ordinary Men"

Kelman argues that normal persons respond to social influences in three basic ways: compliance, identification, and internalization. In *compliance,* one accepts influence, doing what one perceives that others want done. One does so to earn reward or acceptance or to avoid punishment or rejection. Compliant behavior has little to do with one's private beliefs. In *identification,* one adopts behavior associated with a satisfying, self-defining relationship. Such a role relationship becomes part of one's self-image. One copies behavior that seems to go with the role. Kelman sees identification as a key part of normal socialization processes, including professionalization, and of the forming of group identities. It differs from compliance in that one gradually believes in the adopted behavior. Yet the behavior is acted out only when one is playing the role. Though accepted personally, the behavior may not become part of one's personal value system. In contrast, in *internalization* one accepts influences because they are congruent with one's value system. Although a person may be more susceptible to one of these three

153

responses, all may be at work simultaneously. A single response rarely appears in pure form. [2]

Paralleling these three responses are three orientations to political processes: rule, role, and value orientation. These are different ways that one relates to the nation-state or any other unit that commands obedience and loyalty. They also are not mutually exclusive and may work in any combination, although one may be predominant.[3]

A *rule-oriented* person follows rules to avoid trouble. One expects authority to uphold the rules and provide security and order. In return, as a citizen or member, one complies passively and minimally to protect one's interests, because one plays only subsidiary roles and participates only minimally in the benefits of citizenship. Such a person seems to be morally underdeveloped because, in his perception, neither the state's actions nor his actions in response to official demands are relevant to moral principles. One's responsibility here is to follow the rules, while authority is responsible for the consequences. One protests these consequences only when they cause threats to one's security, thus violating the presumed contract of compliance. Although "personality" might produce such an orientation, it more commonly results from a socialization of compliance, produced by life experiences that one feels incapable of affecting. Thus, low levels of education, occupation, or social status are conducive to such socialization.[4]

One sees some rule orientation in the character, roles, and behavior of some SD members. Those among them who were mostly rule oriented would have done their jobs with little sense of responsibility for the consequences. On the other hand, unless other conditioning intervened, they would not have been creative or zealous in committing sanctioned violence. Such an orientation should have been strongest among the lower educated who simply found a secure job in Sipo or SD. Any identification with SS, SD, Gestapo, or Kripo roles would have complemented their responses with role orientation.

A *role-oriented* person feels that one must obey and support authority because it maintains the legitimacy of the system and secures the status of the nation, the unit, and one's self. One supportively executes policies because one identifies with one's role, which one sees as significant to society's affairs. One also perceives one's share in the benefits of the system as significant. Such a person's moral development also seems incomplete, because he perceives that the system operates under a special set of moral principles and that one's moral obligations to the system override personal morality. One protests only against consequences that threaten one's status. Socialization through identification shapes this orientation and results commonly from the life experiences of those with middle levels of education, occupation, and social status.[5]

If as many Sipo and SD members were role oriented as the data on them would indicate, their identities with their police or SD positions were especially compelling motives. Those positions restored any lost status and provided a sense of serving Germany much more appropriately to their abilities. Such men should have dutifully participated in sanctioned violence as part of maintaining the order with which they identified. They would have been as creative as necessary in doing so; however, their responses could have been complicated by value orientations.

A *value-oriented* person takes an active part in formulating and evaluating policies. One expects legitimate authority to uphold true values and to pursue policies reflecting those values. One sees one's duty as being both active and critical toward policies because one sees oneself as sharing ownership and management of the system from which one benefits greatly. The actions of the system and one's duties must be consistent with one's personal moral principles. Thus, such a person would seem to be morally mature. One's support of the system can be firm, but conditional, for one will object to consequences that violate one's values. Socialization that produces a value orientation occurs more easily among those who benefit from high levels of education, occupation, and status.[6]

The description of the higher-educated subset of SD members would argue for the presence of both role and value orientation among them, most likely simultaneously. Their patterns of withdrawal from the SD reinforce the sense that with each step up in educational level, they tended to have formed more value identities with the SD rather than simply a status (role) identity. Thus, there was a corresponding tendency to experience conflicts between those identities and emerging realities.

Complicating the functioning of a value orientation, the values of any system (the Nazis in general or the SS or SD in particular) are not singular, objectively identifiable, and universally shared. Some may be widely shared, others are shared by different groups to different degrees. Even those considered basic by everyone in the system can be subject to sharply differing interpretations. Even mutually contradictory values can claim authenticity in the same system.[7] Thus, a value orientation can bind one to a system without the need for an ideological consensus. There need only be an ideological conjunction that enables one to overlook the violation or endangerment of some values as long as one's more pressing needs and values seem to be served.

Although there seems to be a class bias in Kelman's theories about what encourages each orientation, he actually warns against such interpretation. His research indicates that although there are significant correlations between levels of education or status and orientations, they are neither absolute nor unilateral. Also, to emphasize lower-class availability for crimes of obedience "is to ignore the central part that higher status . . . actors play in producing such crimes. . . . Thus, any analysis implying that crimes of obedience result from the moral deficiencies of the lower classes misses the social-structural realities within which these crimes take shape."[8]

Kelman and associates conclude that although other factors like personality or moral development will affect how one responds to authority's orders, political orientation plays the more significant role.[9] Furthermore, one *single* such orientation rarely acts in isolation. A complex synthesis of forces usually produces the individual's response to a specific order or complex of orders. The value of identifying the different orientations is that they enable one to hear the several voices with which an actor may have been speaking when he gave the rationalization, "I had to obey orders."

All three orientations encourage one to obey legitimate authority under most circumstances. They vary in the quality of the obedience and the circumstances under which one is likely to resist. The rule-oriented obey blindly, but stand outside of authority and do not necessarily share its definitions. They may not obey unless closely observed and subject to punishment. Likewise, the value oriented may stand apart from authority in the sense that they feel empowered to judge it or question its definitions. They demand consistency with their internalized values. Only the role oriented have so identified with authority that they may not be able to stand outside its definitions and see any reason to question. The value oriented are more likely to have the cognitive skills or motivational inclinations to challenge authority, but only if they see it deviating from their most fundamental values.[10]

As the analysis of rule orientation reveals, the popular image of the blindly obedient SS automaton does not provide an ideal orientation for building a dynamic organization. And as we shall see, the SS did not especially pursue it. By the same token, the fanatic true believer would be value oriented, a dynamic but not necessarily reliable agent. Instead, we shall see that SD leaders employed a combination of role and value appeals in their efforts to socialize Sipo and SD members. When this approach worked, the members could be harnessed together into a truly dynamic "instrument of power and terror." But the resultant dynamic also meant that the organization and its members rarely functioned as controlled and disciplined men in the traditional authoritarian sense.

The analysis of the police showed that although some may have submitted to Nazi command compliantly and acted only out of rule orientation, their socialization was mostly that of their role-oriented professional subculture. The purpose of fusing the police with the SD was to infect their role orientation with the SD's value orientation. So infected, their role orientation would bind them to the NS leadership. Kelman argues that the role oriented "may obey without question and often with enthusiasm to the point of committing crimes of obedience. Their sense of obligation to obey may be linked to an overriding loyalty to their leader or to commitment to a transcendent mission in which they see themselves as active partners."[11]

Obviously, the role of the transcendent mission can be reinforced by a value orientation on which that mission centers. When role and mission become fused in one's identity, a truly powerful force can obscure other value conflicts. Thus, one acquires an overriding obligation to obey, especially when one has a higher mission that supersedes other moral scruples. National well-being, national security, and stopping godless Communism qualified as transcendent missions for many professional policemen and SS men alike. "Racial health" qualified equally well as a mission for many educated men in early twentieth century western societies.[12]

Erik Erikson provided insight into the needs that can make role identity or value orientation overwhelmingly powerful. His description of the development of ego autonomy explains how people are driven to develop social roles and status that support the ego. As Kelman emphasized, when an individual identifies with an organization or its mission, he generates internal pressure to advance within the organization and to protect and expand its jurisdictions.[13] Clearly, from the beginning, each branch of Sipo and SD provided its members with highly positive role identities. We shall see how the members sought to enrich those identities with even more gratifying roles, missions, and ideals.

By the same token, the division of labor among the several branches shunted the more distasteful aspects of sanctioned violence onto another group whose different organizational identity did not taint one's identity. Here the combining of several seemingly incompatible groups into Sipo and SD contributed to the process, for it was "the other guy" or "that other organization" that did the dirty work. Since the value oriented believe that each is responsible for the consequences of his own actions, division of labor can enable them to deflect responsibility onto others, as contradictory as that may seem. The lower-status rule obeyers and role players can be held responsible for some undesirable aspects of their action, seen by the value oriented as peripheral to the larger transcendent mission that motivates them.[14]

Nevertheless, all involved had to succumb to dehumanization or brutalization to play their ultimate roles in sanctioned violence. Labeling the SS and Gestapo as criminal organizations has led to theories about mechanisms that transformed their members into mass murderers. For instance, some organized criminals require that their members "be blooded"—commit murder—thereby bonding them to the in-group as unacceptable to normal society. It has been alleged that Hitler was taken with this idea of Blutkitt (blood bonding), and that the SS adopted it, as illustrated by the practice of training recruits at concentration camps.[15]

Unfortunately, this theory distorts the nature of the training and presumes a conscious, official policy of criminalization within all branches of the SS that is not consistent with the evidence, especially for Sipo and SD. Although men like Otto Ohlendorf claimed that Heydrich assigned them to lead Einsatzgruppen as a policy of Blutkitt, that may be the rationalization of a brutalized executioner trying to explain his own failure. Such possibilities bring into focus the historian's problem of delimiting the extent to which mechanisms like authorization, bolstering, routinization, and dehumanization were consciously employed or merely natural extensions of functional processes.

Studies of "normal" murderers, as opposed to professional or serial killers, suggest that their moral restraints collapsed suddenly in a crisis that unleashed murderous violence. They were not necessarily dehumanized in ways that facilitate repetition of murder. In contrast, most Sipo and SD executioners differed from this pattern on two points. First, reaching their "crisis point" usually involved a gradual process. Although the experience had to differ greatly among individuals, there were undoubtedly cohorts who shared experiences. For instance, some early cohort-generating experiences were physical combat during the "time of struggle," the "wild" terrorizing of enemies during 1933, and then the Röhm purge. Finally, "legally" eliminating public enemies became their sanctioned role.

Such group involvement had the added effect of bolstering, but the uniquely extreme incentive for conformity provided by a police-state atmosphere generated both extraordinary pressures and an alibi for those who succumbed. Such pressures worked especially on the non-Nazi professional policemen and bureaucrats who continued to "do their jobs." Already under role pressure to do their duty, they experienced an escalation of pressures with the arrival of growing numbers of men in their ranks wearing NS uniforms and openly professing their Nazism. These interlopers were perceived as informers. Thus, both conformity and identity pressures spiraled upward into a competition to parrot the correct ideas and show appropriate behavior. One had to see the "rightness" in all this or break under the strain. One could not simply be a parrot, one had to believe and act out those beliefs.[16] However, this did not preclude seeing the baseness and stupidity in the acts and beliefs of others in Sipo and SD and feeling morally and intellectually smug about one's superiority over them, a posture typical in the testimonies of former members.

Testing for "Abnormal Men"

Social-psychological theories minimize the significance of "personality" for explaining mass susceptibility to sanctioned violence. In contrast, a well-established tradition has sought explanations in the flawed character of the Nazi participants. No broadly accepted analyses have emerged, however.[17] Psychohistorians have focused on Hitler and Nazi leaders, revealing their psychopathologies. Expanding upon such psychohistorical contributions has required establishing convincing connections between the psychopathology of the leader, the masses he mobilized, and the historical events that ensued. Much of this literature has focused on authoritarian and compulsive character structure that alleg-edly explains German receptiveness. Unfortunately, all such efforts founder on the problem that the identified personality traits or shared experiences were held in common by Germans and non-Germans, by pro- and anti-Nazis.[18]

Nevertheless, opinion remains polarized over how pathological the Nazi membership was, especially SS men. Given the nature of Nazi in-humanity, one easily assumes that the perpetrators had to be sick. They constituted an aberrant minority, mobilized by Nazi leadership to domi-nate and direct the more passively receptive majority and to perform criminal acts.[19] Although almost all serious scholars realize that only a few SS men were "abnormal," the assumption of some pathology often prevails.[20]

Others argue that the vast majority of perpetrators were men who under most conditions would have led normal lives had not environ-ments, such as those in the SS, criminalized them. This might be called an argument for marginal pathology, for most such approaches assume that the perpetrators were more susceptible to criminalization because of characteristics such as those of "authoritarian personalities." Thus, organizations like the SS supposedly recruited such personality types and criminalized them in a high-pressure environment that perverted norms and submerged the individual under total discipline.[21]

Such analyses founder on the reality of Sipo and SD. Most members of Sipo were neither the products of SS discipline nor devoted Nazis. Some at worst jumped on the bandwagon early, but most joined late or never. The SS men among them were SD members, few of whom ac-quired the blind "cadaver obedience" through the model training pro-cesses of the Waffen SS. Recent studies[22] and this book question gener-alizations about their self-submerging obedience and blind loyalty to certain leaders or the Movement. The diverse ways in which Sipo and SD drew together heterogeneous personnel militated against any special appeals to certain personality types.

Given the persistence of "authoritarian personality" theories, how-ever, one should test them against the evidence about early SD mem-bers. Original formulators of the authoritarian personality model now acknowledge that personality is more subject to development through-out life than originally presumed.[23] For instance, some sociocultural en-vironments are more conducive to underdeveloped social flexibility and empathy, and that produces the personality. The roots of these defi-ciencies lie not just in the authoritarian family but in any environmental deprivation: lack of education, rural isolation, or membership in a dis-advantaged minority, an isolating dogmatic religious organization, or an isolating socioeconomic stratum.[24] These more observable phenom-ena offer possibilities for testing arguments that authoritarian personali-ties prevailed among the members.

Low Level of Education

Paralleling Kelman's theories, studies of authoritarian traits usually indicate strong reverse correlations with levels of education: the higher the level of education, the lower the scores on tests for authoritarianism. At first sight this would indicate a marked division within the SD, but the problem is more complex. Some research questions the correlation between education and authoritarianism, and also the presumed advantage of liberal studies over career-oriented education.[25] Research on intellectual development explains this apparent lack of correlation by demonstrating that the effectiveness of education in broadening thought patterns depends more on the quality of instruction and the general institutional environment than on quantity or subject matter.[26] Developmentally, educational effectiveness requires confronting students with conflicts among authorities, and with instructors who model the role of learner more than that of intellectual authority. Instructional or institutional authoritarianism or negative student peer environments can destroy the developmental potential of higher education. Recent analysis of the university environments of the late Empire and the Republic suggest that their graduates received mostly illiberal socialization.[27]

Consequently, education is not the great divider one might expect. It should have decreased authoritarian tendencies—how significantly, no one knows—in early twentieth-century Germany, probably less than today. Too many other possible influences intervene, however.[28]

The significance of these considerations becomes greater when one adds research and theory about relations between intellectual and ethical development.[29] For one example, research focused on the theory of William Perry[30] suggests that most of the characteristics labeled "authoritarian" are also functions of how reality appears to one in an immature or "dualistic" stage of intellectual development. Perry's model describes three major stages of intellectual development occurring from adolescence throughout adulthood, a progression that can be altered by retreat, temporizing, or escape, including, presumably, indefinite regression or stagnation. Growth proceeds as a natural human tendency, subject to stimulation and discouragement. Cognitive dissonance provides stimuli when the person can integrate the dissonant perspectives into a higher synthesis or perception of reality rather than deflecting the dissonance. Maturation apparently occurs best in environments that balance structured conflicts with support, thus encouraging growth. Highly stable, isolating, authoritarian environments do not normally stimulate maturation.

In contrast to theories like Perry's that describe development as a sequential process (cumulative stages through which everyone must pass), other theories perceive growth as a more dialectical and highly variable process. However, maturation is still defined as developing an increasingly more inclusive way of thinking—an ability to deal with more of the apparent contradictions with which reality confronts us. Most significantly, all these studies show close correlations between intellectual development and the ability to make independent moral judgments and to act on them, while accepting responsibility. Unfortunately, the field of adult or post-Piagetian developmental psychology is so young that it has gained neither recognition nor strong coherence among its separate theories.[31] Nevertheless, it already points to richer perspectives from which to view human susceptibility to sanctioned violence, and to new ways of measuring that susceptibility. Specifically, research on Perry's theory has established markers or "flags" of intellectual immaturity. One can use them to detect symptoms of relative intellectual immaturity in the ideas of historical figures. Of course, this requires a solid grasp of the historical context of the words and the cultural relativity of the flags, to guard against misinterpretation.[32]

Specifically, the initial or *dualistic* stage in Perry's model resembles most definitions of one type of intellectual immaturity. In that state one perceives knowledge as absolute. One lives in a world of Right and Wrong, True and False, We and They. Education is the process of learning the right answers that authority gives us. On the positive side, dualism teaches that there are values that must be observed. Such dualistic perceptions complement Kelman's rule orientation.

Perry's second stage, *multiplicity,* is also generally accepted as a type of intellectual immaturity. "All things are relative," "there is no truth," and "everything is just a matter of opinion" characterize the multiplistic perception of knowledge and reality. On the positive side, multiplicity can ultimately depict education as the process of learning "how" to know.

As one matures by integrating dualistic and multiplistic perspectives, authority may become divided into valid and invalid authority depending on supposed ability to see and reveal clearly where true and false are distinguishable. The good teacher (leader) provides clear and simple answers.

In nonhierarchical models, dualism and multiplicity are not sequential stages, but two of the poles among which one evolves. In common, however, all theories have similar models of immature thinking. Thus, despite the formative level of these theories about adult intellectual development, there is a clear consensus on the symptoms of intellectual immaturity and the empowerment that comes with maturity.

This brief summary obscures the subtle complexities of such models. They are plagued by potentials for cultural and historical relativity, but they complement both social and personality theory. Research on different rates of maturation among students suggests that personality probably affects the rate or course of intellectual maturation. Nevertheless, the total developmental experience of most adults seems to enable them to assert some autonomy in relation to behavioral determinants.

Most significantly, research suggests that social and ethical development are functions of intellectual and cognitive development.[33] But the resultant orientations are not predictable. For instance, one in dualist stages might experience high levels of conflict between traditional moral commitments and any contradictory position. A "Catholic peasant" could be value oriented in a way that would lead to early and total alienation from Nazism. In contrast, the seeming lack of ambiguity in Nazi pronouncements about traditional values could lead a "confused urban youth" to reject other authorities and values as false or weak. He could retreat from ambiguity into the complete security of the True authority, Hitler, acquiring a value orientation to Nazism. On the other hand, development heavily oriented toward multiplicity often entails moral relativism. Without the dualist's catechism or any consciously evaluated ethical commitments that come with maturity, a "university student or young graduate" might have fewer qualms about surrendering such an ephemeral thing as moral responsibility to responsible officials or about sacrificing a "traditional humanistic value" in a "struggle for survival."[34]

Research shows that in the United States the process of adult intellectual development begins in adolescence, develops slowly, and rarely reaches mature levels among those studied. Research on a similar idea, cognitive complexity, suggests that only 15 percent of the population is cognitively complex.[35]

In addition to adding new dimensions, development theory also provides a corrective for a possible bias in Kelman's theory that comes from his reliance on Kohlberg's scale of moral maturity. Kelman's rule-role-value orientations are linear to the extent that his research indicates a correlation with Kohlberg's three levels of moral development—preconventional, conventional, and postconventional, respectively. Thus, the rule oriented (lower educated, lower class) seem to operate at a lower level of moral development, despite his warnings against such presumptions. The value oriented (higher educated, etc.) seem to operate at mature levels of moral development. Only they will resist on the grounds of principle.[36] The trap is that the data do indicate a correlation. Kohlberg's postconventional stage of moral development may be a modal characteristic of the value oriented, but should not be a part of the definition. As the model for dualistic ethical immaturity indicates, strong value orientation can also relate to moral immaturity and lower levels of education. Such complexity illustrates why no single likely determinant correlates strongly with a particular political orientation. It may also help us understand in later analysis how some of the highly educated, socially privileged, apparently value-oriented members of Sipo and SD could be so complexly different in their responses. Some examples illustrate the scope of the problem.

Eduard Strauch studied law through the assessor's exam, fully qualifying him for his eventual ranks of superior government counselor in the Gestapo and SS lieutenant colonel. As head of Einsatz units in Latvia and White Russia, he won his superior's praise for outstanding ability "to master opposition of all sorts." He was "extraordinarily calm or deliberate" (Kaltblütiger). Other superiors, however, criticized him severely for his lack of empathy ("Er vermag sich schlecht in andere Menschen einzufühlen"), which hindered his judgment of men and his leadership ability, and led to conflicts with colleagues that could have been avoided. He was suspicious and distrustful, especially of subordinates, and excessively judgmental.[37] Both positive and negative commentary describe the traditional qualities of an "authoritarian personality." Strauch's performance record shows that he succumbed to legitimized violence.

Obviously, his route through classical gymnasium and university, with its highly vaunted emphasis on Bildung, had little humanizing effect on him. Whatever predispositions or acquired traits had made him susceptible to ethical breakdown, such Bildung did not sufficiently develop him to overcome them and prepare himself to cope successfully with the moral crises he would confront. Whatever level of intellectual maturity the student might achieve in academic affairs, very little in the educational experience induced transference to a more pervasive level of intellectual and ethical maturity in the person. Not only was he unprepared to resist legitimized violence, but his "coldbloodedness" in no way shielded him from the resultant psychic strain. He lapsed into alcoholism and finally epilepsy.

Another example indicates that higher education can fail to induce mature thinking even in the academic realm itself. Friedrich Polte would also become an SS lieutenant colonel, heading SD Superior Region Vienna after the Anschluss. Over a six-year period, he had attended several universities, studying history, geography, political economy, and sociology, until he abandoned work on his doctorate for SD employment. When he wrote an SS autobiographical sketch, he described his studies as a "revolutionary mission." By studying the "racial forces in history," he expected to extract the "factual evidence" to expose international conspiracies.[38] This advanced student perceived education, learning, and knowledge as the extraction of discrete facts from a welter of less-relevant facts to prove what valid authority already knew. Such an attitude is not unique among scholars today, and may have been more prevalent then.

In another revealing passage, Polte admitted that his judgment had retarded entry into the Party, because he had been overly critical at not finding "clarity" in its position vis-à-vis religion and Rome. Only in the winter of 1931 to 1932 did he settle the issue with himself and join.[39] In both passages, he wrote like one coping unsuccessfully with transition from dualistic to more sophisticated levels of awareness. At first he had doubts about the legitimacy of the Movement, because of its ambiguous stance on such a "black-and-white" issue as religion. Perhaps when he abandoned his doubts and embraced the authority of the Movement, he had retreated from even greater ambiguities he was discovering in his world.[40] Obviously, the universities failed to facilitate significant development in his case.

Some of Peter Merkl's quotations from autobiographical sketches of early Nazis focus strikingly on students whose rigidly dualistic perspectives made them uncomfortable in educational environments that sought vainly to develop their maturity. Such students became susceptible to teachers or peer groups that stood out as valid authorities by propagating the "right" line. These students repeatedly clashed with what they saw as closeminded, wrongheaded authority.[41] All levels of education failed to help them.

Such examples raise serious questions about the "intellectuality" of the SD in general. Not only the college dropouts but perhaps also the graduates and Ph.D.s, even those with honors, were merely intellects adept at proving prejudices. Research clearly indicates that students relatively low on the theorists' scale of intellectual development can perform quite well in school when it rewards rote learning and acceptance of authority. Were the SD academics merely a cadre of prejudiced, uncritical mandarins?

Although it will require an extensive analysis of the writings of SD intellectuals to determine the issue, until that is done it seems unwise to dismiss such a large number of university graduates as low-level intellectuals. The critical posture of the later SD caused it too much trouble. Furthermore, evidence of a critical-minded maturity, such as that revealed by the evaluator of Strauch, indicates an established disdain for the uncritical, conformist, authoritarian mentality.[42] In both cases mentioned here, the men were stopped before advancement to the fully elite levels—in Strauch's case, specifically because of flaws related to extreme authoritarianism.

In short, the educational levels of these men suggest that they should not have been more likely than the general population to have authoritarian personalities. By the same token, they should have been much less likely to have undergone Kelman's socialization for compliance and rule orientation. On this last point, however, there was probably a major split within the membership between those who were rule/role oriented and those who were role/value oriented.

Age

In contrast with developmental theory, which correlates intellectual maturity with experience, social theory predicts higher levels of authoritarianism in random, older populations than in younger ones. This prediction presumes that the elderly are products of a time that offered fewer diversified opportunities. Rather than being simply contradictory, these different perspectives on age add appropriate richness to our understanding of human development. What this particular theory contributes to analysis of the predominantly youthful membership of the SD is a prediction of relatively more social flexibility than among average German contemporaries. This seems verified by their more aggressively modern social behavior. Also, a rejection of old dogmas was a common denominator; although for some it was replaced by an all-embracing new dogma, for others it involved transcending simple dogma.

Rural Backgrounds

Isolating, homogeneous social environments, low on intellectual stimulation, regardless of location, offer fewer opportunities for diversified role playing.[43] Rural environments are merely one example. The quantitative analysis already indicates that on this count SD membership had significant advantages over the general population. Of course, the data beg the question of whether urban dwellers had access to diverse urban stimulation or suffered "ghetto deprivation," but everything in their social backgrounds suggests the contrary.

Membership in a Disadvantaged Minority

This particular brand of deprivation could apply only to those SD members born outside Austria or Germany (Volksdeutsche) or whose homeland was lost to Germany in 1918 (7 percent of the known membership). Since German minorities usually suffered few deprivational disadvantages, however, other factors seem more relevant.[44]

Dogmatic Religion

In research data, the extent of immersion in certain religious groups correlates directly with authoritarian traits. Researchers disagree over whether significant differences exist among the larger denominations, but all agree on great variation within denominations based on degrees of dogmatism and fundamentalism.[45] Thus, except for minority religious groups, religion offers little predictive reliability. The products of both Catholic and Lutheran churches in early twentieth-century Germany (98 percent of SD membership) should have encountered authoritarian indoctrination, but the decisive factor would be the extent of personal immersion in religious dogmatism, to which no available data speak clearly.

On one point, formal withdrawal from church, the membership sample rates extremely high. At least 90 percent changed their religious affiliation to God-believing (Gottgläubig), the preferred, non-church-affiliated profession in the SS. The rate of church withdrawal was strikingly high in the SD compared with the rest of the SS. Beginning in 1935, SD members began to withdraw at an accelerating rate. By the end of 1937, 44 percent had left their churches, compared with only 16 percent of the general SS membership. Even compared with other special units, by 1938, SD withdrawal was growing at the fastest rate. SD members' ultimate 90 percent withdrawal contrasts sharply even with the SS officer corps. Only 74 percent of SS officers who had joined before 1933 and 68 percent of those who joined after eventually declared Gottgläubig.[46]

Without being subjected to the barracks environment or the training camp indoctrination of the armed SS,[47] members of the SD turned from their churches to the "faith" of the SS in greater numbers. Clearly, their identity with the SD was stronger than with their churches, and perhaps their SD ethos was more gratifying than that of any other SS unit. Their workaday immersion in the new consensus reality of internal enemies and ideological and spiritual threats to the new order required them to deal more with contradictions between old and new faiths.

At least two explanations for their behavior come to mind. If the church and its dogma had been a powerful authority for a man, then that idol fell more totally to the "true authority" of the Movement. One total submission to authority replaced another. Alternatively, the church never had an authoritarian hold on the man, and he easily left it behind for either a more transcendent identity and mission or for higher ego status. The split character of the membership suggests that each explanation applied to some of the members.

The question remains whether religious background would have made these men more authoritarian than others. Nothing in the data argues that, from the perspective of dogmatic religion, the SD membership should have been more authoritarian than the general population.

Lower Socioeconomic Origins

The children of poor farmers, laborers, and lower-income families allegedly display greater tendencies toward authoritarianism, all other factors being equal. Presumably this results from combinations of economically related deprivation and a negative class consciousness that turns inward on a homogeneous reference system—one keeps company with one's own and does not try to become what he is not. Antiintellectualism usually comes with such attitudes. To whatever extent such theory has any predictive value, on the social-origins count, quantitative data again suggest that, as a group, SD members should have been less susceptible than the general population. Even those of lower socioeconomic origins were significantly diverse, with a sizable element being aggressively modern in pursuit of socioeconomic advancement.

Authoritarian Family Background

Here the data are not available, for none of the men spoke to interpersonal relations in their homes when they wrote autobiographical sketches. Only economic hardship bore mention, and certainly that was less severe than for the general population.

Using social status to approximate the potential authoritarianism of fathers produces no indicators one way or the other. Allegedly more authoritarian occupations and educational backgrounds seem balanced against those allegedly less so. The problem is complicated by the image that the German Mittelstand (old, independent middle class) and Berufsbeamten (professional civil servant) fathers were generally stern, demanding, and aloof disciplinarians. Indeed, 54 percent of the fathers of SD members may have fit that broad socioeconomic category. But most recent research is undermining the orthodox images of the German middle class as a homogeneously antimodern, intractable body.[48] It strains credulity to argue that SD members came so disproportionately from significantly more authoritarian homes that they would be more susceptible than the general population.

Military Service

Some research indicates that military experience can increase authoritarian tendencies.[49] On this count, the sample far exceeds national norms, especially the officer corps. They undoubtedly lent a more military air to the organization. However, they also brought with them the trench camaraderie, front socialism, or social egalitarian spirit the war had generated. Furthermore, military discipline and hierarchy involve authoritarian role behavior in specific contexts only. That does not equate to authoritarian personality traits. Finally, as an "informal" education, the military experience can broaden one greatly, especially among officers.

As for their contribution to the brutalization process, as Peter Merkl observed in his study of early stormtroopers, the front soldier generation served better to transmit superpatriotic beliefs than to perpetrate violence.[50] This applied especially to the SD, oriented toward staff work rather than political combat or executive action.

Authoritarian Occupations

Many occupations entail authoritarian behavior (e.g., physicians, police, military, priests, teachers, civil service), and thus their members exhibit authoritarian traits. Given the relative social authority in the career backgrounds of the identified SD membership, they probably underwent more such role conditioning than the general population, but, as with the military, such lately acquired and role-specific behavior did not necessarily affect the full personality. Certainly, the SS or SD involved an authoritarian occupation, but that brings us beyond consideration of preconditioned susceptibility of SD personnel to the roles inherent in Sipo and SD.

Clearly, this quantitatively based sociopsychological analysis of the potential authoritarianism of the early SD membership shows that for every possible trend in one direction, there are countertrends. With respect to all early formative experiences, however, the membership sample should have been subjected significantly less than the general population to deprivations that enhance "authoritarianism." The early SD constituted a relatively privileged and more modernized group. In experiences that could modify earlier personality development (military and occupational roles), conflicting trends at least balance one another, but probably favor development that should have enhanced social flexibility and intellectual maturity.

As for other SS stereotypes, nothing in the data reveals any unique criminality or social pathology. The men had relatively clean civil records. Throughout its entire history, less than 3 percent of the early membership sample were expelled from the SD for any kind of offense, and none were executed. In 1937 alone, more than 1.5 percent of the total SS were expelled, and that was not a year of membership purge.[51] Despite the greatly heightened opportunity to exploit the corruption and the general moral breakdown that SD members later experienced, few can be identified as having been suspected of such involvement.[52] Although at least 31 percent were involved in the brutalization process of the Einsatzgruppen, only three men were charged with killing someone outside the line of duty, and two "executed" an "enemy" personally, outside of a mass execution process. Undoubtedly, the unrecorded incidences far exceed these figures, but consider the scope of brutalization and moral erosion these men had undergone by 1945. Nothing indicates a large number of criminals or immoral riffraff, though some were clearly present in the SD.

The causes of their behavior apparently lie not in defective personalities, but in the processes they experienced that legitimized participation in mass inhumanity. So far, little evidence offers insight into how these men succumbed to those processes and how much susceptibility or resistance they exhibited, but two interesting cases survive from the early years.

An unemployed machinist, who had completed formal schooling at age fourteen, found a home in the SS and a job in the special commando that his unit provided Gestapo Darmstadt. He was on alert on June 30, 1934, when an SA general was brought in under arrest. His commando leader, a senior SS sergeant, told him that he and a colleague were to eliminate the SA officer, under orders. Although in subsequent affidavits, both SS men professed their full willingness to obey orders in this and any other case, they distrusted their sergeant, questioned him on the authority of his orders (which he never adequately revealed), and, when further complications developed, decided to leave all shooting up to him. As things developed, the SA officer survived.[53]

This theoretically susceptible, rule-oriented, lower functionary, whose record indicates otherwise self-serving ethics, should have simply obeyed orders. But both he and his colleague hesitated simultaneously. In this case, bolstering retarded blind obedience, as did the victim's lack of "helplessness"—there could have been serious repercussions, even for mere "functionaries."[54] Later, a gradually escalated process of authorization and brutalization, a more routinized environment, and reversed bolstering would overcome their rule-based reserve.

In the much hotter seat of an SS major and Saxon Gestapo official, Lothar Beutel received unsigned orders from Heydrich for summary executions on June 30. Less free to evade, he sought advice from an older SS commander. At his suggestion, Beutel demanded and got signed orders. This in no way made the act legal or moral, but it clearly revealed the limits of blind obedience. Beutel, a man with a university education and comfortable middle-class origins, showed minimal restraint and succumbed totally to slightly improved authorization: "By order of the Führer and Reich Chancellor," officially stamped and signed Reinhard Heydrich. These orders Beutel dutifully executed.[55]

Ironically, it was a man with an eleventh-grade education who may have risen above the entire process at its full height. SS Sergeant Mathias Graf refused to assume command of a "special action" team on the eastern front, and was relieved of his assignment in the Einsatzgruppen and sent back to Germany. Nevertheless, disciplinary proceedings were dropped, and he subsequently rose to lieutenant's rank. If he had derived his scruples from religious faith, he had abandoned it formally, proclaiming himself Gottgläubig and withdrawing from church membership in 1939.[56]

Perhaps the answer to his immunity lies in relatively less immersion in the processes legitimizing violence and a clear lack of role orientation toward SS or SD. He first joined Party and SS in 1933, at age 30, and was released from the SS in 1937 for general indifference. In 1940, however, recalled under emergency service regulations, he became a supplementary worker in an SD field post. In May 1941, he found himself with Einsatzkommando 6 as assistant to a staff officer responsible for SD work. In his staff service, for which he earned decorations, he knew what was happening, but may have had no direct role. Then, in September 1942, came the command assignment and the crisis of conscience over more direct responsibility. Somehow, Graf had escaped the blind nationalism of most contemporaries, for he twice tried (once after the NS takeover) to emigrate from Germany. Since he had avoided the gradual escalation of authorization and brutalization experienced by Sipo and SD men between 1933 and 1940, the war pressures and sudden immersion in 1941 may have provided insufficient preparation for what he saw in Russia.

"Extraordinary Men" and Institutional Identities

It would seem that rather than looking for explanations in psychological defects or more susceptible personalities, or in social, educational, or intellectual "inferiority," the explanation for the special role that many of these men ultimately played may lie in their social and educational "superiority." Theories that explain the susceptibility of "ordinary men" to sanctioned violence are not sufficient, for there must have been "extraordinary men" with intellectual maturity among the victimizers. The connections between their egos and the missions they helped establish for Gestapo, Kripo, or SD may complete the package and help explain their failures to resist.

Earlier theories of mobilization argued that the trauma of the First World War, the inflation, the Great Depression, and the general social and economic tensions of modernization affected the entire world, but they had unique twists for the Germans.[57] Authority had sanctioned the war, yet the great German nation suffered defeat and humiliation. The validity of Wilhelmine institutions came into question, generating both rebellious calls for more autonomy and the counter urges to reestablish traditional authority or to rebuild a more valid authority. This heightened and politicized the social and economic disorganization that Germany suffered in the 1920s and 1930s. Everyone suffered to some degree from the unemployment and frustration of social aspirations, producing insecurity and disorganization of personality. In whatever direction one's ego was developing, it suffered dissonance and disorientation, intensifying the normal needs for recognition, acceptance, mastery, and security, and tendencies to identify and project upon an external or alien agent the source of one's problems. Under such severe pressure, even the strongest, most autonomous personality becomes more susceptible to exonerating, simplistic explanations that promise prompt relief. The intellectually mature retreat into dualism, the cognitively complex revert to simplicity under severe stress.

Observing that "one of the major reasons that individuals become affiliated with sociopolitical movements is a widespread desire for a new, more acceptable psycho-social identity," John Steiner focused attention on the individual-organizational link in the SS.[58] "A damaged identity" can find group affiliation therapeutic. Thus, he argues that many were attracted to the SS because they anticipated that membership would facilitate a socially acceptable shedding of their unwanted identity and the acquisition of a more satisfying self.[59] Unfortunately, Steiner depicted the majority of SS men as "Philistine" personality types, especially susceptible to Hitlerian images and SS identities.[60] He also argued, however, that the SS hardly offered a monolithic appeal or identity.[61] Although he specifically listed the SD and the Gestapo as branches of the SS, his general descriptions of the appeals, recruitment, and conditioning of SS men fit neither the SD nor the police too neatly.[62] Elsewhere, he seems to exclude SD members specifically from his generalizations about the SS.[63] In short, Steiner hits on a key note with his focus on ego-organizational links, but goes astray by generalizing about the SS and looking for flawed personality types. It seems far more productive to talk about ordinary, even strong egos under stress, and to focus on the identity potentials for them in specific organizations.

Defining "the identities" sought in Sipo and SD poses problems. Men drawn originally to police careers may have sought a role identity, or simply a secure career. Those among them who turned to the Party, SA, or SS for reasons other than conformity or opportunism must have sought additional identity. Many SS men who infiltrated Sipo had originally sought an SS identity, then turned to the police for either a political mission or a career. Men drawn directly to the SD before SS membership sought one or more of its images, or just a salary. Not only does this multitude of potential identities require exploration and analysis, but their interrelations demand attention. How did they contradict or complement one another, generating what forces and tensions? How did these identities relate to psychopolitical orientations and retard or reinforce the mechanisms for authorization, bolstering, routinization, and dehumanization?

The authoritarian nature of the SS demands specific attention as an "identity." A typical model argues:

> Every member of the SS was, of course, but one link in a tightly knit, hierarchically structured chain of command composed of men organized in clusters of multipurpose departmental agencies. Each member was expected to strictly obey orders and be only concerned with matters related to his position and role.[64]

One cannot deny the truth in such a generalization; yet, simultaneously, it is the sort of half-truth that plagues efforts to describe the SS. Granted, SS men often played the role expected of them. Especially when wearing the uniform that symbolized the image, they experienced a merger of role and person, but the individual still existed and reacted as one.[65]

Loyalty to the true leader stood at the center of the SS image, but the focus of that loyalty and the qualifications of the true leader could and did shift. For most SS men, Hitler could remain the exalted yet fatherly Führer who deserved loyalty and provided the final authority for any order, even to the end. But Hitler occupied that position precisely because most held him to be above and, therefore, not responsible for the errors, evils, nonsense, and corruption. What is more important, despite their loyal focus on Hitler, removal from him made the "Führer's will" an increasingly abstract reality, subject to much interpretation. As Bernd Wegener now concludes, "There is much evidence that the 'Führer's will' degenerated increasingly into a magic formula which allowed the various SS agencies to further their very different, in part even opposing, departmental interests." [66]

Recent research has revealed that even for those who underwent the discipline of SS training camps and schools, SS obedience was not to be based on abuse and fear, but rather on respect and admiration, as it allegedly had been in the romanticized Germanic warrior bands. [67] If the alleged "cadaver obedience" of the military SS did not grow from dehumanizingly authoritarian experiences, we shall see that early SD members experienced even less such indoctrination.

Practically every memoir and study of the Gestapo or SD shows that neither Himmler nor Heydrich generated blind loyalty. The contempt expressed by SS memoirists like Schellenberg may be after-the-fact exaggerations, but they reveal a more normative relation to authority figures. The Nazi infighting so often depicted shows the lack of monolithic hierarchy within the Movement, including the SS. The very nature of competing elites, each generating inner-elites with contradictory elite images, disrupted loyalty foci and often created considerable leeway in obedience.

The quantitative social data help unravel the ego-organization linkages that not only enhanced susceptibility to legitimizing processes but may also have involved members in contributing inadvertently to those processes. Obviously, a high percentage of the sample belonged to the privileged segment of society that should have developed less susceptibility to sanctioned violence either from authoritarianism, from intellectual and ethical immaturity, or from compliance socialization and rule/role orientation. It seems that Heydrich achieved reasonably well his ideal of recruiting respected, public-spirited citizens who would actively influence developments in their society. Among higher civil servant recruits, recruiters like Werner Best used a similar appeal. [68] Many academics turned to the SD as a vehicle for influencing rather than obeying or identifying with the leadership. Recruiters like Reinhard Höhn looked for other-minded critics of certain tendencies in the regime. [69] Although many career opportunists undoubtedly numbered among the "better sort" who joined the SD after January 1933, these recruits also included many who assumed an active responsibility for shaping the future of the Reich. Many even resembled the resister-from-within.

This returns us to the problem of defining the SD mission, left dangling at the end of chapter 5. By the end of 1934, the roles of "supplement to the political police" and "ideological intelligence agency" formed the focus in the search for suitable images. If, as suggested, an insecure membership felt driven to find a mission distinct enough from political police work to give the SD a secure raison d'être, organizational image became a pressing concern, especially among upper- and middle-level functionaries. If a significant number of these men had turned to the SD for an institutional identity that gratified ego needs, then definition had to become a compelling, transcendent issue for them. If they succeeded in developing a mission or organizational image that furthered their ego needs, then their ego-organization linkages could become extremely powerful, enough to account for an inability to risk any loss of that identity. Idealized mission grown from ego needs would become the sort of transcendent mission that compelled otherwise less susceptible men to play their roles in sanctioned inhumanity. Their ego-organization linkages provide the best hope of explaining how mature, strong personalities could have involved themselves in processes legitimizing violence.

The evidence for such ego-organization linkages is compelling, though circumstantial. Given their backgrounds, the membership had reason to expect far more upward social mobility than it experienced despite its relatively good record. These men suffered along with their fellow Germans from both a national and personal sense of degradation. Such ego-damaging experiences drive people to a therapeutic, elite or otherwise ego-gratifying organizational identity. Men like Heydrich and those he recruited had been threatened with loss of status before they found a place in the SD. One such man would profess that his loss of status and related "social embarrassment" did not suit his self-image, and he was happy "that through my activity for the SD, I have finally found a new life mission." [70]

More frequently, however, the numerous jurists, like Werner Best, and academics, like Otto Ohlendorf, found a status beyond that likely under the old system. Perhaps more important, they found levers for affecting the system. More than an ego-gratifying power over many little people, they found access to the power above them and the hope of actively shaping their society through this channel. Precisely because that access was so tenuous, its centrality to one's ego-organization linkage made it that much harder to calculate its value rationally. It was not so easy to cast aside when it proved ephemeral. Confronted with its undeniable loss because of conflict with Heydrich in 1939, a man like Best had to stop balancing on the edge as number-two man in Sipo and SD. But someone like Ohlendorf, who had parlayed his position into a network that he still hoped could influence the new Germany, would continue the balancing act until he plunged into the deep end as Einsatzgruppen commander. He would vainly try to preserve his illusory position of influence by conducting mass inhumanity. Although he rejected this distasteful role as "counter-productive," he could separate it from his ego-role in the SD as a peripheral assignment.[71]

Thus, this self-entrapment of multiple, sometimes conflicting, sometimes complementary missions and identities was created by strong egos who sought idealistic missions. One could do dirty work (at least directly supervise it) as a "peripheral" assignment in order to continue pursuit of his transcendent, ego-fulfilling mission. One could be "affiliated" with other men in branches of Sipo and SD whose missions were more direct, but "necessary," dirty work. One could even support their work as long as it was not directly related to one's transcendent mission. One could achieve insulation from their dirty work, if he could disdain those others. One's transcendent mission allowed him that illusion of moral superiority or some rectitude.

Clearly, SD men represented no pathological or psychically susceptible group. Few were wild or extreme Nazi fanatics. In those respects they were "ordinary men." Yet in most other respects, they were an extraordinary mix of men, drawn together by a unique mix of missions. From that point of view, one can explore the problem of defining SD missions and their contributions to the processes that legitimized violence. One can unravel a number of specific organizational images in Sipo and SD and relate them to potential ego identities.

The SD Into 1937

In Search of Image and Mission

From 1934 through 1937, organizational development and the search for a secure raison d'être brought the SD to maturity and expanded its missions. The growing connections with first Gestapo and then Kripo increased the complexity of mission, image, and membership to the point that one can speak of "multiple split (ego-institution) identities." This confusing constellation demands close analysis as a key to how the diverse membership involved itself in sanctioned inhumanity. First, however, surviving evidence from a variety of perspectives reveals much about the continued growth of the SD and makes possible an evaluation of the quality and the real character of its operations.

Organizational Development and Operational Efficiency

In January 1935, to keep up with SS growth, Himmler expanded and reorganized his central command (Reichsführung SS). The former SS offices (Ämter) became SS main offices (Hauptämter). Thus, effective January 30, Heydrich's Security Office became the Security Main Office,[1] subsequently called the SD Main Office to avoid confusion after the creation of Main Office Sipo in 1936.

Meanwhile, the SD evolved broadly conceived intelligence operations and seriously pursued its role of reshaping society. For two years, in pursuit of this evolution, the headquarters underwent constant reorganization until a stable SD Main Office structure emerged sometime during 1936. (see Appendices B.4 and B.5).[2] It consisted of three offices designated by Roman numerals (Ämter I–III), each subdivided into central departments (Zentralabteilungen), main departments (Hauptabteilungen), departments (Abteilungen), and principals or desks (Referate).

Office I, responsible for organization and administration, also provided general control of SD work and significant intelligence support facilities, doing some of the exploitative work for the other offices. For instance, Central Department I 3 monitored all publications, feeding the results to all other branches. Consequently, Office I was by far the largest. Werner Best had been responsible for its initial development, but Gestapo responsibilities took priority in early 1935, and Wilhelm Albert eventually replaced him.[3]

Office II, SD Inland, managed domestic intelligence operations under SS Colonel Herman Behrends. Of its two central departments, II 1, Ideological Evaluation, dealt with the ideological enemies of the Movement. The other central department, II 2, was under SS Major Reinhard Höhn. It concerned itself with the German "spheres of life"—that is, with intelligence not focused on "enemies." Its experts studied what actually happened in German life and what people thought and said.[4] Its primary concern was how the NS revolution was penetrating these "spheres of German life," and the resistance it encountered.

Office III directed foreign intelligence and counterespionage (Abwehr). As such, it conspicuously paralleled the original structure of Main Department III of the Gestapo Office.[5]

Both Offices II and III remained comparatively small. By the beginning of 1937, Office II had ninety-seven people; Office III had only forty-one. Primarily, these men collated reports from material collected by Main Department Press (I 3), the SD field posts, and V-men and experts operating directly under the central department desk chiefs.[6]

The smallness of Office III as late as 1937 testifies to the continued weakness of SD foreign intelligence operations. Nevertheless, by 1935, as SD foreign intelligence began to develop seriously, it evolved its own unique ethos, which must be treated separately.

Despite great strides since 1933, the SD retained many vestiges of its amateurish beginnings. For instance, inconsistent personnel policies produced problems as late as 1937. Men assigned to the same level of responsibility within the Main Office could differ in rank as widely as captain and sergeant. Also, Ohlendorf remembered that when he began work in II 2 in 1936, the staff had to do their own typing, and only Office I was organized systematically.[7]

Since no full SD budgets survive after 1934, we have no measure of financial growth. Fragmentary evidence contradicts the image of Heydrich's growing independence. Instead, Himmler worked to control him and the SD, while shielding it from external monitoring. After Heydrich's maneuvers with Schwarz and Hess in 1934, Himmler, or his SS administrative chief, handled negotiations with the Party treasurer. During 1935, Himmler set his administrative chief firmly in control of SD finances from the Party treasury.[8]

This finally ended Schwarz's efforts to nose into the SD budget. The Party closed its files on SD finances in the spring of 1936, but even before that, the SD budget consisted solely of lump-sum accounts paid to the SS administration by the Party treasurer.[9] Himmler's lieutenants controlled SD finances, which remained limited by Party and SS resources. The funds so available were never enough, and the SD would subsequently pursue government funding, mostly in vain.

SD resources consisted of two budgets: the personnel budget for salaries and the material budget. The personnel budget generally ran twice the size of that for expenses. According to Schellenberg, at their peak, the two together never exceeded twelve million RM a month.[10] There were also occasional budgetary supplements to cover special operations, but these amounted to very little. By the end of 1940, they had totaled only one million RM.[11] The SD remained heavily dependent on the voluntary work of its unsalaried members and associates.

For another measure of growth, during 1935, the SD expanded from about 800 members to more than 1000; then gradual acceleration set in, and during 1936 it exceeded 3000 and approached 5000 by the end of 1937. By the end of 1936, the Main Office had at least 365 personnel.[12]

The bulk of the membership worked below the new main office, where the field structure had expanded greatly. Ten main regions each covered one or more Party Gau. By December 1935, they had under them twenty-seven regions, which were redesignated as sub-regions and increased to thirty-two by December 1936. As the SS and SD field structures grew apart, the SD remained more closely tied to political borders, while the SS conformed to the military districts.[13]

Field-level personnel policies were as irregular as those above. Although all main region heads were officers by 1935, a few subregion heads remained sergeants until at least 1937. In December 1935, the ranks of field office chiefs could range from private to major. Although the respective ranks rose, the disparity remained. By the end of 1936, major region heads ranged from major to lieutenant-general. At least they had eliminated the problem of subregion heads outranking their superiors. The elevated ranks of major region chiefs reflected the SD's growing role in Reich politics. As it grew, tension with Party and state increased, and the SD needed men with standing to negotiate with their counterparts. For instance, in 1936, SS Major General Jakob Sporrenberg would be drafted from the general SS to head Main Region Northeast. As an Old Fighter of high standing, he could better handle the problems the Gestapo and SD had in Gauleiter-Governor Erich Koch's territory.[14] Frequently, the heads of main regions acquired the newly created post of Inspector of Sipo.

Although Heydrich had some leeway to advance his personnel more rapidly,[15] the process of coordinating rank and responsibility made little progress before 1938. One's rank remained more a function of his SS status than of his responsibilities in the SD.

Equally erratic and uncoordinated were the growth and operations of the field posts. When operating properly, a main region (organized comparably to the main office) assembled information from its own agents and from those of its outposts, collated them into periodic or special reports, and forwarded them to the main office. Some sense of their growth pattern and related problems comes from several sources and different perspectives.

During 1935–1936, while this field structure expanded, regional budgets grew accordingly. For instance, between December 1934 and May 1935, one region received a monthly advance varying from 400 to 600 RM, and had material expenses ranging from 284 to 751 RM. By October 1935, its advance had exploded to 2,800 RM.[16]

These same budgets reveal something of work in the field. The bulk of a region's material budget was for mundane matters, such as rent, utilities, transportation, and postage. The only costs directly related to intelligence were subscriptions to publications and small payments (15–30 RM) to reimburse V-persons and members for expenses.[17]

A budget proposed by Subregion Hesse depicts the scale of its operations by the end of 1936. It consisted of five outposts (Aussenstellen) covering nineteen districts. For each outpost, 250 RM covered expenses, including 50 RM to rent each office. Outposts now operated at a level equivalent to the 1934 budgets for regional offices. For the subregion office of 1936, 500 RM covered rent and utilities.[18]

Perhaps nothing better illustrates the new status of the SD than the facilities becoming available through such increased funds. Shoestring operations out of private quarters or rented offices gave way to commodious facilities in pleasant surroundings. Of course, the 50 RM of an outpost still rented merely a modest office or apartment, but the larger subregion and main region offices often occupied substantial houses or apartment buildings. Many such facilities had become available at the expense of Jews and other "enemies."[19]

Presumably, security motivated the choice of such locations. They might have achieved anonymity better among business offices where the comings and goings of personnel would be less obvious. Instead, the SD sought isolation. Physically removed from all other government, Party, or business operations, during their breaks workers could not mix with outsiders, and casual visitors would be conspicuous. At night, a residential building enhanced security, because the available rooms provided quarters for unmarried men who doubled as guards.

As for field post staffing, Major Region Rhein remains the best available case study. In the summer of 1935, it covered the state of Hesse, the Prussian province of Hessen-Nassau, and the districts of Trier and Koblenz from the Rhein Province, and was divided into two regions, XI and XXX. The entire major region had 60 salaried and 45 unsalaried members. The salaried headquarters staff consisted of 31 officers and men, plus 11 probationary members. An additional 24 SD men served as unsalaried members. Since not all were qualified for the responsibilities of one of the thirty or more desks, some staff members still worked several.[20] Nevertheless, major regions seemed reasonably well staffed.

In contrast, the regions had salaried staffs of only one officer and 6 to 8 men, plus a junior officer or sergeant in charge of an outpost. Under them stood 10 or 11 SD men scattered across the region. Clearly, the regional offices could not yet manage a reasonable distribution of the work of thirty desks among such small staffs.

This problem improved only a little between 1935 and 1937. Although Main Region Rhein requested an increase of its salaried members from 63 to 83 by January 1937, the goal was not achieved. The main region staff had grown from 42 to 54. The subregion staffs varied in size from 6 to 23. In addition, within the main region, five Gestapo-SD posts now existed at Kassel, Frankfurt, Darmstadt, Koblenz, and Trier. Each had its Sipo-SD members, ranging from five in Kassel to twenty in Frankfurt. From 105 members, the total had only increased to 127 "working SD," plus 58 Sipo-SD.[21] Below the main region level, there was still no division of labor to allow knowledgeable research.

At the national level, Central Department I 3 provides another concrete picture of growth, strengths, and weaknesses. Simultaneously, it would generate one of the key images of the SD. The SD, like the police, had always relied heavily on publications as a source of intelligence. From the beginning, workers at every office from the central down had scoured newspapers and periodicals and filed clippings.[22] Its intellectual recruits had also focused on literature as a key to ideological influences in the culture; that was the work of a special post at Leipzig.

Until 1935, SD headquarters had no desk (principal) responsible for analyzing literature. The regional office in Leipzig functioned as the SD center for such work. From June 1934, when an SD member with the credentials and zeal to do such work made himself available at the regional office, he exploited the German Library in Leipzig, which became an SD cultural research center, later known as the Leipzig Connection (Verbindungsstelle).

In spring 1935, the SD university recruiting network drew in Franz Six, whose academic credentials in journalism and work with NS presses made him an obvious candidate to head the Press Department. Six had recently received his Ph.D. at Heidelberg, magna cum laude, for a dissertation focused on NS propaganda and couched in NS language. There he had remained, working on his habilitation. A Nazi since 1929, and a student of history and political science, he served as an assistant at the Heidelberg Institute for Journalism, was editor of the *Heidelberger Student* and an official in the German Studentenschaft, advising on journalism. In February 1935, the SD adopted him. During the next year, he completed his habilitation and extensively rebuilt the SD's press service.[23] Over the next two years, he would consolidate personal control over most of the SD's domestic operations and shape one of its primary intellectual images.

In June 1935, six absorbed the Leipzig literature post, giving his department the more ambitious title of Press and Literature Office. He saw the necessity for a complete reorganization, the retraining of all existing personnel, and a major expansion of his entire operation. A pedagogue at heart, he developed an ambitious but well-conceived educational program that reached down through the entire organizational structure. He toured the SD superior regions, where he personally briefed each press principal (Referat). By late September, the subregions had completed the appointment of their principals, and all assembled in Berlin for a week-long training course.[24]

Not only were the trainees thoroughly briefed on the work of the press office, but the staff carefully evaluated them. Six concluded that, at the subregional level, the principals were not suited intellectually or educationally for the work he had in mind. Resources at that level were limited, and their principals usually worked on multiple specialties. They could not handle sophisticated evaluation, but they took to press review enthusiastically, so he decided that such work was mechanical enough for their abilities. The principals at the central department and the superior regions could do the more sophisticated work.[25]

The goal Six had set for his central department was ambitious. He proclaimed that "no newspaper or politically important periodical should appear in Germany . . . without its being garnered and evaluated by the SD." They would report every important development to provide a clear view of German press matters and the men behind them. Each regional office was to assign V-persons to read every local publication and make clippings. These they forwarded daily to the superior region for evaluation. The superior region and central offices also reviewed more important publications and condensed everything into monthly and quarterly reports. Most superior regions also reviewed publications (mostly German language) from adjacent foreign countries. All of this boiled down into two functions: providing Offices II and III with a steady flow of intelligence for their areas of responsibility and maintaining files on every publication and the key personalities involved with them. Six would boast that he converted the haphazard exploitation of the press into the most reliable intelligence source in the entire SD, superior to any reports coming up from the field posts.[26]

Although he profusely praised the "expertise" of subordinates whom he had adopted and trained, Six was realistic enough about the limitations of most SD men in the field to avoid relying heavily on them. By concentrating all evaluation at levels where reasonably competent men were available, he could achieve his ambitious mission to an acceptable degree. In this he was more fortunate than those branches of Office II that had to rely on reports directly from the field. Their work fell short. Furthermore, Six's operations further burdened those field offices, already sorely overextended.

Before July 1935, Superior Region South reported that it had one principal solely responsible for press, and that he had one assistant. This staffing was apparently unusual, for most had none. More typically, however, its regional posts had not made any appointments, for they had few available personnel.[27]

This was an understatement. One regional office reported that it could not possibly assign more responsibilities to the principal whom the superior office had suggested; each of its principals already had several desks to cover. The chances of finding an unsalaried volunteer were slim, especially since the envisioned work was so great. At the outpost level, the proposed press work was even more unrealistic. At that lowest level, there was usually only one salaried man with one helper for the entire outpost, and they could not keep up with their existing load of reports and surveillances. They were especially plagued by lack of cooperation from local officials and outright sabotage by Party offices. The regional officer concluded bluntly that in recent weeks assignments had generated such a load that outpost leaders had become thoroughly discouraged.[28]

Consequently, the superior region assembled a list of press principals at the regional level only.[29] These men would have to work across their entire region, developing their own network of V-persons to carry out the press mission. Although they could perhaps get along without the undeveloped outpost network, this episode reveals the constraints within which SD men worked. As late as the summer of 1935, the SD was still greatly overextended and hardly up to its overblown image as all-seeing eyes.

From all appearances, this had not changed by the end of 1936. The surviving correspondence between Region Aachen and its outpost at Monschau reveals a badly overworked and undersupported post leader, an SS private who probably had no assistant.[30] Between February and December of 1936, Region Aachen sent him at least 66 directives and requests for reports. During the entire period, he typed and forwarded at least 82 reports. Added to these were frequent, routine administrative correspondence and the political evaluations that constituted a large part of an outpost's workload.

Requests from the regional office varied in length from one paragraph to six pages, and some carried five to ten separate assignments, with forms and questionnaires to be completed as part of the report. A typical directive was a guideline for interpreting the Nuremberg laws and identifying violations. A four-page set of instructions accompanied a two-page questionnaire from the press principal who was working up his files on the local presses. One request called for a report on every internment facility in the district and its personnel, and for routine surveillance for suspicious activities. Other typical assignments called for reports on secret Stahlhelm intelligence agencies and on anti-Nazi camouflaged Catholic Youth activities. Outpost leaders also received descriptions of persons at large in the Reich whose appearance they should report.

The poor private may not have been salaried, but if he was he would not have earned more than 125 to 155 RM a month plus a small housing allowance. Nevertheless, until the spring of 1936, he apparently covered all his operating expenses out of his own pocket. In April, when an assignment required more expenses than he could afford, he requested a reimbursement. Yet in May 1936, he had to write to the commander of the superior region to complain that the promised 15 RM per month was not arriving. He finally received his first reimbursement in September and requested an increase to 20 RM. He was now making regular payments on a typewriter he had ordered.[31]

If this private who signed himself 17708 is any example, the SD was able to draw upon dedicated and self-sacrificing men for its exhaustive field work, but few could have brought much sophistication to the task. The picture of the hinterland, outpost level that emerges here is that of an isolated SS man who had limited direct contact with his regional office, and who was poorly briefed on procedures. He merely responded to written directives, and although he gave generously of himself, there were limits to his time and resources. As late as March 1936, he had yet to begin building a significant V-man network.

He was well-enough informed to report on the composition of the district council and the political backgrounds and reputations of its members. On the Catholic young men's movement or the Work Service, for instance, without a V-man net he had knowledge only of his immediate community. He turned to pro-NS priests or a friend in the Work Service. He relied on local SA men with "first-hand knowledge" of illegal and suspect organizations. On unemployment, he made authoritative-sounding statements, but could provide no comparative statistics and blamed problems on one individual in local government. He displayed appropriate paranoia about known and suspected Jews.[32]

The regional office complained that its outposts were dilatory in completing assigned character evaluations, and that their quality was bad. They had to remind field offices of the seriousness of such evaluations, on which a man's career and the well-being of his family rested. Evaluations frequently consisted of single sentences and employed unattributed allegations. To ensure better control, the regional office ordered the compilation of lists of the V-persons who would usually supply the information. No such lists existed as late as June 1936.[33]

By the end of 1937, SD outpost Aschaffenberg in Bavaria, which had at least two workers, was much better organized for evaluating important persons, but even so could not always meet the expectations of higher offices. The leader had developed his network of V-persons, but they did not devote themselves routinely to evaluation. When called on to evaluate someone who had recently left, they were at a loss. He admonished them to admit a lack of knowledge rather than manufacture weak and unobjective reports, and to begin a routine surveillance for future evaluations. A few months later, he indicated that he was still unsatisfied with the quality of his V-net, and admonished his observers to review, purge, and search for better quality associates. At least the outpost leader was in command of an extensively developed net by 1937, and furthermore, he expressed himself to his workers with the force of one well informed about procedures and thoroughly imbued with the SD mission.[34]

Almost six years after its creation, the SD at the level of its outposts and its "all-seeing army of spies" remained unevenly developed and well short of the professional quality to which it aspired. Nevertheless, it clearly saw itself as the shaper of a better Germany. It intended to ensure that the right sort of people occupied all key positions in the new society. Such a mission motivated the expenditure of personal energy demanded of members and affiliates at the field level.[35]

From one Gestapo-SD post comes a report revealing other aspects of amateurishness in the SD field structure. The head of the main Gestapo-SD post in Hesse, SS Technical Sergeant Berges, sent a report to Main Region Rhein about the sloppy prodedures of SD Outpost Darmstadt, headed by SS Second Lieutenant Bonifer. Allegedly, Bonifer's people carelessly lost a secret report where it would be found in a public plaza. Unlike Berges, careful to keep his SD status secret and never putting the names of V-persons on paper, Bonifer and his people were openly known.[36]

The SD could easily keep Berges' report secret and attack such problems discreetly. Not so an incident that occured in Main Region South. There, one Emil Danzeisen had developed a network of V-men in the office of the Munich Police President. Danzeisen, one of the Movement's gangster-like adventurers, had been involved in a sensational attempt to assassinate Röhm in 1932, and had personal contacts among Reich leaders like Hess, Buch, and Schwarz. His exact affiliation with the SD remains unclear, but he had built such an extensive network of agents that he claimed it was an SD outpost, and told his agents that they were members. The agents, disgruntled Old Fighters and nonmember policemen, filed derogatory reports on the Wagner regime and leading officials, even in Himmler's Bavarian Political Police. Rather than forwarding them through the SD, Danzeisen sent reports directly to Hess, Schwarz, and other Party leaders. When this led in 1936 to Gestapo investigation, they broke up Danzeisen's organization and disciplined the involved policemen. The local SD denied their membership, and the Gestapo charged Danzeisen with operating an illegal intelligence operation.[37] By 1937, the resultant scandal forced tighter regulations for field posts and guidelines for the selection of V-persons.

The Danzeisen affair reflects problems that still plagued the SD's V-man network. Between 1934 and 1937, as that network took shape, more formal procedures developed to control it, but they were clearly not effective by Danzeisen's time. Only as late as 1936 did the SD institute significant controls over its V-person system.[38] About the same time, they defined distinctions among the affiliates who worked as V-persons. Typically, however, SD members continued to confuse the categories, partially because of differences between Gestapo and SD terminology.[39]

Outposts and some offices had district observers (BB or Bezirks Beobachter) who served as expert reporters on either a region or a specialization such as the economy. Such unsalaried SD members had their own network of V-persons.[40] They reported to either a desk chief or a field officer.

More ordinary V-persons worked either with such observers or directly with desk chiefs at all levels within the system. At some point, superior regions began to keep file cards on their V-persons.[41] Not until December 1936 do they seem to have been required to send duplicates of their cards to the SD main office, which henceforth maintained a Reich central file.[42]

Regular V-persons took a special oath to serve the SD. For a few years there was an effort to limit them to SS members, except for females, but by 1938, a solid NS commitment remained the sole criteria.[43] To preserve their unreproachable motivations, a V-person was not to be promised any advantages in gaining either SS or SD membership or promotions in any organization.

Also classed as unsalaried SD associates were people titled feeders (Zubringer) and sources (Gewährsmänner). Feeders made occasional, unsolicited reports. Although they took no oath, they knew they were reporting to an SD man and thereby supporting its mission. Unlike a casual police informer, they were screened for ideological commitments and motives and usually had to have some NS affiliation. A "source," on the other hand, was the personal acquaintance of an SD affiliate, to whom he might turn with an occasional question about which the source should be well informed. Unlike the feeder, he or she did not know he was feeding information to the SD. Like the feeder, however, the source was also allegedly screened for commitments and usually had NS affiliations.[44]

V-persons, feeders, and sources were always under consideration for elevation to full membership, if they met the criteria and would be more useful to the SD. Persons in all three categories could be dropped instantly if they were no longer useful or proved in any way unsuitable. Only the V-person would hear of a formal severance, however.[45]

Casual informants from the general population were rare because the SD was much less visible than the Gestapo, barring cases like Riechers and Bonifer, and the public knew much less about SD work. Denouncers usually turned to the police.[46] All of this fit well with the SD's self-image of carefully chosen, well-informed, upright citizens in the service of shaping the new order—a service above employing spies and informers.

The Gestapo maintained a regular listing of unsuitable V-persons for its own, separate system of informers, and the SD distributed these lists to its field posts.[47] SD criteria for suitability were different from the Gestapo's, but unsuitability would have been similarly determined: compromised V-men, producers of inaccurate information, known security risks, and so forth. Gestapo and SD headquarters forbade the sharing of V-persons, but ordered their exchange between branches if they were more appropriate to the other organization's work.

One remaining category of persons used by the SD, but not as associates, were "agents." They worked for the SD as paid informers, but the SD considered the practice so problematic that appropriate experts at the highest levels had to approve any use of them. They were to be employed indirectly to ensure against their having ties with an SD office. They could include persons within enemy circles, such as members of a Jewish or Catholic community, or KPD members.[48]

From all appearances, Danzeisen was an associate working under SD Superior Region South. Since he was not a member, the SD had no problem denying his affiliation and his "V-men." Deniability was one obvious advantage of the SD system. Nevertheless, the Danzeisen affair and similar incidents clearly required much tighter controls. The desire of the outpost leader at Aschaffenburg to purge and rebuild his net probably grew from an SD-wide review of the system, and throughout 1937 and 1938, Superior Region South's files reveal ever tighter, system-wide methods for screening and monitoring V-persons.[49]

Although clues to the rigor of screening are rare, a few survive.[50] The SD did reject candidates for reasons that anyone could admire. They even judged as unsuitable ideally positioned Party members and SS men, if they lacked community respect. The overbearing Nazi who judged others by attendance at all functions or by the enthusiasm of their "Heil Hitlers" served no purpose. If one's family life generated public disdain, he had to be special to qualify.[51]

The quality and all-pervasiveness of the V-person network has been grossly exaggerated for the years under study. It was widely spread, but hit or miss in its coverage—poorly or inconsistently controlled for quality. Nevertheless, from the beginning, V-persons were frequently well placed, knowledgeable, and influential members of their communities. Recruiters must have used the idealistic images of the SD to appeal to these people, who would have seen themselves as shapers of society rather then informers or spies. The network coalesced nationwide during the period between 1936 and 1938.

At the headquarters level, V-person lists survive that reveal an additional focus on experts who provided information. Some were organized according to the positions of influence they occupied. For instance, one file card listed three V-men in the Berlin Racial-Political

Office.[52] One was the official liaison officer, whom the SD used as an open conduit to every Party and government agency, the man responsible for ensuring the officially required cooperation each such agency was obligated to provide. The other two were secret V-men, positioned not only to provide information lacking from the official channel, but also to make suggestions and take actions not known to originate from SD circles. Of course, they also evaluated the other personnel in the office, an activity that outsiders usually "confused" with spying. Clearly, the SD mission was so polymorphous that both its practitioners and their objects could perceive it several different ways.

Mission and Image

Such scandals as the Danzeisen affair continued to focus attention on mission and image. From Himmler and Heydrich's perspective, the problem focused on two interrelated dichotomies. While their SS and police had to terrorize the "enemies," they also had to earn the respect and support of all "good citizens." Finding a balance between terror and respect was no easy exercise. The other conflict lay between the desire for an ideologically reliable agency like the SD, unrestricted by rigidly delimited guidelines, and the need for that agency to work without conflict with the Gestapo and other NS and state agencies it was supposed to purify.

Heydrich recognized that the SD had earned its bad reputation in Party circles, and he disliked the image of spies and informers, although he cultivated the all-seeing-eyes image. In fact, he had another problem beside the SD's image, one which he probably did not fully understand. The SD's paranoid world view of camouflaged internal enemies and its self-righteous drive for purity set the frame of reference for SD operations. Heydrich desired this sort of "ideological insight," but not the related drive to act spontaneously and create problems.

In the fall of 1935, Heydrich issued two directives, trying to limit and channel SD activities in relation to the Party. He criticized his subordinates for being too involved in local relationships, thus impairing their objectivity and producing mistrust in Party circles. The SD would cease all investigation of Party affairs. They would report complaints about the Party directly to the Main Office, which would forward them without elaboration to the Deputy of the Führer.[53]

Heydrich made no effort, however, to square all this with the SD assignment to evaluate all key persons in Party and state. He and SD men obviously did not see this as spying any more than an FBI officer sees doing a security check as spying. For the objects of such reports, it was a different matter. SD work always generated multiple imagery.

Of course, general mistrust of Himmler and Heydrich also lay at the root of the problem, but they blamed the V-persons and field workers and their spontaneous attacks and libelous reports for the bad image of the SD. Cases like Danzeisen's smear tactics against enemies in the Munich police were apparently common, although no others so boldly bypassed SD channels to go directly to higher authority.

Such indiscretions endangered the whole SD operation, leading to demands that the names of V-persons and members be revealed so the accused could defend themselves. Although SD headquarters forbade the release of names, to remove the cause, it continually threatened irresponsible informants with severe disciplinary action. By summer 1936, it also sought to improve relations and operations by establishing liaison officers between SD field posts and their respective local Party leaders.[54]

Himmler and Heydrich could only admonish their subordinates to find the happy medium within the internal contradictions of the system and to walk the line with caution. Such pressures must have heightened the determination of many SD members to find other, more gratifying, missions and images. Thus, they made their contributions to the evolution of their organization below the level of direct involvement by Himmler and Heydrich.

The original SD mission had been observation of enemies and the internal security of the Movement. Although such work implicitly involved spying on the Party, formal arrangements with the Party increasingly denied this as an official function. Furthermore, Himmler's acquisition of the political police had reduced SD observation of the enemy to "ideological intelligence." The development of the two main departments under Office II related directly to the evolution of the SD mission as it expanded from such original foci.

A cursory look at the backgrounds and experiences of the men in these departments and in I 3 reveals more about the internal tensions. The people under Six in Central Department I 3, and under Behrends in Office II, formed a dichotomy typical of divisions within the SD. Many, especially those dealing with ideological enemies, had no special credentials other than in-office training and an ability to parrot shibboleths and to uncover alleged conspiratorial networks. In contrast, most of the men under Höhn in Central Department II 2 had academic credentials, although their intellectual records did not always reveal a critical independence. Where they did, an ideological bias that differed mostly in detail from NS mainlines frequently colored that "independence." Nevertheless they were the sort of academics whom intelligence agencies usually recruit, and who provide well-informed, reasonably "objective" reports.

In other words, among those who held the institutional image of the intellectual information service, there was a split between those who had reason to see themselves as legitimate experts and those they might disdain. Among the latter, there were many who were probably as intellectually proficient at their assigned tasks as their intellectually judgmental counterparts, and who could legitimately resent such biases. Finally, there were certainly intellectually weak, amateurish hacks in both groups.

Although components of Central Department II 1 had existed as a central intelligence agency since late 1933, it apparently developed an extended structure and systematic operation only after 1935. Furthermore, all branches did not grow equally.

Its subordinate main department dealing with political organizations and movements (II 12) was probably the best developed, since it had been the focus of most SD work on enemies before 1934. Since control of its subjects belonged primarily to the Gestapo, its reduction to the role of ideological auxiliary limited further expansion. By the end of 1936, it was a strange hodgepodge of "specialists." Main department head SS Captain Werner Göttsch was one of the previously described unemployed 1932 recruits from Kiel. A business college graduate and victim of the depression, he became one of those jacks-of-all-trades that Heydrich favored for willingness and ability to take on any kind of mission. In 1934 and 1935, he had moved back and forth between Gestapo and SD, most commonly working on espionage and counterespionage. Presumably, this prepared him to run the ideological intelligence service directed at political enemies.[55]

His appointment must have rankled some department leaders under him, for they had developed qualifications for their specialties. SS Lieutenant Martin Wolf was a gymnasium teacher in Saxony who had at least studied history and had worked at SD central since 1934 as a principal, focusing on Marxism. He had worked his way up through the ranks and training courses to assume the head of Department Marxism in October 1935.[56]

The qualifications of SS Captain Horst Böhme were better. He had first-hand knowledge of his subject, having been a member of the now-suspect Stahlhelm, Bund Wiking, and Bund Oberland between 1924 and 1928. He had also completed the detective lieutenant's training course at the Police Institute in Charlottenburg, and served for about one year in the Saxon Gestapo. He had headed Department Rightist Movements since June 1936.[57]

The branches of Main Department II 11, focusing on "alien ideologies" (churches, Freemasons, and Jews), evolved more slowly and reflected more clearly the shifting focus of SD attention in search of a raison d'être distinct from police work. The organization of the 1933 SD Office (Appendix B.3) revealed extensive emphasis on Freemasonry alone among the future components of Main Department II 11. The sole surviving early SD Situation Report of May/June 1934 reflected the rise to preeminence of the "Catholic Movement" as an object of attention. More than half that report focused on this "enemy," with the remainder divided almost equally among the rest.[58] Such shifts in emphasis (but not interpretation) distinguished SD intelligence from Gestapo reports, with their continued emphasis on the left and labor.[59]

SD work on such enemies between 1934 and 1937 shifted from the controlling influence of the "old men," the founding experts like Ilges and Schwartz-Bostunitsch, who were retired by 1937 as too decrepit.[60] A new generation of experts, a mix of outside recruits and inside trainees, replaced them. Less bookish, and undoubtedly more competent managers, they built the organizational structure the SD needed. SS Lieutenant Fritz Hartmann assumed command of Main Department II 11 in February 1936, when he transferred in from the Berlin Gestapo Office. A law-trained civil servant and member of the Gestapo since 1934, he had headed the desk for religious organizations.[61] His transfer from the Gestapo to take over work on religious, Jewish, and Masonic enemies clearly reflected the SD's need for competent management of its work on those enemies as well as its new emphasis on that work.

The major impetus, however, came in spring 1937, when Franz Six took over both central departments, II 1 and II 2.[62] His success in building Central Department Press, overcoming inherent weaknesses of the SD, recommended him for the job. His zeal turned the branches under Main Department II 1 into more competent intelligence agencies supported by trained field operatives and a network of V-persons and agents. On the other hand, his focus on purifying Germany frustrated the plans of those like Reinhard Höhn to redefine the image and mission of II 2.[63] As a result, they remained blurred.

Emphasis on Catholicism under Department Political Churches (II 113) not only reflected Himmler and Heydrich's personal fixations, it also provided an enemy target that the police could attack only when individual clergy or organizations could be charged with endangering Party or state. Thus, the "legal" church offered a fruitful target for ideological intelligence, so that Desk Political Catholicism (II 1131) and other future desks of Department Political Churches had been evolving since early 1934.

The same logic applied to Jewry as an enemy. From 1934, as frustrated elements of the Movement turned their attention to the "Jewish Problem," and attention refocused on that enemy and the need for a "constructive" solution, Himmler, Heydrich, and the SD took notice. As pressure mounted, culminating in the Nuremberg laws, the Gestapo could only arrest Jews who violated laws or seemed involved in some conspiracy. As an ideological intelligence agency, the SD could produce more "concrete information" on Jewish threats and propose more effective action toward the solution of the Jewish problem. To enhance this possibility, the SD shunted aside the "funny old professors" Ilges and Schwartz-Bostunich, and Blaichinger, the principal for Jewry, and replaced them with a newly recruited expert.

Leopold von Mildenstein, a member of the Czech NSDAP, emigrated to Braunschweig in 1932 and joined the SS. From a sideline as a correspondent for the *Berliner Börsenzeitung* and a series of articles published in *Der Angriff* in fall 1934, he established a reputation as an expert on the Middle-East and Zionism. He indeed had personal contacts in Zionist circles, and he came to Heydrich's attention through his pro-Zionist *Angriff* articles advocating emigration. This was already the official SS/SD concept of "the Final Solution for our generation,"[64] so in the summer of 1935, Heydrich recruited him to build up the SD section devoted to Jewry.[65]

Mildenstein would last only one year, but during that time he allegedly made significant contributions to Himmler's ideas about reducing obstacles to emigration, began training several future SD experts, provided a solid picture of Jewish organizations in Germany, and established the SD's "amicable" contacts in Jewish circles, specifically Zionist ones. But his small, still poorly trained staff remained overwhelmed and without any field structure to support it. It relied mostly on the Berlin Gestapo post for its "practical contact with Jews in Germany, which self-evidently was informed only about the local enemy conditions," or so ran the later official line on Mildenstein's shortcomings.[66]

Indeed, Mildenstein's approach was too "theoretical" for success in Nazi circles, and according to him, Heydrich came to view him as too soft. He did not involve his people in Gestapo interrogations and apparently worried over the dissolution of some Jewish organizations. Nevertheless, before his departure, he initiated the practical work of building a field structure, beginning with the appointment and training of desk chiefs at the superior regions and, in April 1936, the beginning of regular monthly reports.[67]

From Mildenstein's departure in July 1936 until the end of the year, Department II 112 consisted of SS Master Sergeant Kuno Schroeder and two SS technical sergeants including Adolf Eichmann, all Mildenstein's young protégés. Schroeder boasted that a harder line emerged promptly as they joined Berlin Gestapo men in monitoring Jewish assemblies and in formulating the definition of "Jewry as enemy of state and Party." The SD was to contribute forcefully to the fulfillment of official NS goals: the removal of Jewish influence from all spheres of public life, and the promotion of emigration. Toward those ends he planned a significant expansion of personnel working directly for Department II 112. Schroeder called for full-time desk chiefs and one to two salaried helpers at the superior region level. They were to build V-man networks, recruit Jews and "pro-Jews" as agents, and train desk chiefs at the subregions.[68]

By February 1937, Schroeder could report little progress on any of his goals. The staff remained the same, and its overload had prevented the mandated reworking of its subject-card-file (Sachkartei). At least its old, persons-card-file (Personenkartei) on important Jews included almost 2,500 entries and would be expanded. He pathetically boasted that their participation in three Gestapo interrogations had garnered valuable information.[69] Even so, much of the department's energy still went into analysis of the Jewish press.[70]

Following Six's spring arrival in Central Department II 1, all of Mildenstein's people except Eichmann departed. Command fell to Lieutenant Dieter Wisliceny, and the staff soon rose to six. Most important, Six's influence led to a complete shift from the former "theoretical" approach to more "practical" action, meaning II 112 worked directly with the Gestapo on arrests and raids. The Gestapo loaned them its material on "international Jewry," and they greatly expanded their focus on Jews outside Germany.[71]

In the field, the network under II 112 had begun to function from the spring of 1936. Superior regions not only produced regular monthly reports but responded to directives for reports on specific subjects such as identifying Jews still in influential positions and assimilationist influences, and providing data on racial pollution cases, emigrations, and returns. They also scoured their areas for suitable V-persons. For support at the subregion level, desk chiefs busily stimulated the imaginations of overworked outpost leaders. They were to uncover Marxist and Catholic contacts with local Jews and to report Jews seen buying NS paraphernalia or pictures of the Führer.[72]

The new emphasis on Department Jewry also grew from the SD need to justify itself independently from the Gestapo. Although both Gestapo and Bavarian Political Police had better developed intelligence sections on Jewry than did the early SD, these police did not combat Jews as such, but only those involved in specific crimes or suspect organizations. Thus, Jewry, like Catholicism, offered another realm for SD development as ideological supplement beyond the Gestapo, so its heightened interest in Jewry may well have grown in part from Gestapo-SD rivalry.[73]

To convert that rivalry into constructive cooperation, in July 1937, Himmler signed the "Functions Order" (Funktionsbefehl), formalizing a division of labor that Gestapo and SD had worked out. Nevertheless, it hardly created the separate SD identity desired by advocates of intellectual intelligence. It merely clarified the SD role as ideological auxiliary of the Gestapo.[74]

Basically, matters related to "executive" actions and threats to national security that could lead to arrest fell to the Gestapo: Marxism, high treason, and immigrants. As the ideological intelligence agency, the SD dealt exclusively with the study of Freemasonry and legitimate German life—that is, most of the objects covered by Central Department II 2. In a gray area fell ideological enemies such as the churches, Jewry, and right-wing opposition, and the economy and the press. The SD researched the fundamental nature and motivation of such "enemies," while the Gestapo worked on specific cases of criminality. When the SD uncovered suspected criminality, it was to inform the Gestapo. By the same token, the SD was to have access to all Gestapo material that could cast light on its work. The Functions Order led to the exchange of intelligence files, agents, and V-persons. Of course, the division of labor was in no way precise, nor could it overcome the ingrained rivalry and distrust. Nevertheless, it increased formal cooperation and opened doors to the SD for more effective operations, especially for work on Jews. The SD was the prime beneficiary, temporarily.

By the end of 1937, Department II 112 had laid the foundations for Eichmann's war-time career, but the organization under it remained minimally developed. Before the Functions Order, Reinhard Flesch, desk chief II B4 of the Gestapo Office, had expedited cooperation with the Gestapo Office and its Berlin main post. The Functions Order elevated the level of cooperation. The SD Main Office integrated the files from Gestapo headquarters into its own, while at the provincial level, Gestapo posts regularly forwarded material to SD superior regions. The SD sent observers during Gestapo raids and interrogations to ensure that SD interests were not overlooked. By 1938, both agencies cooperated in a concerted drive to remove foreign Jews from positions in Germany, and the SD had established liaison with Jewish organizations and every agency of Party and state involved in emigration. It assisted the departure of poor Jews, otherwise unable to leave, and broke down barriers created by the Reich ministry of economics.[75]

Still, II 112 had minimal success in developing its field system. Despite improvements, reports from the superior regions remained unsatisfactory. Even at that level, but especially in the subregions and outposts, adequate people were simply not available. Desk chiefs still had several responsibilities, and training programs and materials remained perfunctory. The field posts had not developed V-man networks for II 112 work, nor had they acquired Jews as agents; only Gestapo agents were available. So Department II 112 decided that it would try to maintain a V-person and agent network only out of the central office, while field posts would rely entirely on Gestapo interrogations for local information. During this year, Hagen and Eichmann began their trips to Palestine, and other men went elsewhere in Europe to recruit V-persons and agents to expand II 112 contact with international Jewry.[76]

Aside from becoming a small Party agency representing Himmler's interests in the overcrowded bureaucracy dealing with Jewish emigration, the SD had garnered little for its self-justification. Its experts had no claims to superior authority except in Himmler's mind and Heydrich's ambitions, which could change. Its fabled network of all-seeing eyes could see far less than the zealous informers who ran to the Gestapo with every tale. Thus, as late as 1938, on the eve of an escalation in the Jewish problem, the SD had achieved no status in Jewish affairs that truly justified its independent existence.

Of course, it would be wrong to attribute the radicalization of NS-Jewish policy to this minor internal tension, for the pressures that produced the pogrom of 1938 and forced emigration developed largely outside Sipo and SD. Ironically, in 1938, when such developments brought executive responsibility for Jewish emigration to Sipo and SD, the executive character of that work ensured its assignment to the Gestapo, leaving the SD once again in an adjunct capacity.[77] Tensions within

Sipo and SD helped to generate a process of competitive radicalization that may have prepared some members for their future roles.

A more exact source of that SD radicalization on the Jewish problem was the gap between their own sense of propriety and the rabid anti-Semitism of elements in the Party whom they believed they should be guiding. To "lead" these elements, they had to have their own brand of radicalism; thus, their policy between 1934 and 1938 was peculiarly ambivalent. For instance, during the heightened tensions of 1935, the SD used *Schwarze Korps* and other organs to criticize anti-Semitic excesses as harmful. The SD and the Gestapo censored some of the more crude anti-Semitic publications. This was hardly the sign of a relatively pro-Jewish stance under Mildenstein, and the "sophistication" of SD experts in their criticism of crude propaganda can also be attributed to a general opposition to any public education that they themselves did not formulate. Their sophistication lay in their self-proclaimed ability to see the more "subtle links" in the great international network of Jewish conspiracy and to neutralize such threats effectively.[78]

By the end of 1936, the SD had clearly proclaimed its goal of shaping NS Jewish policy. They would force Jewish influence out of all spheres of public life, and then promote emigration. In many respects, this program bore the stamp of Mildenstein's interest in Zionism. Although the SD would push emigration as the solution, the Zionist link soon lost favor, because their emigration plan could strengthen Jewry by creating a Jewish state, and because Palestine seemed too problematic. Although the SD's radical solution based on a "respectable" approach was by definition an interim solution, they proclaimed it the "final solution for their generation."[79]

Despite the drive to focus on enemies whom the police could not fully prosecute, the SD work of Central Department II 1 conspicuously paralleled that of Gestapo Main Department II. Given such overlap, friction continued to grow between Gestapo and SD. Well before the Functions Order, all other branches of the Movement including the SS had been forbidden to participate in police actions. Only the SD could participate in Gestapo actions, and only the Gestapo could call on it to do so. The Gestapo had standing orders to turn over to the SD all material not needed for prosecutions. The Functions Order was only one of many efforts to delineate inseparable missions. Behind the formal cooperation remained insurmountable barriers of mistrust and jealousy. Gestapo detectives viewed SD men as Nazi amateur interlopers. SD men doubted the ideological understanding and commitment of the detectives to combating well-camouflaged enemies whose spirit was present even in many Catholic and conservative detectives themselves.[80]

SD evaluation of the political suitability of policemen exacerbated Gestapo suspicions. It was Nazi political interference in police professionalism.[81] Thus, the Sipo-SD, which was supposed to facilitate union, was caught in the middle. The working SD suspected most detective recruits as inadequately imbued with an NS/SS spirit. Professional detectives saw SS-SD recruits into the Gestapo as unprofessional amateurs and spies. They also had doubts about their own men who joined the SS-SD.

Indeed, the tendency of some low-ranking Gestapo-SD to continue to act like the poorly disciplined SS auxiliaries of the early years perpetuated such feelings. For example, in Bavaria in 1935, an SD man serving as teletypist in a local Bavarian Political Police office used his access to files to find suspected Communists. Without informing superiors, he and buddies in the local SD then tried to entrap them. When their plan backfired, subsequent publicity made the police look like amateurs and led to recriminations and open hostility between the local Bavarian Political Police and the SD.[82] Of course the Danzeisen affair greatly discredited the SD among policemen, encouraging negative conclusions about the sort of V-persons upon whom the SD based its evaluations.

The SD had to look for and report nonconformists and petty offenders. When the Gestapo acted on these reports, SD personnel participated in the raids as observers to collect material. Thus, they "encouraged" the Gestapo's executive actions. Although SD men could boast that they thus provided the essential ideological direction to police work,[83] such activity bore the taint of police agents and provided no secure justification for existence as the police came increasingly under SS command.

In contrast, Central Department II 2 represented a different slant on the mission and image emerging from under the vague umbrella of ideological intelligence. Unlike the work of II 1, which focused on enemies, this section's mission dealt with the "good people" in all spheres of German life, ostensibly not as subjects of suspicion, but of study. The SD leaders involved focused heavily on the image of an agency that kept the Leadership informed about the true state of the nation, and they evolved this SD mission more spontaneously than any other. Initially Himmler was less aware of the full significance of their course, and in subsequent years would periodically limit them. This encouraged them to see themselves as separate from Himmler, much of his SS, and what it stood for. Though a logical outgrowth of Heydrich's imagery, this mission evolved without his active initiative. It came primarily from the intellectual types whom he attracted with idealistic images. He encouraged but did not direct their evolution.[84]

Although Otto Ohlendorf, the later head of the relevant branch of the SD, is normally associated with this development, it originated with Reinhard Höhn. Rapidly rising to lieutenant colonel by January 1937, and leading Central Department II 2, Höhn also became a professor in the Faculty of Law at Berlin and Director of the Institute for State Research.[85]

Both Höhn's personality and his ideological positions significantly shaped intellectual tendencies in the young SD. While still a schoolboy in Meiningen, he became a leader in the Youth-Ring South Thüringia, which involved him in the "fight against trash and filth" (Schund und Schmutz)[86] and Communism. Entering university in 1923, he studied law and national economy and began a short affiliation with the NS Movement. After the failure of the 1923 putsch, he joined the Young German Order, but broke with it in 1929, and devoted his energies to the "scientific study of the idea of the national community." "Against his father's will," he began private teaching at the University of Jena to become "financially independent." Unlike most NS members, but like many SD intellectuals, Höhn was an independent thinker who had trouble subordinating himself to any one authority, especially on the subject of future goals. His early writings on the nature of the Volks community shared in much Nazi imagery, but also contained occasional criticisms of Hitler and the Movement. Later discovery of these produced charges against him and forced his removal from leadership in the SD.[87]

When Höhn first began in the Berlin office, his interest was "learning and the universities." From this sort of work, Höhn's new mission sprang. Like many of the SD, he abhorred the image of spy and informer and preferred that of idealistically serving citizen. Using these images, he recruited from faculty and students an informal body of experts known as the "Intellectual SD" (Geistiger SD). Thus, while Behrend's Central Division II 1 continued to concentrate on enemy observation, Höhn's inclined increasingly toward "analytical reporting on the broad spheres of German life" (Lebensgebietsarbeit). He wished to capture the mood of the nation, to measure public responses to the regime, and to analyze them "for the benefit of the leadership," that is, as a way to influence them "positively."[88]

When Ohlendorf entered Höhn's office in May 1936, they were still reporting on suspect persons, but the future direction had emerged. Ohlendorf had become the expert on economic affairs in agriculture, and Höhn found him appealing, particularly because of his outspoken criticism of economic developments. Ohlendorf claimed that he consented to work in the SD with the understanding that their work would involve critical analysis.[89]

Nevertheless, given Himmler and Heydrich's sense of mission, Six's influence over all of Office II, and Höhn's departure in 1937, the intellectual SD would be frustrated in its efforts to "purify" its mission. Although Höhn had managed to establish the idea that II 2 did not focus on enemies, he could not free it from the assumption that it would contribute to SD work against enemies and would report appropriate cases for Gestapo action.

For instance, in December 1936, Office I, responsible for the overall supervision of the SD's intelligence files, ordered their revision. Although the new guidelines acknowledged the difference between II 1's enemy work and II 2's life-sphere focus, Office I's main concern remained the exploitability of the card files for "executive" actions. II 2 was expected to contribute to person-card-files as well as subject-card-files. The typically ambiguous guidelines provided specific examples of what II 1 would contribute, but were vague about what II 2 would provide.[90] Leaders like Six who were preoccupied with the purification of Germany would neither allow nor appreciate the distinctions Höhn sought. Undoubtedly, their own needs to clean out trash and filth and to fight evil influences also prevented the Höhns and Ohlendorfs from achieving the clean break they held in their minds as an idealized self-image.

A surviving set of person-card-files from an SD subregion shows how even as late as the war years, after Ohlendorf commanded RSHA Office III, which allegedly devoted itself to "pure intelligence," its files also included potential reports to Gestapo for executive action. One must admit, however, that SD members' insistence at the Nuremberg trials that they did not spy for and report people to the Gestapo was not entirely unfounded. Frequently the SD employed "constructive educational methods" for dealing with nonconformists who should have been positive role models. Rather than reporting them to the Gestapo, they had their superiors talk to them. If they proved recalcitrant, the SD engineered disciplinary transfers to increasingly isolated, undesirable posts.[91] As the chapters on the Gestapo have shown, the SD provided surprisingly few reports for Gestapo action.

Still, as late as 1938–1939, the field work under Main Department II 23, Economy, focused as much on specific cases as it did on reporting the general mood. Both to gather information and to exercise its influence, its affiliates operated in the Labor Front and other agencies well positioned for such work. In Main-Franken, the subregion desk for II 23 called regularly on its network to investigate economic situations clearly related to suspected enemy activity. Jewish influences and the evasion of Aryanization were prime concerns. It was as interested in the political inclinations of owners as it was in their business, employee relations, and so on. It was not above nosing into the most specific economic details, such as defaults on one particular loan, where it seemed to be concerned with the justice of the case. As in other fields, this SD main department mixed intelligence gathering with an aspiration to instill proper attitudes and behavior among the German people. It presumed to be a moral as well as ideological monitor and mentor.[92]

Clearly, the SD had evolved a variety of distinct, but unfortunately inseparable missions, many of which were related to the ego identities of the membership. Given the insights into that membership developed in chapter 6, one should be able to explore the theory that the ties between mission and identities that these men generated helped make them more susceptible to involvement in legitimized violence. One can also see how these mixed identities could work so well on both role- and value-oriented men, hitting them with a double dose from both appeals. But first, the remaining SD department and its mission, foreign intelligence, requires review.

The Foreign
Intelligence Mission

The third major SD mission, foreign intelligence and counterespionage, continued to develop more slowly than the others, undoubtedly because the SD never had any claim to a monopoly as it had for domestic Party operations. Also, the SD's alliance with the Gestapo was less helpful in this area.

Once Himmler and Heydrich secured their monopoly of political police power in spring 1934, they could curb domestic competition with the SD. The political police curbed all overt activity by Party agencies in both domestic intelligence and counterespionage. They could not totally eliminate it, however, for others could claim a need for information gathering related to their missions. The SD had to negotiate de-limitations and cooperation in the gray areas of overlap with each agency. In the process, however, they won access to the competitions' contacts and information. The same applied to competing state agencies that could not be denied legitimate domestic intelligence operations.[1]

In the realm of foreign intelligence, there were no such advantages. Both the foreign ministry and the military had preeminent claims to legitimacy and expertise, which Hitler respected. Innumerable other public and private agencies had legitimate information gathering needs outside Germany's borders. The Movement had a welter of such agencies.

In this competition, both the Gestapo and SD actually lost ground at first. In January 1934, the Foreign Ministry got Göring's consent to exclude the Gestapo from intelligence gathering outside Germany. It had to limit itself to border surveillance, domestically available sources, and reports from the Abwehr and Foreign Ministry. In the spring, both the military and the Foreign Ministry combined to win Hitler's support for the official exclusion of both SA and SS (SD) from foreign activities. But the legitimate and indispensable role of the counterespionage branch of the Gestapo, the *Abwehr*-police, in support of the military

Abwehr, and the SD's status as its ideological auxiliary provided the decisive wedge for continued operations.[2]

After January 1935, and after Admiral Wilhelm Canaris became head of the military Abwehr, Werner Best headed the Abwehr-police, and Heinz Jost SD counterespionage. The three developed a modus vivendi that led to extensive cooperation. The Gestapo expanded its legitimate overt and its tolerated covert foreign operations, as extensions of its responsibilities inside Germany. The SD gained military recognition as the replacement of all Party agencies in domestic counterespionage and countersabotage, and related intelligence operations inside the borders, but focused outward.[3]

For the next few years, SD counterespionage would bulk larger than more-general foreign intelligence or espionage. Yet the value of its counterespionage role is questionable. It provided no better contacts than the Labor Front inside industry for recruiting field workers (M-Beauftragter) for the Abwehr. Only from the NS ideological perspective could it recruit better than the Gestapo alone. Most of its reports on sabotage paralleled the Gestapo's and derived from former Labor Front networks. Finally, its own field network increased Abwehr and Gestapo coverage only through redundancy. Only Nazis could believe its special attention to Jews and Gypsies as potential foreign agents made it a valuable ideological supplement.[4] Nevertheless, with military approval as a base, both Gestapo and SD expanded into other realms of foreign intelligence.

Until the late 1930s, SS influence in foreign policy remained minimal. Radical imperialism and quick victories for nationalist foreign policy goals were impossible; therefore, their advocates had little appeal to Hitler for the moment. The moderate and cautious had to hold the positions of power and responsibility. Nevertheless, Hitler kept the radicals on the back burner. They all held some position involved in foreign affairs. Himmler found his entry late, through the problem of racial Germans.[5]

The early exclusion of the SS from influence in foreign affairs had its effect on the SD. For instance, although none of the written agreements with the Abwehr explicitly excluded the SD from foreign intelligence (only from military intelligence), those personally involved generally refer to an agreement with both Abwehr and the Foreign Ministry that severely limited the SD's action. By the same token, they officially excluded the Gestapo. Nevertheless, neither the Gestapo nor the SD could be excluded, for they always had the legitimate claim that for defense against internal enemies they needed foreign contacts to trace their foreign connections. As a result, Gestapo and SD foreign intelligence operations developed, but under bothersome limitations. They had free reign for building information collection facilities on borders, in ports, and through immigration agencies,[6] but their competitors curtailed their foreign-based sources, which remained haphazard.

In addition to military and foreign office obstruction, Party authorities also interfered. Alfred Rosenberg's Foreign Political Office (Aussenpolitisches Amt der NSDAP, APA), had well-established intelligence connections, especially through German students abroad, until Heydrich managed to break and absorb its intelligence department late in 1934. Following the June proclamation of the SD's monopoly over domestic intelligence in the Party, the SD absorbed the Party District and APA domestic intelligence services (ND), heretofore coordinated by Arthur Schumann in liaison with Heydrich. From all appearances, Schumann's foreign intelligence branch in the APA might have eluded Heydrich's grasp indefinitely, but through a process that is not entirely clear, Heydrich brought Schumann and his ND under a cloud of suspicion and absorbed his entire operation.[7]

Meanwhile, other Nazis had also taken over some ostensibly private organizations, while consolidating and controlling others. For instance, the Association for Germanism Abroad (Verein für das Deutschtum im Ausland, VDA), worked for the preservation and development of Germanism among racial Germans. The League of the German East (Bund Deutscher Osten, BDO) was a consolidation of organizations working for eastern expansion and influence. Incidentally, such approved organizations owed their monopolies to Gestapo suppression of their competition,[8] which required in turn their cooperation with the Gestapo.

Hess had formed the most significant of these Party agencies in 1931, the Foreign Organization of the Party (Auslandsorganisation der NSDAP, AO), which served as the Party Gau for members abroad, including seamen. In 1933, Ernst Bohle became its head, and Hess gave the organization strong support. In addition to assisting and indoctrinating racial Germans and German citizens abroad, Bohle sought to operate an intelligence service. He reported on attitudes among Germans abroad, and expanded that into general intelligence on foreign attitudes toward Germany. His organization also focused on enemies among Germans abroad, intimidating and even "arresting" them. In short, he had a counterpart to Sipo and SD for Germans abroad.[9]

Of course, the competitors also had to cooperate, giving the Gestapo and SD opportunities to establish foreign contacts for their own work. In November 1935, however, Frick signed an order channeling through the Foreign Organization all ministerial correspondence (including police) with all foreign posts of the Party. Characteristically, Best forwarded the order to all Gestapo officials, telling them to adhere "as closely as possible."[10]

Abwehr, Sipo, and SD developed liaison with the Foreign Organization. Beginning in November 1936, an SS Lieutenant Waneck established liaison for Sipo and SD. Wherever they did not compete, it cooperated closely with them in the spirit of strengthening national security. One took the Abwehr's right to military intelligence so much for granted that local Foreign Organization and Abwehr workers cooperated too spontaneously. Their operations often exceeded control by either headquarters. One finds indications of similar problems for Sipo and SD cooperation with the Organization, especially in some of the cases of Germans "arrested" abroad and smuggled back into Germany. When the Organization functioned as a clandestine police among Germans abroad, it turned its arrestees over to either the Gestapo or the Criminal Police. The branches of the Organization that performed these "arrests" were the Harbor Service and the Seafarer Section, both under Kurt Wermke. He worked closely with Abwehr, Gestapo, and SD, and was adopted into the SS-SD in spring 1936. The Organization people also kept the Gestapo and SD well informed on returning émigrés and businessmen abroad. Despite increasing ties to SS and SD, Bohle clung to the idea that he should have dominance in political-ideological intelligence abroad, and this led to growing friction as SD intentions to extend its Party intelligence monopoly over the "foreign Gau" became apparent.[11]

Fearing international incidents while Germany remained vulnerable, Hitler called for control over such intrigues. He pressed Hess to regulate the problems of Germans abroad, leading to the 1935 creation of the Central Post for Racial Germans (Volksdeutsche Mittelstelle, VoMi). Since initial efforts failed to establish the desired control, Hess turned to Himmler, on whom he had become increasingly dependent for policing the Party. He asked for an SS man to take charge, giving Himmler his entry into foreign affairs. In 1937, SS General Werner Lorenz took over VoMi, and his deputy became Hermann Behrends, facilitating SD use of that office.[12]

For influence in foreign affairs, Himmler had another entry point. Since 1932, he had had close relations with Joachim von Ribbentrop, who became Deputy for External Political Questions on the Staff of the Führer's Deputy. From the summer of 1935, Ribbentrop had developed his influence, and when he took over the Foreign Ministry in 1938, Himmler's SS and SD expanded freely into foreign affairs. Even before that, however, Himmler established SS and SD liaisons by drawing amenable Foreign Ministry personnel into the SS. For instance, when Himmler was in Rome in December 1936, he inducted Legation Counselor Dr. Emil Schumburg, assigning him to the SD Main Office. Schumburg, as head of the German Desk of the Foreign Ministry, went on to serve until 1944 as a liaison for the SS and SD.[13]

Clearly, the highly vaunted Gestapo and SD foreign network was just beginning during the period of this study, and the two organizations had to rely heavily on others for their work. Himmler could exploit his successful penetration of foreign affairs only after 1938–1939. Nevertheless, both Gestapo and SD had laid foundations for this exploitation by 1936.

The SD's foreign missions grew directly out of the observation of enemies, and through 1936, that remained closely tied to the supplemental police status of the SD. By the same token, this sphere of SD operations was suffused with the parallel SD missions of providing a positive influence, of shaping and molding people and institutions, and of purging the unsuitable from positions in which they could do harm to the cause.

Office III of the SD Main Office, which worked closely with the Gestapo Abwehr police, had two central departments (see Appendix B.5). Central Department III 1, Foreign Life Spheres, concerned itself with intelligence about foreign nations, their public opinion, and some espionage. Central Department III 2, External Abwehr, focused on enemy organizations operating in neighboring states.[14]

This organizational split paralleled that in Office II, distinguishing between "pure" intelligence and enemy observation. Nevertheless, such distinctions seem to have acquired less significance in foreign SD work. Foreign intelligence always has a more positive image than spying on fellow citizens, so it did not compel the same pursuit of positive image and separation from Gestapo work that plagued men in Office II.

Because of the early restrictions, SD foreign intelligence had its origins in the field posts in border areas. To develop a more significant central organization for coordinating this work, in July 1934, Werner Best recruited Heinz Jost and recommended him to Heydrich. As a law trained civil servant in Hesse, Jost had worked with Best, who subsequently drew him into the Hessian Gestapo, where they both ran afoul of Gauleiter Springer. In the SD, Heydrich and Best assigned him responsibility for building the small headquarters section for foreign intelligence. By January 1935, he represented the SD Main Office in negotiations among Abwehr, Gestapo, and SD, becoming Best's SD counterpart. In January 1936, he became head of Central Department III 1, and in May took over III 2 as well, serving as deputy to Heydrich, who acted as head of Office III. Nevertheless, as late as January 1937, Office III remained the smallest in the Main Office, with only twelve officers and twenty-nine other personnel. Considering its extensive involvement in Abwehr work, this small staff reveals very little SD emphasis on foreign intelligence not related to counterespionage.[15]

The personnel of Office III tended to be less academic than those in Office II. Instead, they were men who had lived and traveled widely in their areas of responsibility. Their education or training was frequently in business or agriculture, but they had first-hand knowledge of foreign countries. Like their domestic SD counterparts, those specialists focusing on enemies were divided between those who had appropriate backgrounds and those with an NS/SS-inculcated ability to uncover the ideological enemy.

Early SD foreign operations are the hardest to reconstruct because of the fragmentary evidence and the hyperbole that surrounds most espionage work. One gets the impression that it was the least well-developed component, but this might be misleading. Foreign intelligence centered largely on the superior regions, while counterespion-age was mostly field work coordinated with the Gestapo and Abwehr. The smallness of the central department may have reflected a lean efficiency.

In the realm of foreign activities, the SD retained its primitive raison d'être longest. Since domestic police power did not give the Nazis a legal executive arm for crushing enemies in foreign countries, they still needed organizations to conduct clandestine activities more politically focused than those of the military Abwehr. In Abwehr-police work, as in any other, SS-SD cooperation with the police had begun in the auxiliary police capacity, and, after the spring of 1934, such cooperation in foreign matters remained close. The SD performed assignments that could not be trusted to the police. In this way, the Gestapo, as an agency of the state, remained "innocent." Consequently, in foreign activities, the SD developed and retained a capacity for executive action. The SD's support role for the Gestapo also provided an official pretext for liaison with and support from state agencies involved in foreign affairs, the most important being the military Abwehr and the Foreign Ministry.

Our specific knowledge of early SD operations is unfortunately dependent on the thriller stories of SD memoirists who, nevertheless, provide insight. Among its earliest coups, the SD claimed the exposure of a Czech espionage operation that had penetrated the German High Command. Alfred Naujocks took credit for this work. Heydrich involved himself from the beginning, and made all decisions.[16]

According to Naujocks, his original lead came in August 1934, from a double agent. By his own admission, Naujocks performed amateurishly, and his success resulted from unbelievably dumb luck. The Gestapo made the arrests in the general staff and caught the Czech agents. Naujocks described their operations as so amateurish that one can hardly believe they had significant value. According to the official version, the head of the ring supplied his intelligence simultaneously to Czechoslovakia and the Soviet Union. One gets the impression that Heydrich blew the incident out of all proportion as part of his struggle with the pre-Canaris Abwehr.

The killing of Rudolf Formis in Czechoslovakia in January 1935 was another sensational operation also involving Naujocks, and a clear case of SD-Gestapo cooperation. The Gestapo located a clandestine radio transmitter operated by Formis to broadcast propaganda from Czechoslovakia for Otto Strasser's Black Front. According to Naujocks, a special assignment came from Hitler, and Heydrich had promised to kidnap Formis and bring him back alive. The Gestapo provided Naujocks with support: passports, a car, and equipment. Again, Naujocks tells a colorful tale. Unfortunately, he shot Formis fatally when his peculiar scheme backfired, causing embarrassing publicity in the Czech press.[17]

Both of these stories reveal not only a high degree of amateurism and a flair for juvenile cloak-and-dagger adventures, but also a small, hit-and-miss approach to the illegal foreign espionage of the early SD. They explain conservative military and diplomatic concerns about both the Gestapo and SD. They also show how the NS leadership and Gestapo relied on the SD for special assignments, and how Heydrich involved himself directly, tying together Gestapo and SD. But such sensational adventures were by no means typical of SD-Gestapo foreign work, which, like most intelligence work, if done correctly, replaces romantic adventure with dull routine.

Wilhelm Krichbaum, as director of Main Department III of the Saxon Gestapo in Dresden and an operative of the SD, performed the more typical, officially sanctioned work. In December 1933, to screen émigrés for Czech agents seeking to penetrate the Movement, Rudolf Hess had ordered the creation of a Sudeten German Control Post in Dresden under the Foreign Organization. Allegedly, Heydrich got the job for Krichbaum, who made the post an important Gestapo and SD information-gathering center for Czechoslovakia. The post could use its authority to pressure émigrés to become agents or to provide contacts, and Krichbaum's appointment represented one of the earlier SD penetrations of the Foreign Organization.[18]

Until his recruitment into the SS-SD, Krichbaum had not been a Nazi, but an ardent fellow traveler with links to military Abwehr work. Probably through these channels, he had entered the Saxon police in Abwehr work in the summer of 1933. His subsequent appointment as head of Saxon Gestapo Department III, Abwehr, while simultaneously head of the Foreign Organization control post and a member of the SD,[19] reflected a rapid expansion of SD contacts in military, state, and Party agencies involved in foreign intelligence. They also reveal a widespread, informal network that preceded formal organizational development and paper trails that testify to SD activity.

In addition to gathering intelligence, like his counterparts in internal SD work, Krichbaum interpreted freely. With his close collaborator, Hans Krebs, he issued reports highly critical of the moderates around Konrad Henlein, leader of the Sudeten NS Movement. Thus, he and Krebs may have influenced Himmler's attitudes in favor of the more radical wing in the Sudeten Movement and of more radical approaches in Czechoslovakia. Nevertheless, Himmler understood Krebs' role well enough to be on guard against his infiltration of the SD through Krichbaum's operation.[20] As a result, Gestapo-SD attention to Czechoslovakia greatly expanded by 1935, to draw reports from many other sources.

Typical of the uncoordinated informality of SS-SD foreign work, Himmler maintained his own independent sources, although he shared them with Heydrich. One such was Walter von Lierau, another of Himmler's early links in the Foreign Ministry and a consul in Czechoslovakia. An SS member since 1932, he was assigned directly to Himmler, for special duties. He represented another anti-Henlein influence, and another link with the Foreign Organization, with whom he conspired. His many independent ties bothered Heydrich, however, especially as he began to work with both the SD and the Abwehr in such a way that Heydrich finally recommended his expulsion from the SS. Nevertheless, Himmler kept him on his staff for his useful connections.[21]

Given the geographic encirclement of Czechoslovakia by Germany, the SD had three superior regions focusing on that country: South, Middle, and Southeast, coordinated only through the central department. Two examples of the diversity of Superior Region South's feelers emerge from surviving personnel files. Detective lieutenant Fritz Preis led the Bavarian border police post at Eger in Czechoslovakia under the Bavarian Political Police. He served as an SD V-man from April 1933, and became a member in July 1934. He must have worked with Adolf Puchta, who shortly thereafter became department head in SD Subregion Bavarian East Mark. Puchta was a refugee from Czechoslovakia, where, as a longstanding NS member, he had served as a feeder for a Saxon Gestapo outpost until March 1934, when he was forced to flee to avoid imprisonment for his activities. He was instantly taken into the SS-SD and employed on the Czech border.[22]

Within the Sudeten NS Movement itself, SD contacts were strong in anti-Henlein circles. Both Friedrich Brehm and Otto Liebl, active Nazis since the 1920s, had broken with Henlein in 1936. By 1935, both men had established contact with the SD as V-men, and Brehm later claimed that he built a network of agents across Czechoslovakia, serving the SD and the Abwehr. He asserted that his work formed the basis for the SD's organization in Czechoslovakia after absorption. Both men formally joined the SS in 1939, but only Liebl had SD membership, perhaps as early as 1938, suggesting that Brehm exaggerated his SD service.[23]

In SD Superior Region Southeast, the leader since the summer of 1934 was Ernst Müller, born in Moravia. After serving in the Austrian army during the war, he was a farmer in Altenau. His road from there to a salaried position in the SD in March 1934 is unclear. Evidence of his region's work in Czechoslovakia has yet to surface. But as the Czech situation began to heat up, in the summer of 1937, he got a year's leave of absence, allegedly to attend to his farm, during which time he had a special assignment from Heydrich to conduct "ideological research." He played an undefined role in both the Anschluss and the absorption of the Sudetenland, and returned to SD service in September 1938. After a short stint with the RKFDV in Poland, he turned up on Henlein's staff in the Sudeten Gau, working with RKFDV and VoMi.[24]

SD work directed at Czechoslovakia, like much of its work in the Reich, was directed most heavily at the internal affairs of the Movement. Intelligence on Czechoslovakia in general, as opposed to the Sudeten German Movement, remained sketchy and heavily reliant on press service digests until 1937–1938.[25]

Austria should have been the most easily penetrated foreign realm for the SD, given the presence of an Austrian SS. Austrian SS units had their own intelligence sections, referred to as the ND (Nachrichtendienst) and functioning much like the old SS Ic. Yet they had no organizational tie that provided the SD with Austrian field posts—ND men were not SD affiliates—undoubtedly because of the official ban on SD foreign operations. SS headquarters in Vienna established a central ND, which later became a personal intelligence service to Austrian SS leader Ernst Kaltenbrunner, who provided liaison with Heydrich and Jost. Although it forwarded information on request, the ND preserved its autonomy until 1938, and exchanges between ND and SD do not seem to have been as extensive as one would expect. There is also evidence of rivalry. The SD allegedly had its own network in Carenthia, and at least one operation out of Salzburg was exposed in 1935. Unfortunately, most sources are vague, confused, or otherwise unreliable about SD versus ND operations and relations between them.[26]

As another indication of how covert SD operations had to be in Austria, its direct network was limited to associates. One was SS Lieutenant Otto Butting, who from 1935 to 1937 was the Foreign Organization's group leader for Austria. He built the Austrian group while simultaneously serving as an SD operative. He never had any official SD membership, always carried on SS rosters as doctor for an SS regiment. When, in 1937, the AO transferred him to the Netherlands, Canaris drafted him as a Foreign Organization Abwehr agent.[27] Butting was another example of close Foreign Organization, Abwehr, and SD cooperation and sharing of personnel where they were most useful to collective needs.

Recruits from émigrés in the Austrian Legion provided SD superior regions with an ample supply of men to staff their Austrian desks, but most such men were unsuited for SD work and had moved on by 1937. SD failure to recruit suitable sources among Austrian Nazis before they fled across the border adds to the picture of its limited penetration. Dr. Humbert Achamer-Pifrader was a leading Nazi organizer in the Salzburg police from 1931 to his flight in 1935. He was then recruited by the Bavaria Political Police for Austrian affairs and joined the SS, but the SD did not begin his transfer until the end of 1936, and then only as part of the routine expansion of Gestapo-SD membership. Finally, in November 1937, as an SD member he was assigned to Hess's staff to play a role in the upcoming Anschluss.[28]

In May 1935, the Gestapo Office created a special desk for Austrian intelligence (Dezernat II 1C) under SS Lieutenant Franz-Josef Huber. Records of the comparable SD Main Office desk (III 1131) and Huber's SD counterpart have yet to surface, although from 1935 it was receiving reports from the regional posts, and by 1936 regular monthly Austrian Reports (Oka-Berichte) were arriving from Superior Region South.[29] Little remains of Huber's office work, but what does is mostly press analysis and summaries like the SD work done on Czechoslovakia, rather than solid, highly detailed reports.[30]

Recruitment in 1934–1936 also indicates growth in SD foreign interests toward Northeast Europe. Dr. Erhard Kröger was a law-trained civil servant in Riga, Latvia, who became a member of the SD. He had studied at German and Latvian universities, finishing his doctorate in 1927. By 1932, he had become one of many Nazi adherents among the ethnic Germans, forming secret NS organizations. From 1934 to 1939, he did illegal work for the SD and the Liaison Office for Ethnic Germans (VoMi), lost his government position, and was imprisoned in 1936. In 1938 he would become an SS member, and in the following year would lead Himmler's resettlement program from Latvia and Estonia.[31]

Dr. Friedrich Buchardt provided another important contact in the Baltic states. Another Latvian-German and a product of German universities, he spoke Latvian and Russian and had traveled in Russia. As early as 1933–1934, he formed camouflaged NS organizations. After the police banned his press, he moved to Germany. In June 1935, he became head of the Baltic Department of the Institute for East European Economy in Königsberg. There, in early 1936, he became an SD associate, and beginning in January 1937, he held an SD salaried position with a "special scientific assignment." He may have been one of the earliest SD penetrations into the realm of Ostforschung, on which it would tighten its hold in 1937, when Werner Lorenz and Hermann Behrends began to take over through VoMi. He finally became an SS-SD member in 1938 and eventually served SD interests in Baltic resettlement and as a leader of an Einsatzkommando in Russia.[32]

Given its location, SD Main Region Northeast, centered on Königsberg, provided an SD feeler in the midst of other European states. The establishment of an SD subregion office in Danzig further facilitated operations when local NS control of the Free City allowed the SS to operate openly. In September 1935, SD member Kurt Schneider transferred from the Königsberg office to Danzig and later became head of Subregion Danzig, which he apparently established. It did not appear on any lists of SD offices until December 1936. As the only official SD post outside the borders of the Reich, Danzig served ideally for foreign intelligence. Schneider soon assembled a staff, including experts on foreign countries.[33]

Undoubtedly, among such SD foreign experts, many of whom were foreign-born Germans or expellees from lands lost after the war, were some of the most extreme proponents of radical imperialist policies. As in the case of Czechoslovakia, their reports sought to goad the leadership to more extreme action. One case in point was Dr. Klaus Siebert.

Born in Bernburg on the Saale in 1904, he, like many of those who missed the war, entered free corps combat against the Reds and then found involvement in the Kapp Putsch. After a business apprenticeship, at age nineteen he began studying agriculture in east German universities, "out of the belief that Germany's future lay in the East." In 1930, he moved to Austria to fight "Slavic incursions" and to farm. Involved in the July 1934 Putsch, he returned to Germany. All of Himmler's blood and soil and Drang nach Osten ideology motivated this widely traveled man with many personal contacts in numerous European states. In January 1935, he became a salaried member of the SD, and after 1941 helped increase SD influence in VoMi.[34]

Hitler's first territorial gain, the Saarland, lay in the west, however, and had also been the focus of early SD work. The Saar was also a rat's nest of competing Nazi interests and clandestine operations. According to Göring, too many intelligence services fed unverified information, leading to counterproductive actions. He outlawed all such operations from Prussian soil and forbade the Gestapo from having contact with them inside the Saarland. One such was that of SS Lieutenant Otto Lürker, the adjutant of SS Sturm 10 for Saar-Pfalz. Lürker had been Hitler's attendant in Landsburg prison and had close ties with Hess. Nothing indicates who authorized him to move to Zweibrucken and set up his operation; he probably served as (Ic) intelligence officer for Sturm 10 and the SD, for he later claimed that he was then active with the SD. According to "Koehler," an alleged SD and Gestapo operative in the Saar, his operations threatened any systematic work there and greatly bothered Gauleiter Bürckel.[35]

In spring 1934, Werner Best did indeed transfer Lürker to his Superior Region Southwest, where he subsequently led SD post Saargebiet, and then Subregion Baden. He had a full SD career, rising to colonel and leading several SD regional offices. Evaluators generally praised his work as post leader, but in terms typical of evaluations recommending promotion. References to his service in the Saar ranged from fulsome to ambivalent praise. Perhaps Best drew him into the SD both for his influential contacts and to control his problematic Saar operation. He certainly did not trust Lürker as his sole handle on the Saar, for in March 1934, he assigned to Ludwigshafen an old crony from Hesse to establish a border intelligence post for the superior region's work in the Saar.[36] His post, not Lürker's, became the seat for SD focus on the Saar.[37]

As elsewhere, Saar operations existed primarily to fight enemies of the Movement and to report on unsuitable Nazis. Best's foreign intelligence network out of Superior Region Southwest established a reputation for him that led to his command of the Abwehr-Gestapo and his good working relationship with Canaris' Abwehr. In addition to the Saar, Southwest reported primarily on Switzerland and France, especially Alsace-Lorraine.[38]

Also strategically located, Superior Region West covered France,

Luxembourg, Belgium, and the Netherlands. Its surviving records are reports forwarded from Subregion Aachen. These were almost exclusively multipage analyses produced by Dr. Wolfgang Ispert from at least 1936. Ispert was the principal in the (VDA) for political affairs on the western border, and it is not clear if he had official approval for his collaboration. He was apparently trying to use the SD to support his bid for consolidated control over political operations across the western borders. His ten- to twenty-page reports were well-informed assessments from a Nazi ideological perspective.[39]

In one such report, Ispert presented an overwhelming picture of the complexity of Nazi operations across the western border. North of the Saar alone, he identified more than fifty agencies, some as fronts or under umbrella organizations, others as the local operatives of twenty-two major agencies of Party or state, such as the ministries of interior, culture, and propaganda; four Gauleiters; the Hitler Youth; the German Student Body; the VDA, the Foreign Political Office, Bureaus Ribbentrop and von Kursell; the League of Western Germans; and numerous research institutes. They gathered information, propagandized, and spied on and sought to control Germans and fascists in Belgium, Luxembourg, and the Netherlands. These did not include operations from the Saar-Pfalz, Baden, or Württemberg, nor legitimate intelligence operations of the foreign ministry, Abwehr, or Foreign Organization. To this list, the SD subregion leader added the work of the Psychological Department of the War Ministry, and a secret SA intelligence service under Captain von Pfeffer. Interestingly, this SD officer admitted complete ignorance of what the Foreign Organization was doing in his area.[40]

All this activity was revealing. It is not unusual in any country for many different agencies and individuals to have public and private interests across their borders, and complete lack of coordination would be normal. However, a new totalitarian zeal infected those who sought to shape and control everything leading to the new order. That same mentality demanded that these efforts be coordinated for harmony and efficiency. But inevitably, the different power centers disagreed over who would coordinate.

Predictably, the local SD worried over lack of coordination and wanted to know the many independent field operatives, their connections, and their personal convictions. The local leader cited several cases of counterproductive actions, and proposed that the SD intervene in support of Ispert's plan. Ispert wanted himself and SS-General Hoffmeyer, with similar responsibilities for the east, to work directly under Ribbentrop.[41]

Such was the welter of confusion and competition in foreign affairs in which the SD gradually expanded its operations and gained recognition for their legitimacy. By as late as 1937, its intelligence gathering and analysis were not impressive, rarely going beyond exploitation of the press and other public sources. Most of its energy seems directed at the interpenetration of competing agencies and their interlocking contacts among Germans abroad. As in domestic operations, these they sought to observe, evaluate and manipulate.

The SD

Personnel and Images

By 1935–1936, the character of SD membership may have begun to change, but such changes did not involve a "new generation" or new types. Men born after the war, children of the depression who received their formal education during NS dominance, did not appear until 1939 and never became a pivotal force. No new socioeconomic presence emerged. Instead, the change involved shifts of proportional representation among types already present. Although precise analysis will require more extensive research, one can make a few safe generalizations.[1]

Among the 1935–1936 recruits, the trend toward youth continued. The vast majority belonged to the post-1901 cohort, with average age around twenty-six or twenty-seven. Even so, recruit ages still ranged from the early twenties to the fifties. Simultaneously came a decline in status within the Movement. Fewer were Old Fighters, and more than one-third joined after the "power seizure," most in 1933. Lower Party standing was not always a function of increased youth, however. Many younger recruits had been active but underage for Party membership, while many older recruits came from police or government offices where affiliation might have hurt their careers.

One can construct a representative sample of men promoted to officer (or inducted as officers) in 1936 to compare with the SD officer corps of 1934. There are few significant changes.[2] They were only a slightly younger version of the existing corps. In region of birth, they more closely approximated national norms, reflecting the truly national base of recruitment that was now open. Religiously, the skew was ever stronger against Catholic origins, reflecting the increasingly anti-Catholic posture. However, 23 percent would never withdraw from their church compared with 11 percent of the earlier officers, perhaps because the larger percentage of Protestants felt less pressure to do so.[3] Nevertheless, they were subject to the same pressures for withdrawal, for officers who did not were denied further promotion.[4] Thus, this 12 percent difference may indicate an increased number of "less-committed" joiners, willing to go only so far in NS-SS-SD affiliation.

The educational and social dichotomies within the SD seem to have been growing. Educationally, the 1936 officers averaged slightly lower than their predecessors, but included more Ph.D.'s. Coming from all social levels, more of these men were educational underachievers; at the same time, more of those whose fathers held traditional lower-middle-class and transitional occupations pursued higher education more aggressively.

On the average, they were slightly higher in social origins, judging by their father's occupations, and also achieved slightly higher status. Yet, in contrast, a slightly higher percentage had suffered some loss of status at time of entry into the SD.

It is easier to detect the appeal these new officers had for the SD, perhaps because recruitment was becoming less personal and more driven by rational organizational needs. Significantly more (25 percent as opposed to 18 percent in 1934) were drafted to serve as contacts in state, Party, finance, or industry as part of the expanding network of affiliates intended to keep the SD informed and to extend its influence. These newer officers would remain predominantly in the lower ranks, with only 41 percent rising above captain, as opposed to 71 percent of the 1934 officers.

Such generalizations about officers in the total SD are distorted by the shift toward an ever-larger Sipo-SD component. Almost 39 percent were drawn for service in Sipo-SD. A full 34 percent had been SS members in the political police. Half of them had been ordinary SS men who penetrated the Gestapo from the lowest ranks of employees and were not originally professional policemen or qualified civil servants.

Below officer level, one can detect other trends toward recruitment of "base personnel" as opposed to the rapid organization building of the previous years. Most of the recruits who entered in the lower ranks rose more slowly. Their commissions would come in 1938–1939, or, more commonly, later. In other words, the organization focused more on filling its ranks with younger men to be trained as future leaders and staff specialists.

Clearly, the absorption of Gestapo men that began in 1935 brought a major shift within SD membership. With the decision to draw all SS members of the political police into the SD, the police element received a sizable boost—about one-third of all recruits in 1935 and 1936. Of course, only a minority had been professionals before the Nazi era; most were new NS policemen, usually SS men.[5]

Since these Sipo-SD recruits contained many lower class, less educated, unemployed NS youth and Old Fighters who had earned brutal reputations as auxiliary police, they detracted from SD respectability. Consequently, local SD officers recommended rejection of many as "unsuitable for SD." After considerable deliberation, the SD Main Office did reject some, producing their dismissal from the Gestapo, but accepted others.[6] Headquarters had to balance between the desired SD image and the demands of NS-SS brotherhood. Nevertheless, without benefit of theory, the SD strove to weed out those more likely to behave as rule oriented rather than role oriented.

With this influx, the Sipo-SD became a sizable component of the total SD with a special status all its own. These policemen were full-fledged members of the SD, but unsalaried. Their employment was with the state, and they were designated members of an SD section in their state police post. The section was supposed to handle their SS-SD personnel and administrative affairs, but failed to do this well during the rapid growth of 1935.[7] What special assignments they received as SD members within the Gestapo remains unclear, but they undoubtedly evaluated their colleagues. Surely, they received special indoctrination and guidelines to facilitate ideological influence over the rest of the Gestapo.

Thus, in addition to the salaried and unsalaried members who constituted the "working SD," the special category of Sipo-SD emerged formally after June 1936 to contain these policemen. Together, they constituted the total SD. This trend toward different categories of SD membership conflicted with simultaneous efforts to regulate personnel practices within the SS. So did semiautonomous SD recruitment. In the early years, Heydrich had exercised considerable independence, recruiting often outside the SS. During 1935–1936, Himmler and Heydrich initiated steps toward regulating and coordinating SS and SD policies, primarily to bring SD membership into line with that of the SS.

The SD remained partially immune to the physical requirements and even some racial criteria for SS membership. Even so, although the SD suffered little from the purge that allegedly eliminated 60,000 men from the SS between 1933 and 1935, it did respond to Himmler's tightened membership criteria. For instance, in addition to the arbitrary physical requirements, by September 1935, Himmler required all SS, sergeant and above, to have complete genealogical records for themselves and their wives as far back as 1800. All subsequent recruits had to trace back to 1750. Detection of "undesirable" blood lines or failure to complete the chart usually resulted in expulsion.[8]

Himmler's requirements caused many headaches for Heydrich and his staff, already severely hampered in getting qualified personnel. Thus, they persuaded him to treat SD recruits as a special category. From May 1936, SD members did not have to meet the full criteria for physical fitness, and cases of doubtful racial background were treated individually. The SD forwarded to Himmler the records of otherwise unsuitable candidates, and he evaluated each one personally. However, he offered these special dispensations only until April 1938, and said nothing about the fate of those exceptions already in service after that date.[9] This compromise pressured the SD to limit its exceptions.

For example, one who proved unretainable was an Old Fighter who had become an auxiliary police leader with the Braunschweig Political Police. From this position, he had risen to SS major and acquired police civil service rank. In 1935, he transferred to the SD. But by September 1937, incomplete genealogical records for himself and his wife had become such a problem that he had to resign from the SS-SD.[10]

For simple members, Himmler's criteria created extra burdens. Genealogical research requires much correspondence and paperwork. Although the state set severe limits on what a church could charge for documentation, complete documentation costs for one person could run to 25 RM. Costs for both husband and wife could considerably strain a young family's resources, coming to 25 percent of a junior sergeant's monthly salary. Much worse, some men had to chose between "unsuitable" fiancees and their SD career. Their decisions provide clear measures of commitment to the SD, and may have split fairly evenly between those who opted for the SD and those who chose the loves of their lives.[11]

Beginning in 1935, Heydrich's authority to induct full members independently of SS entry became more restricted. Himmler ordered a review of all SD men recruited from outside the SS and, henceforth, required all subsequent recruits to earn simultaneous entry. Heydrich retained some independence, for despite Himmler's tightened control, he could still involve men as associates.[12] Nevertheless, such cases became increasingly rare in the personnel records, suggesting less frequent resort to associate, salaried staff personnel. They represented only temporary expedients for employing badly needed experts before the SS bureaucracy could process their membership.[13] Few held such status indefinitely.

To meet SD needs, the SS frequently cut its own red tape. Since Heydrich could draw upon the large pool of SS members for talent, cases of associate status for experts became rarer. By spring 1936, when they found a desirable expert in the enlisted ranks, any SD main region could detail (kommandiert) him from his SS unit for up to six months. Apparently, only the SD Main Office could detail an officer. If one proved desirable for permanent service, the main region would apply for his final transfer.[14] Thus, his "on-command" or provisional transfer status paralleled his SD probation.

SS promotions continued with little regard for role in the SD. Throughout 1935 and 1936, Himmler promoted almost automatically men with low SS numbers. Nevertheless, to provide some balance, because the SD was "still engaged in its formation," he granted an exception to his rule against non-SS recruits being inducted with officer's rank. Approval of all SS membership and rank still had to go through SS personnel offices.[15]

Beyond all the complications caused by ties to the SS, the SD generated its own irregularities. It probably never achieved anything like the standardized, performance- and suitability-based career scale that usually goes with professional organization. Although Himmler decreed such a system for Sipo and SD in early 1938, Heydrich's staff remained embroiled until the eve of the war in the complications of adopting it. Undoubtedly, it never reached fruition. In the process, Schellenberg revealingly observed that for the early SD, any such system had been entirely outside consideration. Positions were filled on the basis of the suitability of those immediately available and the SD's momentary needs. The results were haphazard advancement, with men of unequal qualifications in comparable positions and much uncertainty about one's potential for advancement. SD careers were unstable. Most suitable SD men allegedly rose with extraordinary rapidity, but some could remain indefinitely in place with no way of determining why advancement was not forthcoming.[16]

Since the SD continued to employ unsalaried, part-time members in positions where it needed full-time staff, it created further problems. For instance, in March 1936, SS Lieutenant Colonel Julius Plaichinger, an economic expert in the SD Main Office since 1933, requested release from his duties. He had begun unsalaried work in Munich with the understanding that he could continue full-time in his profession. With the transfer of headquarters to Berlin, his problems began, and he had to leave.[17]

In contrast to its erratic personnel policies, SS-SD pay and other conditions of work had become attractive, at least until the economy improved and older careers could be resumed lucratively. In 1935–1936, a married SS-staff sergeant could earn from 180 to 215 RM per month. In addition, to encourage fecundity, Himmler provided supplements, 10 to 30 RM for each child, providing a boost for the typical SD family with two to three children. Between 1933 and 1939, the average salaried income in Germany rose from 127 to 188 RM per month, and that of the self-employed from 208 to 480. Secondary school teachers earned from 386 to 661 RM. The average attorney's receipts were 900 RM, while the average physician earned 1,042 RM. An SS captain (Hauptsturmführer), the highest rank most SD men achieved, could earn from 330 to 395 RM, while generals peaked at 1,000 to 1,350 RM.[18] On the negative side, apparently retirement and survivors' benefits were not yet available.

Paid leave was generous, according to the official tables. The workweek was Monday through Saturday, with Sundays off.[19] A few records indicate that men had to forgo vacations to cover their workload at times during SD history, but no consistent data indicate whether the stipulated vacation releases from a six-day workweek were achieved most of the time. Probably not.

By early 1935, members of the working SD were exempt from the work service (Arbeitsdienst) required of the rest of the SS. Such a privilege did not extend to military service. All members of the total SD had to complete military obligations in order to maintain their status.[20] This remained true until the priorities of the war years took hold. Until then, up to 3.5 percent of the total SD was relieved of duty at any given time for military service, usually reserve exercises. Despite exemptions, during the war, from 12 to 20 percent were on leave to the military.[21]

Clearly, although some members achieved positions that might otherwise have eluded them, SD membership garnered for most a secure station at a standard of living at least comparable to what they could have achieved in a "normal" Germany. SD membership probably got some out of the depression faster than those outside NS employment channels, but probably no faster than those within. Less tangible elements like prestige and psychological fulfillment refocus our attention on the SD's image and ego identities.

A corps of underpaid, self-sacrificing, model citizens was part of that image.[22] "Orb" portrayed a less positive version of that image in his insider's exposé. Noting that most high-ranking members allegedly handled "many hundreds of thousands of RM in bribe money," he marveled at SD efficiency at controlling graft, and at the severity of an alleged "secret SD honor court" which dispensed death sentences executed by the "SD-Rollkommando." He also claimed that they were held to an exemplary family life under close scrutiny. One's immediate supervisor allegedly intervened on a wife's first complaint, and a third complaint resulted in an honor court.[23]

Personnel records discredit these images as fancifully embroidered half-truths. Until the war's greatly increased opportunities, incidences of graft and corruption were indeed rare, considering the potential. A few men succumbed, especially to the opportunities offered during Reichskristallnacht.[24] During the war, although the incidence rose, transgressions do not seem extraordinarily common, given the temptations and an environment of moral disintegration.

Private lives and morals were also unextraordinary in every sense. Some SD men involved themselves in extramarital affairs and unseemly confrontations with others, but again the rate seems within norms. The divorce rate seems neither especially high nor low. Such peccadilloes brought undesirable comments in one's evaluations, but the consequent effects on one's SD career seem no greater on the average than in most military organizations. A few outstanding exceptions occurred when the unlucky individuals drew Himmler's personal attention.

All cases of graft, corruption, or other felonies were handled by regular SS courts, of which the SD had a branch. There are no signs of special severity in punishments or of anything like a camouflaged execution, not even an official one in the more than one thousand files examined, and there are only a few arrests, imprisonments, or frontline assignments.

Nothing casts more light on the SD's ethos than its training programs. Throughout, the SS evaluated its men for their military bearing and demeanor. Yet this was not in the spirit of authoritarian martinets, but rather a "new model army" ideal inherited from World War I trench camaraderie. SS soldierly virtues included an open spirit of camaraderie among all ranks, not a class-conscious deference to rank. Officers and NCOs had to command obedience through earned respect, not intimidation and Kadavergehorsam.[25] In addition, the SD especially prided itself on a working environment in which rank gave way to a team spirit. Each man's contribution and viewpoint were to be evaluated on their merits, and all were drawn into participation. Such a format of student-centered learning characterized SD instruction, and participants were called on to render a critical evaluation of the instructors' success in achieving such an atmosphere.[26]

Of course, the SD fell short of its ideals, but probably no further than most institutions. Many SS officer candidates were relegated to the SD precisely because their lack of soldierly qualities were balanced by capacities needed by the SD. Even men initially judged unsuitable in SD evaluations found full careers, because it badly needed contacts, skills, or knowledge insufficiently available in the stock of fully suitable candidates.[27]

In January 1935, the SD initiated a one-week general course for working-level personnel, intended to ensure uniformity of perspective and spirit. Heydrich and Best doubted the sufficiency of local training. The first class assembled at the new SD School in Berlin Grunewald. The top leaders took the mission so seriously that Heydrich gave the inaugural pep talk, defining the spirit of the SD, and Best made the first informational presentation, also emphasizing the SD ethos.[28]

Students responded positively to the balance between soldierly discipline and treatment as "equivalent colleagues." Most specialists from the main office who made presentations maintained this balance and avoided professorial lectures. Only old "Professor" Schwartz-Bostunitsch fell back on reading authoritative conclusions from his research, and stood out as "inappropriate" in style. Only the principal for economics failed to impress the students with a mastery of his subject. Such observations revealed some degree of success in achieving a "criticizing (intellectual) activity in the positive sense."[29]

Of course, Heydrich and Best made the strongest impressions. Yet their presentations contained tensions between values and roles characteristic of polar tensions already uncovered in this analysis. For instance, Heydrich called for open exchanges and positive criticizing to build an SD that would both save NS from corruption and enable each SD man "to represent with iron discipline the will of the Führer and to follow his orders up to the point of self-renunciation." In their private lives, SD men should exhibit uncensorable moral conduct, yet in the pursuit of higher goals for society, they would have to do things otherwise dishonorable if done out of self-interest. "Principle: personal conscience and perception of honor are subordinate to the goal and mission of the SD...."[30] One could not ask for a more clear appeal to Kelman's role orientation. Yet aside from the inherent moral dilemma, one had to square "open" exchanges and "positive" criticism with a blind adherence to a reality defined absolutely by the Führer.

Heydrich also poured out a diatribe against Catholicism that reflected the SD's current preoccupation. Since no ties could hinder the SD man from a full application of the ideas of the Führer, no Catholic attending confession could serve. It was virtually impossible to win reliable collaborators from among members of Catholic communities. Instead, reliable NS youth had to be inserted into such enemy organizations that could not be outlawed, so that within twenty years SD men would lead them. Thus, not immediate successes, but long-range plans were the most pressing missions of the SD.[31]

As the data on newer officers show, in following this logic, the SD had begun to exclude from its ranks many of those other-minded Catholics it had previously drawn upon, and was forcing from the community of the Church those already in the SD who might have served its goals of infiltration. Once paranoid ideological lines were drawn, the "positively criticizing" SD severely constrained pursuit of its own goals.

Best also drew some impossibly fine lines. The SD did not spy on SS comrades. Instead, "when offenses of active SS men or officers were confirmed" (note the use of passive voice), one should inform the appropriate SS superiors directly, without recourse to SD channels. "The SD is also no secret organization. Every German can know of its existence and its local offices." The local leader should be held in such esteem that anyone who felt anything amiss could come to the local SD in complete confidence. Yet the primary duty of each SD member was total secrecy. Their collaborators and informants must never be known to anyone. But since such immunity could lead to irresponsible false witness against honorable persons, such agents had to be constantly warned that they were subject to prosecution for slander or other abuses of their trust. All this would somehow square the circle of contradictions and make the SD an "intelligence service that possessed the trust of the entire Volk."[32] Needless to say, such trust failed to materialize, even within the comradely ranks of the SS.

Examples of both cooperation and friction characterized SS-SD relations and make all generalizations unsatisfactory. Many SS men harbored a growing hostility toward the SD comparable to that felt by Party members and policemen. They simply distrusted spies. Many suspected that SD experts and informers were recruited too freely from "unreliable elements," meaning some group toward which one was hostile, like intellectuals, bureaucrats or policemen. Agreements dating from 1935–1936, formally regulating SD liaison with other branches of the SS, are notably similar to those intended to delimit SD activities vis-á-vis Party and state agencies, suggesting a comparable level of friction.[33]

In contrast, while the SD role in the Röhm purge had reaffirmed its image as spies in some circles, for others it made the SD a beacon of hope that drew idealists. Most such Nazis came from the more established elements of society that had been disturbed by the uncontrolled elements. They had a strong sense of order and of their own obligations to help preserve it. For them an organization like the SD could provide the appropriate sense of direction. This image also drew previously non-NS representatives of the respectable, educated classes, especially their younger sons, just beginning careers.[34]

Such trends brought no abrupt break with the past, however, for the SD's recruitment pool remained as diverse as before. For instance, the SD continued to provide employment for ordinary Party members in need. Typical was Fritz, the son of a Lutheran pastor. He had tried to pursue the legal education that opened doors to government careers, but had to give this up in 1930 because of family finances. From then on, he claimed he could not get employment due to his political reputation, and, therefore, he devoted himself full-time to the Party. Given his involvement with the Movement since before the 1923 putsch, the Party owed him something. In March 1935, at the age of thirty-one, he found his first real salaried position in the SD.[35]

Lest one dismiss all such examples as shiftless, undeserving men who used hard times to excuse failure and exploited political contacts to win sinecures, the case of a diligent, hard worker bears mention. The son of an estate steward, he remembered a hard childhood of war years and the inflation. At age fourteen, family economic problems terminated his schooling, but he remained self-reliant. He became a typesetter, and, while working, continued his education, finally attending university. Meanwhile, he joined the Hitler Youth in 1929 and the SA and Party in 1931. He remained employed until 1935, when he quit for a salaried SD position. Undefeated by hard luck, he had always aspired to more, and an SD career finally offered it. In 1937, he became an officer and rose to captain by 1941.[36] As a source of jobs for loyal Nazis, the SD drew more than ne'er-do-wells.

Furthermore, following the dissolution of the organization of the SA Chief of Training Affairs in January 1935, large numbers of its university men found positions in the SD. Given both that office's role in paramilitary training for school youth and the SA-military conflict,[37] the SD had penetrated it and developed well-established contacts. In turn, SD penetration enhanced its base of recruitment in academic circles.[38]

To achieve its mission of influencing policy decisions and public behavior, the SD recruited from among influential persons. By the beginning of 1936, when Himmler had ordered a survey of SS ranks to identify "intellectually leading men," SD Main Region Rhein reported numerous members in prominent positions—for instance, two university professors and two faculty in teachers' colleges. Uncharacteristically, this region had no public school teachers as members, but its V-net did. Professionals included two states attorneys and a lawyer in private practice. There were two newspaper editors and a member of the German Information Bureau. In government, the head of the district at Koblenz, three city administrators, and a mayor were members, supplemented by numerous similarly placed V-persons. There was also a high administrator in the Railroad Directory at Kassel. Among the Sipo-SD were three Gestapo field post leaders, their assistants, and growing numbers at all levels. They included six additional jurists.[39] Only one of these distinguished men had turned to the SD for employment. The rest served without pay.

This tendency to recruit men for their influential positions also made the SD an early home in the SS for men whom Himmler personally cultivated. For instance, Fritz Kranefuss and Dr. Wilhelm Voss had important positions in or contacts with business and industry and were forming themselves into Himmler's Friendship Circle.[40] Likewise, under Werner Best's leadership, Höhn and SD lawyers sought to reshape German law along "positive" lines. Not only did they court amenable jurists and plant articles to sell ideas about their desired police state, they also sought to dominate influential agencies like the Academy for German Law.[41] Their efforts to penetrate academia and shape educational policy reveal still more links between their identities and the missions they evolved for the SD.

Typical of that educated elite and its ethos was Dr. Wilhelm Spengler, recruited in 1933 as expert on religious affairs for Superior Regions Middle and South-East. He then created the previously mentioned Leipzig Literature Post. Spengler was a freshly minted Ph.D. in German literature, history, philosophy, and art history. He had such conflicts with Catholic authority in high school that he turned in reaction to the study of "the positive counter-influences of the Germanic cultural heritage." He pursued a career in high school teaching to impart an appreciation of *völkisch* culture to German youth. Nevertheless, Spengler was not drawn to the NS Movement. His later excuse for this failure was preoccupation with his educational mission and a sideline in social work with unemployed, young academics. He also claimed that he did not join along with other teachers in spring 1933, because he disdained bandwagon jumping. But in the fall, Beutel recruited him with high talk of the intellectual-ideological mission. Apparently, he saw the SD as a vehicle for achieving his goals, and he proposed that he establish an SD post for the evaluation of German Literature. When it was approved, he gave up teaching and began his ambitious project.[42]

Spengler provides another example of how the SD drew intellectuals into first its mission, and then the full NS cause. He was intellectually competent enough to graduate magna cum laude and get his dissertation published. He was of sufficiently independent mind to reject the dualistic authoritarianism of high school religious indoctrination. The rejection was clearly along intellectual lines. What remains to be tested is whether he turned to the "germanischen und deutschen Geisteserbe" in search of more pluralistic richness or a more monolithic source of authority. His failure to embrace Nazism as *the* answer implies the former—that he was drawn into the Movement through the SD appeal for independently minded intellectualism, then immersed in the SS view of reality. We badly need to study the writings of such SD intellectuals to determine if and when they began using völkisch and NS concepts in reductionist, dualistic terms, or if they employed more pluralistic, mature metaphors.

Since education and culture at all levels interested the SD, it recruited actively among students and professional intellectuals. By no means were SD interests limited to gathering intelligence; their energies focused equally on influencing intellectual developments. Thus, they became active agents in NS student and academic associations and state and Party agencies intended to direct education and scholarly research. They took sides in both intellectual controversies and factional squabbles with their usual mix of antiestablishment intellectuality and self-righteous zeal. They might well have become the directors of German education, had the Reich survived.

Scholars debate the relative success or failure of Nazi penetration of the faculty.[43] Apparently, most faculty were intellectually sympathetic and lent the regime a decisive credibility. Nevertheless, they maintained a degree of intellectual independence that justified hard-line Nazi distrust of academics. Unlike student organizations, academia is deeply entrenched. Only a long-term program of penetration like that of the SD would have won the desired degree of control. Some junior faculty and others outside the conventional establishment clearly drew into SD membership, but we have no serious study of penetration. Most recruits among established faculty were V-persons, which may never be measurable. Early SD reports on various universities express a dissatisfaction indicating lack of the desired influence, although the picture is clouded by their partisan ties to particular academics like Ernst Krieck and his program.[44]

For German students, we have a better picture of the degree of SD success.[45] The prime example of SD penetration and control was Dr. Gustav Adolf Scheel. A medical student at Heidelberg in 1930, Scheel joined the NS Student League and quickly entered SA and Party. In 1931–1932, as leader of the German Studentenschaft in Baden, he led a campaign against a Jewish professor targeted by the Nazis. By 1934, he had risen to Gauführer of the Student League. Then he entered the SD and expanded his career as a professional political student to become head of the new SD school at Berlin Grunewald.[46]

Typically, the SD had no intention of disrupting his work in NS student organizations. He remained active as student leader in Baden, and between 1934 and 1936 helped keep the peace between the Studentenschaft and its rival NS German Student League. While the Reich-wide conflict between these student groups mounted, he may have played a role in discrediting their leaders, and through the SD convinced Himmler and the Reich Leadership to terminate their divisive influence among students. As a result, in November 1936, Hess appointed him Reich Student Leader with authority over both organizations. By this time, Scheel also headed SD Main Region South-West. Thus, to fulfill its joint role as intelligence agency and shaper of the new society, the SD increasingly overextended its key people. While remaining Reich Student Leader, Scheel rose to Inspector of Sipo and SD, and in the Party to Gauleiter. In the end, his personal goal and that of the SD was fulfilled when, in his testament, Hitler named him Reich Minister of Education.[47]

Such a fruition in futility typified SD pursuit of its ego images. To maintain one's influence and status, one had to make so many compromises with the dominant elements of the NS world view and the realities of NS infighting that whatever correctives one achieved became meaningless. This may have been so true of Scheel that it is now impossible to determine what educational and academic ideals he truly pursued. He proclaimed programs to provide educational access for underprivileged students, but grossly underfunded them and did not support similar but potentially more effective programs.[48] Of course, budget realities frustrate educational ideals in the best of societies, and the personal infighting among Nazis frequently prevailed over principles. He subsequently presented himself as a champion of more intellectual freedom for students than other Nazis would allow. He allegedly sought some reintegration of religious students into student activities. Indeed, in 1935, trainees at his new SD school credited him for the critical-egalitarian atmosphere of the program. Yet he was in the forefront of efforts to ensure that students and future academics be the right-thinking products of NS indoctrination, and he used Sipo and SD to purge the universities of unsuitable students. Out of fear of the effects on his position should his enemies carry stories to the Führer, he would even stifle student political humor with the admonition that they "did not have sufficient insight nor above all the right to make apparently humorous remarks in this field."[49]

An inability to include within legitimate intellectual freedom viewpoints that differ too far from one's own is not a unique problem among respected intellectuals in any society. Right, left, and center share a concern that deviant elements will abuse intellectual freedom. Nazis like Scheel certainly abused it, but of course, saw their action as a righteous counterattack against the true abusers. The problem in assessing the commitments of SD intellectuals is that of not being able to immerse oneself in their frame of reference. One cannot juggle together such resonantly conflicting values: egalitarianism and racism; a positively critical evaluation of NS ideology untroubled by its antihumanisitic tenets and its total submission to the will of the Führer. To arrive at such intellectually mature values as Scheel proclaimed yet to behave as he did, one had to arrive at firm intellectual commitments and then shut down the critical processes by which one did so. The psychological pressures that drive one to such extremes would have to be experienced to be fully understood. The parent or teacher who has been caught in a contradiction between his teachings and his behavior, driven by reality, has experienced it on a small scale. To know that a harmless joke told by one's students could destroy a network of imagined influence built at great sacrifice of principles and psychic energy could drive anyone to self-delusion.

The story of one of Scheel's colleagues, Dr. Martin Sandberger, casts a different light on this problem. He had been leader of the Tübingen Studentenschaft, so they had worked together from 1933. By 1935, Sandberger had earned his Ph.D. and was working in juridical service toward his final exam, while simultaneously doing salaried work for the SA Chief of Educational Affairs. Then Scheel recruited him into the SD. In January 1936, he became leader of department II 2 in Scheel's main region.[50] Doing double duty like Scheel, he served also as Commissioner of the South-West Region for the Reich Student Leader. According to Scheel, he wooed Sandberger with the idealistic intellectual image of the SD in which he strongly believed. Its membership, chosen for their dedication and quality, were to provide the Leadership with objective information and positive suggestions.[51]

For several years in the Reich Student leadership, Sandberger disseminated NS/SD influence in university and juridical circles by placing contributions in influential journals. By 1937, the organization extended beyond Reich borders to university students in Austria and east European states. By 1940, however, assigned to the personnel office (Amt I) of the RSHA after rising to highest SD positions and serving a stint as head of an immigrant center,[52] he had become dissatisfied with SD work. Perhaps its idealistic image had tarnished.

There are only a few clues to what might have gone wrong. According to Scheel, from 1936 to 1939 he and Sandberger had dedicated themselves to helping the economically underprivileged qualify for higher education, and had frustrated NS efforts to discriminate against theology students. But historian Geoffrey Giles argues that such work was nowhere as successful as Scheel contended, so perhaps that caused Sandberger's disillusionment. Other friends testified that Sandberger had opposed trends in NS Jewish policy, and had been especially outspoken against the Kristallnacht. According to Scheel, through most of 1939 Sandberger had been on sick leave, and then Scheel had helped him get temporary leave from the SD while he secured his civil service status. But once the war had begun, permanent transfer from SD became almost impossible.[53]

Consistent with theories that Einsatzgruppen assignments were a way of testing one's doubtful commitments, in June 1941, Sandberger was assigned as commander of Einsatzkommando Ia and later commander of Sipo and SD in Estonia. He received praise, in the usual language of promotion recommendations, for doing his job with great industry and better-than-average intensity. On trial, he echoed Heydrich's role-oriented charge to SD trainees: although the Führer's order had offended his personal moral sense, he had to obey it. Yet he claimed to have frustrated by several months orders to execute all Estonian Jews. Characteristically, he described the execution of Communist functionaries as actions by police under Gestapo orders, as though he somehow had no personal responsibility for police actions under his command.[54]

Regardless of how he felt, he had responsibility for all SD and police action in Estonia. In spite of how well he executed orders, there is no reason to doubt that he desired a separation of dirty work from his personal image, even while he "did his duty." Perhaps SD purging of university intellectuals had contributed earlier to his desire to separate from the organization whose value-oriented appeal he had once bought.

A different example of such intellectuals was the previously described Franz Six. In addition to double duty as university lecturer and SD central department leader, he played actively at educational politics. In Scheel's student organization, he served as titular head of the Reich Vocational Contest, part of a program to counter charges that NS influence had negative effects on education.[55] Six's ideological commitments fused with an intellectuality that gave SD work on the enemy a "scientific" cast and, after 1936, infected his Office II with a zealousness that lent their recommendations an air of urgency for dealing with the enemy.[56] If the contrast between the idealistic and purging activities of the SD had turned off some like Sandberger, they fused comfortably in those like Six.[57]

In contrast to Six's mission of purging enemies, Otto Ohlendorf shaped the image that other intellectuals preferred for their SD.[58] At university, he had planned to teach economics in higher education. By 1934, however, his political evolution had made him a self-righteous outcast among Nazis. Coming from a hometown environment of farmers, small-businesses, and artisans, he had subscribed to the völkisch concept of national community. While rejecting Marxism, such a view sought to capture the harmonious sense of collectivism in a society that preserved as its base the small independent economic unit. Since Nazism promised such an order, the Movement drew him as early as 1925.

Meanwhile, Ohlendorf had already discovered differences with Party leaders over "personal and factual views," and he became politically inactive. In 1932, he spent a year in Italy studying the Fascist system and returned even more confirmed against tendencies toward state socialism and economic concentration. In 1933, he found employment with a man of like mind—he became an assistant to Professor Jens Peter Jessen in Economics at the Institute for World Economy, Kiel University.[59]

Unfortunately for the two of them, local Party leaders could not tolerate their outspoken opposition to "national Bolshevist" tendencies in the new Reich. Both men had to resign, and Ohlendorf joined the ranks of Nazis arrested for expressing disappointment over what the new power holders were doing. His disillusionment gave vent to a drive to provide the leadership with scientifically based advice for guidance along the "true path" of National Socialism. In December 1934, he rejoined Jessen in Berlin at his Institute for Applied Economic Science, only to find himself once more under fire when Alfred Rosenberg attacked Jessen. He lost his second position.

At this point, May 1936, the SD drew him in. Höhn had sought Jessen precisely because of his reputation as an unpopular critic. Jessen referred him to Ohlendorf, who, after hearing of Höhn's plans for the SD, saw in that organization the opportunity to play a decisive role in shaping the new order. He soon became Höhn's deputy. Ohlendorf developed a network of experts in the field posts to build a Reich-wide system of economic reporting, and Höhn wanted him to extend it to all the spheres covered by Central Division II 2. Thus, by 1937, this branch of the SD saw itself as evolving away from enemy observation and toward reporting "pure" intelligence. Of course, they had to camouflage their work to avoid opposition.[60]

Although both Himmler and Heydrich saw the value of Ohlendorf's critical reports, they kept such controversial material to themselves. In fact, Himmler criticized any reports he had to forward that were too interpretive. Involved in delicate power struggles, he could not tolerate outspoken subordinates who generated hostility from other quarters, especially on subjects whose complexity exceeded his understanding or whose ideological basis escaped his sense of certainty. Under such pressure, in 1938 he dropped Höhn, and Ohlendorf had to recede into the background. Ohlendorf's control of the SD situation reports came later, but the SD mission he championed had become a vital component by 1936.

Another young recruit with solid academic credentials was Walter Schellenberg. Always cited as typical of "the new generation of SD members," he was one of the respectable young middle class Germans drawn to the SS and SD because they promised to become the new establishment. Actually, men like Schellenberg represented nothing new among SD members. Like Ohlendorf for SD-Inland, he embodied key components of the aspirations and self-images emerging for SD-Ausland, which he would eventually command.

Having pursued preparatory schools in Saarbrücken and Luxembourg, fluent in French and German, he had that sense of cosmopolitan poise that led many Europeans to claim world citizenship despite nationalistic or other contradictory commitments. Like many sons of his class, he aspired to a prestigious professional career or the higher civil service, particularly foreign service. He ultimately studied law and political science. In 1933, when he was to begin his legal apprenticeship and needed a government fellowship for support, his professors advised him to guarantee success by joining the Party and SS. He claimed he did so merely out of conformity and without ideological commitment.[61]

Indeed, nothing indicates significant political or ideological commitments prior to 1933. He had devoted himself to preparation for his future station, and was the sophisticated and cynical free thinker usually described in most accounts. This does not square, however, with the Schellenberg who clearly and forcefully expressed ideological commitments in the surviving documents. Schellenberg absorbed and conformed as necessary to the prevalent values of the environment in which he sought to succeed. Like any successful status seeker, he had acquired this skill as second nature. Although his polish required him to reserve a certain haughty detachment, especially from crude and offensive extremists, he conformed tacitly to dominant values. Although luckier than Ohlendorf in avoiding the evil demands of this ideology, he was not nearly as free of its contamination as his self-image demanded, or as he insisted in his memoirs.

His early impressions of the SS speak of the process that drew him in. Like most other Germans, in the enthusiasm of the time, he thought NS would provide the drastic action Germany needed to lift itself up, and he expected the unreasonable aspects of its creed to fade. In the "elite" SS he found the "better type of people" (feinen Leute) and a glamor that appealed to him. It promised to be the elevating vehicle of the Movement, as opposed to ruffian elements like the SA. Yet despite his claims of ideological aloofness, he admits that SS indoctrination lectures he had been called to deliver, including attacks on the Catholic Church, are what drew the attention of the SD. What Schellenberg had embraced was an intellectual's "critical" brand of National Socialism, making him susceptible to the SD's dedicated-intellectual image. Here was a clear mix that revealed the power of combining role and value orientations.

According to Schellenberg, two SD "members" of his university faculty recruited him. They told him of SD intelligence work, and he expressed an interest in the foreign aspects. They advised him that for an SD career, he should complete his legal education and enter civil service. Until then, he would serve as an unsalaried "member," rendering voluntary reports. Actually he held associate status from sometime in 1934 and became a member in November 1935. Meanwhile, he had been doing his juridical apprenticeship. Through SD intervention, this apprenticeship extended to work with Gestapo posts. At Frankfurt, he got his first foreign mission—to do a report on a professor at the Sorbonne. Further apprenticeship followed in the Gestapo Office, Berlin. In December 1936, he completed the state exam[62] and entered the civil service, Gestapo Office.

He was soon detailed to the SD Main Office. There, working intermittently on organizational affairs, he became Heydrich's right-hand man, a foil against Best's influence and a respectable replacement for Naujocks. The link between his Gestapo training and SD work had been counterespionage, and from this he would eventually become the head of SD-Ausland (Amt VI of the RSHA).

His goal was to turn his branch of the SD into a professional foreign intelligence agency for the new order. Although he claimed that he meant it to be separated from Party and SS and to be a state agency, that does not square with his role in the development of Sipo and SD as a fusion of SS and state. What he apparently intended was an image of intellectual independence and objective reporting, one clearly separated from dirty police work, crude NS dogmatism, and extralegal SS special action. Although he clearly betrayed a flair for the cloak-and-dagger image of a romantic secret service, he disdained Heydrich's dirty-work agents like Naujocks and would seek to purge them from his SD as he sought freedom from their image. He also sought distance from the ideological taint of Himmler's SS-SD.[63]

Clearly, the internally propagated images and missions of the SD are essential to understanding the character and roles of its members. Its external image completes the picture, for it helped determine who might be initially attracted. Despite occasional references in newspapers, the SD was not in the public eye. When Eichmann joined, he had allegedly confused it with a body-guard service.

One "well-informed" Party member left his impression in a 1936 diary entry. Hans-Jörg Maurer was an Old Fighter and a fanatical anti-Semitic journalist who had become disillusioned over totalitarian tendencies.[64] Maurer thought the SD was a new development and had only heard rumors about its place in the power structure. He feared it could become a Cheka. Its members were drawn from "especially tested, dependable Nazis," free to act beyond the law and on their own initiative, even to the point of murder. One of its basic tasks was determining the progress of the NS ideology in winning the people. Thus, it was especially interested in the press, but opposed to the heavy-handed, repressive methods of the Reich Press Chamber.[65]

Although such mixed, external impressions contrasted with some idealistic SD self-images, they did depict an influential elite in a position to shape Germany's future. Such romantic licence-to-kill imagery might draw opportunists and would-be Chekists. But while it might worry some disillusioned NS dissidents, it could attract others. It could appeal to young idealists, ambitious or otherwise, as long as they aspired to having an impact on their world.

Preliminary Conclusions

One should now be able to draw some preliminary conclusions along lines proposed in previous chapters. Obviously, the SD was a complex phenomena, and that complexity may have contributed significantly to the involvement of many members in the "dutiful" execution of increasingly inhumane roles. As late as 1937, it was still coalescing as an organization, while simultaneously evolving so rapidly that it could never fully manage its responsibilities. The goals assigned by Himmler and Heydrich, and those it generated for itself, overextended its capacities. At the same time, different pressures drove its members to search for more satisfactory institutional identities.

Organizationally, the field structure was too under-developed to be all-seeing in all those areas it had targeted. Its reporting remained uneven and erratic. Although often well-placed and well-informed, its sources were unevenly distributed. The field staff that processed and forwarded their information was zealous, but overworked and of limited capacities.[66] The central staff of analysts was hard-pressed to digest and collate the flood of material. Despite several revisions of the central filing system and the impressive-sounding concepts behind it, the relatively small staffs could never have handled the full flood. If today's police and intelligence agencies with the latest in electronic technology cannot control and fully exploit their information, certainly the SD was overwhelmed. Of course, when given a specific assignment, as opposed to total analysis, it could focus to produce an impressive body of information on a person or organization. In this respect, it could always fill its police-state role, but never its chosen, idealized role.

For their evaluations of individuals, reports on local enemy activity, and general reports on "spheres of life," the field posts received frequent criticism. Specifically, a lack of concrete detail and the impressionistic quality of the reports troubled headquarters. But the guidelines they issued were so abstract that they baffle readers today and must have been of little help even to SD workers with a more concrete sense of the work.

Although the SD pursued "objectivity," that never included any questioning of basic NS assumptions that guided their work. One could never question international conspiracies of Marxism, Jewry, Catholicism, and Masonry. One certainly did not challenge the rectitude of anything on which the Führer was specific. Nevertheless, that left a wide range of other things that were debated within the Movement, and even considerable leeway to differ over details within the areas of ideological certainty. Despite admonitions against involvement in local and personal politics, SD members championed many such causes.

As for the quality of its analyses of the effects of NS policies, scholars generally agree that its reports were probably more objectively critical than those of other agencies.[67] This can be attributed to SD other-mindedness, which grew, however, from a complex amalgam. It involved not only higher levels of intelligence and education, but also highly personal adherence to selective parts of the NS world view and a heavy lading of intellectual arrogance that required one to be critical of all others, but especially those who stood in the way of SD influence and control.

All of these characteristics and the roles this organization would play in the evolution of inhumane population and imperialist policies were to some extent products of its unique mix of personnel. Unarguably, a phenomenon like Nazism drew many psychologically unbalanced personalities. They do not, however, seem to have been a dominant presence in the working SD. Its appeals were diverse, and to accomplish its missions, it had to draw upon a wide range of people.

The marked dichotomies among the members suggest inevitable tensions. A wedding of an educated elite with ordinary "little men," of socially aggressive modernists with traditionalists, of confident achievers with damaged egos, of cosmopolitans with provincials—the SD was full of uneasy bedfellows. Surviving documents reveal efforts to plaster over tensions and rivalries with calls for comradeship and teamwork. But it was precisely this mix and the presence of those one might disdain that enabled the SD to enmesh men of any psychopolitical orientation, of any personality type, and of any level of intellectual development.

Members could be more easily drawn into sanctioned violence, whether they had developed to fit Kelman's models of the blindly obedient rule oriented, or the creatively obedient role oriented. Some had found a healing ego identity in the SS ideal, as suggested by John Steiner. Others were "opportunists" who found a suitable status identity in the SD. If their moral or other value-oriented commitments were high enough to prevent them from obeying orders for direct involvement in inhumanity, they either left or found more comfortable SD roles. In those roles, they "merely" facilitated inhumanity indirectly, often an unpleasant but "necessary" side effect of their more respectable roles.

All this provides a moderately satisfactory explanation for the moral failures of the ethically weak, the socially conditioned, the ego damaged, and any others who had not developed sufficient intellectual autonomy. Nevertheless, many among the sort drawn by SD appeals must have achieved sufficient levels of intellectual and ethical autonomy to have risen above being merely drawn into legitimization. Given the extraordinarily high percentage of the educated elite among them, it seems unlikely that psychopathic manipulators could have designed traps sufficiently subtle to have netted them all. More likely, they had to enmesh themselves by inadvertently developing "traps" that were products of their own intellectual identities.

One such image-trap was the promise of influence over national leadership, a powerful combination of role and value orientation. Given the nature of NS leadership, however, that promise of influence was especially elusive and ephemeral. A good deal of intellectual arrogance also helped the would-be advisors fool themselves. Nevertheless, for many healthy intellectual egos, such a goal could be most compelling. Furthermore, the more one had to sacrifice to retain access to the goal, the less rationally one would be able to assess its realizability. Ego commitment got in the way. Thus, as SD leadership evolved their compelling mission of guiding NS leadership and shaping the nation, they had to assume responsibility for solving unpleasant problems that could not be trusted to those they disdained. Although they might succeed in shunting the dirty work onto others, they had to create the solutions and see to their implementation, even if the solutions evolved beyond their sense of what was appropriate. In order to preserve their access to control and influence, they had to get their own hands dirty. In the end, they inadvertently facilitated evil evolutions as much as they became "trapped" in them.

Obviously, even those categories labeled broadly as SD intellectuals lacked a uniformity of either composition or self-image that allows for simple generalization. Among them were indeed paranoid, mystic crackpots who peopled their world with enemies, and "dualistic" intellects whose idea of research was finding evidence to prove their prejudices.[68] But they make it too easy to explain susceptibility, and one cannot dismiss the lot as intellectual misfits.

Intellectual arrogance certainly permeated the drive to purge elements that misdirected the new order. Clearly, arrogance lay in the appeals that SD intellectuals used to recruit one another. They would provide the "objective," "accurate" information, a "valid" assessment of the public mood, and "proper" intellectual guidance for the leadership. Only they could compensate for the loss of contact that occurred when an authoritarian state dispensed with free elections. Only they could displace the self-serving sycophants who sought to isolate the leadership.[69] Obviously, one can find pathology in such a self-image, if one feels a need to do so. One might not, however, if these men had joined the British Secret Service or one of Roosevelt's brain trusts.

Some of these same men expressed motives that would be admirable under any circumstances. Some sought to defend higher education from antiintellectual elements that would replace universities with NS indoctrination and career training.[70] Others expressed an intellectually mature appreciation of free inquiry in academia. Contrary to elitist intellectualism, they would open the doors to higher education for the economically underprivileged.[71] To explain their susceptibility, one must find more than weakness and pathology. One must see how their admirable qualities turned on them.

Like most leaders in the SD who were teachers, jurists, and higher civil-service administrators, Höhn, Ohlendorf, Scheel, Schellenberg, and Six, as intellectuals, liked not only to manipulate and mold ideas but also to shape and fashion society—people's attitudes and values. Although they had an intellectual self-image and approached their mission in life through the realm of ideas, they fit well into that class of SS leadership that Robert Koehl labeled "social engineers." They all saw themselves shaping a new community of harmony and strength. This goal tied together the intellectual teachers, jurists, and writers with technicians, engineers, medical doctors, civil servants, and businessmen. They had all sought esteemed professions to lead in shaping or "serving" society.[72] Among them, a subtle but significant difference divided their self-images and shaped the related roles they played in Sipo and SD.

That subtle distinction was both elusive and illusory. Those involved on one side usually expressed their role in terms like "positive," "intellectual," and "ideological." In making his distinction between ideological intelligence and police functions, Himmler expressed tangentially a difference that for him was simply the difference between SD and Sipo. In fact, the difference created by his subordinates crossed all organizational lines within Sipo and SD. It distinguished those primarily hoping to shape society constructively from those more concerned with cleansing. This went beyond differences between SD (ideological intelligence) and police (executive action); it expressed itself within SD in the distinction between "enemy intelligence" and "positive intelligence." Since one needs some label to express the difference between SD work directed at revealing the enemy in Central Division II 1 and that which emerged from Central Division II 2 under Höhn and Ohlendorf, the label "cultural intelligence" may serve best.[73]

Of course, the need to purge and the desire to shape are never clearly separable, and both found expression in the imagery of all branches of the SD and of Sipo as well. Both formed components of the personalities and self-images of practically every articulate member. Thus, both Höhn and Six would create new "intellectual intelligence" roles while never really separating themselves from "enemy intelligence" functions. Nevertheless, "negative purging" and "positive shaping" emerged increasingly as opposite poles on a continuum formed by the missions and images of the various branches of Sipo and SD. To complete an analysis of the consequences of these SD self-images, one must put them in the context of the totality of Sipo and SD.

Conclusion

Sipo and SD: The Significance of Organization and Image

Several modifications of scholarly and popular images have emerged from this analysis. As late as 1937, the SD had not achieved anything like its image of all-seeing eyes. It had not outgrown its amateurish origins, and it remained overwhelmed by its missions. Its role in penetrating and turning the political police was more subtle and initially far less direct than previously described. Under the pressure of wartime demands, it would never overcome its problems.

The growing consensus among scholars that the Gestapo's image was in many ways a myth has been reinforced.[1] It grew so rapidly that it too remained overwhelmed by its responsibilities. Among its personnel, the professional detectives were sandwiched between Nazified administrators and SS superiors above and an unhealthy leaven of SS toughs in the lowest ranks. Thus, the Gestapo was simultaneously the embodiment of its police-gangster image and the professional police force to which it aspired. It was one of those syntheses of opposites that make many institutions impossible to describe satisfactorily.

One must remember, however, that the functional, internal perspective on Gestapo work provided by this study cannot stand alone. The Gestapo was only part of the total apparatus of Sipo and SD. That in turn was only part of the much larger SS-police-concentration-camp system. All of that was supported by a vast network of surveillance provided by Party and state agencies. Together this made for a massive structure of police-state efficiency sufficient to do the job of keeping German society in line behind Hitler's war and the Nazi crimes of inhumanity, even after it all went sour. Even so, the important role of spontaneous, self-serving informants in all this makes it clear that the terror did not operate entirely under control or as intended. The efficiency of the Gestapo is yet another aspect that is almost impossible to analyze and describe satisfactorily.

Since Kripo was subjected to "SS-ification" later than the Gestapo, it had a reputation for immunity to Nazification and involvement in NS crimes. Yet Kripo detectives became as thoroughly involved in the NS Movement as Gestapo detectives, their work was polluted by NS ideology, and many participated in the crimes of the regime. These detectives joined only three years later than their Gestapo counterparts the real amalgam created by Sipo and SD.

The members of Sipo and SD were initially drawn together by their roles in purging society of all nonconformity. One sees a strong parallel here with Detlav Peukert's observation that for the middle class by the mid–1930s the elusive appeal of Volksgemeinschaft had to be supplemented increasingly by the discovery and elimination of internal and external enemies.[2]

Perhaps more significant are new insights into the men of each component. For most of these men, one can dismiss the image of sadists and misfits. The revealed membership contradicts theories that the SD or the police attracted predominantly those personalities highly susceptible to sanctioned violence. Equally doubtful is the argument that the more normal personalities in these organizations were driven to criminality by a psychologically predisposed hard-core element, although a similar but more self-induced process may have been at work.

These organizations drew diverse types, many of whom had two things in common: idealistic self-images and goals, and a need to protect their organizations from disreputable elements. Their positive human characteristics were admirable, and their weaknesses were in no way extraordinary. Yet they succumbed to sanctioned violence as extremely and thoroughly as psychopaths, while their involvement was far more deadly for the victims. They contributed their significant talents to the escalation of Nazi tendencies from mere rhetorical outbursts and random violence to previously unimaginable levels of execution.

I have proposed that the explanation for this enigma lies as much in the otherwise admirable qualities of these men as in any psychic weaknesses or pathologies. They built organizations and set goals that matched their positive qualities, although the marriage was often perverted. In so doing, they tied their egos to the organizational images they created. Unfortunately they had grown up immersed in a culturally defined reality that gave their world views powerful conjunctions with those of Nazism. From there, they could be more easily drawn close to the extremes of Hitlerian and Himmlerian ideological variants. Together, ideological conjunctions and their powerful ego-institution links within Sipo and SD enmeshed them in their fateful roles.

I have described Sipo and SD as an entity—as a coherent whole—but have shown that in many respects it was not. This is another example of a synthesis of contradictions, but one that lies at the root of the role Sipo and SD played in drawing otherwise respectable men into sanctioned violence. Sipo and SD was an entity, and that was its true significance. It was far more than an administrative convenience through which Heydrich managed his separate commands. It bound together its three components to such an extent that none of them can be properly studied nor fully understood in isolation.

Sipo and SD as a Dangerous Liaison

The SD had a mission to infiltrate key institutions of society and guide them along proper NS lines toward the future Reich. Sipo-SD emerged within the total SD as those men who would infiltrate and guide Sipo detectives toward the true State Security Corps. But many SD leaders developed other missions and an ethos that conflicted with the taint of a police spy-enforcer image. By the same token, even if the professional policemen shared an ideological conjunction with the NS revolution, they had problems with their marriage to SS-SD. For good reasons, all these men denied any true fusion of SD with police, while each branch of the police denied identity with the other.

Yet they were one, especially after the 1939 creation of the RSHA (Reichssicherheitshauptamt), a common headquarters to coordinate integration. They were one in a conglomerate within which each man could be transferred to different branches or temporarily assigned to common missions. This meant that no matter how distinct they might have remained either de jure or in their minds, de facto they were tied together in their inhumane roles. Yet the perverse power of Sipo and SD lay in the distinct, contradictory institutional images that separated Kripo from Gestapo from SD, and even the components of the SD from each other in the minds of their members. That facilitated denial of their marriage while they moved together toward their ultimate roles.

By 1936, Himmler had legal control of all the police. No longer preoccupied with strategies for gaining control, he prepared to create the Staatsschutzkorps, a term that came into common usage during 1936–1937 to express the matured version of his vision.[3] We may never know who contributed most to the concept. It clearly grew from Hitlerian imagery and took its general form in the grand dreams Himmler began evolving before 1931. It got much of its specific form from refinements of Heydrich and the SD leadership, including the newly recruited professional policemen. For Himmler, it was to be a union of the police, the SS (and SD), and parts of the administration, into "a corps for the defense of the realm." In 1935, Heydrich spoke of the need to propagate an inner discipline and loyalty to bind together its diverse components. He turned to his SD as the vehicle for propagating that bond within his agencies.[4]

SS-SD penetration of the police had originally been sporadic and largely uncoordinated. The process had gone two ways: policemen joined the SS-SD, and men from these organizations entered the police.

After 1935, the process became more organized and deliberate, as some policemen were pressed to take SS membership. Although a total fusion of SS and state was Himmler's goal, it was only loosely achieved. Sipo was never a part of the SS. SD membership among Sipo may never have exceeded 18 percent. Although most men in command positions were SS-SD members, many of those commanders were late joiners from the ranks of the police. Many Kripo men distanced themselves from SS identity even if they formally joined. Even the more thoroughly "SS-ified" Gestapo only identified selectively with the SS. Despite the rhetoric of SS camaraderie, Gestapo and Kripo men often disdained their SD partners, and vice versa. Himmler and Heydrich knew they needed at least a generation to overcome this resistance. Initially, the SS would indoctrinate the existing policemen, but ultimately, the new recruits, Hitler Youth, drawn simultaneously into the SS and police, would bring the ideal corps to fulfillment. These men of the future would be free of old traditions and "reactionary" police professionalism.

With the development of this concept of State Security Corps, the SD function of penetrating the police supplemented its ideological intelligence mission. That in turn added further complexity to the SD and gave it that "multiple personality" that drew and bonded together its diverse membership.

When Himmler created the SD in 1932, its image was already self-contradictory. The open mission of observing and analyzing the enemy included a focus on "the enemy within." That meant a negative SD image of spies and informers among the brotherhood, ferreting out undesirable elements. In contrast, Himmler and Heydrich conjured a counterimage. They rejected the mode of police spies, and chose instead an idealized secret service that every citizen willingly supported. Heydrich wooed such people by describing an SD that would provide the leadership with broadly based information, thereby affecting policy decisions. This mixed image drew a diverse body of men. On the one hand, it appealed to those who aspired to provide intellectual guidance for the Movement, while on the other, its cloak-and-dagger component drew in men who ranged from sophisticated romantic adventurers to the crudest of activists. Despite its negative connotations, the internal spy image also drew men with an "idealistic" mission to purge and purify.

Since the SD grew parallel to the more significant political police, it underwent tensions that exaggerated the contradictions in its mission. An SS-commanded political police raised the question of whether the SD was needed. The answer, that it performed ideological intelligence functions supplemental to yet distinct from police work, was not wholly adequate. Although this mission implied an elite role as ideological guide to the police, it also involved that negative image of enforcers. Consequently, they pursued still further the more positive intelligence functions in which they would guide the leadership and shape national policy. This led to "cultural intelligence," providing information on domestic conditions and moods, and to foreign intelligence, Ausland-SD. It also included infiltrating and controlling the key institutions of society, not to spy, but to provide positive influences.

From 1935, these positive images drew men who preferred roles separate from police functions. Consequently, in the SD image, the internal division widened between "negative purging," or police work, and "positive shaping." Less clearly involved in this split image, the foreign intelligence branch had an additional ethos of romantic derring-do. The distinct image of this branch would take longer to emerge, but would eventually include a posture above SS and police and apart from "ideology." The intensification of these split images within the SD resulted primarily from its ties to the political police.

The Police and Society in Crisis

The professional policemen of Sipo pose a special problem. Analyzing them from the perspective of the police in contemporary industrial society links the Nazi police state to more universal problems of the police in modern societies. Although this is not a new idea, much more work is required in this direction.

Specifically, the application of police-subculture theories to early twentieth-century Germany requires more thorough testing to reveal the historically specific German police subcultures that probably existed. We need data on the social backgrounds of the professional police and of the real changes in personnel that occurred between 1919 and 1945. We need deeper analysis of changes in both the public images and professional self-images of these police. We need to know more about changes in their training programs and ideological orientations. Until then, the following interpretation might provoke such research.

In any society, "police science" must be in tune with the predominant assumptions, or the society will have problems with its police. When a society is in transition, such a harmony becomes especially problematic. If that society does not successfully redefine the ethos and image of the police and their relation to society, the gap between the prevalent forces of change and the policeman's sense of propriety will grow to a crisis point. Social change without regard for its impact upon the police is especially dangerous, because the police exist to *preserve* society. Disruptive changes can alienate the police from the direction of change in their society. The police will become more susceptible to reactionary appeals, or worse, to extremist appeals that cloak themselves in the preservation of society and its traditional values.

The police are not the problem. The problem grows from the innate ability of reactionary and right-wing extremists to appeal to them and to any other elements alienated by too rapid a change. It also grows from the general tendency of left-wing and liberal elements either to ignore the police, to perceive them as part of the problem, or to push them counterproductively. The society's conservatives may play the key role, for if they are progressive they can smooth the transitions, but if not, they will entrench the police in a righteous opposition. Unfortunately for Germany, that was the course their history took.

While undergoing rapid change, societies often suffer from a hysteria over the "breakdown of law and order." This exaggerates the crisis of the police, for they are charged with failure to defend society. Enthusiasm mounts for an effective rooting-out of the "basic sources of crime and deviancy." In Germany, the police were wooed by Nazis who promised to give them freedom from restraints that prevented them from eliminating those criminal and deviant elements. Once under Nazi command, fear of the Red menace, of criminal elements, and of sexual offenders worked together to create a common thread for the logic of all Sipo work. The general acceptance of popular genetic theories about degeneracy fused arguments for "euthanasia" and crime prevention with fears of racial pollution. Ideas about final solutions followed naturally.

The policemen became willing participants in the first steps toward the police state. They gladly threw off the restrictions imposed by the liberal constitution and served the Nazi state well as long as their professional integrity did not seem threatened. However, as the realities of SS penetration became apparent and the NS world view perverted their "free hand for police work," they also suffered an identity crisis. A few ended their involvement. Most remained and deluded themselves with false images of their organizations, roles, and relations with the SS-SD. From there, they participated in the escalation process that led to mass inhumanity.

Ironically, the ideal image of the Gestapo, different from the now-common one of brutal police terrorism, contributed to these processes. The leadership from Göring, Himmler, and Heydrich down wished to build the image of their police as honored and trusted by the people. Not only did the professional police aspire to such an image, but they also denied anything beyond a nominal fusion with the SS-SD.

They clung tenaciously to the belief that they were a legal instrument of the state, doing only what had to be done to serve the nation. Furthermore, they twisted their real tie to the SS-SD into yet another alibi. It enabled them to deny "police responsibility" for actions besmirching their professionalism, by shifting blame onto SS-SD men among them. Thus, for those who refused to see their prostitution to Nazism, the very police subculture that should have generated forceful resistance to NS penetration created a mythical self-image of professional autonomy. That in turn enabled them to perform their work without asking themselves so many troubling questions. The work they could or would not perform fell to others whose presence they had to tolerate.

Strangely, what applied to the Gestapo applied even more to Kripo. These professionals not only saw themselves as free of SS-SD contamination, but also stood aloof from the Gestapo. They preserved an exaggerated image of professional autonomy. Their leaders constantly boasted that their membership in the SS-SD was only nominal and that this sacrifice saved Kripo's true professional autonomy. Yet, like the Gestapo, the Kripo served in the Einsatzgruppen, applied NS racial theory to its criminological work, assumed responsibilities for euthanasia, and would submit all future generations of Kripo recruits to SS indoctrination and conformity to all SS standards.

Thus, no matter how much distance police and SD men might have sought between their identities, they were drawn together in processes legitimizing inhumanity by the common denominator of those identities—Sipo and SD. Since those processes continued throughout the history of Sipo and SD, one needs to establish their course not only for 1933–1937, but beyond, as a context for understanding the institutions in which they would occur.

Sanctioning Inhumanity

I do not accept the idea that the important thing to discover is *what* these men did and *how* they went about doing it. Indeed, that allows us to see clearly the evil of the Nazi world view and all who contributed to it. But it is not enough to pass judgment on those evil individuals. "It"—the Nazi solution—can and will happen again if we do not understand our own vulnerability to similar phenomena. To be sufficiently educated to function in our world, each of us must understand how, not just "ordinary men," but *we* could have participated.

The only psychologically comfortable way to deal with the Nazi experience is from the heights of moral condemnation. Clearly, it was a product of evil values and beliefs inherent in the ideology. But all those responsible were not simply evil—fundamentally immoral, sociopathic, psychopathic, the scum of society, or weak, susceptible personalities. When all perspectives come together, those responsible emerge more like Jekyll and Hyde.

Any effort to explore how good Dr. Jekyll turned into Nazi Mr. Hyde is an unsettling activity. Was he a victim, trapped by the poison he brewed with good intentions? This is especially troubling since, if the perpetrators were victims, what then of their victims? Do we put them on the same level? No, for the basic difference lies in the problem of "responsibility."

I tread the dangerous waters of approaching the men of these organizations as normal, basically decent people whose fate was also tragic. As the Greeks understood tragedy, it made no difference what he intended, the tragic character destroyed himself and all around him. Fate played a role. If these men had been born in the Allied countries, they might have been heroes of that war. But in the Nazi camp, they played the roles of terroristic enforcers and mass murderers. That, however, does not make them victims. They were not just the hapless victims of fate; they failed to exercise their moral judgment. The important knowledge we must dig for here is how and why they blinded themselves, and what encouraged them in that process.

Few members of Sipo and SD ever decided to commit "murder" for any personal reason. They obeyed orders to kill, or most often to facilitate killing, and although they usually perceived that these deaths differed from normal war-situation killings or legal executions, they obeyed by viewing them as analogous to such normally sanctioned violence. They obeyed the ostensibly "lawful" orders of the leaders of their nation. Thus, they had created a context in which they could not perceive their acts as criminal. Even after Nuremberg and in a different frame of reference, most of them still could not make such an equation. This is not to say that they had no moral qualms about their orders—they often did. No one can live without compromising and violating values, yet one copes without thinking of one's self as an immoral person for having done so. To the extent that they thought of their organization as above traditional laws or values, there is an analogy with the criminal organization, but such a belief in a higher cause characterizes most revolutionary movements and religions, which offer better analogies than criminal organizations.[5]

If we leave behind assumed pathology or criminal analogies and introduce models of norm distortion and legitimization processes that help us understand what happened to the "normal" participants, we gain some sense of how it could happen to us.[6] We can reestablish an empathy with our subjects—that element so essential to the historian's scholarly creativity, but generally denied us by the nature of Nazi inhumanity. With such an approach, however, one enters the treacherous waters of Historisierung, best advocated by Martin Broszat.[7] By "empathy" I do not mean either sympathy or uncritical empathetic identity with one's subjects. Historians must balance empathy with critical distance. Most of all, however, one cannot hope to capture the moral problem presented by the Nazi experience without applying an empathy founded in intellectual maturity and grown from the experience and knowledge that one has also walked treacherous paths, but failed with far less serious consequences.

For both policeman and SD member, the first step toward sanctioned inhumanity involved legitimization and brutalization. It generally came during the uncontrolled, "revolutionary" violence directed at the Red enemies. Each performed zealously roles he could justify as legitimate, while distancing himself from acts he could not justify, but which the rabble would perform extremely well. Distrust, even fear of that uncontrollable rabble subsequently led to another step that brutalized some and set the pattern for the rest to follow. The Röhm purge affected members of the SD and Gestapo in ways difficult to unravel. To begin with, most were not privy to any manipulation at the top. In the context of the reports they had forwarded or received, evidence of a pending coup must have been convincing.[8] Many of them had problems with the alleged conspirators, so when they were unleashed on these newly exposed enemies of the Volk, they behaved as they had against the Reds. Afterward came promotions, and, of course, everyone benefited from the elevation of the Gestapo and SD that resulted. Most men probably felt self-righteous satisfaction about their service. Some apparently relished their role of radical enforcement. Almost all had relied on the cruder SS men for the actual dirty work.

Nevertheless, many later looked back on June 30 and saw a fatal turning point. For some, the questioning began as soon as the rumors of Himmler and Heydrich's roles became common. For others it occurred more gradually. For many, it occurred only when called to account after the war. In every case, however, the net result was the same.

Having involved themselves in an escalating process of evidence gathering until they believed their victims were the enemy, and having projected such evil on the enemy that they self-righteously destroyed him, they contributed to the process. Whenever they encountered their sense of guilt, however, they had a convenient scapegoat. By seizing upon rumors and by accepting the images of Himmler or Heydrich as the Machiavellian manipulators who engineered such things as the Röhm purge, they could project their guilt onto their chiefs and salve their consciences. Even Göring and the military leadership employed such rationalization, producing almost unanimous postwar testimonies that everyone was duped by these evil geniuses. It is now impossible to separate such rationalizations from reality, to determine where mutual escalation ended and manipulation began.

If such a sense of betrayal developed before the end, it became the turning point of one's career. For some early members, June 30 marked that awareness. Henceforth they were unable to serve with self-righteous zeal and became misfits in the ranks of Sipo and SD. Some terminated their careers voluntarily, but few gave explanations for doing so. Dr. Joachim Mrugowski merely said he withdrew "owing to certain developments which were divergent from his ideas of what an information service should be."[9] Some clung to their positions, but increasingly resisted changes desired by Himmler or Heydrich. Others merely degenerated, slipping into alcoholism or corruption. A few voiced accusations against their chiefs and were broken. In the files of many SD members, there are signs of disillusionment. For most, however, such developments came too late to save them.

After 1934, the shifts of focus from one enemy to another involved more SD and policemen in authorization, routinization, and dehumanization that prepared the stronger characters for the next step and totally destroyed the resistance of the weaker. Whether it was homosexuals or political priests, conservative military and financial circles that could sabotage the new Germany, or the Jews, the logic of one's ideological or professional commitments required some action, and authority called for just a little more. Often, some uncontrollable element forced an action one might otherwise have stopped short of, for one had to preempt their initiatives. Frequently, such steps pushed men beyond their sense of propriety and drove them to seek separation from police or SD, but the war and its transcending call to serve the nation drew them back more firmly. Somewhere along the way, some would develop a sense that all they believed in had been betrayed, but by then it was too late.[10]

For example, the "Jewish Problem" involved complex evolutions. Until 1938, neither the Gestapo nor SD played any significant role in shaping national policy about Jews. The SD refined the line espoused by the SS—emigration. But such policy received no executive force until the Gestapo acquired responsibility for furthering emigration in 1938.

If anything, most members of the Gestapo or SD were "moderates" among Nazis on the Jewish question. That moderation, with its concomitant "scientific and professional" research into the problem, made the trap so deadly for victim and victimizer alike. No matter how cynical one was about Nazi brands of anti-Semitism or how low Jewry was on one's list of threats to the nation, one lived in a milieu in which the fundamental assumptions of anti-Semitism constituted reality. As one historian put it, the Nazis created a framework in which questioning the existence of a "Jewish problem" became tantamount to questioning the emperor's new clothes.[11] Nowhere was this more true than in Sipo and SD, where Himmler had defined good police or intelligence work as revealing the Jewish connection behind the problem. The detective won praise by finding a Jewish element in any crime or plot. The SD operative built elaborate charts revealing the network of Jewish connections and their relevance to everything un-German. To function within these systems, one had to accept the existence of "at least some truth" in all such conjuring, thus preparing oneself intellectually for the authorization.

Meanwhile, from 1934–1938, the more "unreliable elements" of the Movement agitated the "Jewish problem." Their agitation led to the Nuremberg Laws and on to the pogroms of November 1938, often embarrassing the NS state at inopportune moments and disrupting economic affairs. From the beginning, both Gestapo and SD felt pressures to assert their authority in such actions. The SD leaders, with a self-image as intellectual guides for the Movement, felt compelled to stand for more respectable and regulated solutions, while they also felt pressure to provide dynamic direction rather than abdicating policy formulation to irresponsible elements. This dichotomy drove them to seek more thorough solutions. The years 1935 to 1936 witnessed contradictory actions within both the SS and the police based on ambivalent desires to retain a radical stance on the Jewish problem while trying to maintain order. This was the link between the pressures generated by NS radicals and the ad hoc problem solving of bureaucrats or functionaries who laid piecemeal the foundations for many different "final solutions."

After 1938, any action that facilitated emigration and, therefore, eliminated an increasing source of conflict was justifiable, especially if the more brutal side effects fell in the domain of some branch of Sipo and SD that lay outside one's realm of identity. For the intellectual SD, the job fell to the Gestapo. For the professional detective, the job fell to Sipo-SD men under Eichmann. Ultimately, routinization meant the true dirty work fell to someone in the Einsatzgruppen, or, better yet, entirely outside Sipo and SD in the camps.

Meanwhile, other contemporary experiences had prepared some for the ultimate step. "History"—that is, World War I—had taught the reality of modern total war: victory now requires the destruction of the enemy nation, for all men and women will be mobilized. As one SD man put it, total war meant "war without mercy, . . . destroying the enemy nation . . . with all means without any regard and without consideration of existing conventions." Total war, national security, enemy nations, and the Jewish problem all became part of the emperor's new clothes, providing rationalization for what would come. As early as 1938, some SD men foresaw, with greater clarity and enthusiasm than most others, that the process could lead to genocide.[12] At some point, Heydrich and some of his lieutenants, sensing the likely outcome, may well have begun planning options and pushing in directions that would guarantee that they would be the ones ready to do whatever the Führer decided.[13]

Others could look down on uncontrolled brutality like November 1938 as "a shame and a scandal" because they occurred "without orders." One would prosecute unreliable elements in Sipo and SD who participated in such undisciplined outbursts. But authorization made even a morally offensive action a different matter. By 1941, the cushions of routinization and rationalization facilitated even the "deplorable" killing of women and children. Nevertheless, at the peak of the process, even brutalization could not defuse the tension, for many functionaries of genocide broke under the strain or sought escape through transfer.[14]

The major developments that legitimized genocide lie outside the scope of this book, which explores instead the preparatory phase and the creation of the institutional environment in which it would occur. With this sketchy perspective, however, one can look back with a better appreciation of the significance of the institutions and their psychosocial environments as a key to the processes that legitimized such inhumanity.

Mutual Escalation

Whether one focuses on either branch of Sipo (Gestapo or Kripo) or on any SD office, the full membership clearly belied the images of either professional detective or intellectual leadership. The spectrum ran from those with respectable credentials, through a marginal set, to the shady characters who were available for the dirty work. The marginal set could rise to middle and even higher functionary status, but both civil service and SS-SD leadership strove to keep them from fully elite ranks. Both detectives and SD members would combine to weed out some of the shady element. For instance, the 1935–1936 screening process of SS-Gestapo employees denied SD membership on the grounds of a "lack of requisite knowledge" (Fachkenntnisse), or of the "necessary intellectual talents," or on the basis of character. Others would survive, however, despite their flaws, for someone had to fill the lower ranks. But such men encountered a definite ceiling in middle functionary status.[15]

Such people undoubtedly helped brutalize their "betters." Once present, even in small numbers, they added steam to the pressure cooker. To the professional policeman, the uniformed NS infiltrators challenged his zeal and goaded him to take the extra step that proved patriotism and dedication. To the SD intellectual, that element who would obey any order became a standard by which loyalty and dedication were measured. Such elements also gauged the "radicalism" of a true revolutionary's solution to ideologically defined problems. But one should not overemphasize the significance of this presence as a catalyst to sanctioned inhumanity. Other forces were probably more decisive.

The respectable members' need to purge disreputable elements also revealed the depth of their identities with the organizations they would purify. Most of those with respectable credentials, either academic or detective, were bound to a profession of public service. Professional detectives had little hope of shifting to any other career of equal prestige. Few of those with legal degrees could hope for comparable prestige outside the civil service. When confronted with the unfortunate side effects of the Nazi system, they could only preserve their self respect by psychologically distancing their public service from those involved more directly in the "side-effects." The Gestapo official served the nation by defending it against un-German pollutants. The Kripo detective served society by controlling its criminal elements and maintaining law and order. The SD functionary provided the leadership with the objective, accurate information they needed to keep the nation on the right track. The lower ranks, who had no hope whatever of a more prestigious service career elsewhere and found self-respect in one branch or another, had to have more tolerance for involvement in some of the necessary side effects.

The more privileged, professionally credentialed members of Sipo and SD who did have alternatively prestigious service-career options could seek them when the side effects negated the service they performed in Sipo and SD. They could withdraw honorably to resume their professions. But then the war changed priorities, and only public service was again acceptable. Thereafter, only the military offered a respectable option. Many would seek that escape from the contaminating side effects, but usually it involved much lower rank and, therefore, service below one's ability and status.

An identity bound up in a need to serve significantly hardly represents a quality that one would condemn. Yet it drew these men into at best complicity in, and at worst direct commitment of horrible crimes. Perhaps worst of all, these side effects became the central reality while the idealized mission became increasingly illusory.

The political detective increasingly terrorized the innocent or innocuous and persecuted the truly good citizen driven to any outward resistance. The scientific work of the detectives gave way to racial theories of criminality, and they were sent out to perform more ideologically defined roles. The SD intellectual never influenced the decision-making process of the Third Reich in any direction except perhaps the escalation of imperialism and encouragement of the Final Solution. On the contrary, when SD reports revealed the unacceptable, Bormann, Goebbels, and Himmler obstructed their circulation and finally denied the SD access to official sources of information.[16] The SD dream of reshaping the nation by infiltrating key institutions never rose much above spying and imposing a deadly conformity that contradicted any ideal of critical dynamism.

When one is confronted with such conflicts between his central ideals and the realities of his life, one often retreats even deeper into mythical self-images and can become enmeshed even more tightly in organizational identities. As the ethical crises mounted, the mythical image became one's only prop to self-respect and even sanity. One bonded totally with one image of one component of Sipo and SD, and that fused overall with a sense of membership in a special fighting force against all that threatened a proper Germany.

In that respect, one sees a strong parallel between Sipo and SD and the image of the Wehrmacht painted by Omer Bartov.[17] The military was a most diverse body of men from all strata and walks of life, welded into a disciplined, effective fighting force that held together to the last moments of the war. They "were among the regime's strongest supporters . . . accepting the regime's view of Germany's mission in the world and its perception of the Reich's enemies as consisting mostly of inferior beings unworthy of life."[18] Yet while the Generals could depict the rank and file as "National Socialists through and through, . . . at the same time they tried to present the Wehrmacht as a professional organization quite indifferent to ideology." [19] The Volksgemeinschaft had failed to materialize for them, but a Kampfgemeinschaft against the enemies of the Volk bonded them together.

For Sipo and SD, indoctrination was reinforced by the evidence they themselves generated in their ideologically guided police and security operations. They thus converted ideological images of the enemy into reality. They had prepared themselves for brutalization and dehumanization before they encountered their victims as vermin on the eastern front. Once a real total war had materialized, war against such enemies became a transcendent mission that could bond together men with conflicting and mutually hostile self-images into a "disciplined," effective instrument of extermination.

This book has elaborated those self-images in Sipo and SD. Explaining their significance far exceeds contributing to our picture of the internal rivalries and hostilities that characterized the Third Reich. Their true significance lies in the synthesizing abilities of Sipo and SD that held together such diverse and mutually antagonistic groups so that they performed functions essential to fulfillment of the NS world view. Sipo and SD, bound together by the cement of the total SD, allowed many contradictory types to perform their specialized and idealized functions in their separate compartments. One could extol his egalitarian combat community without acknowledging a common identity with disdained colleagues.

Such a perverse system of bonding exceeds the capacities of any leaders to create. Its dynamic tensions actually ran counter to the ideals of both Himmler and Heydrich, who constantly exhorted their subordinates to closer cooperation and a more genuine brotherhood. They wished a true fusion of SS and police. Instead, the bonds that Sipo and SD welded were examples of the autonomously operating, psychosocial mechanisms of contemporary societies—mechanisms that obscure realities while facilitating the entrapment of idealistic people into severe moral crises. In Sipo and SD, they offered the ultimate in authorization and routinization, paving the way to brutalization. These mechanisms and the blindness of SD intellectuals, of civil servants, and of professional policemen to these mechanisms worked to the advantage of Himmler and Heydrich. It strains credibility to argue that they consciously constructed such mechanisms. Explaining how well they may have realized and consciously exploited these mechanisms in the evolution of imperialistic and racial programs lies beyond this study.

Such problems form the central issues in the history of the SS and the Third Reich. To what extent did Nazi aggressions and racial programs grow from the deliberate and preconceived plans of the NS leadership, and to what extent from pressures from below and from the forces that leaders unleashed by expressing their evil fantasies? This book has delineated the ways in which directions from above and spontaneous pressures from below complemented one another in the creation of Sipo and SD. Furthermore, it has shown how forces unleashed in Sipo and SD helped generate "semispontaneous" pressures, encouraging more radical foreign and racial policy.

Of course, such radical policies were "intended" all along in an abstract sense. Both the ideology and the general goals espoused by the leadership created the new consensus reality in which ideological conjunctions drew the lower level functionaries toward an ideological consensus with the leadership. In this way, less clearly formed intentions synthesized with functional pressures generated by those intentions to coalesce the actions of all involved into increasingly more clearly defined goals and plans for their fulfillment.

Clearly, Sipo and SD attracted some sadistic and criminal personalities, but they were too few to account for what tens of thousands of men ultimately did. Perhaps psychosocial descriptions of processes that legitimize inhumanity and theories about how the bulk of any modern population is so "psycho-politically oriented" that it is susceptible to such processes explain how Nazi criminality could occur in any society. But one must still explain the involvement of those better than "ordinary," psychically and intellectually more healthy personalities. They should have been at least as prevalent—if not more so—in Sipo and SD than in the general population, because of their relative social and educational privileges.

This book has offered theories about ego-institutional identities to explain how such otherwise healthy people could be blinded by mechanisms that produce cohesion in complex modern societies, sometimes by obscuring moral crises. To explore such mechanisms, I have emphasized the idealistic and normative aspects of Sipo and SD, for that part of the historical reality is what most participants seized upon. This emphasis denies neither the inhumanity nor the corruption that also formed part of that reality. Nor does such an analysis exonerate any participant, "healthy" or otherwise.

People entrap themselves in both tragic and evil roles—not only because of their character weaknesses or pathologies, but even if they possess strong personalities and character. Sometimes, such qualities drive one into roles in which one's ethical awareness can be blindsided. That is the process of true moral failure. If history is to serve the role of moral education that was once attributed to it, historians must probe the processes of such moral failures.

Although many of the men studied here drew into Sipo or SD purely to advance themselves, at least an equal number pursued an ideal. It made no difference whether it was racist, aggressive-nationalist, exclusive-ideological, or a more admirably patriotic or socially constructive mission, they were willing to risk their souls for a transcendent purpose. Whether they realized that they supped with the Devil or not, they entered his trap when they identified with the image and mission of any component of Sipo and SD in order to use that component to pursue their higher aims. While they worked diligently toward their tantalizing ideals, all they were ever allowed to achieve was ultimately evil. Their failure to perceive the nature of the trap or to abandon their goals at any time before the end constituted their degree of guilt and responsibility.[20]

"The pathology of modernity" that the Nazi experience has revealed is a poem in which Holocaust rhymes with the little injustices and the occasional inhumanities we inadvertently inflict in the everyday pursuit of our higher goals. These pursuits become most dangerous when they are backed by the absolute certainties provided by science, ideology, or religion. They can entrap the best-intentioned along with the morally indifferent. The danger is so great because the mechanisms are so well camouflaged in responsibilities that mix banal routine with sanctified ends. This danger remains greatest as long as society fails to educate its members against its own inherent tendencies, about their responsibility to be active rather than passive agents within it, and about the resultant moral enigmas with which they must be prepared to deal. Nowhere in society is this perhaps more serious than in the domain of the state's police and security activities. A heightened awareness is essential for all who serve within that domain, all who must direct and control them, and all of us when we deal with them.

Modern society has created complex, deceptive mechanisms that obscure the ethical and practical significance of our daily affairs. Perhaps these are more overwhelming than those of simpler times. If so, that neither excuses modern people nor protects them from any consequences. Members of industrialized society accept both the demand for higher levels of technical skill and knowledge and the consequences of failure to achieve such education. If modern society also requires higher levels of ethical and psychological awareness than simpler times, then one must also accept the demand for a higher education to develop that awareness and the consequences of failure to pursue it.

Appendix A
Table of Comparative Ranks

SS	German Army	U.S. Army	German Police
Reichsführer SS	Generalfeldmarschall	General of Army	Chef der Deutschen Polizei
Oberstgruppenführer	Generaloberst		Generaloberst der Polizei
Obergruppenführer	General	General	General der Polizei
Gruppenführer	Generalleutnant	Lieutenant General	Generalleutnant der Polezei
Brigadeführer	Generalmajor	Major General	Generalmajor der Polizei
Oberführer		Brigadier General	
Standartenführer	Oberst	Colonel	Oberst der Schupo
			Reichskriminaldirektor
Obersturmbannführer	Oberstleutnant	Lieutenant Colonel	Oberstleutnant der Schupo
			Oberregierungs- und Kriminalrat
Sturmbannführer	Major	Major	Major der Schupo
			Regierungs- und Kriminalrat
			Kriminaldirektor
Hauptsturmführer	Hauptmann	Captain	Hauptmann der Schupo
			Kriminalrat
Obersturmführer	Oberleutnant	First Lieutenant	Oberleutnant der Schupo
			Kriminalkommissar
			Kriminaloberinspektor
Untersturmführer	Leutnant	Second Lieutenant	Leutnant der Schupo
			Kriminalinspektor

(continued)

Appendix A
Table of Comparative Ranks (*continued*)

SS	German Army	U.S. Army	German Police
Sturmscharführer	Stabsfeldwebel	Master Sergeant	Obermeister
			Kriminalobersekretär
			Meister
			Kriminalsekretär
Truppenführer/	Oberfeldwebel	Tech Sergeant	Hauptwachtmeister
Hauptscharführer			Kriminaloberassistent
Oberscharführer	Feldwebel	Staff Sergeant	Kriminalassistant
Scharführer	Unterfeldwebel	Sergeant	Oberwachtmeister
			Kriminalassistant
Unterscharführer	Obergefreiter	Corporal	Wachtmeister
			Kriminalassistant Anwärter
Rottenführer	Gefreiter	Private, First Class	Rottwachtmeister
Sturmmann	Obersoldat		Unterwachtmeister
SS-Mann	Schütze/Soldat	Private	Anwärter
Anwärter		Recruit	

Note: Police ranks underwent changes during the period 1932–1937, and they cannot be consistently correlated with military or even SS ranks. Correlations here are approximate.

Appendix B

Chart B.1 The Geheime/Staatspolizeiamt
Organization Plan for September 1, 1933

Chief: *Ministerialrat Diels* ─────────┐
Deputy: *Oberregierungsrat Volk* ───┘── *Special Commando Henze*
                                           SS-Sturmf. Rodde

Propaganda Post: *von Lützow*

Department I. Organization and Administration—*RA Dr. Schnitzler*
    Desk A: Organization
    Desk B: Personnel Office, Security, Holding Cells
    Desk C: Management

Department II. Legal department—*ORR Volk*
    Desk A: Judicial Affairs, Law
    Desk B: Reduction of Personal Freedom (Protective Custody)
    Desk C: Disposition of Seized Property
    Desk D: Press Police (Subversion)
    Desk E_1:   Economic Politics, Work Sabotage
    Desk E_2:   Cultural & Social Politics
    Desk F: Riots, Explosives, Assassinations, Weapons, Protection, Foreigners, Immigrants, Jews, Freemasons
    Desk G: Foreign: Foreign Germans, Borderlands, National Minorities, Saar, Memel, Danzig, Austria

Department III. Movements Department—*KPR Nebe*
   Information Service—KK Nussbaum
   Secret Service—KOK Otto
    Desk A: Police Squads—*KK Lipik*

249

Desk B: Marxism
    B1:   Communism
    B2:   Labor Affairs (esp. RGO)—*GA Dr. Gisevius*
    B3:   Socialist Party—*GA Dr.Gisevius*
    C: Counterrevolutionary Efforts
    D: Russians

Department IV. Treason and Espionage—*PCapt. Ölze*
    Commission 1:   Industrial & Economic Espionage
    Commission 2:   Aerial, Coastal, Military, England, Special
    Commission 3:   France, Foreign Legions, Belgium
    Commission 4:   Poland, Polish Deserters, Danzig
    Commission 5:   Soviet Espionage, Soviet Border States
    Commission 6:   Czechoslovakia, Austria, Balkans, Pacifists

Department V. Liaison Officers
            To the SA—*SA Sturmf. Blumenthal*
            To the SS—*SS Oberf. Henze; SS Sturmf. Rodde*
            To the ND of the NADAP—*SA Standf. Aumüller*
            To the Schupo—*PMaj. Ilgen; PCapt. Schünemann*

Note: For the sake of brevity, only the names of the more significant personnel are given in these charts.
Sources: Chart, Organisation des Geheimen Staatspolizeiamts, Stand: 1.9.1933, OA 500/1/38a/269; a similar chart (n.d.), 267.

Chart B.2   Geheime Staatspolizeiamt Organization Plan of October 1,1935

Chief: *Pr. Minister President Göring*
    Deputy Chief and Inspector: RFSS Himmler
         Deputy & Leader of Gestapo Office: SS-Gruppenf. Heydrich
            Deputy Leader: SS-Standartenf. ORR Dr. Best

Main Department I—SS-Standartenf. ORR Best
    Principal IA: Organization & business; personnel affairs of middle and
                        lower civil servants and employees, Gestapa
    Principal IB: Budgetary affairs of the Gestapo
    Principal IC: Economic affairs of Gestapo
    Principal ID: Organization and business of the field posts
    Principal IE: Personnel affairs (except as covered by IA)
    Principal IF: Non-Prussian political police
    Principal IG: Material law of the political police
    Principal IH: Seizure of property
    Principal IJ: Justiciary; disciplinary testing and discharging
    Principal IK: Special organizational affairs
    Principal IL: Foreign political police

Main Department II—SS-Gruppenf. Heydrich

Subdepartment II 1:	Enemy movements; Party affairs; protective custody; economic affairs; archive; identification service; weapons affairs *SS-H'Sturmf. Flesch* Deputy: *SS-H'Sturmf. Müller*
II 1 zbV.:	Special assignments; observations; assassinations; weapons and explosives affairs
II 1 A:	Communist and Marxist movements and their affiliated organizations—*SS-H'Sturmf. Müller*
II 1 AI:	Communism; subversion
II 1 A1:	Communism
II 1 A3:	Subversion; factory work of the KPD; Am-Apparat
II 1 AII:	Marxism other than KPD and affliiated organizations; Comintern; GPU; right Russian movements, etc.
II 1 A2:	Marxism and affiliated organizations
II 1 A4:	Comintern; GPU; Russian constitution; right-Russian movements; returnees from USSR; foreigners file
II 1 B:	Churches; confessional leagues; sects; Jews; Free Masons; emigrants—*SS-H'Sturmf. Flesch*
II 1 B1:	Churches; confessional leagues; sects
II 1 B2:	Jews; Free Masons; emigrants—*RR Dr. Hasselbacher*
II 1 C:	reaction; opposition; affairs of Austrian refugees *SS-O'Sturmf. Huber*
II 1 C1:	Reaction
II 1 C2:	Opposition
II 1 C3:	Austrian affairs
II 1 D:	Protective custody; concentration camps—*KR Futh*
II 1 E:	Economic, agrarian and social politics; work sabotage; political unions
II 1 F:	Card files; reports; document administration
II 1 G:	Identification service
II 1 H:	Party, SS, SA, HJ, BdM, NSKK affairs—*KR Meisinger*
II 1 H1:	Party, HJ, BdM affairs
II 1 H2:	SA, SS, NSKK affairs
II 1 H3:	Combatting phenomena hostile and to the state
II 1 S:	Special desk (homosexuality?)—*KR Meisinger*
Subdepartment II 2:	Press affairs—*RR Dr. Gotthardt*
II 2 A:	General press affairs
II 2 B:	Domestic press and publishers (except church presses)
II 2 C:	Church confessional press
II 2 D:	Domestic editors, publishers, reporters
II 2 E:	West European and non-European press
II 2 F:	East European press
II 2 G:	Emigrant press and hate propaganda
II 2 H:	Film; theatre; art; science
II 2 J:	Library; lector of press police for compiling books

Main Department III: Abwehr Office
> Deputy: *RR Damzog*

Subdepartment III 1:   High treason and counterespionage EAST
> *KR Kubitzky*

III 1 A:	Poland; Danzig
III 1 B:	Czechoslovakia
III 1 C:	Russia and its eastern rim states
III 1 D:	Marine, coastal defense; high treason; special foreign and unknown hostile states

Subdepartment III 2:   High treason and counterespionage WEST
> *KR Geissel*

III 2 A:	France; Belgium; Switzerland
III 2 B:	Italy; Austria; Hungary; Balkan states; work and economic espionage
III 2 C:	America; Holland; England; Scandanavian states; Wehrmacht; SS; SA; FAD
III 2 D:	High treason, pacifists; separatists; deserters; Foreign Legionnaires; refractures
III 2 E:	Air transport affairs

Subdepartment III 3:

III 3 A:	General preventive measures; special assignments
III 3 B:	Foreigner and border control
III 3 C:	Minorities inside the Reich

Subdepartment III 4:   Communications; card files; statistics

Department IV added 26 October 1935
> *SS-Sturmbannf. Schupo Capt. Staudinger*

IV A:	Vehicular affairs
IV B:	Report management and forwarding
IV C:	Flight affairs
IV D:	Technical weapons office

Source: Geschäftsverteilungsplan des GeStapa, Stand vom 1 October 1935; and GeStapo, re Errichtung einer Abteilung IV beim GeStapa, 26.10.1935, BA/R-58/840/50-66.

Chart B.3   Organization of Security Office, 1933–1934

Chief of Sicherheitsamt (SHA)
Adjutant

Department Z *(Zentral)* (registry and correspondence of CdSHA)

Department I. Organization
  1. Personnel
  2. Personnel file

3. Civil service reinforcements for state organizations
4. General organizational matters; activity reports
5. Training officer

Department II. Administration (pay, finances, supplies)

Department III. Information (Domestic Political)
1. NS, *völkisch,* monarchical opposition, etc.
2. Religion and ideology, including separatism
3. Marxists
4. Science and education
5. Constitution and law
6. Strengthening of ideological awareness of the public

Department IV, Counterespionage and Foreign Inquiry
1. Foreign intelligence
2. Jews; pacifists; hate propaganda; emigrants
3. GPU; espionage; immigrants
4. Counterespionage, military and economic
5. Armament
6. Economy and corruption

Department V, Freemasonry
1. Freemasonry card file (domestic—foreign)
2. Evaluation
3. Lodge file
4. Archive
5. Museum

Independent Desk (VI), Press
1. Monitoring and evaluating
2. Information service

Independent Desk (VII), Technical Support and Radio
1. Enemy organizations file
2. Photography; laboratory; drafting
3. Statistics
4. Library
5. Radio (wireless communications)

Sources: Carbon copy from files of SD OAb Rhein, n.d.(1934), HStA Wiesbaden, 483/ 625/70-80; and Best letter, 2.4.1977.

Chart B.4 Organization of the Sicherheitshauptamt, 1935

Chief of the Sicherheitshauptamt

Zentralamt 1, Central Chancellery
   Hauptabteilung 1: Service supervision
   Hauptabteilung 2: Registry
   Hauptabteilung 3: Radio and technical support

Zentralamt 2, Personnel Office
   Hauptabteilung 1: Personnel and promotions
   Hauptabteilung 2: Assignments
   Hauptabteilung 3: Training, education and recruitment
   Hauptabteilung 4: SS-Court and disciplinary affairs, welfare
   Hauptabteilung 5: SD-School

Zentralamt 3: Administrative Office

Zentralamt 4: Press Office
   Hauptabteilung 1: Press
   Hauptabteilung 2: Literature
   Hauptabteilung 3: Film and radio

Sachamt 1: Culture Office—politically important developments in all spheres
   of public life

Sachamt 2: Information Office—Identification and analysis of all enemies of
   the NS ideology

Sachamt 3: Abwehr Office—Counterespionage and countersabotage

Sachamt 4: Staff Office—Reporting to the relevant offices of Party and state
   all important developments in the state and Party apparatus as well as in the
   economy and foreign affairs

Note: The author has not yet been able to determine what, if any, numeric and alphabetic designations may have been used; the numbers given above are simply sequential.

Source: CdSHA, Vorläufige Geschäftsordnung, 1 September 1935, OS/500/3/9/10–14.

Chart B.5   Organization of SD Main Office, 1936–1937

Chief of SD Main Office [SD-HA]—Heydrich
Staff Command: *SS-Brigf. Taubert*
Adjutant: *SS-O'Sturmf. Neumann*
(Office z.b.V., coordination of unsalaried affiliates in other agencies)

Office I: Administration and Organization—SS-Standf. Albert

Central Department I 1: Staff chancellery
  I 11: Service supervision
    I 111: Organization and inspection
      I 1111: *SS-O'Scharf. Schellenberg*
    I 112: Management
  I 12: Objective supervision
    I 121: Reporting [Berichterstattung]
    I 122: Special commission [Sonderaufträge]
  I 13: Registry
    I 134: Reich central card file
  I 14: Technical support—*SS-Sturmbf. Sohst*
  I 15: Staff command

Central Department I 2: Personnel
  I 25: Court

Central Department I 3: Press and museum—SS-Sturmbf. Six
  I 31: Press and literature—*SS-U'Sturmf. Spengler*
    I 311: Central press bureau—*SS-Scharf. Hagen*
    I 312: Monitoring of press and literature—*v. Kielpinski*
      I 312-1: Freemasons and Jewry; 2, confessional tendencies; 3, Marx-
        ists; 4, emigrants; 5, rightist circles; 6, sciences; 7, Volk-
        stum and race; 8, arts; 9, law & administration; 10, ed-
        ucation; 11, Party and state; 12–14, economy; 15,
        Poland and Russia; 16, northern states; 17, England;
        18, France; 19, Italy and Spain; 20, Austria and Swit-
        zerland; 21, special Abwehr; 22–24, Germany daily
        press
    I 313: Analysis of press and literature by life spheres
  I 32: Museum, library and scientific research, Ehrlinger

Central Department I 4: Administration, SS-Standf. Bork

Office II: SD-Inland—SS-Standf. Dr. Behrends
  Central Department II 1: Ideological analysis—*Behrends*
    II 11: "Ideologies,"—*SS-O'Sturmf. Hartmann*
      II 111: Freemasonry—SS-O'Sturmf. Christensen
        II 1111: Humanitarian lodges—*SS-H'Scharf. Ehlers*
        II 1112: Christian-national lodges—*H'Scharf. Wisliceny*
        II 1113: Angle lodges and Masonic-like lodges
        II 1114: Freemasonry in foreign countries
      II 112: Jewry—SS-H'Scahrf. Kuno Schröder
        II 1121: Zionists/assimilationists
        II 1122: Neutrals/orthodoxy and Karatative
        II 1123: Assimilationists/Zionist affairs—*Eichmann*
      II 113: Religious-political currents—SS-O'Sturmf. Hartl
        II 1131: Political-Roman Catholicism
        II 1132: Protestantism/orders and missions
        II 1133: Sects/protestantism
        II 1134: Völkisch religious groups/sects
    II 12: Political enemies—SS-H'Sturmf. Göttsch
      II 121: Left movements/Marxism—*SS-O'Sturmf. Wolf*
        II 1211: Communism
          II 121 11: Comintern
            II 121 116: Special auxiliary internationals
              II 121 1161: Profintern
                II 121 11612: Interntl. Transport Workers Federation
        II 1212: Social Democracy
        II 1213: Special Marxists
      II 122: Middle movements—*SS-U'Scharf. Radunski*
        II 1221: Democratic organizations
        II 1222: Pacifist organizations
      II 123: Rightist movements—*SS-H'Sturmf. Böhme*
        II 1231: Reaction
          II 123 11: Stahlhelm
          II 123 13: Soldiers organizations
        II 1232: Völkisch oppostion
        II 1233: National Bolshevism [Strasser's Black Front]

  Central Department II 2: Analysis of Spheres of Life—SS-Sturmbf. Höhn
    II 21: Cultural life (Volkstum)—*SS-O'Sturmf. Rausch*
      II 211: Sciences—*SS-O'Sturmf. Beyer*
        II 2111: Teachers and university affairs
        II 2112: Research
        II 2113: Political intellectual directions
      II 212: Volkstum and Volkskunde
      II 213: Race and Volksgesundtheit—*SS-U'Sturmf. Kurreck*
      II 214: Arts/citizens—*SS-H'Scharf. Hennig*
    II 22: Community life—*SS-U'Sturmf. Brauns*

II 221: Constitution and law

II 222: Administrations

II 223: Youth, education—*SS-O'Scharf. Koch*

  II 2231: School affairs

  II 2232: Student organizations

II 224: Party and state orgainzations/press and literature

II 225: National Socialism/Party and state [1937?]

II 23: Material life [economy]—*SS-O'Sturmbf. Heuckenkamp*

II 231: Food economy—*SS-H'Sturmf. Ohlendorf*

II 232: Commerce and transportation

II 233: Currency, banks, markets, and insurance

II 234: Industry and commerce—*SS-O'Sturmf. Eilers*

II 235: Crafts and trades/revenue—*SS-O'Scharf. Seibert*

II 236: Finance/labor and social welfare

II 237: Labor (industry)—*SS-U'Sturmf. Leetsch*

Office III: Abwehr—SS-Standf. Jost

Central Department III 1: Foreign spheres of life

III 11: Europe

  III 111: East: Russia and border states; far East [1937?]

  III 112: South-East/West

    III 1121: Hungary; 1122, Balkans

  III 113: South (South-East)

    III 1131: Austria; 1132, Italy; 1133, Switzerland

  III 114: South-West (South)

    III 1141: Spain; 1142, Portugal

  III 115: West

    III 1151: France; 1152, Belgium; 1153, Netherlands

  III 116: North

    III 1161: England; 1162, Denmark; 1163, Scandinavia

III 12: Non-European states

  III 121: Americas (North-West)

III 122: Australia

III 123: Asia

III 124: Africa

Central Department III 2: Foreign political Abwehr

III 21: Espionage

  III 211: Military espionage

  III 212: Political espionage

  III 213: Economic espionage (Freemasonry)

III 22: Enemy intelligence services

  III 221: West (Jewry)

  III 222: North (political churches)

III 223: East (Communism and Marxism)
III 224: South (liberalism)
III 225: (Legitimacy, right movements)

The first listed responsibility of each office, department, or desk is based on organizational structure effective 1/15/36. Information in parentheses is based entirely on Ramme. Frequent redesignations and reorganizations make designations below the Amt level problematic for any specific date (changes in title are designated by a slash, i.e., early/later). Amt III was significantly reorganized, apparently in spring 1937, which may account for Ramme's differences. Personnel for each position are based on the 1/15/37 Signenzeichnung, and were changed occasionally.

Pattern: Office (Amt)   I
       Central Department (Zentralabteilung)   I 1
         Main Department (Hauptabteilung)   I 11
           Department (Abteilung)   I 111
             Principal or Desk (Referent)   I 1111

The "principal" was the lowest organizational level; numbers beyond that represented subcatagories of an area of research under that principal. A few are added for illustration.

Sources: Befehl d. CdSHA, reorganization of SHA, (n.d., effective 1/15/36), OA/500/3/5/1–18; RFSS, CdSHA, I 112, re "Signenzeichnung," 15.1.1937, StAwshft.b.d.KG Berlin; Ramme, Sicherheitsdienst, 54–57, 248; Aronson, *Heydrich,* 202–203, 206; numerous BDC/SSO and RuSHA files; RFSS, CdSHA, Stabskanzlei: I/1111, "Sachkartei und Sachakten," 8.12.1936, HStA Düsseldorf, RW 33/1/139/1–17; and Peter Brommer, *Die Partei hört mit: Lageberichte und andere Meldungen des Sicherheitsdienstes der SS aus dem Grossraum Koblenz, 1937-1941* (Koblenz: Verlag der Landesarchivverwaltung Rheinland-Pfalz, 1988).

Appendix C

Quantitative Analysis of SD Members

The Samples

My analysis employs three overlapping samples: a sample from all ranks of the SD, from its origins in 1932 to the end of 1934; a sample of all members holding SS officer's rank by the end of 1934; a random sample who were either promoted to SS officers rank or entered with SS officers rank in 1936.

The main sample consists of 518 men identified as members of the SD before the end of 1934, plus 8 who were significant associates before the end of 1932 and who subsequently became full members. This sample of 526 early affiliates represents a mix of all ranks, men who would hold key leadership positions in Sipo and SD, men who would remain in the rank and file, and men who would leave the SD. Specifically, it includes 180 who became officers before the end of 1934, 319 who subsequently became officers, and 27 who never rose above noncommissioned rank.

This is not a random sample. Since there are no known surviving, complete rosters of members for any period, a random sample cannot be established. Official lists of all SS officers *(Dienstaltersliste* or *DAL)*, published annually between 1934 and 1938, have survived, along with some supplementary lists and a roster of senior officers for 1944.[1]

Every man in the DAL promoted to officer before the end of 1934, plus a few others identified from other records, constitute the sample of 180 SD officers by end of 1934. They represent perhaps 99 percent of the total. Thus, this sample of SD officers by 1934 is for all practical purposes a total population.

The sample of SD members by 1934 is simply the best available sample. Although it overrepresents men who became officers by 1938, that does not skew the sample significantly. Most early members who remained active long enough eventually became officers. Surviving rosters for particular times and places indicate that the representation of men who never achieved officer's rank may be proportional in this sample.[2] The most underrepresented would be those who rose to officer between 1938 and 1945. The most overrepresented are the officers by 1934.

This sample contains approximately 62 percent of the estimated membership by the end of 1934, and 78 percent of that by the ends of both 1933 and 1932.[3] Although not technically a representative sample, it is certainly representative of the men who played formative roles in the SD. One must pursue the total population rather than settling for the easily identified officer corps, because of the lack of correlation between SS rank and status in the early SD.

The third sample for the early SD is a random sample of 120 men from among those whom I identified in the 1936 DAL as new SD officers. This process was problematic, and 16 turned out to have been promoted as SD members to officer in 1935. Nevertheless, they have been retained in the sample which remains representative of men promoted to officer later in the period under study. They provide a comparative analysis against the men promoted to officer before the end of 1934. I pursued randomness by selecting every fifth man identified as not appearing in previous DAL as SD members. This process guaranteed an even distribution among the ranks, by date of promotion and SS number, since that is the order in which entries in the DAL occur. For obvious reasons, I prefer this guaranteed distribution achieved by stratified-systematic sampling over the more conventional process employing random number tables.

Source of Data

The primary source of data has been the SS and other biographical files in the former U.S. Document Center at Berlin, commonly referred to as the BDC.[4] I usually limited the search for quantifiable data to the SS Officers' (SSO) files, the Rasse und Siedlungshauptamt (RuSHA) files, and SS miscellaneous files, supplemented by comparable collections of SS personnel documents removed from the BDC collection for the various Nuremberg trials (housed originally as part of RG-238 of the U.S. National Archives and subsequently microfilmed in several collections). In addition, I exploited collections of SD and SS personnel records not integrated into the BDC that survived in the Landeshauptarchiv at Koblenz and the Hauptstaatsarchiv at Wiesbaden. In a few cases, biographical publications listed in the bibliography contain relevant entries that flesh out basic data. The Nuremberg records also contained interrogations of some of these men and persons who worked with them, filling in some missing holes.

The BDC files confront one with several problems. Specifically, the SSO files are an artificial collection created for the trials and de-Nazification process. They consist of miscellaneous SS documents filed together under the names of the officers. They include, for instance, standard personnel forms and questionnaires, evaluations written by superiors, disciplinary records, transfer and promotion orders, and personal and official correspondence. In contrast, the RuSHA files are an original collection of that office responsible for the health and genealogical evaluation of SS men and their brides. Both collections often contain one or more handwritten autobiographical statements (Lebens-läufe), composed at different times.

The problems posed by these documents begin with frequent lacunae or an almost complete lack of information. Files vary in size from one document to several folders up to six inches thick. In some cases the standard forms appear not to have been kept up to date. Some entries are illegible or nearly so. As with all personnel records, errors are not uncommon. Fortunately, there is enough duplication that many errors can be detected. Given my own experiences with the U.S. military and government agencies, I conclude that the data in these records are as reliable as most official personnel records. The source for potential GIGO (garbage in, garbage out) is probably not significantly greater than in any other study based on official records. Problems relating to specific types of data are outlined below.

The Nature of the Data and Methodology

Another possible source for GIGO is my own interpretation and coding of the more problematic data. Additionally, as explained below, much of the tabulated data about personal histories and SS-SD careers has to be treated as impressionistic. It can be quantified only in the sense that it is counted and tabulated to provide "comparative impressions." It cannot bear the weight of statistical analysis.

Since I never intended to limit myself to conventional sociopolitical analysis, and since I always suspected that the men were an especially heterogeneous and unique mix of unconventional Nazis and accomplices, I collected a wide range of information. I not only wanted to know the men, but also the personnel politics of Sipo and SD. Consequently, I coded 114 entries for each case: 110 are data on the individual; 4 are identification and source codes. Each entry exploited for this study is listed below with an explanation of its inherent problems, strengths and weaknesses.

Of course, not all 110 items are available for each case. In most, at least one item is missing or illegible. This may upset purists who prefer to throw out or replace cases with incomplete data. I rejected such a strategy because of the number of problematic entries, and because the total population, particularly that of many subsets, is already small. The absence of SSO files on men who never rose above NCO would require dropping them entirely. So I have kept all cases no matter how incomplete, even negative BDC searches that leave me with only limited data. To help the reader see the possible significance of missing data, in the tables, missing data are usually indicated, unlike in the text, where only valid percentages are given. When simple statistical frequencies, means, and modes, are derived from these data, the percentage of the missing data provides adequate warnings about reliability.

Most items selected for entry were available consistently, however, and many lend themselves to reliable quantification. On the other extreme, items like expressions of personal prejudice, disciplinary actions and involvement in significant events like the Röhm Purge, the *Kristallnacht* and the *Einsatzgruppen* are not recorded consistently or in enough detail to lend themselves to reliable quantitative manipulation. I include them because of their relevance to the analyses attempted here, but they allow only minimal, cautious usage, primarily as impressionistic rather than scientific data.

In between these extremes lie uneven data such as occupation and employment records. Some files contain sufficient detail to define occupational status and history clearly. In other cases, a few vague, inconsistently employed terms provide the only clues. Thus, relatively clear data mix with vague information. For each data category described below, I explain such problems.

For this study, only relatively simple frequency and cross-tabulation analyses seem necessary. More sophisticated efforts may be employed later to reveal aspects of personnel politics over the extended history of Sipo and SD.

The chi-square test for association reveals which of the following tables exhibit distinctive characteristics among the subcategories in SD membership. In most cases, there are no significant differences among the subcategories, so I have not encumbered the text with the test data. When determining significance, I have required that $\alpha \leq .05$. Wherever that occurred, the relevant data accompany the table. Unfortunately, in the most interesting cases of apparent differences, specifically such things as expressed prejudices or prior involvements in NS violence, the data are too "impressionistic" to warrant statistical testing and analysis, and are merely tabulated for clarity of presentation.

Since space does not allow publication of all tabulated data, scholars who need access to either the raw data or printed tables should contact the author.

Personal Background

Item 1. Date of Birth (Age Cohorts)

Items 2 & 3. Place of Birth and Size of Community in 1925   Community size in 1925 was chosen as a median date for the maturity of the sample and because of readily available statistics.[5]

For comparative data, I used Ziegler's figures for the pre-1933 SS officer corps[6] and the distribution of the German population in 1910.[7] Because I coded by SS-Abschnitt, my distribution (like Ziegler's) is slightly skewed to the numbers counted as southerners. I included in the "south" Abschnitt Rhein, which contained RB Wiesbaden and all of Land Hesse. The figures for the German population are that of 1910 within the 1929 borders. From that set of statistics, I could not separate RB Wiesbaden from the count for the north. This can account for less than 2 percent of the deviation between SS/SD data and that for the Reich. Again, for comparison in size of birth place, I have used Ziegler's data on the pre-1933 SS officers,[8] and the general German population for 1925.[9]

Items 4 & 5. Religion (see tables C.1)   On most standard forms, when religion is recorded, only gottgläubig may be given. When that was the case, to obtain comparable data, I followed Ziegler's pattern of assigning the father's religion, when available. Even after such efforts, many remain unknown. Date of withdrawal of church membership (item 5) is indicated on standard forms.

For comparative data, for the pre-1933 SS officer corps, I used Ziegler[10] and the German population in 1933.[11] The calculations for the 1933 population excluded practicing Jews from the data. Percentages in parentheses are valid percentages.

For comparative data on church withdrawal, I have used data on SS membership for September 1937 and December 1938[12] and Ziegler's samples of pre-1933 and 1938 SS officers.[13] The estimated final figure for the SS-Totenkopfverbinde is extrapolated from Ziegler's chart for his sample of 1938 SS-TV officers.[14] My data are in valid percentages (except for the missing data percentage in parentheses).

Items 6-8. Level of Education (see tables C.2)   Level of formal education is a standard entry on all personnel forms, and when a Lebenslauf is available, details about apprenticeships (item 7) are available. From Lebensläufe one can also learn about interruptions (item 8) and frustrated educational goals.

For comparison of educational levels, I used Ziegler's data on pre-1933 and 1938 SS officers.[15] Unfortunately, in my initial coding, before I was fully aware of the nature of my population and what might prove to be the more important distinctions, I made too many fine distinctions

Tables C.1 A. Comparative Religious Origins

Religion	Pre-1933 SS Officers	1934 SD Officers	1934 Other Ranks	1934 Total	1936 SD Officers	1933 General Population
Evangelical		52.3	61.8	58.5	67.5	
Lutheran	70.9	(66.7)	(75.9)	(72.8)	(81.0)	62.7
		23.9	17.6	19.8	15.0	
Catholic	28.8	(30.5)	(21.6)	(24.6)	(18.0)	33.3
Other		2.3	2.1	2.2	0.8	
or none	0.3	(2.8)	(2.5)	(2.6)	(1.0)	4.1
unknown		21.7	18.5	19.6	16.9	
N		180	346	526	120	65.5 million

Chi-square could be calculated with validity only for the two major denominations. With the df = 1, chi-square had to be calculated with Yates' correction. For the 1934 membership, chi-square = 4.041; df = 1; P < .05. For the officers, chi-square = 5.306; df = 1; P < .05.

B. Church Withdrawal

Withdrawn by	SD Sample	SS-TV	General SS	33 SS Officers	38 SS Officers
1934	8.2				
1935	18.1				
1937	44.1	51.7	16.2		
1938	50.6	69.0	21.9		
1945	90.1	85?		74.4	68.1
Unknown	(32.7)				
N	526				

at lower levels of education, and not enough at the higher. Persons who attended but never completed university cannot be distinguished from those who attended lesser Hochschule such as Akademie. For comparison with Ziegler's statistics, valid percentages are given in parentheses.

Many apprenticeships involved simultaneous attendance at Fach- or Gewerbeschule, which are counted as completion of a "middle school" level, unless completion of grade level O-II (Ober-Sekunda, second-highest class) or above is indicated. Reasons for disruption of education or training before entering the SD have been compressed. "Economic" includes loss of father, inability of family or student to finance, or having to support the family. "Other" is another "nonfault" category that includes reasons of health, noneconomic hardships, going to war, or the

Tables C.2   A. Education—Comparative Levels

Level	34 Other	SD Samples 34 Officers	36 Officers	SS Officer Samples Pre-1933	1938
Less than 8 years	0.6	1.1	1.7		
	(14.3)	(14.5)	(21.1)	48.1	37.0
Volksschule OIII	13.3	11.1	18.3		
Mittelschule-UII	30.0	16.2	19.2		
	(31.1)	(19.1)	(20.2)	5.9	4.9
Höher OII-OI	16.8	14.4	14.2		
	(17.3)	(17.2)	(14.9)	28.3	27.4
Attended Hochschule	13.6	14.4	15.8		
Universität mit	9.0	13.9	10.8		
(University total)	(36.7)	(49.3)	(43.9)	17.7	30.0
Doktorat	13.0	13.3	15.0		
Unknown	3.2	15.6	5.0		
N	526	180	120		

For 1934 ranks, Chi-Square = 11.732; df = 5; P < .05

B.   Education—Apprenticeships and Disruptions By Educational Subsets

Apprentice	Lower	High School	Higher	Unknown
Completed	69.3	53.6	10.1	
Incomplete	2.0	4.8	2.5	
None	13.7	25.0	80.3	
Unknown	15.1	16.7	7.0	

Disruptions				
Econ/family	9.3	6.0	9.6	
Failed/quit	0.0	0.0	0.5	
Political	0.0	1.2	3.5	
Other	3.5	3.6	1.0	
None	70.7	71.4	74.7	
Unknown	16.6	17.9	10.6	
N	205	84	198	39

family moving to where the desired education/training was unavailable. "Political" includes claims of persecution, turning to full-time political commitments/activities, or taking up a salaried position with the Movement, including the SD (which might have been driven as much by economic as by political motives).

Occupation and Social Status

Items 9–16. Occupation or Social Status   These are problematic data at two levels. First, wherever a Lebenslauf is unavailable, only a vague one- or two-word title indicates the occupation. Even with Lebensläufe, the father's occupation frequently remains vaguely identified. Furthermore, since occupation and social status were so closely interrelated in such a class-conscious society as Germany, one can anticipate either the use of inflated terms (Kaufmann for sales clerk) or conversely, due to the Nazi egalitarian posture, modesty in self-labeling (Arbeiter or Bauer instead of skilled worker or foreman or Gutsbesitzer). Consequently, one has to use a number of other characteristics to evaluate the given information, such as level of education. Therefore, the exact occupation, especially one's level within it, cannot always be coded with a high level of confidence.

The second, more difficult, problem is calculating social status from occupation, level within it, education, and other miscellaneous symptoms. Social status or class is an elusive concept in any society, not least in Germany between 1870 (when many of the fathers in the sample were establishing their status) and the 1930s.

My exploration and analysis of the available data evolved simultaneously with most of the current debate over social analysis of the membership and support of the Nazi Movement. Although I have benefited considerably from such debate, my objectives have not been entirely the same as most participants. I share one of the emerging conclusions that social background does not explain Nazism, and certainly not its worst consequences.[16]

Most efforts at organizing people into social classes according to their occupations have centered around debates over the social roots of Nazism or around the so-called German Sonderweg in modern socioeconomic development. Such approaches offer little help in understanding the men of Sipo and SD. My concern has been exploring the self-images, motivating ideals, and sociocultural baggage of the membership. From early on, I detected strong symptoms of self-deceiving organizational identities in the expressions of leading members both during their involvement and subsequently in memoirs and interrogations.[17] Consequently, I collected and coded all consistently available data that might reflect self-images, the nature of the ego (whether strong or weak, threatened or damaged), and motivating or proclaimed ideals and missions. Simultaneous reading in the emerging literature of psychohistory and in social and psychological theory suggested possible connections among the psychological and valuational phenomena, sociocultural backgrounds, and the life experiences in Germany of the men in question. Consequently, I have organized my occupational-social analysis somewhat differently than most.

Despite differences, like most attempting a socioeconomic analysis of early twentieth-century Germans, I have found guidance in work ranging from Theodor Geiger's through Michael Kater's and beyond.[18] Based on three dimensions of analysis—education, occupation, and independent versus salaried income—I divided subjects initially into three gross categories: upper, lower middle, and lower.

Earlier efforts to distinguish among old and new elites and secure upper-middle-class members foundered on the vagueness of the data. Now "upper classes" consist of high civil servants and public office holders, regular officers and reserve officers of field grade, academics from university through public school administrators to Studienräte, pastors, priests, editors, free professionals (mostly medical or legal), owners of large businesses and industry or corporate executives, managers, large landowners, technical professions (holding Diplom and self-employed or in managerial positions), and students in programs preparatory for such occupations (Kater's occupational subgroups 10–14).

The concept of "lower-middle class" requires flexibility to include both older and newer occupational groups that seem to have held such status by the 1920s and 1930s. Included are middle civil servants; reserve officers of company grade; public school teachers; lesser clerics; journalists; most artists; medical technicians and nurses; small-business owners; junior managerial positions and wholesale sales; small landholders or peasants, plus Landwirtsbeamten; technical professions (without Diplom); master craftsmen who may have owned a shop or business, or supervised in larger concerns; students in training for such positions; and skilled laborers in supervisory positions. As a special subset that could be split out, I included the full range of lower white-collar employees: lower (einfach) civil servants and government employees; NCOs in the military; service, clerical, sales and technical employees; and trainees for such positions. (All together, these equal Kater's subgroups 4–8.)

The "lower class" consists of two subgroups. Skilled labor includes all those ranging from salaried workers in old guild or artisan skills; industrial workers who had formal training programs of three years or more; workers in agriculture or forestry with similar formal training; such trainees not likely to inherit a family business; and unskilled workers in supervisory positions (Kater's subgroups 2 and 3). Semi- and unskilled labor includes corporals and below in the military; farm hands; workers without formal training programs; domestics without supervisory status; and any elementary school graduate or worker trainee who never achieved higher status outside the SS-SD (Kater's subgroup 1).

The separable lower white-collar and skilled labor subgroups allow for analysis of status from more than one theoretical perspective. Efforts at analysis of German society before World War II have produced debates over proper classification of these subsets. Disagreement covers those who treat them as lower-middle and working class respectively, those who treat them collectively as a new social component of the lower-middle class, and those who class them together as "workers." Arguably, most white-collar employees in Germany rejected working-class identity and aspired to middle-class life-styles and status, copying them in every way they could. However, many, especially those of working-class origin or inhabitants of working-class neighborhoods, identified with workers or at least joined Socialist or Communist unions and parties. Some had apparently begun the modern western trend toward what some ironically call the new "classless society," consisting of a predominant "salaried estate," distinguishable within its ranks only by education, income, and personal life-style, and greatly homogenized under the influence of modern mass media.[19] In the Lebensläufe, I encountered many sons of traditional lower-middle-class-fathers (i.e., artisans, peasants, and small shopkeepers) who pursued not only white-collar but even skilled labor occupations without any signs of feeling a loss of status (at least not before depression-era unemployment). Treating them as having lost status by one or two steps denies new attitudes and obscures "structural mobility," i.e., movement from old and dying to new occupational opportunities. Such new jobs offered at least equal salaries and standards of living—and often more long-range upward mobility.

To be able to view the data from such alternative perspectives, I can keep each subgroup in its original gross class, rearrange them up or down as theory demands, or unite them in a "transitional class." That class falls "between" lower-middle and lower as a compromise between what was arguably still the dominant perception of social status in 1930, and the growing perception of those within that "transitional class." I use the "transitional-class" arrangement for a conservative measure of social mobility. Thus, movement from lower-middle-class fathers to "transitional class" sons would count as a *possible* loss of one step in status. For sons of unskilled workers, it would count as one step up, but as no upward movement for skilled workers' sons. Thus, I have deliberately minimized signs of upward mobility that might not have been perceived as such by many contemporary Germans. At the same time, this specific change of status can also be seen as a possibly aggressively modern act of social mobility, subject to frustration (especially in the depression) and to condescending behavior from less-modern mentalities. Such men should have had more strong than weak or flawed egos, though much bruised and battered in many cases.

Having hit late upon this solution and the significance of "structural mobility" as a symptom of possible ego strength and of ego threats particular to Germany in the Weimar era, I regret not having made allowances for finer coding distinctions between traditional and modern components of some other occupational groups. Nevertheless, from the (I) upper, (II) lower-middle, and (IV) lower classes as presently coded, upward or downward movement from father's to son's first and second careers and status may signal similar symptoms. The result of these classifications is the two-dimensional social-occupational structure in Chart C.

Regrettably, such categorizations still obscure significant distinctions, especially within the "upper class" conglomerate. Unfortunately, in my estimation, the data belie the meaningfulness of any efforts to quantify such distinctions. On the other hand, I did make distinctions missing in other approaches. For instance, all students, military, or civil servants should not be lumped together in one or two classes. The obvious differences between Universität, Handelschule, and Gewerbeschule students, between reserve and regular officer, between sergeant and corporal, among Kriminaldirektor, Kriminalkommissar and Kriminalassistent demand distinctions. The combination of career and more-precise educational information on standard SS forms and their usual consciousness of distinctions in military and civil service ranks made more-accurate categorization possible than in Nazi Party records, for instance.

Nevertheless, the final balance between precision and lack of reliability leaves me skeptical about sophisticated statistical analysis of my social data. All class-based analysis, especially social mobility, is offered here as better than impressionistic evidence, but not as scientific proof or testing. So many subjective decisions have been made along the way that GIGO lurks in the wings.

9 & 10. Father's Occupation & Status   Except for additional clues found occasionally in a Lebenslauf, there is usually only a one-word title given.

Items 11–12. Member's Learned Occupation & Status

Item 13. Length of Time in First Career   This is time before changing careers, before changing status within career, or before entering the SD.

Items 14–15. Member's Second Occupation & Status   If more than two second occupations, the longest practiced was chosen.

Item 16. Time in Second Occupation before Entry into the SD

Chart C

SOCIAL - OCCUPATIONAL STRUCTURE

OCCUPATIONAL FIELDS	I UPPER	II LOWER MIDDLE	III TRANSITIONAL	IV LOWER
Government & Civil Servants	Elected Officials, Higher Civil Servants	Middle Civil Servants	Lower Civil Servants	Workers
Military	Regular Officers	Reserve Officers	NCOs	Other Ranks
Education Religion	University Gymnasium Clerics	Teachers, Lesser Clerics		
Arts and Letters	Editors Artists with Diplomas	Journalists most Artists		
Professions Service	Physicians Lawyers Architects	Medical Technicians Nurses	Hair Dressers	Hospital Attendants
Banking & Commerce	Large Owners Executives	Small Owners Managers Representatives	Sales Clerical	Stock Workers Porters
Agriculture	Large Owners	Peasants Farm Administrators		Farm Labor
Industry and Transportation	Large Owners Executives Engineers	Small Owners Indep. Artisans Technicians	Skilled Workers	Unskilled Semiskilled Workers
Students & Trainees			White-collar Blue-collar	

Social Mobility

Social mobility is an extremely culture and period relative concept. It is too easy to impose contemporary American conceptions of advancement onto Weimar Germany, where significantly different social values prevailed. What is more, that society, like most western industrial societies in the twentieth century, was undergoing radical changes in such perceptions.[20] Even if one can agree on the prevalent measures of status at the time, one can rarely know how an individual or those whose opinions affected him felt. Such feelings are far more important for my purpose of assessing self-image. Despite all these problems and the problematic nature of my assessments of social status, I feel it necessary to look at what is available as evidence of socio-economic achievement (tables C.3).

To do this I performed several calculations:

1. Change in occupational area from father's occupation to son's learned occupation as a crude measure of attempted occupational mobility
2. Changes in the social status from the father's to the son's, including changes between status achieved in the learned occupation and in a second occupation, if any
3. Cross-tabulations among these changes
4. Net changes in the social status of the sample of fathers versus that of members at time of entry into the SD
5. Cross-tabulations of father's status by son's level of education as another measure of attempted mobility
6. Specific examination of sons of lower-middle-class families, since that class has always been a focus of study to explain Nazism as well as the object of many stereotyping assumptions

Of course, all of this had to be compared against published studies of social mobility in Germany during this period, which unfortunately contain little comparable data, but which do provide some sense of relative achievement.[21]

7. Other Personal Information

Items 17–19. Economic Disruptions   Where Lebensläufe exist, it is possible to get some sense of whether or not a subject was unemployed or underemployed, when, and for how long.

Items 20–22. Military Record

Item 23. Paramilitary Activity   This covers activity in groups such as Freikorps.

Tables C.3   A.   Indicators of Social Mobility—Education Attempted as a Measure of Social Aspirations

Father's Class	Educational Level Attempted				Total %
	1	2	3	4	
Upper	2	14	14	77	107
% of Row	1.9	13.1	13.1	72.0	20.3
Lower-Middle	33	56	38	62	189
% of Row	17.5	29.6	20.1	32.8	35.9
Transitional	15	47	20	18	100
% of Row	15.0	47.0	20.0	18.0	19.0
Lower	6	7	1	2	16
% of Row	37.5	43.8	6.3	12.5	3.0
					114
Unknown					21.8
					(412)
N	56	124	73	159	526
% of Known	13.6	30.1	17.7	38.6	100

Ed. Level 1 = Volksschule or less, with or without Lehrzeit
2 = Volks- to Mittelschule, plus vocational schools, to U II
3 = Hoehrer Schule, O II to O I
4 = Attempted any type of Hochschule
Given the small numbers per cell in the lower class, the chi-square test was performed only for the top three classes. Chi-Square = 78.207; df = 6; P < .001.

B.   Indicators of Social Mobility—Class Change by Father's Class

Father's Class	Movement Up or Down in Social Class							Total
	+3	+2	+1	None	-1	-2	-3	
Upper				73	16	13	2	104
% of Row				70.2	15.4	12.5	1.9	100
Lower-Middle			59	54	69	8		190
% of Row			31.1	28.4	36.3	4.2		100
Transitional		15	21	57	6			99
% of Row		15.2	21.2	57.6	6.1			100
Lower	1	4	10	1				16
% of Row	6.3	25.0	62.5	6.3				100
Unknown								117
N	1	19	90	185	91	21	2	(409)
% of Row	0.3	4.6	22.0	45.2	22.2	5.1	0.5	100

C.   Indicators of Social Mobility—Class Change by Change in Occupational Area

Compare to Father	Movement Up or Down in Social Class							
	+3	+2	+1	None	-1	-2	-3	Total
Area Different	1	17	69	129	72	18	1	307
% of Row	0.3	5.5	22.5	42.0	23.5	5.9	0.3	100
Valid % of Total	0.2	4.1	16.8	31.5	17.6	4.4	0.2	74.8
Area the Same	0	2	21	56	20	3	1	103
% of Row	0.0	1.9	20.4	54.4	19.4	2.9	1.0	100
Valid % of Total	0.0	0.5	5.1	13.7	4.9	0.7	0.2	25.1
Unknown								116
Total	1	19	90	185	92	21	2	(410)
% of Row	0.2	4.6	22.0	45.1	22.4	5.1	0.5	100
Total Sample								526

D.   Indicators of Social Mobility—Gross Social Changes, Fathers to Members

	1	2 Traditional Lower-Middle Class	3a White-Collar Workers	3b Skilled Workers	4 Unskilled Workers	Total N
	Upper					
Fathers	25.8	46.1	16.0	8.1	4.1	100.0
%/N	108	193	67	34	17	419
Members	36.8	23.5	27.3	8.4	4.0	100.0
%/N	175	112	130	40	19	476
Changes	+11.0	−22.6	+11.3	+0.3	−0.1	0.0

Item 24. Civil Punishment   Some standard forms have entries for convictions. Usually, these are cursory or undecipherable due to abbreviations or extremely small handwriting. Consequently, one cannot always be sure if they refer to felonies or misdemeanors. In Lebensläufe, subjects might brag of their involvements in political crimes, although no criminal record was indicated because there had been no charges or convictions, so I treat this item as countable impressions rather than reliable data.

Family Status   Although dates of engagement, marriage, separation and divorce, and the births of children and their sexes figured prominently in Himmler's measures of an SS man's suitability and affected SS promotions,[22] I saw no reason to include them in my analysis, for there

E.   Indicators of Social Mobility—Movement of Sons of Lower-Middle Class Families

Learned Class	Upper	Second Class Lower-Middle Class	Transitional	Unskilled Workers	Total N% Learned
Upper	46	2	1		49
	24.2	1.1	0.5		25.8
Traditional	5	31	3	1	40
Lower-Middle	2.6	16.3	1.6	0.5	21.1
Class					
Transi-	8	21	64	6	99
ional	4.2	11.1	33.7	3.2	52.1
Unskilled			1	1	2
Workers			0.5	0.5	1.1
Total	59	54	69	8	190
% Second Class	31.1	28.4	36.3	4.2	100

are no overt symptoms of uniqueness in family status among members of the SD.

Pre-SS/SD Political Involvements

Item 25. Involvement in Political Violence   This covers all references to violent political activities from the civil war through the Kampfzeit. I was looking for symptoms of early brutalization, and used a scale of 0–5 to represent degree of violence;

    0 = None
    1 = actions against property only
    2 = physical violence
    3 = emphasizes injuries suffered in 2
    4 = killing opponents or bombings
    5 = 3 plus 4

Given the heterogeneous nature of the sources and the subjectivity of the assessment, I also treat these data as countable impressions or indicators, rather than scientific measurements.

Items 26-37. Indicators of Prejudice (table C4)   This covers all references in Lebensläufe to most of the enemies, hates, and fears characteristic of the NS Weltanschauung, but especially those targeted by Sipo and SD. I was searching for attitudes held before membership. Using a scale of 0–7, I coded severity, but since the expressions in each category were so few, to get a significant measure of differences, I collapsed the scale into four units:

None expressed
Mild statements: Formulaic expressions, shibboleths only; personal observations of the allegedly negative effects of enemy activities; claims to have begun studying the enemy or to have been enlightened about the enemy at some point
Strong statements: Claims to have suffered personally from enemy activity; active involvement in combating the enemy or threat
Virulent statements

The list of enemies, fears, or threats includes:

- *Enemy States:* Other nations' efforts to keep Germany down, to persecute or treat her unfairly or disrespectfully; any zenophobic statements
- *Miscegenation:* The weakening of the German nation by the pollution of German blood with that of other "races"
- *Jews:* Fear/hate of Jews as a major threat to the German nation
- *Catholicism:* Conflicts with or hostility toward Catholic clergy; belief that Catholic Christianity is an internationalist, pacifist, alien ideology detrimental to the strength of the German spirit; belief that the Catholic Church is an international, conspiratorial power working against the German nation
- *Freemasonry:* Belief that the Masonic order is a society of internationalist, liberal conspirators through which Germany's enemies operate to undermine natural German culture and society
- *Communism:* Fear/hate of the KPD, Communist (Marxist) ideology, or an international Communist conspiracy
- *SPD:* Fear/hate of the Social Democratic Party, its labor organizations, and its influence in the Weimar "system"
- *The Republic:* Hostility directed at the liberal republican constitution or form of government, politicians of the ("non-Marxist") pro-Republic parties, partisan politics in general, and the corruptions of the "system," and any *expressed* desire or *act* to overthrow the Republic
- *Homosexuality:* Fear/hate of homosexuality or homosexuals as corrupting, weakening influences
- *Moral Decay:* Concern with other symptoms of "moral decadence" as threats to the strength of the German nation
- *Capitalists*: Hate/fear of economically powerful combinations or individuals as unjust, corrupting, undermining influences and forces in German society
- *Old Guard:* Hate/fear of traditionally powerful influences and institutions of the old society as unjust, retarding influences in German society

Table C.4 Prejudices in Approximate Order of Severity

| | 1934 Members | | | | | | 1936 |
| | Educational Level | | | | | | |
Prejudice	Lower	High School	University	Working SD	Sipo-SD	Total	Officers
Liberal Republic	86.6	87.0	87.5	88.2	81.6	86.8	83.9
Mild	0.6		0.7	0.3	1.2	0.5	1.1
Strong	12.8	13.0	11.9	11.5	17.2	12.7	15.1
Communists	89.4	91.5	86.9	91.1	80.9	88.9	90.3
Mild	0.6	1.4	2.0	0.9	2.2	1.2	1.1
Strong	10.0	7.0	11.2	8.0	16.9	9.9	8.7
Enemy States	94.4	88.6	90.7	92.6	89.7	92.0	91.4
Mild	1.1	2.8	2.0	1.9	1.1	1.7	3.2
Strong	4.5	8.6	7.3	5.5	9.1	6.3	5.5
Socialists	96.6	100.0	97.4	98.1	95.3	97.5	97.8
Mild	0.6		0.7	0.3	1.2	0.5	0.0
Strong	2.8		2.0	1.6	3.5	2.0	2.2
Jews	97.2	98.6	96.0	96.1	100.0	97.0	98.9
Mild	2.8		1.3	1.0		0.7	0.0
Strong		1.4	2.7	2.9		2.3	1.1
Catholicism	99.4	97.1	95.3	98.1	95.3	97.5	98.9
Mild	0.6		1.4	0.6	1.2	0.7	0.0
Strong		2.8	3.4	1.3	3.5	1.8	1.1
Old Guard	98.9	98.6	100.0	99.4	98.8	99.2	100.0
Mild	0.6			0.3		0.3	
Strong	0.6	1.4		0.3	1.2	0.5	
Capitalists	99.4	100.0	100.0	99.7	100.0	99.7	100.0
Strong	0.6			0.3		0.3	
Homosexuals	100.0	98.6	100.0	100.0	98.8	99.7	100.0
Strong		1.4			1.2	0.3	
Freemasonry	100.0	100.0	100.0	100.0	100.0	100.0	98.9
Mild							1.1
Moral Decay	100.0	100.0	99.3	99.7	100.0	99.7	100.0
Strong			0.7	0.3		0.3	

The first percentage given = no written expression of prejudice.
All data are in valid percentages; missing data for the total population (526) ranges from 23.2 to 24.5 percent per cell. Missing data for the 1936 officers (126) was consistently 22.5%.

Since the men were instructed not to discourse on ideology in their Lebensläufe, I presume such references represent either strong feelings intimately related to the subject's sense of his own development, or efforts to ingratiate himself with superiors. A third alternative, of course, is the general tendency of persons completing standardized forms to ignore instructions and to express what they feel is important. Even if their statements were calculated purely for effect, they represented an awareness of the consensus reality in which the writer would be expected to perform, and his willingness to conform to that reality. Thus, the data being recorded here are symptoms of either role or value orientations, worth counting as indicators, but merely "soft" rather than "hard" data.

Since most writers of the Lebensläufe were terse and inexpressive, I supplemented their commentary with other indicators of attitudes before to SD membership, encoding any comparable, surviving written expressions made before their membership. Beurteilungen that testified to involvements in non-NS organizations or to activities primarily directed against one of the enemies or concerns were encoded as "Strong."

Item 38. Pre-NS Political Memberships   Aside from entries in standard forms and elaborations in Lebensläufe, any suspicion of involvement in enemy organizations usually produced extensive detail in SS and Party files.

Items 39–41. Earliest NS Involvement   This covers subsidiary NS organizations, and "involvements" short of official membership in the Party or a major affiliated organization. Item 39 is the earliest mentioned (in any source) date of affiliation or cooperation with any NS group, whether alleged or verified. If clandestine, the reason was coded as item 40. Alleged or verified affiliation was coded as item 41. In addition to the individual's earliest identity with the movement, I was attempting to get some measure of the real extent of NS penetration of key institutions in German society, particularly the police.

Item 42. Party Membership Date

Item 43. Party Membership Number

Item 44. Date of Entry into SA   This may be negative.

Item 45. Date of Exit from SA

SS, Sipo, and SD Career

Item 46. SS Entry Date

Item 47. SS Membership Number

Items 48–49. SS Punishment Record   This includes the date of first offense for which formal punishment was recorded and the number of such recorded offenses. Since recorded offenses ranged from minor infractions to embezzlement and murder, the coded data is a crude measure of the degree of nonconformity and/or criminalization within the SS frame of reference. Expulsion data provide a better measure of serious SS discipline problems among Sipo and SD members.

Items 50–52. Early Involvements in SS Violence or Para-Police Organizations   This includes involvements in the "wild" phases of the Machtergreifung/Gleichschaltung, such as Hilfspolizei, Sonderkommando, or Polizei Angestellen (item 50); involvement with one of the concentration camps (item 51); and involvement in the Röhm purge (item 52). Only item 50 appears in the records with any consistency. Item 52 is extremely problematic and provides only an indicator of the extent of collective involvement.

Items 53–60. Police Career   Items 53–56 encode the nature of the police career before 1933 and any contacts with the NS Movement. Items 57 and 58 detail the career after 1933 but before SD membership. Items 59 and 60 encode the police career after SD entry.

Item 61. Experience in Security or Intelligence Work Prior to SD Membership

Items 62–63. Associate SD Experience   This covers the nature and date of first involvement.

Item 64. SD Region of Formal Entry

Item 65. Date of Kommandierung from SS into SD   This may be null.

Items 66 & 67. First and Second Dates of Ehrenamtlich Mitgliedschaft   This may be null.

Items 68 & 69. First and Second Dates of Hauptamtlich Mitgliedschaft   This may be null.

Items 70 & 71. Apparent Appeal to SD as Useful Member & First Use in SD as Member

Item 72. Einsatzgruppen Involvement   This information is not consistently available.

Items 73 & 74. Date of Temporary Withdrawal from SD & Reason

Item 75. Date of Return

Items 76 & 77. Date of Termination of SD Membership and Reason

Items 78–81. Involvement in Later SS/SD Violence   This covers the apparent nature of involvement in the Kristallnacht (item 78), the euthanasia program of 1940 (item 79), the initial mass shootings on the eastern front in the summer of 1941 (item 80), and any aspects of the later full-scale genocide programs (item 81). Since such records survive erratically, I deduced from the position held at the time the probable nature of involvement—a crude measure of the population's involvements.

Item 82. Symptoms of Psychic Strain   This indicates whenever a subject suffered from stress-related illness (including alcoholism), had frequent accidents, attempted suicide or any self-destructive act, or committed punishable acts; also requests for transfer into front line military units. Evidence survived erratically—again, this is a crude measure.

Item 83. Murder   This covers any record of personally killing an individual apart from the mass killing processes, regardless of whether or not the victim was a designated target for extermination. The probability of charges and an investigation were low despite Himmler and SS Court officials' diligence. What I seek here is some measure, no matter how crude, of the full criminalization of members involved in mass extermination.

Item 84. Corruption   This includes any record of suspected corrupt behavior at any time during a Sipo or SD career. Himmler and SS Court officials diligently sought to maintain "high standards of personal morality" in the SS, as did many high officials in Sipo and SD concerned with "professionalism." It is impossible to determine whether their detection rate was higher or lower than that in comparable agencies. This is another measure of the full criminalization of members.

Item 85. Date of Formal SD Membership

Item 86. SS Rank at Time of Entry into SD

Item 87. Time in Other Ranks after Joining SD

Item 88. Time in NCO Ranks in SD

Items 89–90. Date and First Officer's Rank in SD

Item 91. Interval Before Promotion to Obersturmführer

Items 92–99. Dates of Promotion and Intervals from Hauptsturm- to Standartenführer

Items 100–103. Intervals Between Promotions from Ober- to Obergruppenführer

Items 104–105. Highest Rank and Date of Promotion in SD

Items 106–107. Highest Subsequent SS Rank and Date of Promotion If Transferred

Items 108–110. Führer- or Junkerschule Record   This includes Jahrgang (item 108); SS units from which entered and to which assigned (item 109); and status at end of involvement (item 110).

Notes to Appendix C

1. *Dienstaltersliste der Schutzstaffel der NSDAP* (DAL), T-175/204 and 205, also at BDC and Bundesarchiv.

2. For example, unidentified SD personnel rosters, circa June 1944, T-175/241/2730305-97.

3. Estimated 840 members by end of 1934, 247 by end of 1933, and 40 by end of 1932. George C. Browder, "The Numerical Strength of the Sicherhertsdienst des RFSS," *Historical Social Research*, 28: 30–41; see table 2, p. 35.

4. George C. Browder, "Problems and Potentials of the Berlin Document Center," *Central European History* 5(1972): 362–380.

5. Statistischesreichsamt, Germany *Statistisches Jahrbuch für das Deutsche Reich, 1930* (Berlin: Reimer Hobbing, 1930), 10–12.

6. Herbert F. Ziegler, "The SS Fuehrer Korps: An Analysis of its Socioeconomic and Demographic Structure, 1925–1939."(Ph.D. diss., Emory University, 1980); see table 7, p. 57.

7. Calculated from *Statistisches Jahrbuch, 1930, 5.*

8. Ziegler, "SS Fuehrer Korps," see table 6, 55.

9. Calculated from *Statistisches Jahrbuch, 1931, 11.*

10. Ziegler, "SS Fuehrer Korps," table 11, 69.

11. Calculated from *Statistisches Jahrbuch, 1938, 22.*

12. *SS Statistische Jahrbuch, 1937,* T-175/205/4042280; and for 1938, 4042345.

13. Ziegler, "SS Fuehrer Korps," see table 10, 66; and 166–167 describing his sampling and weighting procedures.

14. Herbert F. Ziegler, *Nazi Germany's New Aristocracy: The SS Leadership, 1925–1939* (Princeton: Princeton University, 1989); see figure 3.4, 87.

15. Ziegler, "SS Fuehrer Korps," see table 14, 89; also Gunnar C. Boehnert, "An Analysis of Age and Education of the SS Führerkorps, 1925–1939." *Historical Social Research* 12(October 1979): 4–17.

16. Allen, "Farewell to Class Analysis;" Madden, "The Social Class Origins of Nazi Party Members," p. 277; and Peter Baldwin, "Social Interpretations of Nazism: Renewing a Tradition." *Journal of Contemporary History* 25(January 1990): 5–37.

17. George C. Browder, "The SD: The Significance of Organization and Image." In *Police Forces in History,* edited by George L. Mosse (London: SAGE Publications, 1975).

18. Theodor Geiger, *Die soziale Schichtung des Deutsches Völks* (Stuttgart: Ferdinand Enke, 1932); Michael H. Kater, "Quantifizierung und NS-Geschichte: Methodische Überlegung über Grenzen und Möglichkeiten einer EDV-Analyse der NSDAP Sozialstruktur von 1925 bis 1945." *Geschichte und Gesellschaft* 3(1977): 453–484; Konrad H. Jarausch, "Occupation and Social Structure in Modern Central Europe: Some Reflections on Coding Professions," *Quantum-Information* 11 (July 1979); Juergen Kocka, "Theories and Quantification in History." *Social Science History* 8(1984): 169–178; Michael H. Kater, The Nazi Party: A Social Profile of Members and Leaders, 1919–1945 (Cambridge: Harvard University Press, 1983): 1–13. Also cf. Baldwin, "Social Interpretations;" Madden, "Social Class Origins," 263–268; and Daniel I. Greenstein, "Standard, Meta-Standard: A Framework for Coding Occupational Data." *Historical Social Research* 16(1991): 3–22, for more recent summaries of the debate.

19. Summaries of the debate, see n. 18; Richard Bessel and Mathilde Jamin, "Nazis, Workers and the Uses of Quantitative Evidence." *Social History* 4: 111–116; Conan Fischer, "The Occupational Background of the SA's Rank and File Membership during the Depression Years, 1929 to Mid–1934," in Stachura, *Shaping of the Nazi State* (London: Croom Helm, 1978), 131–159; Hans Speier, *German White-Collar Workers and the Rise of Hitler* (New Haven: Yale University Press, 1986); Hartmut Kaelbe, "Social Mobility in Germany, 1900–1960." *Journal of Modern History* 50 (September 1978): 441–42.

20. *The Journal of Interdisciplinary History* 7(1971), especially Franklin F. Mendels, "Social Mobility and Phases of Industrialization," 193–216, and Donald J. Treiman, "A Standard Occupational Prestige Scale for Use with Historical Data," 283–304; and Kaare Svalastoga, *Social Differentiation* (New York: Van Rees Press, 1965).

21. See n. 21, chapter 6.

22. Herbert F. Ziegler, "Fight Against the Empty Cradle: Nazi Pronatal Policies and the SS-Fuehrerkorps." *Historical Social Research* 38(1986): 25–40.

Notes on Document Citation and Abbreviations

For every archive or microfilmed document collection, I have employed an appropriate variant of a standard citation format, as follows:

Archive/fund/folder/(subfolder-if-any)/page(s)
Microfilm-designation/reel-number/(folder-if-any)/frame(s)

Archival Abbreviations Within both archival and microfilm citations, numerous abbreviations will appear that are not listed below. These will refer either to specific funds that are listed in the bibliography under each archive, or to standard archival terminology.

BA	Bundesarchiv (Federal Archive)
BA-MA	Bundesarchiv-Militärarchiv-Freiburg
BDC	Berlin Document Center (U.S. Document Center Berlin)
By(H)StA	Bayerisches (Haupt)staatsarchiv, Munich
GLA	Generallandesarchiv Karlsruhe
GStA	Geheimes Staatsarchiv Berlin-Dahlem
GStAnwlt.b.d.KG	Generalstaatsanwaltschaft bei dem Kammergericht Berlin
HStA	Hauptstaatsarchiv (Central Land Archive)
IfZ	Institute für Zeitgeschichte, Munich
LC	Library of Congress
LHA	Landeshauptarchiv Koblenz
NA	National Archives
OA	Osoby Archive Moscow
PIH	Polizei Institut Hiltrup (Polizei-Führungsakademie)
StA	Staatsarchiv (Land Archive)

| USHRIA | U.S. Holocaust Memorial Research Institute Archive |
| Wolfbtl | Wolfenbüttel |

Book and Journal Abbreviations

AHR	*The American Historical Review*
CEH	*Central European History*
GSR	*German Studies Review*
HSR	*Historical Social Research/Historische Sozial-forschung*
IMT	*Trial of the Major War Criminals before the International Military Tribunal*
JCH	*Journal of Contemporary History*
JCL&C	*Journal of Criminal Law and Criminology*
JCL, C&PS	*Journal of Criminal Law, Criminology and Police Science*
JMH	*Journal of Modern History*
JPS&A	*Journal of Police Science and Administration*
MBliV	*Ministerialblatt des Reichs- und Preussischen Ministeriums des Innern*
TWC	*Trials of the War Criminals*
VB	*Völkische Beobachter*
VJfZ	*Vierteljahrshefte für Zeitgeschichte*

German and Nazi Abbreviations The following abbreviations will frequently appear in combination with one another; e.g., RuPrMdI, Reichs (R) und (u) Preussischen (Pr) Ministerium des Innern (MdI).

Ab	Abschnitt
Abtl.	Abteilung
aM	am Main
AO	Auslands Organisation
ASt.	Aussenstelle
ADSt.	Aussendienststelle
AW	Ausbildungswessen
b.	bei
BDR	German Federal Republic
Br.	Braunschweig
By.	Bayerisch
bzw.	beziehungsweise
Cd	Chef der
CdDP	Chef der Deutschen Polizei
CdS	Chef der Sipo
d.	der, die, das, des, dem
DAF	Deutsche Arbeitsfront
DAL	Dienstaltersliste der SS

DDR	German Democratic Republic
dienstl.	dienstlich
Dt.	Deutsch
Erl.	Erlass
f.	für
Fd	Führer der
GeStapa	Geheime Staatspolizeiamt
GeStapo	Geheime Staatspolizei
GL	Gauleitung, Gauleiter
HA	Hauptarchiv der NSDAP
HA-Sipo	Hauptamt Sicherheitspolizei
HAbtl.	Hauptabteilung
Hohenz.	Hohenzollern
HPFiW	Höherer Polizeiführer im Westen
i.	in, im
Id	Inspekteur der
IM	Innen Ministerium
KBDPB	Kameradschaftsbund Deutschen Polizeibeamten
Kd	Kommandeur der
KDAL	Dienstaltersliste der höheren Kriminalbeamten
KI	Kriminalinspektion, Kriminalinspektor
KK	Kriminalkommissar
KL	Konzentrationslager
kom.	kommissarisch
KPD	Kommunistische Partei Deutschland
Kripo	Kriminalpolizei
KSt	Kripostelle
KStL	Kripostellenleiter
L	Land, Länder
Ld.	Leiter der
LKD	Landes Kriminaldirektor
LKPA	Landes Kriminalpolizeiamt
LKPSt	Landes Kriminalpolizeistelle
LPI	Landes Polizei Inspektor
MD	Ministerialdirektor
MdI	Ministerium des Inner
MinPräs	Ministerial Präsident
MR	Ministerialrat
n.	nach
ND	Nachrichtendienst
NF	Nachrichtenführer
NS	National Sozialist (Nazi)
NSDAP	National Sozilistische Deutschen Arbeiter Partei
OAb	Oberabschnitt
OPG	Oberst Parteigericht
ORR	Oberregierungsrat
O'Stubf.	Obersturmbannführer

PD	Polizei Direktion, Polizei Direktor
Pol. Präs.	Polizei Präsidium, Polizei Präsident
polit.	politisch
PP	politische Polizei
PPK	Politische Polizei Kommandeur
Pr.	Preussisch
R	Reichs
RB	Regierungsbezirk
RdErl.	Runderlass
Reg.	Regierung
RegPräs.	Regierungs Präsident
RFM	Reichs Finanz Ministerium
RFSS	Reichsführer SS
RJM	Reichs Justiz Ministerium
RL	Reichsleitung, Reichsleiter
RSF	Reichsstudentenführer
RSHA	Reichssicherheitshauptamt
RuSHA	SS Rasse und Siedlungshauptamt
SA	Sturmabteilung
Scharf.	Scharführer
Schwab.	Schwabisch
SD	Sicherheitsdienst des Reichsführers SS
SD-HA	Sicherheitsdienst Hauptamt
SHA	Sicherheitshauptamt
Sipo	Sicherheitspolizei
SLSt	Stapoleitstelle
SPD	Socialistische Partei Deutschland
SS	Schutzstaffel
SSF	SS-Führer
SS-HA	SS-Hauptamt
SSt	Staatspolizeistelle (Stapostelle)
SStL	Stapostellenleiter
stadl.	stadtlich
Stapo	Staatspolizei
stl.	staatlich
stelv.	stellvertretend
StV	Stellvertreter
StMin	Staatsministerium
StR	Staatsrat
u.	unter or und
UAb	Unterabschnitt
UAbtl.	Unterabteilung
v.	von, vom
VA	Verwaltungsamt
VM	Vertrauensmann
Würt.	Württemberg
WVHA	SS Wirtschafts- und Verwaltungs-Hauptamt

Notes

Introduction

1. George C. Browder, *The Foundations of the Nazi Police State: The Formation of Sipo and SD* (Lexington: University Press of Kentucky, 1990).

2. Ibid., 248–249.

3. Robert Gellately, "Rethinking the Nazi Terror System: A Historiographical Analysis," *German Studies Review (GSR)*, 14 (1): 23–38 (1991); Gellately "Situating the 'SS-State' in a Socio-Historical Context: Recent Histories of the SS, the Police, and the Courts in the Third Reich," *Journal of Modern History (JMH)*, 64 (June 1992):338–365; Gellately, *The Gestapo in German Society: Enforcing Racial Policy, 1933–1945* (Oxford: Oxford University Press, 1990); Reinhard Mann, *Protest und Controlle im Dritten Reich: Nationalsozialistische Herrschaft im alltag einer rheinischen Grossstadt* (Frankfurt: Campus, 1987); Bernd Hey, "Zur Geschichte der westfälischen Staatspolizeistellen und der Gestapo." *Westfälische Forschungen* 37 (1987):58–90; and subsequently, Klaus-Michael Mallmann and Gerhard Paul, *Herrschaft und Alltag: Ein Industrierevier im Dritten Reich. Widerstand und Verfolgung im Saarland, 1933–1945* (Bonn: J.H.W. Dietz Nachf., 1991); and *Terror, Herrschaft und Alltag im Nationalsozialismus: Probleme einer Sozialgeschichte des deutschen Faschismus,* edited by Brigitte Berlekamp and Werner Röhr (Münster: Westfälisches Dampfboot, 1995).

4. Gellately, "Rethinking," 32.

5. Christopher Browning, "Beyond 'Intentionalism' and 'Functionalism': A Reassessment of Nazi Jewish Policy from 1939 to 1941." In *Reevaluating the Third Reich,* edited by Thomas Childers and Jane Caplan (New York: Holmes & Meier, 1993), 211–233; and Richard Breitman, "The 'Final Solution'." In *Modern Germany Reconsidered, 1870–1945,* edited by Gordon Martel (London: Routledge, 1992), 197–210; these works reveal the degree of synthesis and the gaps that remain. Detlev J.K. Peukert, "The Genesis of the 'Final Solution' from the Spirit of Science," also in Childers and Caplan, *Reevaluating,* 234–252.

6. Continued research has modified my original position in detail, but enriched rather than altered it.

7. Erwin Staub, *The Roots of Evil: The Origins of Genocide and Other Group Violence* (New York: Cambridge University Press, 1989), 66; and Marijana Benesh and Bernard Weiner, "On Emotion and Motivation: From the Notes of Fritz Heider." *American Psychologist* 37(August 1982): 887–895, especially p. 891 on tension toward aggression.

8. Raul Hilberg, *Perpetrators, Victims, Bystanders: The Jewish Catastrophe, 1933–1945* (New York: HarperCollins, 1992), 3–19, especially Hitler's 1919 paper distinguishing between emotion (Gefühl) and reason (Vernunft).

9. Browder, *Foundations*, 248. See also William S. Allen, "The Collapse of Nationalism in Nazi Germany," In *The State of Germany: The Role of Nationalism in the Making, and Remaking of a Nation-State,* edited by John Breuilly (London: Longmans, 1992), 141–153, on "the common vocabulary"; Browning's "overlap in ideological outlook," in "Beyond 'Intentionalism'," 219–220; and Mallmann and Paul's "terrain of opposition" in *Herrschaft und Alltag.*

10. I shall establish this argument as specifically relevant to members of Sipo and SD. Sarah A. Gordon, *Hitler, Germans and the Jewish Question* (Princeton: Princeton University Press, 1984); Michael H. Kater, "Everyday Anti-Semitism in Prewar Nazi Germany: the Popular Basis." *Yad Vashem Studies* 16(1984): 129–159; Michael R. Marrus, *The Holocaust in History* (Hannover: University Press of New England, 1987), 9–18, 47; Donald M. McKale, "Traditional Antisemitism and the Holocaust: The Case of German Diplomat Curt Pruefer." *Simon Wiesenthal Center Annual* 5(1988): 61–76; and Sybil Milton, "The Context of the Holocaust." *GSR* 8(May 1990): 269–283.

11. Peter Baldwin, "Social Interpretations of Nazism: Renewing a Tradition." *Journal of Contemporary History (JCH)* 25(January 1990): 21–23.

12. Fred E. Katz, "Implementation of the Holocaust: The Behavior of Nazi Officials." *Comparative Studies in Society and History* 24(July 1982): 510–529; Juergen Kocka, "German History before Hitler: The Debate about the German *Sonderweg*." *JCH* 23(January 1988): 3–16; and John Sperber, "Master Narratives of Nineteenth-Century German History." Review article in *Central European History* 24(Spring 1991): 69–91.

Chapter 1

1. John F. Galliher, "Explanations of Police Behavior: A Critical View and Analysis." *Sociological Quarterly* 12(1971): 308–318; John P. Clark, "Isolation of the Police: A Comparison of the British and American Situations," *Journal of Criminal Law, Criminology and Police Science (JCL,C&PS)* 56(1965): 307–319; A.J. Butler and Raymond Cochrane, "Examination of Some Elements of the Personality of Police Officers and Their Implications." *Journal of Police Science and Administration (JPS&A)* 5(December 1977): 441–450; "Report to the Neuffield Foundation on a Seminar on the Sociology of the Police held at Rodney Lodge, Bristol, from February 25–28, 1971." *The Police Journal* 44(1971): 227–243; Johannes Feest and Rüdiger Lautmann, *Die Polizei: Soziologische Studien und Forschungsberichte* (Opladen: Westdeutscher Verlag, 1971); Arbeitskreis Junger Kriminologen, *Die Polizei, Eine Institution öffentlicher Gewalt* (Neuwied: Luchterhand, 1975); and Tom Bowden, *Beyond the Limits of the Law: A Comparative Study of the Police in Crisis Politics* (Harmondsworth: Penguin, 1978).

2. Robert W. Balch, "The Police Personality: Fact or Fiction?." *JCL, C&PS* (1972): 108; John L. Genz and David Lester, "Authoritarianism in Police as a Function of Experience." *JPS&A* 4 (1):9–13 (1976); and David Lester et al., "The Personalities of English and American Police." *Journal of Social Psychology* 111(June 1980): 153–154.

3. Genz and Lester, "Authoritarianism in Police;" and Balch, "Police Personality."

4. William A. Westley, *Violence and the Police: A Sociological Study of Law, Custom, and Morality* (Cambridge: MIT Press, 1970); Ellwyn R. Stoddard, "The Informal 'Code' of Police Deviancy: A Group Approach to 'Blue-Coat' Crime." *JCL,C&PS* 59(June 1968): 201–213; Leonard D. Savitz, "The Dimensions of Police Loyalty." *American Behavioral Scientist* (May–June, July–August, 1970): 693–704; Hans H. Toch, "Psychological Consequences of the Police Role." In *Readings in Criminal Justice,* edited by Edward Eldefonso (New York: Glencoe Press, 1973), 85–92; and James Q. Wilson, "The Police and Their Problems: A Theory." *Public Policy* 12(1963): 189–216. For Statistical verification, even across cultures, see Butler and Cochrane, "Examination of Some Elements of Personality."

5. Everett C. Hughes, "Good People and Dirty Work." *Social Problems* 10(1962): 5; and Robert J. Friedrich, "Police Use of Force: Individuals, Situations and Organizations." *The Annals of the American Academy* (November 1980): 82–97.

6. Wilson, "A Theory," 192.

7. Balch, "Police Personality," 112.

8. David H. Bayley, *Patterns of Policing. A Comparative International Analysis* (New Brunswick: Rutgers University Press, 1985).

9. Richard J. Evans, "In Pursuit of the *Untertanengeist:* Crime, Law and Social Order on German History." In *Rethinking German History: Nineteenth-Century Germany and the Origins of the Third Reich* (London: Allen and Unwin, 1987), 156–187; Elaine Glovka Spencer, "State Power and Local Interests in Prussian Cities: Police in the Düsseldorf District, 1848–1914." *Central European History (CEH),* 19 (3): 293–313 (1986); and Herbert Reinke, " 'Armed as if for War': The State, the Military and the Professionalization of the Prussian Police in Imperial Germany." In *Policing Western Europe: Politics, Professionalism, and Public Order, 1850–1940,* edited by Clive Emsley and Barbara Weinberger (Westport, CN: Greenwood Press, 1991), 66–68.

10. James Q. Wilson, *Varieties of Police Behavior* (Cambridge: Harvard University Press, 1968).

11. Bowden, *Beyond the Limits,* 42–48.

12. Emsley and Weinberger, *Policing Western Europe,* vii–xiii; David H. Bayley, "The Police and Political Development in Europe." In *The Formation of National States in Western Europe,* edited by Charles Tilly (Princeton: Princeton University Press, 1975), 328–379; and James F. Richardson, "Berlin Police in the Weimar Republic: A Comparison with Police Forces in Cities of the United States." In *Police Forces in History,* edited by George L. Mosse, (London: SAGE, 1975), 79–93.

13. Richard Bessel, "Policing, Professionalism and Politics in Weimar Germany." In *Policing Western Europe,* 187–219; Richardson, "Berlin Police;" James H. McGee, "Political Police in Bavaria, 1919–1936" (Ph.D. diss., University of Florida, 1980); and Bowden, *Beyond the Limits.*

14. Westley, "Secrecy and the Police." *Social Forces* 34(March 1956): 254–257.

15. Bayley, "The Police . . . in Europe;" and Richardson, "Berlin Police," 80–86. Contemporary comparisons, Raymond B. Fosdick, *European Police Systems* (1915, reprinted Montclair, NJ: Patterson Smith, 1969); and *American Police Systems* (1920, reprinted Montclair, NJ: Patterson Smith, 1969).

16. Lothar Barck, *Die Organisation des staatlichen Sicherheitsdienstes in Baden* (1931), p. 7, carried the image of objectivity to the point of insisting that the police mission was even independent of the economic and social relations of the time. Hsi-Huey Liang, *The Berlin Police Force in the Weimar Republic* (Berkeley: University of California, 1970), 10, 20–29; Eric D. Kohler, "The Crisis in the Prussian Schutzpolizei 1930–32." In *Police Forces in History*, 131–135; and McGee, "Political Police in Bavaria," especially chapters 3–5.

17. Liang, *Berlin Police*, 81–94. HStA Stuttgart, E 151c II, Bü 566/82–89, especially P.P. Stuttgart to IM re Artikel in *Der Schwab. Tagwacht* "Nazizellen bei der Polizei," 84; and E 151a, Bü 1180. E.g., BDC/SSO, Rudolf Löffel (b. 6.7.87).

18. George C. Browder, *Foundations of the Nazi Police State: The Formation of Sipo and SD* (Lexington: University Press of Kentucky, 1990) 41–42.

19. Wilson, "A Theory," 205–207, 209 (for quote); Westley, "Violence and the Police," 34–41; Toch, "Psychological Consequences," 85–92; Friedrich, "Police Use of Force." For an exchange on violence and respect for the police between Polizei-Oberstleutnant Rühle von Lilienstern, Leiter der Landespolizei Thüringen, and Polizei-Kommandeur Heimannsberg of Prussia, "Ist die Polizei richtig bewaffnet?" *Die Polizei* 26(May 16, 1929): 400–402. Rudolf Diels, *Lucifer ante Portas* (Zurich: Interverlag, 1950), 117.

20. McGee, "Political Police in Bavaria," chapter 1; Diels, *Lucifer ante Portas,* 117, on "solidarische Leugen der Beamten."

21. Siegfried Zaika, *Polizeigeschichte. Die Exekutive im Lichte der historischen Konfliktforschung* (Lübeck: Schmidt Römhild, 1979).

22. Wilson, "A Theory," 205–207; Harold J. Gordon, *Hitler and the Beer Hall Putsch* (Princeton: Princeton University Press, 1972), 120–36, 138–39; and cf. McGee, "Political Police in Bavaria."

23. Harold Gordon, "Police Careers in the Weimar Republic." In *Proceedings of the Citadel Symposium on Hitler and the National Socialist Era*, edited by Michael B. Barrett (Charleston: The Citadel Development Foundation, 1982, 160–169).

24. Gitta Sereny, *Into that Darkness* (New York: Random House, 1974), 28, on the "Vienna School" of police training. Unfortunately, Jürgen Siggemann, *Die kasernierte Polizei und des Problem der inneren Sicherheit in der Weimarer Republik: Eine Studie zum Auf- und Ausbau der innerstaatlichen Sicherheitssystems in Deutschland, 1918/19–1933* (Frankfurt aM: R.G. Fischer Verlag, 1980), did not address this aspect directly.

25. Anonymous, *Volk und Schupo* (Cologne: Gilde Verlag, 1929); and KPD, Kursusdisposition, "Die Arbeit unter der Polizei," BA/R-58/547.

26. Robert Harnischmacher and Arved Semerek, *Deutsche Polizeigeschichte* (Stuttgart: W. Kohlhammer, 1986); Report to the Neuffield Foundation, "Sociology of the Police," 229; Hans-Heinrich Hülke and Hans Etzler, *Verbrechen, Polizei, Prozesse. Eine Verzeichnis von Büchern und klieneren*

Schriften in deutscher Sprache (Wiesbaden: Bundeskriminalamt, 1963). Reinke, " 'Armed as if for War'," on the Imperial background.

27. For the perspective of a former German policeman, Tonis Hunold, *Polizei in der Reform* (Düsseldorf/Vienna: Econ Verlag, 1968). E.g., BDC/SSO Löffel, Lebenslauf, n.d. Another case study is Erika S. Fairchild, "Women Police in Weimar: Professionalism, Politics and Innovation in Police Organization." *Law and Society Review* 21 (3): 375–402 (1987).

28. Karl D. Bracher, Wolfgang Sauer, and Gerhard Schulz, *Die nationalsozialistische Machtergreifung* (Cologne: Westdeutsche Verlag, 1960), part 2, 429; Werner Feld, "The German Administrative Courts." *Tulane Law Review* 36(April 1962): 496–497; Heinrich Nagel, "Judicial Review in Germany." *American Journal of Comparative Law* 3(Spring 1954): 236–238.

29. A policeman on being caught in the middle, Lothar Danner, *Ordnungspolizei Hamburg: Betrachtung zu ihrer Geschichte, 1928 bis 1933* (Hamburg: Verlag Deutsche Polizei, 1958), 195–208.

30. Ibid.; and see nn. 42–43, 45–46.

31. Liang, *Berlin Police,* 64–73; and Kohler, "Prussian Schutzpolizei," 131–142.

32. Liang, *Berlin Police,* 72–73.

33. Ibid., chapter 4, for the Kripo in Prussia; and McGee, "Political Police in Bavaria," revealing differences among the Länder; as does *Beförderungsgrundsätze für des staatlichen Sicherheitsdienstes in Baden,* 1931, StA Freiburg, LRA Konstanz (XXII-Polizei)/1462.

34. Liang, *Berlin Police,* 121–123, 127–129. Cf. Walter Schellenberg, *The Schellenberg Memoirs* (London: Andre Deutsch, 1956), 32, and 91 on Müller with evaluations by Müller's colleagues; "Bestimmungen über Annahme, Ausbildung, Prüfung und Beförderung in der staatlichen Kriminalpolizei," Nr. 7019, Pr. Landtag, 3 Wahlp. 1. Tg. 1928/31; and Pr. MdI, re "Kriminalkommissarlaufbahn. Zulassung und Ausbildung," StA Stade, Rep.80P/1648.

35. Liang, *Berlin Police,* 134–135.

36. "Nachweisung über die seit dem 1. Mai 1925 auf Preussischen Gebiet begangenen kriminellen Schwerverbrechen," Nr.5185, Pr. Landtag, 2 Wahlperiode 1.Tag. 1925/27, StA Stade, Rep.80P/1646; Liang, *Berlin Police,* 116–119.

37. Ibid., pp. 122–125; and testimony of Friedrich Rehmstedt, "Bremen Kripo and political police," 5.9.1947, M395/24/429–32.

38. Wilson, "The Police and Their Problems," 196–197.

39. Toch, "Psychological Consequences," 85–92.

40. Liang, *Berlin Police,* 148–149.

41. Zaika, *Polizeigeschichte,* 212; and Polizei Kommandeur Heimannsberg, "Der 1. Mai und seine Folgererscheinnungen in Berlin." *Die Polizei,* 26 (10): 229 (1929).

42. Liang, *Berlin Police,* 84; Chris Bowlby, "Blutmai 1929: Police, Parties and Proletarians in a Berlin Confrontation." *The Historical Journal,* 29 (1): 153–154 (1986).

43. Official vacillations on the subject, Ilse Maurer and Udo Wengst, eds., *Staat und NSDAP. 1930–1932. Quellen zur Ära Brüning* (Düsseldorf: Droste Verlag, 1977).

44. Cf. Zaika, *Polizeigeschichte,* with Bowlby, "Blutmai." Rodney Stark, "Police Riots: An Anatomical Report." *Urban Life* 1 (1): 7–38 (1972).

45. KPD leadership, which had optimistically monitored dissension within the police through 1931 (*Information*, No. 6, Oktober 1931, T-175/357/ 2867568–78), began to worry about increased pro-NS influences in early 1932 (*Information*, No. 2, February 1932, T-175/357/2867532–33).

46. T-175/343/EAP 173–b-16–105/360 for official reports and newspaper clippings. Bowlby, "Blutmai"; Thomas Kurz, "Arbeitermörder und Putschisten. Der Berliner "Blutmai" von 1929 als Kristallistionspunkt des Verhältnisses von KPD und SPD vor der Katastrophe." *Internationale Wissenschaftliche Korrespondenz zur Geschichte der Deutschen Arbeiterbewegung* 22 (3): 297–317 (1986); Eva Rosenhaft, "Working-Class Life and Working-Class Politics: Communists, Nazis, and the State in the Battle for the Streets, Berlin 1928–1932." In *Social Change and Political Development in Weimar Germany*, edited by Richard Bessel and E. J. Feuchtwanger (London: Croom Helm, 1981), 207– 240; and cf. Zaika, *Polizeigeschichte*, 217–230.

47. StA Nürnberg, Rep.270IV/690–94, covering 1931–1932. Reich-wide studies, *Generalübersicht über die staatsfeindliche Zersetzungstätigkeit in Reichswehr und Schutzpolizei in der Zeit vom 1. Januar bis zum 30. Juni 1932*, compiled by I4, T-175/R589/78–79; and Der Pol.Präs., LKPA, *Jahresbericht der Zentralstelle zur Beobachtung und Bekämpfung der staatsfeindlichen Zersetzungstätigkeit in Reichswehr und Polizei für das Kalenderjahr 1932*, StA Stade, Rep.90P/1866.

48. Polizeimajor Ratcliffe, Pr. Polizeiinstitut, "Denkschrift über Kampfvorbereitung und Kampfgrundsätze radikaler Organizatinen," December 1931, in Maurer and Wengst, *Staat und NSDAP*, 235, assessed possibilities of SA support against KPD uprising.

49. T-175/330/EAP 173–b-16–05/309, 344/EAP 173–b-16–05/361, 344/ EAP 173–b-16–05/365, 345/EAP 173–b-16–05/369 and 372, 357/EAP 173– b-16–05/356, and 368/EAP 173–b-16–05/427 for reports from the countersubversion offices, captured directives of the KPD AM-Apparat, and sample propaganda.

50. Browder, *Foundations*, 43–47.

51. Herbert Jacob, *German Administration since Bismarck: Control vs. Local Autonomy* (New Haven: Yale University, 1963), 124, 128–131, 142; Kohler, "Prussian Schutzpolizei," 142–149; Christoph Graf, *Politische Polizei zwischen Demokratie und Diktatur* (Berlin: Coloquium, 1983), 49–91; Albert C. Grzesinski, *Inside Germany* (New York: E.P. Dutton, 1939), 157–161; and Diels, *Lucifer ante Portas*, 77–78, 122–124.

52. "Der Geist der Polizei," von einem Polizeibeamten. *Der Polizeioffizier* 9(1930): 490–491; Polizeimajor Lettow, Höhere Polizeischule Eiche, "Wie lange noch?", and Polizeioberstleutnant Demoll, "Wie lange noch?" *Die Polizei* 30(1933): 105, 186–188; Diels, *Lucifer ante Portas*, 122–124.

53. "Die Schupo und wir," *Völkische Beobachter (VB)*, January 17, 1930.

54. Ig to die NS Korrespondenz, 9 March 1932, HA/77/1565; also Ig re "Offizierssäbel bei der Pr. Schutzpolizei," 18.11.31, Ibid.

55. "Der Nationalsozialismus in der hamburgischen Polizei," *VB*, October 14, 1932.

56. Daluege, "Die deutsche Polizei" under cover letter of RuPrMdI, November 1935, BA/R43II/391.

57. Liang, *Berlin Police*, 12–13, 90; Danner, *Ordnungspolizei*, 223; BA/ Schu 456 for correspondence about Saxon police unions and Nazi success; and

PrMdI, 28.4.1931, StA Stade, Rep.80P/1424. NS Arbeitsgemeinschaft, W'haven-Rüstringen to GL Bremen, 25.3.1933, BA/NS-10/69/249–50. StA Bremen, 4,65–17–4, reports from summer 1932.

58. BDC/SSO and RuSHA, Erich Vogel (b.13.7.89); and NA/RG238/787–PS, and 788–PS.

59. BDC/SSO Gommlich (b. 11.7.91); and Rausch (b. 14.10.98).

60. See Christoph Graf, *Politische Polizei*, 96–98.

61. Ibid., pp. 364; and cf. Liang, *Berlin Police*, 148 (quotation), 167, 227; *Dienstalteslliste der höheren Kriminalbeamen*, 1935 (hereafter *KDAL*); and Pol.Präs. Berlin to Staatssekretär, 6.4.1934, GStA/Rep.90,P/Nr.3/62b.

62. BDC/SSO and RuSHA, Philipp Greiner (b.27.12.95); and Liang, *Berlin Police*, 167.

63. BDC/SSO, and RuSHA, Dr. Rudolf Braschwitz (b. 18.1.00).

64. Diels, *Lucifer ante Portas*, 77–78, 120–122; and Hans B. Gisevius, *Bis zum Bittern Ende* (Hamburg: Classen & Goverts, 1947), 1:132. On the purge, Bericht der Polizei-Abteilung des PrMdI über ihre Arbeiten im Jahre 1933 . . . , 1.2.1934, BA/R-43I/ 2290. Johnpeter H. Grill, *The Nazi Movement in Baden, 1920–1945* (Chapel Hill: University of North Carolina Press, 1983), 244–245.

65. Bericht der Polizei-Abteilung . . . , 1.2.1934, BA/R-43 I/2290. On Liebermann, *KDAL*, 13, 70. On attitudes, Diels, *Lucifer ante Portas*, 124–25.

66. Diels, *Lucifer ante Portas*, 133–135.

67. Liang, *Berlin Police*, 170–171.

Chapter 2

1. On the history: Dieter Fricke, *Bismarcks Prätorianer: Die Berliner politische Polizei im Kampf gegen deutsche Arbeiterbewegung* (Berlin: Rütten & Löning, 1962); James H. McGee, "Political Police in Bavaria, 1919–1936." (Ph.D. diss., University of Florida, 1980); and Peter Fricke, "Anfänge und Organisation der Nachrichtenstelle bei der Polizeidirektion Bremen," unpublished dienstlicher Bericht im Rahmen der Laufbahnprüfung für den gehobenen Archivdienst des Landes Bremen, 1966. On double-duty, e.g., correspondence of 1931–1932 on polit.Abtl.d.PD Wesermünde, StA Stade, Rep.90P/1926.

2. In addition to McGee: Shlomo Aronson, *The Beginnings of the Gestapo System: The Bavarian Model in 1933* (Jerusalem: Israel University Press, 1969); and *Reinhard Heydrich und die Frügeschichte von Gestapo und SD* (Stuttgart: Deutsche Verlags-Anstalt, 1971); Christoph Graf, *Politische Polizei zwischen Demokratie und Diktatur* (Berlin: Colloquium, 1983); Johannes Tuchel, *Konzentrationslager. Organisationsgeschichte und Funktion der "Inspektion der Konzentrationslager" 1934–1938* (Boppard aR: Harald Boldt, 1991), 45–60; Joerg Schadt, ed., *Verfolgung und Widerstand unter dem Nationalsozialismus in Baden* (Stuttgart: W. Kohlhammer, 1976), 28–36; and Adolf Diamant, *Gestapo Leipzig. Zur Geschichte einer verbrecherischen Organisation in den Jahren 1933–1945* (Frankfurt aM: Graphica-Druck, 1990).

3. George C. Browder, *Foundations of the Nazi Police State: The Formation of Sipo and SD* (Lexington: University Press of Kentucky, 1990).

4. Herbert C. Kelman, "Violence without Moral Restraint: Reflections on the Dehumanization of Victims and Victimizers." *Journal of Social Issues* 29 (1973): 25–62; Kelman and V. Lee Hamilton, *Crimes of Obedience: Toward a*

Social Psychology of Authority and Responsibility (New Haven: Yale University, 1989); Nevitt Sanford and Craig Comstock, *Sanctions for Evil* (San Francisco: Jossey-Bass, Inc., 1971); Stanley Milgram, *Obedience to Authority: An Experimental View* (New York: Harper and Row, 1974); and Fred E. Katz, "Implementation of the Holocaust: The Behavior of Nazi Officials." *Comparative Studies in Society and History* 24(July 1982): 510–529.

5. Kelman, "Violence," 618–652; Henry V. Dicks, *Licensed Mass Murder: A Social-Psychological Study of Some SS Killers* (New York: Basic Books, 1972), 253–255; Viola W. Bernard, Perry Ottenberg, and Fritz Riedl, "Dehumanization." In Sanford and Comstock, *Sanctions*, 102–124; P.G. Zimbardo, "The Human Choice: Individuation, Reason, and Order Versus Deindividuation, Impulse, and Chaos." In *Nebraska Symposium on Motivation*, edited by W. J. Arnold and D. Levine (Lincoln: University of Nebraska Press, 1970).

6. Roger Brown, *Social Psychology: The Second Edition* (New York: Free Press, 1986), part VI, especially chapters 15 and 16.

7. Graf, *Politische Polizei*, chapter 4; and Bernd Hey, "Zur Geschichte der Westfälischen Staatspolizeistellen und der Gestapo." *Westfälische Forschungen* 37(1987): 58–90.

8. Geschäftsverteilungsplan des GeStaPA, gültig ab 19. Juni 1933, BA/R-58/840; Graf, *Politische Polizei*, doc. 12a, 415–416. Gestapo preoccupation with the left: GeStapa, Mitteilungen Nr.8, 26.6.1933, OA/519/3/19. Nachrichtenkonferenz at Gestapa, 16/17. 10.1933, mentioned in Pol.Präs. Frankfurt a.M. to PrMdI, 21.10. 1933, HStA Wiesbaden, 483/714.

9. Geschäftsverteilungsplan der Abteilung I des Polizeipräsidiums Berlin vom Herbst 1931, reprinted in Graf, *Politische Polizei*, document 2, 401–403.

10. Organisation des GeStapa, n.d. and Stand 1.9.1933, OA/500/1/ 38a/ 267, 269; and Geschäftsverteilungsplan des GeStapa for 22.1. 1934, GStA/ Rep.90P/2,2/91–107.

11. Rudolf Diels, *Lucifer ante Portas* (Zurich: Interverlag, 1950) 168; Graf, *Politische Polizei*, 174–178; Kurt Schilde and Johannes Tuchel, *Columbia-Haus: Berliner Konzentrationslager 1933–1936* (Berlin: Druckhaus Hentrich, 1990), 29; and Aufbau der GeStapo Pr., Stand 1.2.34, GStA, 90P/ 1,2/128.

12. Robert Thevoz, et al., eds., *Die Geheime Staatspolizei in den preussischen Ostprovinzen, 1934–36: Pommern, 1934/35* (Cologne: Grote, 1974), I:18–28, II:212–220; Thomas Klein, ed., *Die Lageberichte der Geheimen Staatspolizei über die Provinz Hessen-Nassau 1933–1936* (Cologne: Böhlau, 1986), I:1–50; Klaus Mlynek, *Gestapo Hannover meldet . . . Polizei und Regierungsberichte für das mittlere und südliche Niedersachsen zwischen 1933 und 1937* (Hildesheim: August Lax, 1986); Hans-Jürgen Döscher, "Geheime Staatspolizei und allgemeine Verwaltung im Regierungsbezirk Stade." *Stader Jahrbuch* 42(1972): 70–90; Jörg Kammler, "Nationalsozialistische Machtergreifung und Gestapo: Am Beispiel der Staatspolizeistelle für Regierungsbezirk Kassel." In *Hessen unterm Hakenkreuz: Studien zur Durchsetzung der NSDAP in Hessen*, edited by Eike Henning (Frankfurt a.M.: Insel Verlag, 1983), 506–535; Hey, "Geschichte der westfälischen Staatspolizeistellen"; Adolf Diamant, *Gestapo Frankfurt a.M.* (Frankfurt: W. Steinmann & Boschen, 1988), 1–53. Pr.MdI, 21.2.1933, BA, Schu 465; Karl Schäfer, *20 Jahre im Polizeidienst (1925–1945)* (Frankfurt aM: Decker & Wilhelm, 1977), 21–23; and Besoldungsbedarf für das SSt Frankfurt a.M. nach dem Stande vom 1.6.33, HStA Wiesbaden, 483/714.

13. Thevoz, et al., *Pommern*, 2:199–200; Pr.MdI, "Vorläufige Dienstanweisung für die Landespolizeiinspektionen Schleswig-Holstein und Hannover, 26.4.1933; "Aufgabengebiet der SSt," n.d., StA Aurich, Rep.21a/Reg.Aurich/10009; and SSt Hannover, 8.5.1933, "Neuorganisation der politischen Polizei," StA Hannover, 122a/ VIII/430/370. For Dortmund, PP Dortmund, "Personalbedarf für die SSt in Dortmund," 28.11.1933, StA Munster, Reg.Arnsberg/14601/7–14; and Hey, "Geschichte der westfälischen Staatspolizeistellen."

14. Hey, "Geschichte," 10.

15. Ibid., 14–15; and SSt Köln, "Politische Polizei und SSt," 29.7.1933, HStA Düsseldorf, RW18/2/46–47.

16. Pr.MinPräs., GeStapo, "Haushalt der GeStapo für das Rechnungsjahr 1934," 12.3.1934, and "Vorläufige Anweisung für die Rechnungs- und Wirtschaftsführung in der GeStapo," 20.3.1934, HStA Wiesbaden, 483/714; and to the same, Anlage A, StA Düsseldorf, RW36/35. On the personnel politics of SSt Dortmund, StA Munster, Reg.Arnsberg/14601/32, 40, 42–47, 53–55, 59–61. SSt Düsseldorf, "Neuorganisation der Stapo im RB Düsseldorf," 29.3.1934, StA Düsseldorf, RW36/33/1–7; and Pr.MinPräs., "Organisation der GeStapo," 16.7.1934, StA Munster, Reg.Arnsberg/14601/ 1–3. Mlynek, *Gestapo Hannover*, 21–25; and Hey, "Geschichte der westfälischen Staatspolizeistelllen," 59–63, 69–72.

17. Vorschlag f.d. Organisation d. GeStapo im RB (Dortmund), n.d. (March 1934); and PP Dortmund, "Haushalt der GeStapo f.d. Rechnungsjahr 1934," 26.3.1934, Anlage 1, StA Munster, Reg.Arnsberg/14601/37–38; 46–47.

18. Ibid., Anlage 2, 48.

19. Ibid., Anlage 5 and 6, 51–52.

20. Der kom.Reg.Präs., Aurich, 8.5.1933 "Zusammenarbeit zwischen SSt Wilhelmshaven und Reg.Aurich, StA Aurich, Rep.21a/10009; PD Wilhelmshaven, SSt, "Etatnachweisung der SSt," 21.10.1933; Pr.Min Präs., GeStapo, to RegPräs. Aurich, 8.12.1933; and stelv.Reg Präs. Aurich, "Personalbedarf der SSt," 16.12.1933, StA Aurich, Acc.22/89,207,460. Stelv.RegPräs. Aurich, "Verlegung d. SSt f.d. RegBez.Aurich . . . ," 25.11.1933, HStA Hannover, 122a/ VIII/430. Kassenanschlag . . . GeStapo . . . 1934, StA Munster, Reg.Augsburg/14601.

21. Meldungen des Geheimen Staatspolizeiamts, 1. and 2.8.1933, USHRIA, RG-11.001M.10, 91/109/1–10.

22. Ibid., 1.–2. and 4.8.1934, 5, 10, 19.

23. Kammler, "Nationalsozialistische Machtergreifung und Gestapo," 521, citing Erl. v. 29.5.1933, re "Vernehmung in politischen Gewahrsam befindlicher Personen durch Angehörige der SA und SS," StA Magdeburg 180/9408 Bad Hersfeld. See also Kammler, 520; and Johannes Tuchel and Reinhold Schattenfroh, *Zentrale des Terrors. Prinz-Albrecht-Strasse 8: Hauptquartier der Gestapo* (Berlin: Siedler, 1987) 166.

24. Tuchel and Schattenfroh, *Zentrale des Terrors*, 163–200; Erwin Nippert, *Prinz-Albrecht-Strasse 8* (Berlin: Militärverlag der DDR, 1988); and Schilde and Tuchel, *Columbia-Haus*, chapter 4.

25. Diels, *Lucifer ante Portas*, 134–135, 168–230; Hans B. Gisevius, *To the Bitter End* (London: Alden, 1948) 60–61, 68–74. Franz von Papen, *Memoirs* (New York: Dutton, 1953), 294–295; and the accounts of Ambassador Dodd and his daughter, William E. Dodd, Jr., and Martha Dodd, *Ambassador*

Dodd's Diary (New York: Harcourt Brace, 1941); and Martha Dodd, *Through Embassy Eyes,* (New York: Harcourt Brace, 1939).

26. Tuchel and Schattenfroh, *Zentrale des Terrors,* 139–144.

27. Politische Beurteilung of Huber, GL München-Obb., 17.3.1937, BDC/ RuSHA, Franz-Josef Huber (b. 22.1.02).

28. Aronson, *Beginnings,* 5–6, 25, citing Huber's testimony of 3.10.1961 in Aktenversammlung gegen Heinrich Müller, assembled by the Ludwigsburg Center for the Investigation of War Crimes and now on file in the GlStAnwlt.b.d.K. Berlin, 1 Js 1/68 (RSHA), hereafter cited as Müller Collection.

29. "Müllers Laufbahn," Bd. XI, and summation of information on Müller by Sichting, 24.5.1962, Bd. VI, Müller Collection.

30. Politische Beurteilung, 12.12.1939, BDC/RuSHA, Müller.

31. Müller to Best, Aüsserung zu der vorläufigen Formulierung des Polizei-Begriffes, 5.5.1937, T-82/25/ADR-26/5224/4/37. Eichmann on Müller, in Joachen von Lang, *Eichmann Interrogated: Transcripts from the Archives of the Israeli Police* (New York: Random House, 1984), 80, 84.

32. Personal letters from Mrs. Freya von Molke, January 25 and March 13, 1990. The quotation is Mrs. von Molke's approximation.

33. Aronson, *Beginnings,* 14, 16; and PD München to StMdI betr.: Erhö-hung des Personalstandes der PD München, 27.3.1934, ByHStA, Abt I, MdI, 71881. Further growth: StMdI, PPK By. to Württ.IM. betr.: Polit. Polizei, 22.3.1934, HStA Stuttg. E 151a/Bu 1452/52.

34. Aronson, *Beginnings,* 16–18, 32–37; and "Die Lehre von Dachau." *Völkische Beobachter (VB),* 24/25.5.1933.

35. Aronson, *Beginnings,* 33, 38–45; Broszat, "Concentration Camps," 414–415; Niederschrift, Ministerratssitzung vom 16. Mai 1933, ByHStA, Abt.II, MA 99–525; StA Bamberg M30/785; and Lawrence Walker, " 'Young Priests' as Opponents: Factors Associated with Clerical Opposition to the Nazis in Bavaria, 1933." *Catholic Historical Review* 65(1979): 402–413.

36. Martin Broszat, "The Concentration Camps 1933–45." In *Anatomy of the SS State,* edited by Hans Buchheim, et al. (New York: Walker and Company, 1968) 414–415; StA Bamberg, M30/785; Edward N. Peterson, *The Limits of Hitler's Power* (Princeton: Princeton University Press, 1969), 377–378; and Walker, "Young Priests," 405–409.

37. Peterson, *Limits,* 377–378.

38. Bund Deutscher Polizeibeamten e.V., "Die Beamten der Geheimen Staatspolizei. Die geschichtliche Entwicklung und Organisation der politischen Polizei und der Geheimen Staatspolizei. Die Rechtsstellung der Beamten der Geheimen Staatspolizei im Gesetz zu Artikel 131 GG und im Regierungsentwurf der Bundesbeamtengesetzes," Kassel, January 1953, 13–15, reveals how far this logic had been internalized by these policemen.

39. Aronson, *Beginnings,* 27–28. SS and Police training material, "Geschichte-Aufgaben-Aufbau der deutschen Polizei," T-175/247/2738615ff.; and "Politische Polizei," T-175/277/5487511 ff.

40. McGee, "Political Police in Bavaria," 277–279.

41. Schäfer, *20 Jahre.*

42. Ibid, 37–38.

43. For Württemberg, Württ.IM, "Verwendung von Beamten des Polizei-präsidium Stuttgart bei der Württ. Politischen Polizei im Innenministerium," 26.5.1933, StA Ludwigsburg, E188c/lfd. Nr.104/ Bauer, Friedrich.

44. Browder, *Foundations,* 94–96, 112–113; and Braunschweigische MdI,

re "Braunschweigische Politische Polizei, 4.5.1934, StA Wolfenbuttl., 12A Neu/13/16075/6–8.

45. Br.MdI, re "Br.polit.Polizei Aussenstellen-," 11.6.1934; "Zulassung vom Zivilanwärter zum staatlichen Kriminalpolizeidienst," 10.7.1934; Br.PP, re "Prüfung von Angehörigen der Br. Politischen Polizei für den staatl. Kriminalpolizeidienst," 4.3. 1935; Br.MdI, re "Befreiung von Angehörigen . . . von verschiedenen Vorschriften der Prüfungsordnung für den staatl. . . . ," 13.3.1935, StA Wolfenbuttl., 12a Neu/13/16072/16,42,52.

46. Gestapo, SSt Braunschweig, "Namentliches Verzeichnis der Angestellten, die für eine endgültige Übernahme in die Geheime Staatspolizei in Betracht kommen," plus 2 Nachtrage, StA Wolfenbuttl., 12a Neu/13/16072.

47. ORR Dr. Perey, "Geschichte der Bremischen Polizei seit 1800," typescript, 1936, Anhang, "Geheime Staatspolizei", StA Bremen, 33Ac.

48. Reconstructed from StA Bremen 124–72–01/2, Geschäftsverteilung i.d.Kripo v.1.10.33, 11, and 1.10.34, 16; and 3.P.1.a./ 1223, Schulz? to CdSipo, 13.1.1937, re "Aufstellung der Beamten und Angestellten."

49. BDC/SSO, Erwin Schulz (b. 27.11.00); and M-395/9 and 24 on Schulz from the Einsatzgruppen case.

50. Affidavits of Friedrich Rehmstedt, Hans Hafemann, Hans Wülfers, Alfred Schwasting, and Heinrich Schnitger, M-895/24/429–615.

51. Der Polizeisenator, Bremen, 7. and 11.3.1933, StA Bremen, 3–P.1.a./40.

52. T-175/422/2949916 and -943 show changes between April 19 and May 17. The first Geschäftsverteilungsplan is 25.10.1934 (BA/R-58/840), but filing plan of 28 June shows nearly completed reorganization, T-175/422/2950047–049, 2950004–05.

53. Cf. Aronson, *Heydrich,* 225–229; and Graf, *Politische Polizei,* 176–178, 182–185, 216–220. BDC/Mappe Polizei, Namentliches Verzeichnis der bei der Pr. GeStapo . . . beschäftigten männlichen Personen nach dem Stande vom 25. Juni 1935 and KDAL 1935 produce more complete pictures of personnel changes.

54. Namentliches Verzeichnis . . . vom 25. Juni 1935, BDC/Mappe Polizei. Female clerical personnel could not yet have accounted for the difference of 62.

55. Pr.GeStapo, Kassenanschlag über d. planmässigen Einnahmen u. Ausgaben d. GeStapo f.d. Rechnungsjahr 1934, StA Munster Reg. Augsburg/14601; Namentliches Verzeichnis; and "Die Polizei," n.d. (circa June 1936), 34, with cover letter, RFSS u.CdPP, 21.9. 1936, BA/R43II/391.

56. Ansprache des RFSS vor den Beamten und Angestellte des GeStapa am 11. Oktober 1934, 4–8, BA/NS-19, H.R.2.

57. Ibid., 6–7.

58. E.g., Heydrich, "Wandlungen unseres Kampfes" (1935), T-175/247/2738620–34; "Die Bekämpfung des Staatsfeinde." *Deutsches Recht* 6(15 April 1936): 121–123; Best, "Die Geheime Staatspolizei," loc. cit., 125–128; and "Rede des RFSS vor dem Staatsräten im Haus der Flieger, 5.3.1936," BA, NS-19/H.R.3.

59. E.g, ORR Erich Vogel, 787 and 788–PS. *Trial of the Major War Criminals Before the International Military Tribunal (IMT)* 26: 322–327; and BDC/SSO, Erich Vogel (b. 13.7.89), and cases of erratic discipline described by SS-Oberf. Günther Reinecke, *IMT* 20: 433–459.

60. Werner Best, *Die Deutsche Polizei* (Darmstadt: L. C. Wittich Verlag,

1941); and exchanges between Best and Schellenberg on training for Sipo, T-175/239/EAP 173–b-05/2J.

Chapter 3

1. Christoph Graf, *Politische Polizei zwischen Demokratie und Diktatur* (Berlin: Colloquium, 1983) 216–220, provides the most balanced picture of the changes.

2. Karl D. Bracher, Wolfgang Sauer, and Gerhard Schulz, *Die National-sozialistische Machtergreifung* (Cologne: Westdeutsche Verlag, 1960), 540, n. 108. BDC/SSO, Edmund Trinkle (b. 15.5.91), especially Lebenslauf.

3. Records of those purged: GStA/90/951/48–64. On Nebe, Hans B. Gisevius, *To the Bitter End* (London: Alden, 1948), 149. On Heller, Rudolf Diels, *Lucifer ante Portas* (Zurich: Interverlag, 1950), 139, 149, 182; and GStA/90/951/93–104. BDC/SSO, Dr. Karl Hasselbacker (b. 7.10.04).

4. Compare Geschäftsverteilungsplan, January 1934, with KDAL 1935.

5. Gisevius, *To the Bitter End,* 149.

6. Graf, *Politische Polizei,* 216–217, for the example of Volk.

7. Ibid., 392–398.

8. Since Graf mixes NS affiliation and Party membership, and seems to contradict himself, I am not sure I have summarized these data accurately.

9. BDC/Mappe Polizei/Namentlisches Verzeichnis.

10. BDC/Sammelliste 49/1–12, 20–164/Namentlisches Verzeichnis for the respective SSt.

11. Shlomo Aronson, *Reinhard Heydrich und die Frühgeschichte von Gestapo und SD* (Stuttgart: Deutsche Verlags-Anstalt, 1971), 189; and Günter Plum, "Staatspolizei und innere Verwaltung, 1934–1936." *Vierteljahrshefte für Zeitgeschichte (VJHfZ)* 13:196–197. L.d.GeStapa, "Schriftverkehr mit übergeordneten Behörden," 28.6.1934, T-175/229/2767268–269; Erl.u.d. Ernennung und Entlassung der Beamten der GeStapo," 28.2.1935, GStA, 90P/1,2/132; and PP Berlin, 6.4.1934, GStA, 90P/3/62–3, interfering in appointment of SStL Berlin.

12. Namentliches Verzeichnis . . . GeStapa, BDC/Mappe Polizei. References to SS-OAb Rhein directive of 6.5.1935 in 83. SS-Standarte, Stellenbesetzung . . . Färber . . . , 17.4.1936 (BDC/SSO, Wilhelm Färber, b. 13.1.94); and 33. SS-Standarte to SS-Ab XI, 16.4.1936 (HStA Wiesbaden, 483/678).

13. BDC/Mappe Polizei/Namentliches Verzeichnis, GeStapa and Sammelliste 49, for 34 SSt., Stande von 25 Juni 1935.

14. See appendix C, items 26–37.

15. Graf, *Politische Polizei;* and George C. Browder, *The Foundations of the Nazi Police State: The Formation of Sipo and SD* (Lexington: University Press of Kentucky, 1990), 62, 83–89, 118–120, 124.

16. Pr.MinPräs., 8.11.1933, HStA Hannover, 122a/VIII/430; GeStapa, "Nachwuchs der politischen Polizei," 15.3.1934, T-175/422/2950062–4; and GeStapa to MinPräs, C.d.GeStapo, 24.3.1934, and I.d.GeStapo, to Pr.MinPräs, C.d.GeStapo, 24.5.1934, GStA, 90P/1, 1/94–97.

17. RFSS, SS-Ergänzungsamt, Tgb.Nr.2369/35, 4.7.1935, BDC/SSO Färber (see note 12).

18. Erl.u.d.Ernennung und Entlassung der Beamten der GeStapo, vom 29.6.1936, GStA, 90P/1,2/180; and StA Munster, Reg.Arnsberg/14602, personnel regulations.

19. PrGeStapo, GeStapa, to LKD Thille, 18.9.1936, BA/R-58/853; Ge-Stapo, d.Inspekteur to Pr.MinPräs, C.d.Gestapo, 1.10., and response, 19.11.1934, GStA, 90P/1,2/29–33.

20. Übersicht über die Laufbahn der Kriminalbeamten der GeStapo, under cover letter, SSt Karlsruhe, "Aufnahm von Kriminal-Kommissaranwärter," 4.10.1937, GLA Karlsruhe, 345/G2026.

21. Ibid., 3–4.

22. GeStapa, SA Verbindungsführer to Pr.MinPräs, 13.4.1934; GeStapa, der Inspekteur to Pr.MinPräs, 16.6.1934; GeStapa to StR Neumann, MD im Pr.StMin, 12.7.1934, GStA, 90P/1,2/89–100, 217–219.

23. RFSS, CdSHA to FdSD-OAb, re Namhaftmachung von Verwaltungs-beamten, 5.12.1934, HStA Wiesbaden, 483/714.

24. BDC/SSO, Dr. Hans Fischer (b. 21.8.06).

25. BDC/SSO, Hans Blomberg (b. 27.9.06).

26. BDC/SSO, Dr. Emanuel Schäfer (b. 20.4.00).

27. Comparisons of the careers of NS and non- or late-NS detectives up to 1935, *Dienstaltersliste der höheren Kriminalbeamen (KDAL)*. The prelimi-nary work of Jens Banach, "Das Führungskorps der Sicherheitspolizei und des SD 1936–1945," paper presented at the Gestapo-Tagung, October 4–7, 1995, in Salzau bei Kiel, appeared too late for integration into this book, but his results seem consistent with mine.

28. BDC/SSO, Pomme; SSO, Reinhold Heller (b. 15.7.85); GeStapo, der Inspekteur, 16.4.1934, GStA/90/951/99–100; BDC/SSO, Hans Gippert (b. 12.11.05); and SSO, Kurt Riedel (b. 17.8.03).

29. E.g., BDC/SSO, Karl Döring (b. 24.5.05); SSO, Erwin Krause (b. 14.7.06); SSO, Oskar Schmidt (b. 1.6.01); and SSO and RuSHA, Wilhelm Wächter (b. 18.7.09).

30. BDC/SSO and RuSHA, Fritz Krause (b. 9.5.12).

31. BDC/SSO, Wilhelm Färber (b. 13.1.94).

32. Ibid., correspondence re Färber, 17.4.1936, 28.1.1937, and 16.9.1943.

33. E.g., BDC/SSO, Dr. Wilhelm Harster (b. 21.7.04); SSO Erwin Schulz (b. 27.11.00); and Dr. Walter Stahlecker (b. 10.10.00), LdWPP.

34. RMdI, "Nationalsozialistische Erziehung der Polizei," 3.7. 1934, StA Bremen, 3–P.1.a./1171.

35. Elisabeth Kohlhass, "Die Mitarbeiter der regionalen Staatspolizeistel-len. Quantitative und qualitative Befunde zur Personalausstattung der Ge-stapo." In *Gestapo: Mythos und Realität,* edited by Klaus-Michael Mallmann, and Gerhard Paul (Darmstadt: Wissenschaftliche-Buchgesellschaft, 1995), 223–225, 232–235.

36. E.g., GeStapa, Rundschreiben, 30.5.1934, T-175/414/2949981; IdGe-Stapo, "Nachrichtendienst des Partei," 25.6.1934, T-175/405/2928200; PPK Bayerns, "Die Zusammenarbeit der stl. Polizeibehörden mit dem SD RFSS," 7.12.1934 (ref. to Verfügung d.PPKuLdGeStapo, 4.7.1934) T-580/93/457; HAbtl.III, "Zusammenarbeit mit dem SD und Adjutant a.V.," 20.6.1935, T-175/250/2742150; PrGeStapo, der StVCuI, "Zusammenarbeit der GeStapo mit dem SD des RFSS," 10.8.1935, T-175/250/2742238–39; and similar order of 20.12.1939, Ibid., 2742504.

37. Der PPKdL, PrGeStapo, der StVC, re Festnahmen von Angehörige des SD, 29.5.1936, T-175/414/2939948.

38. PPKdL, PrGeStapo, der StVC, 6.5.1936, calling such a meeting for 12 and 13.5, and attached Tagungsplan, T-175/423/2950977–78.

39. Reinhard Mann, *Protest und Kontrolle im DrittenReich* (Frankfurt: Campus, 1987); Robert Gellately, *The Gestapo in German Society* (Oxford: Oxford University Press, 1990); and Klaus-Michael Mallmann and Gerhard Paul, *Heerschaft und Alltag.* (Bonn: J. H. W. Dietz Nachf., 1991). *Terror, Herrschaft und Alltag im Nationalsozialismus,* edited by Brigitte Berlekamp and Werner Röhr (Münster: Westfälisches Dampfboot, 1995), for some of the debate over the work of Mallmann and Paul.

40. Typed guidelines, SSt Aachen, 8.3.1935, HStA Düsseldorf, RW 35/1/116–44, or T-175/432/2962497.

41. Mann, *Protest und Kontrolle,* 82–83.

42. Ibid., 184–185.

43. Ibid., 180, 251–258.

44. Ibid., 180, 236–251, 258–270.

45. Gellately, *Gestapo,* 49; and "Enforcing Racial Policy in Weimar Germany: The Polish Workers, the German People, and the Nazi Police," paper presented at the annual American Historical Association convention, December 28, 1992. Mallmann and Paul, *Herrschaft und Alltag,* 229–245, paint a similar picture for SSt Saarbrücken.

46. Mann, *Protest und Kontrolle,* 182, 241, 252.

47. Halbmonatsberichte of SD-Oberabschnitte for 1.–15.4.1937, USHRIA RG-15.007M, 33/398/25, 29, 31–33, 36.

48. Guidelines (see n.39), 5–30 (120–145 in folio).

49. Guidelines, 5.

50. Mann, *Protest und Kontrolle,* 292.

51. Gellately, *Gestapo,* 162; and "Enforcing Racial Policy." Mallmann and Paul, *Heerschaft und Alltag,* similar conclusions for SSt Saarbrücken.

52. Mann, *Protest und Kontrolle,* 163–172.

53. Gellately, *Gestapo,* 163.

54. E.g., GeStapa, on cooperation with Forschungsamt, 18.11.1933 and 7.5.1934, PPKdL, "Zusammenarbeit mit der Deutschen Arbeitsfront," 23.10.1935; DAF, RLdDAF, "Zusammenarbeit mit dem GeStapa . . . , 24.9.1935; T-175/422/2949895, 922, and 706–709; RFM, *Reichszollblatt,* Ausgabe A, Nr. 35, 16.4.1936, T-175/423/2950964; ByPP, "Berichterstattung," 11.5.1936; and ByPP, "Auskunftserholung bei Finanzämtern, 1.7.1936, T-580/106/14. See Mallmann and Paul, *Herrschaft und Alltag,* 224–229, 284–287.

55. Ludwig Eiber, "Zur "Effektivität" der Gestapotätigkeit und der Funktion der Gestapo im faschistischen Terrorsystem." In *Terror, Herrschaft und Alltag,* edited by Berlekamp and Röhr, 184–185.

56. Mann, *Protest und Kontrolle,* 293–294. Denunciations, pre-NS political police, Anonymous, *Die Politische Polizei,* Berichte, June 1930, 27, PIH, PG 4-23-7PR.

57. Mann, *Protest und Kontrolle,* 295–296; and Mallmann and Paul, *Herrschaft und Alltag,* 229–234.

58. Gellately, *Gestapo,* 164.

59. E.g., Baden MdI, "Bekämpfung des Denunziantentums," 12.6. 1934, StA Freiburg, LKK/1529; and von Pfeffer, "Denunziantentum," 6.9.1933; Thomas Klein, ed., *Die Lagebericht der Geheimen Staatspolizei über die Provinz Hessen-Nassau 1933–1936* (Cologne: Böhlau, 1986), 618. See also Martin Broszat, "Politische Denunziationen in der NS-Zeit," *Archivalische Zeitschrift,* 73(1977): 221–238.

60. Cf. Guidelines, 14–18, 19–20, and GeStapa, stlv.CuL, to RJM, 28.3.1935, GStA, Rep.90P/104/115–25. Mallmann and Paul, *Herrschaft und Alltag,* 234–238; and Frank Dingel, "Die Gestapo—'Alibi der Nation' oder gesellschaftliches Problem?" in *Terror, Herrschaft und Alltag,* edited by Berlekamp and Röhr, 205.

61. E.g., a case in SSt Aachen, 1937, HStA Düsseldorf, RW35/12/22–35, especially GeStapa Schnellbrief, 6.1.1938, outlining criteria by which cases would be judged.

62. Mallmann and Paul, *Herrschaft und Alltag,* 234–245; and Paul, "zur Sozialgeschichte von Verfolgung und Widerstand am Beispiel des Saarlandes (1935–1945)," in *Terror, Herrschaft und Alltag,* edited by Berlekamp and Röhr, 51–52, 56–58.

63. E.g., 3rd U.S.Army, IR/20/13–14.

64. David Martin Luebke and Sybil Milton, "Locating the Victim: An Overview of Census-Taking, Tabulation Technology, and Persecution in Nazi Germany." *IEEE Annals of the History of Computing* 16(3): 1–14 (1994).

65. GeStapa, "Dienstanweisung für die HAbtl. III—Ausland—." 5.6.1934, OA/500/3/8/199–228, esp. 16–23 (214–221); UAbtl. III/4, "Dienstanweisung," 11.5.1934, USHRIA RG-11.001M 1/38a/13b-14b; Johannes Tuchel and Reinhold Schattenfroh, *Zentrale, des Terrors. Prinz-Albrecht-Strasse 8: Hauptquartier der Gestapo* (Berlin: Siedler, 1987) 125; and 3rd U.S. Army/IR 20/13.

66. Tuchel and Schattenfroh, *Zentrale,* 126.

67. SSt Dortmund, ASt Hagen, "Funkspruch Nr.105 Berlin, v.24.10.34 u. Funkspruch Nr. 85 Berlin v.1.11.34. Einrichtung von Listen (an das Gestapa Berlin) solchen Personen, die irgendwie in homosexueller Hinsicht in Erscheinung getretten sind," 24.11.1934, StA Münster, Politische Polizei III. Reich/Nr.369/103516–20.

68. Tuchel and Schattenfroh, *Zentrale,* 146–149; Burkhard Jellonnek, *Homosexuelle unter dem Hakenkreuz: Die Verfolgung von Homosexuellen im Dritten Reich* (Paderborn: Ferdin and Schöningh, 1990); and cf. Geoffrey Giles, " 'The Most Unkindest Cut of All': Castration, Homosexuality and Nazi Justice." *Journal of Contemporary History (JCH)* 27(1992): 41–61.

69. Browder, *Foundations,* 157, 247–248.

70. Pr.GeStapo, stlv.C, PPKdL, "Schutzhaft," 5.2.1936, HStA Düsseldorf, RW34/26/2–4.

71. SSt Köln, 5.2., n.d. October, and 28.10.1936, loc.cit., 5, 16–17, 25–26.

72. GeStapa, "A-Kartei," 8.1.1937; and SSt Aachen, the same, 11.2.1937, HStA Düsseldorf, RW35/7/31, 28–30.

73. Tuchel and Schattenfroh, *Zentrale,* 128.

74. David Irving, *Das Reich hört mit. Görings "Forschungsamt": Der geheimste Nachrichtendienst des Dritten Reiches* (Kiel: Arndt, 1989).

75. UAbtl.III/4, "Dienstanweisung," 6–7; 3rd. U.S. Army/IR 20/14–15; Mallmann and Paul, *Herrschaft und Alltag,* 225.

76. CI-CIR/15, 17–21, on the agents of SLSt München and their classification, post 1939. Cf. Walter O. Weyrauch, "Gestapo Informants: Facts and Theory of Undercover Operations." *Columbia Journal of Transnational Law* 24(1986): 554–596. Mallmann and Paul, *Herrschaft und Alltag,* 215–223.

77. "Criminal Informants." In *The Encyclopedia of Police Science,* edited

by William G. Bailey (New York: Garland, 1989), 108–111; and Dr. Erich Anuschat, "Kriminalistik." *Die Polizei* 38: 97–100.

78. Weyrauch, "Gestapo Informants."

79. Erlasse über Agenten und Vertrauensleute (Stand vom 15.10. 1935), all originating in GeStapa, T-175/405/2928178–80.

80. LdGeStapo, 1.6.1934; GeStapa, 16.6.1934; PPKdL, 14.2.1935, T-175/422/2949989, 2950027, 2950632.

81. CI-CIR/15, 17; and Adolf Diamant, *Gestapo Frankfurt a.M.* (Frankfurt: W. Steinmann & Boschen, 1988), 21–22.

82. Bailey, *Encyclopedia*, 110, on informant control; and 393–396, "Intelligence."

83. SSt Düsseldorf, "Dienstanweisung der SSt Düsseldorf," 11.11.1935, HStA Düsseldorf, RW36/8.

84. BrPP, "Räumliche Vergrösserung der Braunschweigischen Politischen Polizei," 9.11.1934, StA Wolfenbuttl., 12a Neu/13/16073.

85. Ibid.

86. Ibid.; BrPP, "Personensuchanlage in der Braunschw. Politischen Polizei," 20.3.1936; and SSt Braunschweig, "Zusammenstellung über die laufenden Dienstgeschäfte in der SSt... vom 12.3.1937," 13.3.1937, StA Braunschweig, 12a Neu/13/16073 and 16076.

87. ADSt Bückeburg, "Gestellung einer Hilfskraft für den Dienst der Stapo . . . ," 31.3.1936, StA Bückbg., L4/9179.

88. 3rd U.S. Army/IR 20/3, "The Gestapo in Frankfurt/Main," 14.

89. Mallman and Paul, *Herrschaft und Alltag*, 210–214, 224, 245.

90. Tuchel and Schattenfroh, *Zentrale*, 118–124.

91. BPP, Halbmonatsberichte, 2. and 16.5.1934, 1. and 16.6.1934, USHRIA RG-15.007, 7/61/36, 60, 90, 112; Rapport, January and June 1936; SLSt München, November 1936, T-175/421/2948377–418, -573–600, -708–732.

92. SSt Düsseldorf to ASt Essen, 21.7.1936, citing RFSS Erl. v. 23.3.1936; GeStapa, "Konzentrierung der Jüdischen Schutz- und Schulungshäftlinge im KL Dachau," 17.2.1937, T-175/423/2958667; and Hans-Günther Ricardi, *Schule der Gewalt. Die Anfänge des Konzentrationslager Dachau, 1933–1934* (Munich: Verlag C.H. Beck, 1983).

93. GeStapa, "Inschutzhaftnahme von Betriebsführern," 29.12.1934, T-175/422/2949506.

94. Tuchel and Schattenfroh, *Zentrale*, 124–125.

95. Erich Wollenberg, "Der Apparat - Stalins Fünfte Kolonne," *Ost-Probleme*, 3: 578–580; and interrogation of Hans Helmut Wolff, 18.6.1945, NA/RG-238/L-178/5–7; Detlev Peukert, *Die KPD im Widerstand. Verfolgung und Untergrundarbeit am Rhein und Ruhr, 1933 bis 1945* (Wuppertal: Peter Hammer, 1980); and Allen Merson, *Communist Resistance in Nazi Germany* (London: Lawrence and Wishart, 1985). Cf. Mallmann and Paul, *Herrschaft und Alltag*, 215–223, 249–251.

96. E.g., Bericht der SSt Kassel über politische Lage . . . , 29.8. and 20.10.33, Klein, *Die Lageberichte*, 66, 71.

97. Mlynek, *Gestapo Hannover*, and Klein, *Lageberichte . . . Hessen-Nassau*, vol.1.

98. Klaus Mlynek, *Gestapo Hannover meldet . . . Polizei und Regierungsberichte für das mittlere und südliche Niedersachsen zwischen 1933 und 1937* (Hildesheim: August Lax, 1986), 25–29.

99. Ibid., Reports of 4.12.33, 83; 4.5.34, 166; 9.8.34, 196; 7.1.35, 289;

4.2.35, 314–315; 4.3.35, 319–321; 4.6.35, 360–362; 3.8.35, 393–395; 3.8.35, 408–409; and 4.10.35, 431–433.

100. Klein, *Lageberichte* 1: 5–13.

101. Bericht, 28.7.33, Klein, *Lageberichte*, 1: 60.

102. PPräs.i.Frankfurt a.M. to PrMdI, 21.10.1933, HStA Wiesbaden, 483/714/23–24; GeStapa, 11.7.33; SSt Kassel cover letter, 24.7.33; SSt Kassel 23.10.33; ibid., 2: 614–615; and Bericht, 9.11.33, ibid., 1:74–76.

103. "Auszug aus dem Erl. . . . Heydrich," 24.5.1934; Robert Thevoz, et al., eds. *Die Geheime Staatspolizei in den preussischen Ostprovinzen, 1934–36: Pommern, 1934/35* (Cologne: Grote, 1974), 209.

104. GeStapa, 19.2.1935, T-175/422/2950243–44.

105. GeStapa, "Judenkartei," 17.8.1935, BA, R-58/276/22; for Hessia, GeStapa Darmstadt forwarded his subsequent elaborations on 30.8. and 18.9.35, 16.1. and 3.3.36, HStA Wiesbaden, 483/305.

106. Lagebericht Hannover, 3.7.35, 3.8.35, 4.10.35, 4.12.35, Mlynek, *Gestapo Hannover*, 374, 394–395, 432–433, 459; Übersicht Kassel, 1.6.33, 4.8.34, 5.11.34, 5.12.34, 5.1.35 and 5.10.35; Klein, *Lageberichte* 1: 110–111, 135, 182–183, 195–196, 210–211, 320–321.

107. GeStapa, "Zusammenarbeit mit den Finanzbehörden bei Vorbereitungen zur Auswanderung," 17.12.1935, and subsequent directives, HStA Düsseldorf, Reg. Düsseldorf/45361/81–90; "Massnahmen gegen zurückkehrende Emigranten," 3.7.1935; Klein, *Lageberichte* 2: 729–730; Arthur Prinz, "The Role of the Gestapo in Obstructing and Promoting Jewish Emigration." *Yad Vashem Studies on the European Jewish Catastrophe and Resistance* (1958): 205–218.

108. Gellately, *Gestapo*, tables, 3 and 4, 162, 164.

109. Helmut Krausnick, "The Persecution of the Jews," in *Anatomy of the SS State* edited by Hans Buchheim, et al. (New York: Walker and Company, 1968), 32–43; and George C. Browder, "Sipo and SD, 1931–1940," Ph.D. dissertation, University of Wisconsin, Madison, 1968, 251–257.

110. BDC/SSO, RuSHA, Albert Reinke (b. 29.10.77), especially 80 201, re "Reinke . . . ," 24.10.1935.

111. Martin Broszat, "The Concentration Camps 1933–45," in *Anatomy of the SS State*, 425.

112. Gunnar C. Boehnert, "The Jurists in the SS-Führer Korps, 1925–1939." In *Der "Führerstaat:" Mythos und Realität*, edited by Gerhard Hirschfeld and Luther Kettenacker (Stuttgart: Klett-Cotta, 1981), 361–373.

113. Ibid., 366–73; and Browder, "SIPO and SD," 242–243, 272–273, 276–282.

Chapter 4

1. For 1932, Horst-Adalbert Koch, "Zur Organisationsgeschichte der Deutschen Polizei, 1927–1939." *Feldgrau* 5(1957): 169. Data for ratios, Präs.d.Polizeiinstituts, to PD Nürnberg, 9. and 11.9.1928, StA Nürnberg, Reg.218/1¹/655; and Hsi-Huey Liang, The *Berlin Police Force in the Weimar Republic* (Berkeley: University of California, 1970), 125, citing Grzesinski.

2. PrMdI, Bericht der Polizei-Abteilung . . . , 1.2.1934, 2–3, BA, R-43/I/2290; and Allgemeine Verteilung der Stärken der deutschen Polizei (Stand: 1.Dezember 1933), StA Bückbg., L4/12525.

3. Daluege, "Die Deutsche Polizei . . . ," November 1935, 2, BA, R-

43II/391; (RuPrMdI?) III B 1, 11.5.1935, Thiele? memo, BDC/PK, Othmar Toifel (b. 12.7.98); and cf. RuPrMdI, "Stärke und Aufgaben der staatl. Polizei," 21.9.1935, 1, BA, R-18/5627/201; and RFSS, "Die Polizei," n.d. (circa spring 1936), 8, BA, R-43II/ 391, for slightly different figures. SSt Wilhelmshaven to IdGeStapa, 26.6.1934, StA Aurich, Acc.22189/207/460.

4. III B 1 memo of 11.5.1935, 2–4.

5. "Einheitliche Gemeindepolizei im ganzen Reich." *Völkische Beobachter (VB)*, November 7 1935; and RdErl.d.RuPrMdI, 25.10.1935, *Ministerialblatt des Reichs und Preussischen Ministeriums des Innern. (MBliV)*, 1327. For 1939, Wolfgang Ullrich, *Verbrechensbekämpfung. Geschichte, Organisation, Rechtsprechung* (Berlin: Luchterhand, 1961), 254.

6. "Nachweisung über den in der Zeit vom 1. Oktober 1931 bis 31. Dezember 1931 abgeleisteten Dienst der staatl. Kripo," StA Detmold, L75/IV/ 7,2,III; and "Übernahme stadtl. Polizeibeamten in den Staatsdienst," n.d., L80Ie/I,2,1,II/Anlegeband.

7. Attachment to PP Hannover, LKPSt to Herrn RegPräs., 8.11.1935, StA Aurich, Acc.22/89, Dezernat 201/161, Kriminalpolizei. Jahrbuch Amt V (RSHA), 1939/1940, USHRIA RG-11.001M.01, 17/26/94.

8. RMdI, "Vergleichende Darstellung der Kripo d.dt. Länder," 7.2. 1933, StA Detmold, L80Ie/I,2,1,II/Anlagebund, or StA Bremen, P.1.a./1143; RMdI to IMd.Länder, 18.9.1934, StA Detmold, L80Ie/P/2.II; and Memo to Pfundtner, 29.5.1934, and from Pfundtner, 28.5.1934, BA, R-18/Rep.320/627/65–66, 71. Karl-Leo Terhorst, *Polizeiliche planmässige Überwachung und polizeiliche Vorbeugungshaft im Dritten Reich* (Heidelberg: C.F. Müller Juristischer Verlag, 1985), 43–45.

9. RdErl.d.RuPrMdI, v. 20.9.1936, *MBliV*, 1936, 1339; RdErl.d. RFSSuCdDtPol, v. 1.9.1937, *MBliV*, 1937, 1483; and RdErl.d.RFSSuCdDtPol, v. 16.5.1938, *MBliV*, 1938, 883.

10. Daluege, "Bericht . . . ," 2.2.1934, 5; and Daluege, "Die Polizei" (under RuPrMdI cover letter, November 1935), 16–17.

11. Terhorst, *Polizeiliche . . . Vorbeugungshaft*, 9–109; and Bernd Wehner, *Dem Täter auf dem Spur: Die Geschichte der deutschen Kriminalpolizei* (Bergisch Gladbach: Gustav Lübbe Verlag, 1983), 193–196, 198–202.

12. Terhorst, *Polizeiliche . . . Vorbeugungshaft*, 15–40.

13. Ibid., 9–19, 49–54, 76, 99–100.

14. Ibid., 61–96. For police arrest authority, 1931–1934, "Die polizeiliche Verwahrung (Sec.15.PVG vom 1.6.1931);" and cf. for 1934–1935, "Vorbeugende Polizeihaft gegen Berufsverbrecher," T-175/277/5487631–37, -655–57

15. Terhorst, *Polizeiliche . . . Vorbeugungshaft*, 97–99.

16. Ibid., 85–86, 100–109.

17. E.g., SS indoctrination building on these developments: "Die Staatsfeinde und ihre Bekämpfung," T-175/277/5487521–24; "Geschichte—Aufgaben—Aufbau der Deutschen Polizei;" and SS-O'Stubf. MR Werner, "Fragen zur Kriminalpolitik," T-175/247/2738615–20, -884–86.

18. Wehner, *Täter*, 204.

19. RuPrMdI?)III B1 (Thiele's?) notes, 11.5.1935, 2–4, BDC/PK, Othmar Toifel (b. 12.7.98).

20. Wehner, *Täter*, 204.

21. Cf. Nebe, "Stellungnahme zu der Formulierung des Begriffs "Polizei," 8.3.1937; and Müller, "Ausserung zu der Formulierung des Polizei-Begriffs," 5.5.1937, T-82/25/ADR-26(5224/4/37).

22. Wehner, *Täter*, 196–98; Frank Arnau, *Das Auge des Gesetzes. Macht und Ohnmacht der Kriminalpolizei* (Düsseldorf and Vienna: Econ, 1962), 64; and Rudolf Augstein, et al., "Das Spiel ist aus—Arthur Nebe." *Der Spiegel* (November 24, 1949): 28.

23. CdS, 17.10.1936, StA Bremen, 3–P.1.a./1200/39a; and CdS, 4.3.1937, T-175/423/2951744.

24. Wehner, *Täter*, 206.

25. Daluege, "Bericht . . . ," 1.2.1934, 2, BA, R-43I/2290/28.

26. Kripo Karlsruhe, Personalkartei f. Angestellte u. Beamte, Tag der Ausstellung: 18.3.38, GLA Karlsruhe, 465d/1435.

27. *Dienstaltersliste der höheren Kriminalbeamen (KDAL)* 1935 yielded 39 KStL and similar post directors; Namentliches Verzeichnis . . . , 26.6.1935 (SSt personnel rosters, BDC/Sammelliste 49), compared with *KDAL* and other records, identified 31 SStL.

28. Daluege's report, "Die deutsche Polizei," BA/R43 II/391.

29. Namentliches Verzeichnis, June 1935 (see n. 27).

30. Jarbuch Amt V (RSHA), 1939/1940, 3–4, USHRIA, RG-11.001M.01, 17/26/8. The preliminary work of Jens Banach ("Das Führungskorps der Sicherheitspolizei und des SD 1936–1945," paper presented to the Gestapo-Tagung, October 4–7, 1995, in Salzau bei Kiel) seems to bear this out.

31. BDC/SSO, Thiele (b. 22.3.90); and 1935 *KDAL*. See also nn. 3–4.

32. BDC/NS, PK, Kattolinsky (b. 28.12.01).

33. BDC/SSO, RuSHA, Braschwitz (b. 18.1.00).

34. Impressions based on the BDC files of 29 Kripo Beamten in höheren Dienst who were not SS members: four were allowed to wear the SS uniform; one was a contributing member of the SS.

35. BDC/SSO, RuSHA, NS, PK, Wolfgang Berger (b. 20.1.97); and same files, Josef Menke (b. 12.11.05).

36. Hans Mommsen, *Beamtentum im Dritten Reich* (Stuttgart: Deutsche Verlagsanstalt, 1976); Martin Broszat, *Der Staat Hitlers: Grundlegung und Entwicklung seiner inneren Verfassung* (Munich: Deutscher Taschenbuch Verlag, 1973); Jane Caplan, *Government without Administration: State and Civil Service in Nazi Germany* (Oxford: Oxford University Press, 1988); "Civil Service Support for National Socialism: An Evaluation." In *Der Führerstaat, Mythos und Realität: Studien zur Struktur und Politik des Dritten Reiches,* edited by Gerhard Hirschfeld and Lothar Kettenacher, (Stuttgart: Kett-Cotta, 1981), 167–191; and a summary emphasizing "special cases," Dan P. Silverman, "Nazification of the German Bureaucracy Reconsidered: A Case Study." *Journal of Modern History (JMH)* 60 (3): 496–539 (1988).

37. George C. Browder, *The Foundations of the Nazi Police State: The Formation of Sipo and SD* (Lexington: University of Kentucky, 1990), 44–45, 77; and Caplan, *Government*, 134, 184–188.

38. RMdI, der Reichskommissar f. Beamtenorganisation, to Luckner, 7.7.1933; and Kameradschaftsbund Dt. Polizeibeamten (KBDPB), to MdI v. Lippe, 26.7.1933, StA Detmold, L80Ie/P,2,III. KBDPB, to RMdI, 31.7.1933, with draft of Frick's article, BA, R-18/5268.

39. Frick's article.

40. MdI, Karlsruhe, "Ausbildung der Polizei: hier Fachschriften," 18.9.1933, StA Freiburg, LRA Konstanz/1462; Wehner, *Täter*, 195–196, 199.

41. PD Wesermünde, "Pflege des NS bei der Kripo," 10.4.1934, with attached "Nachweisung u. abgehaltene Vortrags- und Aussprachsstuden bei der

KI Wesermünde;" and LPI Mitte, Magdeburg, "Unterricht u. NS Weltanschauung," 9.7.1934, similar assemblies, 6.7.1933, StA Stade, Rep.80P/1424.

42. Silverman, "Nazification," 535–536.

43. "Nachweisung . . . , see n. 41.

44. "Polizei und Wehrmacht," Köln, 8.4.1936, HStA Düsseldorf, Polizeibehörden vor 1945.

45. Milton Mayer, *They Thought They Were Free: The Germans, 1933–45* (Chicago: University of Chicago, 1955), 40–41, 56–57, 71, 99, 128.

46. RMdI, "Nationalsozialistische Erziehung der Polizei," 3.7.1934, StA Bremen, 3–P.1.a./1171; and RMdI, an die Innenministerien der Länder -ohne Preussen-," 6.10.1934, with attached article by Wilhelm Kube, "Polizei und Nationalsozialismus," *Der Märkische Adler*, 28.9.1934, HStA Stuttgart, E151aII/566/197, 198.

47. Silverman, "Nazification," 528–530.

48. Daluege, "Bericht," 1.2.1934, 2, 5, BA, R-43I/2290/28, 31.

49. "Prüfungsordnung f. d. staatl. K-K-Anwärter," 1, under PrMdI cover letter of 24.11.1933, StA Stade, Rep.80P/1403.

50. Collection of Prussian decrees, curricula, and testing guidelines, from early Weimar to early NS, StA Stade, Rep.80P/1403.

51. "Lehrordnung und Prüfungsordnung für die Polizeischulen," Anlage zum RdErl.vom 7.9.1933, 3–4, StA Stade, Rep.80P/1403. Topic outlines on aspects of law, 1937, T-175/277/5487492–508.

52. "Lehrordnung und Prüfungsordnung für die Polizeischulen," Zweiter Teil, Prüfungsordnung, Anlage zum RdErl.vom 22.July 1934, 10–11, 14–15; "Prüfungsordnung f.d.staatl.K-K.Anwärter," 24.11.1933, 1–3, StA Stade, Rep.80P/1403.

53. E.g., dienstl. Beurteilungen of individual Beamten, StA Nürnbg., Abg.1978/1445.

54. "Richtlinien f.d. Dienstlaufbahn d. oberen Kriminalbeamten . . . Zusammengestellt n.d.z. Zeit geltenden ministeriellen Bestimmungen," n.d. (latest regulation dated 1935), BA, R-58/259.

55. RdErl.d.RFSSuCdDP, vom 6.4.1937, "Führerschule der Sipo," T-175/248/2740085.

56. *Trial of the Major War Criminals before the International Military Tribunal* 21: 507–508.

57. Richtlinien für die Dienstlaufbahn der oberen Kriminalbeamten, n.d. (circa 1935), BA/R-58/259. See exchanges between Schellenberg and Best, February and March 1939, T-175/239/2728208–13, -408–419, -431–442, -453–457.

Chapter 5

1. George C. Browder, *The Foundations of the Nazi Police State: The Formation of Sipo and SD* (Lexington: University Press of Kentucky, 1990), 23–24.

2. Richard Breitman and Schlomo Aronson, "Eine unbekannte Himmler-Rede vom Januar 1943," *Vierteljahrshefte für Zeitgeschichte (VJfZ)*, 38 (April 1990): 343.

3. Richard Breitman, *The Architect of Genocide: Himmler and the Final Solution*, (New York: Knopf, 1990), 4–17, 33–39.

4. Elke Froehlich, ed., *Die Tagebücher von Joseph Goebbels: Sämtlich Fragemente* (Munich: K.G. Sauer, 1987), 30.6.31 and 3.7.31, 84–86.

5. Breitmann and Aronson, "Himmler-Rede," 343; and Lina Heydrich, *Leben mit einem Kriegsverbrecher* (Pfaffenhofen: Verlag W. Ludwig, 1976), 25–29.

6. BDC/SSO Hans Kobelinski (b. 2.6.00).

7. Shlomo Aronson, *Reinhard Heydrich und die Frühgeschichte von Gestapo und SD* (Stuttgart: Deutsche Verlags-Anstalt, 1971) 56; and Heydrich to Schwieger Eltern 11.8.31, in Heydrich, *Leben,* 32–33.

8. HA/4/83 for material SA or SS Ic men forwarded, August–December 1931. RFSS, SS-Befehl-A-Nr.53, 10.10.1931, BA/R-58/1151.

9. P.N.D., Nr.748, Führerbesprechung der SS-Münchens am 26.8.31 im Braunen Haus, HA/72/1546.

10. RFSS, SS-Befehl-D-Nr.43, 4.9.1931, HA/28A/1773.

11. Browder, *Foundations,* 30–32; BDC/SSO/Heydrich; and Heydrich, *Leben,* 32–33.

12. RFSS, Gesamt-Stärkemeldung der SS für den Monat Dezember 1931, 25.1.1932, HA/28A/1773.

13. NSDAP, RL, "Nachrichtendienst," 26.11.1931, HA/89/1849.

14. Nachrichtensammelstelle, 18.3.1932, re "Nachrichtendienst der NSDAP," HA/28A/1774, and Polizeiamt, Oldenburg, Abt. Exekutive, to PH Wilhelmshaven, 27.2.1932, HA/71/1533.

15. Abteilung Ic, "Liste ab 1.12.31," Stettin, 12.11.1931, T-580/220/62.

16. "Auszug aus einem Bericht des Dipl.-Ing. Paul Leffler über den SD," from Werner Best, made available by Aronson. BDC/SSO, August Simon, (b. 14.12.98), Lebenslauf.

17. Aronson, *Heydrich,* 61–62, n. 155; and Heydrich, *Leben,* 34–35.

18. Aronson, *Heydrich,* 270, n. 157; and Paul Leffler, "Auszug aus dem Bericht des Dipl.-Ing. Paul Leffler über des SD." Made available by Best through Aronson.

19. SS-Übersichts-Karte, 13.IV.32-17.VI.32 and 15.XI.32, T-175/200/2741062–63.

20. Based on BDC SS personnel records; Browder, "Die Anfänge des SD: Dokumente aus der Organisations geschichte des Sicherheitsdienstes des Reichsführers SS." *VJfZ* 27(1979):299–324. On SD Gebiet Nord-Ost, BDC/SSO Karl Appel (b. 25.8.08); on Danzig, BDC/SSO Kurt Schneider (b. 30.4.04), and T-175/423/2951554.

21. BDC/SSO, August Simon (b. 14.12.98), Lebenslauf.

22. Werner Best, "Beantwortungen des Fragebogens (Aronson)," unpublished materials, B.1-3. BDC/SSO, Paul Blobel (b.13.8.94); SSO, Erich Rasner (b. 7.3.05); SSO, Erich Körting (b. 22.1.02), Lebenslauf of 17.12.1934; SSO, Wilhelm Pallas (b. 1.3.97). "Deckadressen für ausgehende Post," n.d. (1933); and "Chiffre-Nummern" (1932 or 1933), HStA Wiesbaden, 483/625/117–18.

23. Alwin Ramme, *Der Sicherheitsdienst der SS* (Berlin: Deutsche Militärverlag, 1970), 260; BDC/SSO, Lothar Beutel (b. 6.5.02); SSO, Gerhard Närger (b. 4.9.06); and SSO, Dr. Otto Rasch (b. 7.12.91).

24. BDC/SSO, Horst Böhme (b. 24.8.09); and SSO, Rasch.

25. Meldung, Leffler, 18.9.1933, 1; and interrogation of Leffler, 20.9.1933, 3. BDC/USchla, Leffler.

26. BDC/USchla, Leffler.

27. BDC/SSO, Leffler, Meldung; and Heydrich, *Leben*, 37.

28. BDC/SSO, Kobelinski; and RuSHA, Werner Göttsch (b. 23.10.12), Lebenslauf.

29. BDC/SSO, Willy Falkenberg (b. 5.1.00), Lebenslauf, 31.5.1933; and Falkenberg to SD OAb Ost, 6.9.1937, RuSHA, Falkenberg.

30. George C. Browder, "The Numerical Strength of the Sicherheitsdienst des RFSS." *Historical Social Research* 28(October 1983): 30–41.

31. Heydrich, *Leben*, 35–37; Leffler, "Bericht," 2–3; and cf. Aronson, *Heydrich*, 61–62; and Günther Deschner, *Reinhard Heydrich: Staathalter der totalen Macht* (Esslingen: Bechtle, 1977), 55–57.

32. Leffler, "Auszug," 2.

33. Ibid., 2–3.

34. SDdRFSS to SS-Gericht, 23.11.1933, BDC/USchla, Leffler.

35. BDC/SSO, Leffler.

36. BDC/SSO, Arthur Bork (b. 13.4.92); and SSO, Karl Albrecht Oberg (b. 27.1.97).

37. Heinrich Orb, *Nationalsozialismus, 13 Jahr Machtrausch* (Olten: Verlag Otto Walter, 1945), 63, 127, erroneously identifying Sohst as Johst; BDC/SSO Sohst (b.23.9.98); and Geschäftsverteilungsplan Gestapa, 33.1.1934, GStA 90P/2,2/107.

38. Hansjürgen Koehler, *Inside the Gestapo* (London: Pallas, 1940), 37–38, 210–236; and BDC/SSO Sohst.

39. Heinz Höhne, *Der Orden unter dem Totenkopf: De Geschichte der SS* (Gütersloh: Sigbert Mohn, 1967), 97.

40. OPG, 20.2.1934, Beschluss und Begrundung, BDC/USchla, Leffler.

41. Protokoll, Erklärung Leffler, 9.2.1934, BDC/OPG, Dietrich Klagges (b. 1.2.91). SDdRFSS to Schwarz, 19.7.1933, T-580/93/457.

42. BDC/SSO, Walter Böhlke (b. 13.12.06). Examples of problems: SSO, Behrends, RFSS to SDdRFSS, 10.1.1934, and RFSS to SS-OAb Nordwest, 13.1.1934; SSO, Heiner Kurzbeim (b. 31.1.10), promotion proposal dated 26.8.1933; and SSO, Wilhelm Wiebens (b. 17.3.06).

43. BDC/SSO, Friedrich Bauer (b. 18.1.03); and SSO, Heiner Kurzbeim (b. 31.1.10).

44. BDC/SSO, Leo Hausleiter (b. 9.1.89); SSO, Dr. Ernst Kaussmann (b. 11.9.05); SSO and RuSHA, Wilhelm Paul (b. 18.8.08); and SSO, Karl Spiewok (b. 13.12.92).

45. BDC/SSO, Dr. Wilhelm Patin (b. 25.6.79); and SSO, F. Walter Ilges (b. 31.5.70).

46. BDC/SSO, Herbert Mehlhorn (b. 24.3.03).

47. BDC/SSO and RuSHA, Dr. Georg Hagen (b. 16.3.89); SSO, Benedikt Karg (b. 22.6.01); SSO, August Meier (b. 8.10.00); SSO and RuSHA, Alfred Meissner (b. 7.2.96); SSO and RuSHA, Helmut Pommerening (b. 19.10.02); SSO, Kurt Walter (b. 14.7.01); and SSO, Dr. Richard Wendler (b. 22.1.98).

48. Aronson, *Heydrich*, 153; and BDC/SSO, Walter Potzelt (b. 16.7.03).

49. BDC/SSO Bruno Streckenbach (b.7.2.02), especially Beurteilung by Reichsstatthalter Hamburg, 27.4.1937.

50. Undated, tissue-paper copy from files of OAb Rhein, HStA Wiesbaden 483/625/70–80, verified by Lebensläufe of early members, and Werner Best (letter of 2.4.1977).

51. 1,III/4, re Kartei, 9.5.1934.

52. SDA, Abtl. V?, "Personal für Abteilung V," 17.10.1934, OA, 500/3/38/2.

53. Johannes R. von Bieberstein, "Aufklärung, Freimaurerei, Menschenrechte und Judenemanzipation in der Sicht des Nationalsozialismus." *Jahrbuch des Institut für Deutschen Geschichte* 7(1978): 339–354; BDC/SSO, Erich Ehlers (b. 24.2.12), Lebenslauf; Schwartz-Bostunitsch BDC/SSO (b. 1.12.83); and Jochem von Lang, ed., *Eichmann Interrogated* (New York: Random House, 1984), 22.

54. "Bericht SS Scharf. Kaulard über den Besuch der SS Schule in Berlin," 15.2.1935, LHA Koblenz, 662.6/45/10; and Hauptsturmführer Julius Blaichinger, 1934 *Dienstaltersliste der SS (DAL)*; no records at the BDC.

55. 1 an alle SD-Oberabschnitte re Anweisungen für Berichterstattung, n.d., HStA Wiesbaden 483/625/42–59.

56. BDC/SSO, August Meier (b. 8.10.00); and SSO, Adolf Blunck (b.19.8.09).

57. Günter Peis, *Man Who Started the War* (London: Odhams, 1960), 32–36.

58. Ibid., 35–36.

59. Ibid., 37–40; and BDC/SSO, Naujocks.

60. Chiffre-Nummern Liste in HStA Wiesbaden, 483/625/20–23, 68, 117–119; Klare and Leffler reports, BDC/USchla, Leffler; Klare affidavit, 11.8.1933; and Weichardt's statement, February 1932, attached to PD Wilhelmshaven to K.d.Marinestation Wilhelmshaven, 1.3.32, HA/71/1533.

61. T-175/200/2741059, -055; and BDC/SSO, Dr. Wilhelm Spengler (b. 19.3.07), Lebenslauf, 13.7.1936.

62. Aronson, *Heydrich*, 152.

63. Best, "Beantwortung des Fragebogens (Aronson)," B:1–3. Orb, *Nationalsozialismus*, 74–75; and Koehler, *Inside the Gestapo*, 31, 86.

64. BDC/SSO, Dr. Otto Rasch (b. 7.12.91).

65. BDC/SSO, and PK, Wilhelm Albrecht (b.8.9.98); and Orb, *Nationalsozialismus*, 65 for SD traditions. Group West's records survive at HStA Wiesbaden: Aufteilung der Chiffre-Nummern, circa 1934, 483/625/21–23, on the Saar.

66. BDC/SSO and RuSHA, Franz Glende (b.27.2.06); and SSO and RuSHA, Wilhelm Pallas (b.1.3.97).

67. Deckadressen für ausgehende Post, n.d., HStA Wiesbaden, 483/625/117. On SS-Gruppe, T-175/200/2741059, -055. "Liste der NF. im Bezirk des SS-Oberabschnitte West," n.d., 483/625/81–82; and Mitarbeiter list, n.d., 90–91.

68. Liste der NF. im Bezirk des SS-OAb West, 483/625/81–82; and BDC/SSO, Julius Bechthold (b.14.3.98), Lebenslauf.

69. Mitarbeiter, n.d. (late 1933 or early 1934), 483/625/90–91.

70. SD-Vertrauensleute im Unterbezirk I/2, n.d. (late 1933 or early 1934), 483/625/83–84.

71. SS Übersichtskarte, Stand von 1.6.34, T-175/200/2741048; and *Nationalsozialistische Jahrbuch* (Munich, 1934), 161. George C. Browder, "Sipo und SD, 1931–1940" Ph.D. diss., University of Wisconsin, Madison, 1968, 278, 283–286.

72. Nachrichtenreferent der SS-Gruppe West beim HPFiW, 5.5.1933 to Dr. Simon (SD Group West), StA Darmstadt G-12B/15/11; and Best, "Beantwortung des Fragebogens," B:2–3.

73. BDC/SSO and RuSHA, Alexander Maitre (b. 11.5.99), Lebenslauf, 26.6.1938.

74. Werner Best, "Beantwortung des Fragen im (Aronson) Schreiben vom 3.12.1964." Unpublished materials, 2.

75. StMdI, der PPK Bayerns, re "die Zusammenarbeit der staatl. Polizeibehörden mit dem SD," 7.12.1934, T-580/93/457.

76. Hoeppner testimony, *Trial of the Major War Criminals before the International Military Tribunal (IMT)*, 20: 190–191; and Ohlendorf testimony, *IMT* 4: 352–353.

77. Himmler speech to Reichswehr officers, January 1937, 1992(a)-PS, *IMT* 29: 223–224.

78. Johannes Tuchel and Reinhold Schattenfroh, *Zentrale des Terrors. Prinz-Albrecht-Strasse 8: Hauptquartier der Gestapo* (Berlin: Siedler, 1987); and Reinhold Rürup, ed., *Topography of Terror* (Berlin: Verlag Wilhelm Arenhövel, 1989).

79. Undated "Registraturverzeichnis;" and Best letter of 2.4.77.

80. RFSS, CdSHA, CdAbtl.I, re "Namhaftmachung von Verwaltungsbeamten," 5.12.1934, HStA Wiesbaden, 483/714.

81. Registraturverzeichnis. "Kartei," n.d.; and "Vorläufige Richtlinie für die Einrichtung einer Verbändekartei," n.d.(1934), HStA Wiesbaden, 483/625/94–98, 115–116.

82. SS Ab.I, re "Stimmungsbericht," 16.11.1932, and one such report to Herrn Richard Hildebrandt (LAb.I), HA/28A/1774; and RFSS, CdSHA, Lagebericht Nr. 123, May/June 1934, T-175/408/2932449–520.

83. The Anweisungen für Berichterstattung (attachments for Abteilungen III and IV only) devoted 4.5 pages to Katholizismus and less than 1 each to Protestantismus, Sekten, Deutsche Glaubensbewegung, and Gottlosenbewegung, 2.5 to right opposition, 2 to Marxismus, and 1.5 to Judentum. RFSS, CdSHA, Lagebericht Nr. 123, devoted 36 pages to katholische Bewegung, 7 to evangelische Bewegung, 9 to der Judenfrage, 8 to Lage und Tätigkeit des Marxismus, and 8 to Freimaurerei. Surviving reports of SD Abschnitte Erfurt and Weimar are devoted entirely to monitoring Catholic priests and organizations; they begin with 1934, but become more frequent from 1936, OA 1241. In December 1934, the SD produced a 41 page study on "Die staatsfeindliche Tätigkeit des politischen Katholizismus," OA 500/1/194. BDC/SSO Karl Hönscheidt (b. 26.2.03), Beförderungsvorschlag, 28.2.1936.

84. Registraturverzeichnis, HStA Wiesbaden, 483/625/85.

85. Interrogation of Justus Beyer, 30.4.1947, 5, 8–9, OCCWC, NA/RG 238. Alan E. Steinweis, "Weimar Culture and the Rise of National Socialism: The *Kampfbund für deutsche Kultur*." *Central European History (CEH)* 24 (4): 402–423 (1991).

86. Beyer Interrogation, 6–7; BDC/SSO Beyer (b. 16.4.10); and Reinhard Höhn (b. 29.7.04).

87. Dienststellenbesetzung des SD-Oberabschnitts Rhein an 1.12.34, HStA Wiesbaden 483/11286; and 3rd U.S. Army Interrogation Report Nr. 20, 8, NA/RG 238.

88. Orb, *Nationalsozialismus*, 87–89; and PI 10125, betr.: den SD des RFSS, July 1933, BDC/SSO, Daluege.

89. NSDAP Reichsleitung, Reichsschatzmeister to Reichskassenverwal-

tung, 26.1.1934, T-580/93/457; and notations on SDdRFSS to Schwarz, 19.7.1933, T-580/93/457.

90. NSDAP, StVdF to Schwarz, 9.10.1934; and 1.12.1934, re Finanzierung des SS-SD, T-580/93/457.

91. NSDAP, StVdF to Schwarz, 9.10.1934; Reichsschatzmeister to RFSS, CdSD re Finanzierung-SS-SD, 26.10.1934; RFSSuCdSD to Reichsschatzmeister, 15.11.1934; and Reichsschatzmeister to RFSS, CdSHA, re Etat Sicherheitsamt, 28.11.1934, T-580/93/457.

92. Reichsschatzmeister to RFSS, CdSHA, and to Stabsleiter des StVdF, 28.11.1934, T-580/93/457.

93. NSDAP, StVdF to Reichsschatzmeister, 1.12.1934, T-580/93/457.

94. Schellenberg memorandum, 24.2.1939, T-175/239/2728160; and Pohl, WVHA, 10.1.1941, Sondermittel für den SD, T-175/59/2574394.

Chapter 6

1. RFSS, Personal-Referent, "Beförderungen von Angehörigen der Schutzstaffel mit des SS-Ausweisnummer . . . ," 10.4.1934, HStA Wiesbaden G-12 B, 4/2. On SS heterogeneity: Erminhild Neusüss-Hunkel, *Die SS* (Marburg: Norddeutsche, 1956); Heinz Höhne, *Der Orden unter dem Totenkopf: Die Geschichte der SS* (Gütersloh: Sigbert Mohn, 1967) Robert L. Koehl, *The Black Corps The Structure and Power Struggles of the Nazi SS;* (Madison: University of Wisconsin, 1983) Robert L. Koehl, "Was There an SS Officer Corps?" In *Proceedings of the Citadel Symposium on Hitler and the National Socialist Era, 24–25 April 1980,* edited by Michael B. Barrett (Charleston: The Citadel Development Foundation, 1982), 97–106; and Bernd Wegner, *The Waffen-SS, Organization, Ideology, and Function* (Oxford: Basil Blackwell, 1990) ix–x, 139–50.

2. George C. Browder, "The Numerical Strength of the Sicherheitsdienst des RFSS." *Historical Social Research* 28(October 1983): 30–41; chart and table 1, 31–33.

3. Based on sample described in Appendix C.

4. Browder, "Numerical Strength."

5. BDC/SSO, Erich Ehlers (b.24.2.12), Lebenslauf; and RFSS, CdSHA, Die Voraussetzungen der Aufnahme bzw. der Versetzung in den SD, 28.6.1934 (HStA Wiesbaden, 483/173).

6. CdSHA, "Vorläufige Geschäftsordnung," 1.9.1935, OA, 500/3/9/10; and RFSS, CdSHA, Stabskanzlei, "Befehl für den SD Nr. 76/36, "Nachrichtenerfassung," 15.12.1936, OA, 500/1/3/12–15.

7. 30001, re "Mitarbeiter zur kommissarischen Verwendung," 30.10.1933, HStA Wiesbaden 483/625/25.

8. RFSS, CdSHA, re "Die Voraussetzungen der Aufnahme bzw. der Versetzung in den (SDdRFSS)," 28.6.1934, HStA Wiesbaden 483/173.

9. Browder, "Numerical Strength," chart 2, 34.

10. On the war generation, Robert G.L. Waite, *Vanguard of Nazism: The Free Corps Movement in Postwar Germany, 1918–1923* (New York: W.W. Norton & Company, 1969); and Robert Wohl, *The Generation of 1914* (Cambridge: Harvard Univ. Press, 1979). On the younger generation, Peter Loewenberg, "The Psychological Origins of the Nazi Youth Cohort." *American Historical Review (AHR)* 76 (December 1971): 1,457–1,502; and Peter D. Stachura,

Nazi Youth in the Weimar Republic (Santa Barbara: CLIO, 1975). Michael L. Ladeen, "Fascism and the Generation Gap." *European Studies Review* 1(1971): 275–283; Paul Madden, "Generational Aspects of German National Socialism, 1919–33." *Social Science Quarterly,* 63(3): 443–461 (1982); and Michael H. Kater, "Generationskonflikt als Entwicklungsfaktor in der NS-Bewegung vor 1933." *Geschichte und Gesellschaft* 11 (1985): 217–243.

11. On the Party, Michael H. Kater, *The Nazi Party* (Cambridge: Harvard University, 1983), 141, and table 13, 261. On the SS, Gunnar C. Boehnert, "An Analysis of Age and Education of the SS Führerkorps, 1925–1939," *Historical Social Research (HSR),* 12 (October 1979): tables 1 and 2, 9; Herbert F. Ziegler, "The SS Führer Korps: An Analysis of its Socioeconomic and Demographic Structure, 1925–1938." (Ph.D. diss. Emory University, 1980); Herbert F. Ziegler *Nazi Germany's New Aristocracy: The SS Leadership, 1925–1939* (Princeton: Princeton University Press, 1989). Unfortunately, neither Boehnert's nor Ziegler's data on age are organized comparably to mine.

12. Ziegler, *New Aristocracy,* 59–79.

13. 1925 national data, *Statistisches Jahrbuch,* 1931, 11; and Kater, *Nazi Party,* table 9, 255.

14. On the problems of socioeconomic classification and the available data, see Appendix C.4. On social class in the Party, Kater, *Nazi Party,* 19–115, and figure 2, 264; Herbert D. Andrews, "The Social Composition of the NSDAP: Problems and Possible Solutions." *German Studies Review (GSR),* 9(2): 293–318 (1986); Paul Madden, "The Social Class Origins of Nazi Party Members as Determined by Occupations, 1919–1933." *Social Science Quarterly* 68(2): 263–280 (1987); or Detlaf Mühlberger, *Hitler's Followers: Studies in the Sociology of the Nazi Movement* (New York: Routledge, 1991). On the German nation in 1933, Kater, *Nazi Party,* 12, and table 1, 241.

15. Fritz K. Ringer, *Education and Society in Modern Europe* (Bloomington: Indiana University Press, 1979), table 1.1, 54.

16. Boehnert, "Analysis of Age and Education," 13–14.

17. Ziegler, "SS Führer Korps," 72–87; and *New Aristocracy,* 104–105, citing, Kater, *Nazi Party,* 152 and 241. Appendix C.5, items 11–13.

18. Appendix C.7, items 17–19.

19. Konrad H. Jarausch, *The Unfree Professions: German Lawyers, Teachers, and Engineers, 1900–1950* (New York: Oxford University Press, 1990), 86, 204–205, 250.

20. Appendix C.4, items 6–8.

21. Appendix C.6.

22. Appendix C.6; and Hartmut Kaelble, "Social Mobility in Germany, 1900–1960." *Journal of Modern History (JMH),* 50 (September 1978): 439–461; and *Social Mobility in the 19th and 20th Centuries: Europe and America in Comparative Perspectives* (New York: St. Martin's, 1986). Richard F. Hamilton, "Braunschweig 1932: Further Evidence on the Support for National Socialism." *Central European History (CEH),* 17(1): 31 (1984).

23. Appendix C.8, items 39–41, 44; and C.9, item 46.

24. Appendix C.8, item 38.

25. Peter H. Merkl, *Political Violence under the Swastika: 581 Early Nazis* (Princeton: Princeton University Press, 1975), 358–363.

26. Appendix C.9.

27. BDC/SSO and RuSHA, Rolf Mathes (b. 1.10.10).

28. BDC/SSO and RuSHA, Wilhelm Rämisch (b. 30.5.13), RuSHA Lebenslauf.

29. Lonnie L. Lorance, "General SS Membership in Main Sector Rhein, 1934–1936" (Seminar paper, University of Wisconsin, 1970), 8–16.

30. BDC/PK and RuSHA, Kuno Schröder (b. 29.10.14); and der Abtl.L. II/112, 26.3.1936 re "Zurückstellung des SS-Scharführer Schröder vom Arbeitsdienst bis 1.4.1937," BA/R-58/1156.

31. BDC/SSO, Erich Ehlers (b. 24.2.12).

32. BDC/SSO, PK and RuSHA, Alfred Naujocks (b.20.9.11); and Günter Peis, *Man Who Started the War* (London: Odhams, 1960), 28–35.

33. BDC/SSO, Alfred Riechers (b. 2.3.95): 20.8.1937 Bericht re Riechers; and RFSS,CdSHA, Strafverfügung to Riechers, 6.9.1937.

34. BDC/SSO and RuSHA, Herbert Voshagen (b. 11.8.00), Lebenslauf, 22.3.1938.

35. SSO, PK and RuSHA, Voshagen, PK report dated 12.4.1943; and SSO Straf-Sache.

36. E.g., BDC/SSO, Friedrich Zimmermann (b. 14.8.93); and Lebenslauf in Leon Poliakov and Josef Wulf, *Das Dritte Reich und seine Denker* (Berlin: Arani, 1959), 368.

37. BDC/SSO and RUSHA, Alfred Filbert (b. 8.9.05), RuSHA Fragebogen und Lebenslauf, 11.1.1937, and Personal-Bericht und Beurteilung, n.d.

38. BDC/SSO Franz Xaver Helldobler (b. 19.4.89).

39. BDC/SSO Ferdinand Gottersman (b. 25.8.05).

40. See Appendix C.8, items 26–37.

41. Appendix C.7, item 24; C.8, items 25, 50–52. Given the "impressionistic" quality and the smallness of most cells, tests for significance of these data are pretentious exercises; the data have no statistical weight.

42. For the disproportionately severe barriers to employment among the apprentice-trained and unskilled, especially in the 1900–1914 cohort, and some comparable records that indicate that SD members fared better than average, Detlav Peukert, "The Lost Generation: Youth-Unemployment at the End of the Weimar Republic." In *The German Unemployed,* edited by Richard J. Evans and Dick Geary (New York: St. Martin's, 1987), esp. 181–182. It is less clear how the lower white-collar-employee component of this SD group fared compared with peers outside the SD; Dieter Petzina, "The Extent and Cause of Unemployment in the Weimar Republic." In *Unemployment and the Great Depression in Weimar Germany,* edited by Peter D. Stachura (New York: St. Martin's, 1986), 38. On unemployment and NS appeal, Richard Evans, "Introduction," in *German Unemployed,* 16–17; Juergen F. Falter, "Unemployment and the Radicalization of the German Electorate," in Stachura, ed., *Unemployment,* 187–208; Jürgen Kocka, *Angestellte zwischen Faschismus und Demokratie. Zur politischen Sozialgeschichte der Angestellten: USA 1890–1940 im internationalen Vergleich* (Göttingen: Vandenhök & Ruprecht, 1977); and Hans Speier, *German White-Collar Workers and the Rise of Hitler* (New Haven: Yale University Press, 1986).

43. Arno J. Mayer, "The Lower Middle Class as Historical Problem." *JMH* 47(1975): 409–436.

44. BDC/SSO Hermann Müller (b. 30.5.91), especially Lebenslauf. Kater, "Professionalization and Socialization of Physicians in Wilhelmine and Weimar Germany." *Journal of Contemporary History (JCH)* 20(1985): 677–701 and

"Hitler's Early Doctors: Nazi Physicians in Predepression Germany." *JMH*, 59(1987): 25–52, for Müller's context.

45. Konrad H. Jarausch, "The Perils of Professionalism: Lawyers, Teachers, and Engineers in Nazi Germany." *GSR* 9(1): 107–137 (1986).

46. Kaelble, "Social Mobility," table 5, 449; or Michael S. Steinberg, *Sabers and Brown Shirts: The German Students' Path to National Socialism, 1918–1935* (Chicago: University of Chicago Press, 1977), table 2, 35; Gerhard Arminger, "Involvement of German Students in NS Organizations Based on the Archive of the Reichsstudentenwerk," *Historical Social Research (HSR)* (1984)80: 3–34; Jarausch and Arminger, "The German Teaching Profession and Nazi Party Membership: A Demographic Logit Model." *The Journal of Interdisciplinary History* 20(2): 197–225 (1989); Anselm Faust, *Der Nationalsozialistische Deutsche Studentenbund. Studenten und Nationalsozialismus in der Weimarer Republik*, 2 vols (Düsseldorf: Schwann, 1973); Alice Gallin, *Midwives to Nazism: University Professors in Weimar Germany, 1925–1933* (Macon, Ga., Mercer University Press, 1986); Geoffrey J. Giles, *Students and National Socialism in Germany* (Princeton: Princeton University Press, 1985); Jarausch, *Students, Society, and Politics in Imperial Germany: The Rise of Academic Illiberalism* (Princeton: Princeton University Press, 1982); Jarausch, *Deutsche Studenten, 1800–1970* (Frankfurt a.M.: Suhrkamp Verlag, 1984); Kater, *Studentenschaft und Rechtsradikalismus in Deutschland 1918–1933* (Hamburg: Hoffmann & Campe, 1975); Reese C. Kelly, "German Professorate and Nazism: A Failure of Totalitarian Aspirations." *Higher Education Quarterly* 25(3): 261–280 (1985); and Wolfgang Zorn, "Student Politics in the Weimar Republic." *JCH* 5(1): 128–143 (1970). William Janner, "National Socialism and Social Mobility." *Journal of Social History* 9(3): 339–366; 347–348, on the SS appeal.

47. Jarausch, *Unfree Professions;* Charles E. McClelland, *The German Experience of Professionalization: Modern Learned Professions and Their Organizations from the Early Nineteenth Century to the Hitler Era* (Cambridge: Cambridge University Press, 1991); and Geoffrey Cocks and Jarausch, eds., *German Professions, 1800–1950* (New York: Oxford University Press, 1990). On ego identity, Harvey Goldman, *Max Weber and Thomas Mann: Calling and the Shaping of the Self* (Berkeley: University of California Press, 1988).

48. William S. Allen, "Farewell to Class Analysis in the Rise of Nazism: Comment." *CEH* 17(1): 60–61 (1984); Richard F. Hamilton, "Reply to Commentators." *CEH* 17(1): 75, 85 (1984); and Hamilton, "Braunschweig, 1932," *CEH* 17(1): 20–24, 32–33 (1984).

Chapter 7

1. Herbert C. Kelman and V. Lee Hamilton, *Crimes of Obedience: Toward a Social Psychology of Authority and Responsibility* (New Haven: Yale University, 1989).

2. Ibid., 103–110.

3. Ibid., 118–119.

4. Ibid., 120, 269–276.

5. Ibid., 120–121, 268–276.

6. Ibid., 121–122, 268–276.

7. Ibid., 122.

8. Ibid., 262–263, 303, 316.

9. Ibid., 267, 305.

10. Ibid., 272–274, 322.

11. Ibid., 328.

12. Joseph W. Bendersky, "Psychohistory before Hitler: Early Military Analyses of German National Character." *Journal of the History of Behavioral Sciences* 24(2): 166–168, 176–178 (1988); Everett C. Hughes, "Good People and Dirty Work." *Social Problems* 10(1962): 5; Michael H. Kater, "Everyday Anti-Semitism in Prewar Nazi Germany: The Popular Basis." *Yad Vashem Studies* 16(1984): 129–159; and Donald M. McKale, "Traditional Antisemitism and the Holocaust: The Case of German Diplomat Curt Pruefer." *Simon Wiesenthal Center Annual* 5(1988): 61–76.

13. Erik Erikson, "Identity and the Life Cycle: Selected Papers." *Psychological Issues* 1 (1959), and " 'Identity Crisis' in Autobiographic Perspective." In *Life History and the Historical Moment* (New York: W. W. Norton & Company, Inc., 1975), 15–47; Peter Loewenberg, "Psychological Perspectives on Modern German History." *Journal of Modern History (JMH)*, 47(June 1975): 250–251; and Fred Weinstein and Gerald M. Platt, "The Coming Crisis in Psychohistory." *JMH* 47(June 1975): 207.

14. Kelman and Hamilton, *Crimes of Obedience*, 319–320.

15. Leo Alexander, "War Crimes and their Motivation." *Journal of Criminal Law and Criminology (JCL&C)* 39(September 1948): 300–301; and Richard Breitman, *The Architect of Genocide: Himmler and the Final Solution* (New York: Knopf, 1990), 39–44.

16. Henry V. Dicks, *Licensed Mass Murder: A Socio-Psychological Study of Some SS Killers* (New York: Basic Books, 1972) 255.

17. Terry G. Mensch, "Psychohistory of the Third Reich: A Library Pathfinder and Tropical [sic] Bibliography of English Language Publications." *The Journal of Psychohistory* 7(1979/80): 331–354; Louise E. Hoffman, "Psychoanalytic Interpretations of Adolf Hitler and Nazism, 1933–1945: A Prelude to Psychohistory." *Psychohistory Review* 11(1982): 68–87; William J. Gilmore, *Psychohistorical Inquiry: A Comprehensive Research Bibliography* (New York: Garland, 1984); George M. Kren, "Psychohistory, Psychobiography and the Holocaust." *Psychohistory Review* 13(1): 40–45 (1984); Bendersky, "Psychohistory before Hitler"; and William McK. Runyan, ed., *Psychology and Historical Interpretation* (New York: Oxford University Press, 1988) critique most of the relevant literature. Harvey Asher, "Non-Psychoanalytic Approaches to National Socialism." *Psychohistory Review* 7(3): 13–21 (1979).

18. Charles R. Bambach, "Fascism and Family Structure: A Critique of the Institut für Sozialforschung's *Studien über Autorität und Familie*." *Michigan Journal of Political Science* 2(2): 1–15 (1983); Theodore Adorno, et al., *The Authoritarian Personality* (New York: Harper, 1950); Dicks, *Licensed Mass Murder;* Peter Loewenberg, "The Psychological Origins of the Nazi Youth Cohort." *American Historical Review (AHR)* 76(December 1971): 1,457–1,502; Lawrence Walker, "The Nazi 'Youth Cohort': The Missing Variable." *The Psychohistory Review* 9 (Fall 1980): 71–73; and Michael Selzer, "Psychohistorical Approaches to the Study of Nazism." *Journal of Psychohistory* 4 (Fall 1976): 215–224, with comments by Martin Wangh, Helm Stierlin, and Peter Loewenberg, 225–230.

19. Florence R. Miale and Michael Selzer, *The Nuremberg Mind: The Psy-*

chology of the Nazi Leaders (New York: Quadrangle, 1976); Selzer, "Psychohistorical Approaches;" and cf. Gerald L. Borofsky and Dan J. Brand, "Personality Organization and Psychological Functioning of the Nuremberg War Criminals: The Rorschach Data." In *Survivors, Victims, and Perpetrators: Essays on the Nazi Holocaust,* edited by Joel E. Dimsdale (Washington: Hemisphere Publishing Corp., 1980), 359–403.

20. E.g., Frank Chalk and Kurt Jonassohn, *The History and Sociology of Genocide. Analyses and Case Studies* (New Haven: Yale University Press, 1990), 28.

21. Dicks, *Licensed Mass Murder;* Elie A. Cohen, *Human Behavior in the Concentration Camp* (New York: Grosset and Dunlap, 1953); George M. Kren and Leon Rappoport, "SS Atrocities: A Psychological Perspective." *History of Childhood Quarterly* 3 (1975): 130–137; George M. Kren, "Psychohistory and the Holocaust." *Journal of Psychohistory* 6 (1979): 409–417; and John M. Steiner, "The SS Yesterday and Today: A Sociopsychological View." In Dimsdale, ed., *Survivors,* 405–456.

22. Albert Breton and Ronald Weintrobe, "The Bureaucracy of Murder Revisited." *Journal of Political Economy,* 94(5): 905–26; David H. Ketterman, "Those Who Said "No!": Germans Who Refused to Execute Civilians during World War II." *German Studies Review (GSR)* 11(2): 241–254 (1988); and Bernd Wegner, *The Waffen-SS: Organization, Ideology, and Function* (Oxford: Basil Blackwell, 1990), ix–x.

23. Milton Rokeach, *The Nature of Human Values* (New York: Free Press, 1973); Herbert Kelman and J. Barclay, "The F Scale as a Measure of Breadth of Perspective." *Journal of Abnormal and Social Psychology* 67 (1963); David A. Fabianic, "Authoritarianism in Criminal Justice Literature." *Journal of Police Science and Administration (JPS&A)* 7 (1979): 55–59; and Nevitt Sanford and Craig Comstock, *Sanctions for Evil* (San Francisco: Jossey-Bass, Inc., 1971), 141.

24. Don Stewart and Thomas Hoult, "A Social-Psychological Theory of the Authoritarian Personality." *American Journal of Sociology* 65 (November 1959): 274–279; and Susan Benack, "The Development of Relativistic Epistemological Thought and the Growth of Empathy in Late Adolescence and Early Adulthood" (Ph.D. diss., Harvard University, 1981).

25. E.g., Fabianic, "Authoritarianism in Criminal Justice Literature," 59–60.

26. Nn. 29–31 and 33–35.

27. German educational institutions propagating völkisch prejudices and chauvinism: George L. Mosse, *The Crisis of German Ideology* (New York: Grosset & Dunlop, 1964), 150, 152–169, and 190–203; Peter H. Merkl, *Political Violence under the Swastika: 581 Early Nazis* (Princeton University Press, 1975), 306–309; Konrad H. Jarausch, "Liberal Education as Illiberal Socialization: The Case of Students in Imperial Germany." *JMH* 50 (December 1978):609–630 and *Students, Society, and Politics in Imperial Germany: The Rise of Academic Illiberalism* (Princeton: Princeton University Press, 1982); and Frederic Lilge, *The Abuse of Learning: The Failure of the German University* (New York: The Macmillan Company, 1948). Comparative studies: James C. Albisetti, *Secondary School Reform in Imperial Germany* (Princeton: Princeton University Press, 1983), esp. 304–313; Fritz K. Ringer, *Education and Society in Modern Europe* (Bloomington: Indiana University Press, 1979); Lilge, *The*

Abuse of Learning, v–vi; and Thomas Alexander and Beryl Parker, *The New Education in the German Republic* (New York: The John Day Company, 1929); revealing the problems of evaluating curricula and professed institutional philosophies versus actual environments.

28. Merkl, *Political Violence*, 300–306, 308.

29. Herbert H. Hyman and Paul B. Sheatsley, " 'The Authoritarian Personality'—A Methodological Critique." In *Studies in the Scope and Method of "The Authoritarian Personality*," edited by Richard Christie and Marie Jahoda (Glencoe, Ill.: The Free Press, 1954), 93–96; Nevitt Sanford, "Authoritarianism and Social Destructiveness," in Sanford and Comstock, eds., *Sanctions*, 147; and Fred Weinstein and Gerald M. Platt, *Psychoanalytic Sociology* (Baltimore: Johns Hopkins University Press, 1973), 69–73. William Runyan, "Reconceptualizing the Relationship between History and Psychology." In Runyan, ed., *Psychology and Historical Interpretation*, 247–295, for a summary of applications of cognitive theory. Barbel Inhelder and Jean Piaget, *The Growth of Logical Thinking from Childhood to Adolescence* (New York: Basic Books, 1958); Piaget, *The Moral Judgment of the Child* (New York: Free Press, 1965); Lawrence Kohlberg and R. Kramer, "Continuities and Discontinuities in Childhood and Adult Development." *Human Development* 12(1969): 93–120; and for an evaluation of related research and its relevance to the Nazi experience, Carol Gilligan, "Moral Development." In *The Modern American College*, edited by Arthur W. Chickering (San Francisco: Jossey-Bass Publishers, 1981), 139–157; and see also nn. 33–35.

30. William G. Perry, *Forms of Intellectual and Ethical Development in the College Years: A Scheme* (New York: Holt, Rinehart and Winston, Inc., 1968); and "Cognitive and Ethical Growth: The Making of Meaning." In Chickering, ed., *The Modern American College*, 76–116.

31. Michael L. Commons, Francis A. Richards, and Cheryl Armon, eds., *Beyond Formal Operations: Late Adolescent and Adult Cognitive Development* (New York: Praeger, 1984), especially John M. Broughton, "Not Beyond Formal Operations but Beyond Piaget," 395–411; Michael Basseches, *Dialectical Thinking and Adult Development* (Norwood, N.J.: Ablex, 1984); and James T. Tedeschi and Svenn Lindshold, *Social Psychology* (New York: John Wiley & Sons, 1976).

32. Runyan, "Reconceptualizing," 275–280.

33. See n. 29, especially Gilligan; and Benack, "Development."

34. Lawrence Kohlberg, "Stage and Sequence: The Cognitive-developmental Approach to Socialization." In *Handbook of Socialization Theory and Research*, edited by David Goslin (Chicago: Rand McNally, 1969), 347–480; "Continuities in Childhood and Adult Moral Development Revisited." In *Life-Span Developmental Psychology: Personality and Socialization*, edited by Paul B. Bates and K. Warner Schaie (New York: Academic Press, 1973); "Moral Stages and Moralization: The Cognitive-developmental Approach." In *Moral Development and Behavior*, edited by Thomas Lickona (New York: Holt, Reinhart and Winston, 1976); and Kohlberg and D. Candee, "The Relation of Moral Judgment to Moral Action." In *Morality, Moral Behavior and Moral Development*, edited by William Kurtines and Jacob Gewirtz (New York: Wiley, 1984). Also James R. Rest, *Development in Judging Moral Issues* (Minneapolis: University of Minnesota Press, 1979).

35. Ann B. Salyard, "The Educated American: A Study of Intellectual De-

velopment in Adulthood" (Ph.D. diss., University of California, Los Angeles, 1981); Tedeschi and Lindshold, *Social Psychology*, 128, citing Streufert and Fromkin, 1972, on cognitive complexity.

36. Kelman and Hamilton, *Crimes of Obedience*, 263, 267, 269, 273.

37. RSHA, betr.: . . . Strauch (n.d., post August 1943), NO-2966, M-895/9/0739–41.

38. BDC/SSO and RuSHA, Friedrich Polte (b. 20.1.11), Lebensläufe, 24 May 1934 and 15 December 1939.

39. Ibid., Lebenslauf, 24.5.34.

40. Perry, *Intellectual and Ethical Development*, 75, 182–185.

41. Merkl, *Political Violence*, 303–304.

42. On intellectuals attracted to Nazism and its appeals: Mosse and Steven Lampert, "Weimar Intellectuals and the Rise of National Socialism." In Dimsdale, ed., *Survivors*, 79–105; Weinstein, *Dynamics*, 1–32; and Jarausch and Gerhard Arminger, "The German Teaching Profession and Nazi Party Membership: A Demographic Logit Model." *The Journal of Interdisciplinary History* 20(2): 225 (1989).

43. Merkl's evidence (*Political Violence*, 72–75) seems to support this theory for the early 20th-century German experience.

44. Valdis O. Lumans, *Himmler's Auxiliaries: The Volksdeutsche Mittelstelle and the German National Minorities in Europe, 1933–1945* (Chapel Hill: University of North Carolina Press, 1993), chapters 5 and 6.

45. Stewart and Hoult, "Social-Psychological Theory," 276; Arthur Niederhofer, *Behind the Shield* (Garden City, NY: Anchor Books, 1967), 142; and Daniel J. Levinson and Phyllis E. Huffman, "Traditional Family Ideology and Its Relation to Personality." *Journal of Personality* 23 (1955):251–273.

46. Appendix C.4, items 4–5.

47. On SS religious policy and pressures on members, Herbert F. Ziegler, *Nazi Germany's New Aristocracy: The SS Leadership, 1925–1939* (Princeton: Princeton University Press, 1989), 83–88.

48. David Blackbourn, "The *Mittelstand* in German Society and Politics 1871–1914." *Social History* 2 (1977): 409–433; Jane Caplan, *Government without Administration: State and Civil Service in Nazi Germany* (Oxford: Oxford University Press, 1988); Geoff Eley, *From Unification to Nazism: Reinterpreting the German Past* (Boston: G. Allen & Unwin, 1985); Richard Evans, *Rethinking German History: Nineteenth-Century Germany and the Origins of the Third Reich* (London: Allen & Unwin, 1987); Robert G. Moeller, *German Peasants and Conservative Agrarian Politics, 1914–1924* (Chapel Hill: University of North Carolina Press, 1986); Thomas Childers, "The Social Language of Politics in Germany: The Sociology of Political Discourse in the Weimar Republic." *AHR* 95(2): 331–358 (1990).

49. E.g., John L. Genz and David Lester, "Military Service, Education and Authoritarian Attitudes of Municipal Police Officers." *Psychological Reports* 40(April 1977): 402.

50. Peter Merkl, *The Making of a Stormtrooper* (Princeton: Princeton University Press, 1980), 110.

51. "Secret" inserts, *Statistisches Jahrbuch der SS*, 1937, T-175/205/4042236. James J. Weingartner, "Law and Justice in the Nazi SS." *CEH* 16 (September 1983): 281–282.

52. 16 percent of the relatively small sample of 84 for whom the author feels confident of having sufficiently complete records.

53. BDC/SSO, Otto Kipka (b. 14.12.10), statement of August 15, (Ernting) 1935; and statement of Erich Hinkel, August 13, 1935.

54. BDC/SSO Oskar Glauning (b. 7.3.06).

55. Von Eberstein testimony, *Trial of the Major War Criminals before the International Military Tribunal (IMT)*, 20: 290; and BDC/SSO, Lothar Beutel (b. 6.5.02).

56. BDC/SSO, Mathias Graf (b. 8.5.03); *TWC* 4:15, 584–87; and NO 4855, M895/9/1,205–6.

57. William Kornhauser, *The Politics of Mass Society* (Glencoe, Ill.: Free Press, 1959); Seymore M. Lipset and Earl Raab, *The Politics of Unreason* (Chicago: University of Chicago Press, 1978); Anthony Oberschall, *Social Conflict and Social Movements* (Englewood, NJ: Prentice-Hall, 1973); and Charles Tilly, *From Mobilization to Revolution* (Reading, Mass.: Addison-Wesley, 1978).

58. Steiner, "The SS Yesterday and Today," 407–408, 416.

59. Ibid., 416; Roger Brown, *Social Psychology: The Second Edition* (New York: Free Press, 1986), 551–571, summarizes the research.

60. Steiner, "The SS Yesterday and Today," 408.

61. Ibid., 416–417.

62. Ibid., 432, 434.

63. Steiner, *Power Politics and Social Change in National Socialist Germany: A Process of Escalation into Mass Destruction* (Atlantic Highlands, NJ: Humanities Press, 1976), 120.

64. Steiner, "SS Yesterday and Today," 414–415.

65. Ibid., 435. On autonomy and competition within the SS: Fred E. Katz, "Implementation of the Holocaust: The Behavior of Nazi Officials." *Comparative Studies in Society and History* 24(July 1982): 510–529; and Breton and Weintrobe, "Bureaucracy of Murder."

66. Wegner, *Waffen-SS*, x.

67. Weingartner, "Law and Justice," 280–281.

68. Best affidavit, JOST 10, M-895/23/42–45.

69. Lawrence D. Stokes, "Otto Ohlendorf, the Sicherheitsdienst and Public Opinion in Nazi Germany." In *Police Forces in History*, edited by George L. Mosse (London: SAGE, 1975) 234–235; and see also Shlomo Aronson, *Reinhard Heydrich und die Frühgeschichte von Gestapo und SD*, (Stuttgart: Deutsche Verlags-Anstalt, 1971) pp. 210–216; and Hanno Sowade, "Otto Ohlendorf—Nonkonformist, SS-Führer und Wirtschaftsfunktionär." In *Die Braune Elite: 22 biographische Skizzen*, edited by Ronald Smelser and Rainer Zittelman (Darmstadt: Wissenschaftliche Buchgesellschaft, 1989), 188–200.

70. BDC/SSO, Ludwig Pfester (b. 10.5.11), Lebenslauf, 13.9.1938.

71. On Ohlendorf's self-image and "autonomy" in "bureaucratic" roles, Katz, "Implementing the Holocaust," 522–527.

Chapter 8

1. SS-Befehl, Nr. 2, 25.1.1935, SS-Befehls-Blatt, 1, T-611/4/ 430.

2. "Vorläufige Geschäftsordnung," 1.9.1935 (OA 500/3/9/1–21); "Aufbau der SS Verwaltung," 27.9.1935 (HStA Wiesbaden, 483/173); Befehl d. CdSHA,

re organization of SHA, n.d. (effective 15.1.1936), OA 500/3/5/1–18; and RFSS, CdSHA, Stabsführer I 112, Stabsbefehl für SD-Hauptamt Nr. 3/37, re Signenzeichnung, 15.1.1937 (hereafter SD-HA Stabsbefehl 3/37).

3. Ibid.; and BDC/SSO Albert. RFSS, CdSHA, Bericht über den Schulungs-kursus des Amtes Presse und Schrifttum . . . 22.–29.9. 1935, n.d., T-175/411/2934847; and Best Beantwortung 3.12.1964, unpublished materials.

4. Stabsbefehl 3/37; Shlomo Aronson, *Reinhard Heydrich und die Frühg-eschichte von Gestapo und SD* (Stuttgart: Deutsche Verlags-Anstalt, 1971) 212–213; and Ohlendorf testimony (29. 0.1945), 2, NA, RG-238.

5. Stabsbefehl 3/37, 11–12; relevant personnel files, BDC; and Aronson, *Heydrich,* 203.

6. Stabsbefehl 3/37, 8–12.

7. Ibid., and Ohlendorf testimony (29.10.1945), 1–2, NA, RG-238.

8. RFSS, Verwaltungchef d.SS, "Aufbau der SS Verwaltung," 27.9.1935, HStA Wiesbaden, 483/173. See also, Ohlendorf interrogation, 9.11.1945, 1445–1705 pm, 15–19.

9. Aktennotiz (NSDAP, RL, Stabsleiter), "Akt SS-Sicherheitsdienst," Munich, 31.3.1936, BA, NS-1/296; and Haushaltsplannung der SS d NSDAP für Rechnungsjahr, 1937, T-175/205/4042303.

10. Vernehmung Schellenberg, 26.3.1947, 1100–1115, 2; and SDdRFSS, SD-OAb Rhein, UAb Hessen, "Etatgestaltung," 25.11.1936, StA Darmstadt, G-12B/4/2. For SS salaries, "Haushaltsplannung 1935 für die Allgemeine SS, Besoldungs-Ordnung der SS der NSDAP," T-611/47.

11. VA SS, SD, "Sondermittel für der SD," 10.1.1941, T-175/59/2574394.

12. Stabsbefehl 3/37; George C. Browder, "The Numerical Strength of the Sicherheitsdienst des RFSS." *Historical Social Research* 28(October 1983): 32; and *Statistisches Jahrbuch der Schutzstaffel der NSDAP,* 1937, T-175/205/4042259.

13. Übersicht über die SD-OAb und die SD-Ab, n.d., forwarded to Gestapo offices, 5.12.1935, T-175/250/2742482-86; and Dienststellen-Verzeichnis, forwarded 14.12.1936, T-175/423/2951553-59. SDdRFSS/UAb Württ.-Hohenz., re Neugliederung des SD-RFSS, 13.6.1936, StA Ludwigsburg, K110/Bü 34.

14. Dienststellen-Verzeichnis, 14.12.1936, T-175/423/2951554; and BDC/SSO, Jakob Sporrenberg (b. 16.9.02), Lebenslauf.

15. HStA Darmstadt, G-12B, 4/2: SS personnel directives, 1934–1936.

16. Abrechnungsbuch of SD-OAb Süd-West, Dec. 1934–Oct. 1935, T-175/507/9372682–705.

17. Ibid.

18. UAb Hessen to OAb Rhein, re Etatsgestaltung, 25.11.1936, StA Darmstadt, G-12B/4/2.

19. BA/NS-1/2427, 2428, 2429, Reichsschatzmeister records of purchases, remodeling and rental for SD use.

20. Rosters, Hauptamtliche Mitarbeiter, SD-Männer, etc., SD-OAb Rhein, HStA Wiesbaden, 483/173.

21. SD-OAb Rhein, Stärkemeldung für Monat Januar 1937, HStA Wiesbaden, 483/176; and SDdRFSS, OAb Rhein, "Sollstärke des SD am 1.1.1937," 25.9.1935, ibid., 11286.

22. "Richtlinien für die Bearbeitung der Auslandspresse bzgl. der Gegnerformen," n.d., OA 500/4/45/50-55.

23. BDC/SSO and RuSHA, Six (b. 12.8.09); M-895/10/NO 4768; and cf. Julius Mader, "Eichmanns Chef ist Bonner 'Gesandter z. WV,' " *Deutsche Aussenpolitik,* 8(5): 405–409 (1963). RFSS, CdSHA, draft of Six's "Bericht über den Schulungskursus des Amtes Presse und Schrifttum in der SD-Schule Berlin in der Zeit vom 22.–29. September 1935," n.d., 1, T-175/411/2934847.

24. Six, "Bericht," 1–4.

25. Ibid., 2–7.

26. Ibid., 4–5; "Dienstanweisung für die Pressereferenten der Abschnitte," attached to 101 (SD-OAb Süd), "Durchführung der Dienstanweisung für P.," 5.7.1935, and later revision, T-175/271/2768126-37, -101-5; and Six's "Die Entwicklung des Amtes II (1935–1939)," cover letter dated 17.7.1939, USHRIA RG-15.007M 23/295/1–9.

27. 101, "Durchführung der Dienstanweisung P.," 5.7.1935, T-175/271/2768126; and Six's Bericht, 1.

28. 4001 to 101, "Durchführung der Dienstanweisung für P.," 10.7.1935, T-175/271/2768116–17.

29. OAb Süd to CdSHA, "Pressereferenten—Schulungslehrgang," 30. 7.1935, T-175/271/2768106.

30. HStA Düssledorf, RW33/10.

31. 17708, "Arbeitsdienst," 20.3.1936; 17708 to 57242, 7.4.1936; 57241 to 17707, 18.4.1936; Rodenbusch to Blobel, 27.5.1936; and 17708, "Nachrichtenmittel für September," 9.9.1936, HStA Düsseldorf, RW33/10/95, 106–108, 160.

32. Reports from 17708, 27.6.1935; 9. and 14.4.1936; 9. and 15.12. 1936, HStA Düsseldorf, RW 33/10/2–3, 62, 79, 81–86, 206, 211–212.

33. 56001, "Organisation (Bearbeitung der Leumundzeugnisse)," 17. 6.1936; and the same, n.d., HStA Düsseldorf, RW33/1/138–39, 158.

34. 105 451, "Beurteilung von führenden Männern und Beamten," 31. 12.1937, T-175/276/5486068, -74; and UAb Mainfranken, "Nachrichtenerfassung," 12.12.1938, StA Wurzburg, Rep. III.8.0.1/919.

35. "Nachrichtenerfassung."

36. SD-Dienststells Stapo Darmstadt to SD-OAb Rhein, re Aussenstelle des SD in Darmstadt—Wahrung der Dienstgeheimnisse, 19.2.1936, HStA Wiesbaden, 483/678.

37. BDC/PK, Emil Danzeisen (b.6.10.97); and records of the investigations, T-175/R257/173-b-10-14/23 and 467/173-b-2-05/06.

38. StA Würzburg, III.8.0.1/901 from UAb Mainfranken: Br.B: 2134/36, "Organisation," 17.4.1936; response of 3502, "Beurteilung der V-Männer," 11 April; SD-UAb IX, "V-Männer," 22 June; SD Befehl Nr. 76/36, "Nachrichtenerfassung," 15.12.1936, OA 500/1/3/12–15; and SDdRFSS, OAb Süd, UAb Mainfranken, "Nachrichtenerfassung," 12.12.1938, StA Würzburg, NSDAP Gau Mainfranken/919/1–6.

39. E.g., Georg Sensenbrenner, "Bericht über Einsetzung und Gewinnung von VM für das Referat II 121," 5.8.1937, USHRIA RG-15.007M, 1/38a/223–27; cf. Leiter II, "Unterscheidung zwischen Zubringern, Agenten, Vertrauenspersonen und Beobachtern," 16.9.1938, 4/26/2–3.

40. E.g., 105451, "Beurteilung von führenden Männer und Beamten,"

31.12.1937; "Lageberichterstattung," 17.1.1938; and "Nachrichtenerfassung," 3.2.1938, T-175/276/5486068, -70, -74.

41. Br.B.:2134/36, "Organisation," 17.4.1936, StA Würzburg seems to be initiating such a file.

42. "Nachrichtenerfassung," 15.12.1936, OA 500/1/3/6–8.

43. Br.B.:2134/36 "Organisation," 17.4.1936; and Leiter II, "Unterscheidung . . . ," 16.9.1938, USHRIA RG-15.007M, 4/26/2b.

44. "Listen von V-Männern, 1936," HStA Wiesbaden, 483/11299; and UAb Mainfranken, "Nachrichtenerfassung," 12.12.1938, 5.

45. UAb Mainfranken, "Nachrichtenerfassung," 12.12.1938, 3.

46. Best Beantwortung 3.12.1964, unpublished materials; and Robert Gellately, *The Gestapo in German Society: Enforcing Racial Policy, 1933–1945* (Oxford: Oxford University Press, 1990), especially chapter 5.

47. E.g., GeStapa, "Erfassung unzuverlässiger Vertrauenspersonen," 26.10.1935, HStA Wiesbaden, 483/171; and Erl.d.PPK vom 14.2.1935, T-175/422/2950632.

48. UAb Mainfranken, "Nachrichtenerfassung," 12.12.1938, 4–5.

49. StA Würzburg, III.8.0.1/920; and T-175/276/5486095–97, questionnaires to determine V-man reliability, beginning 1938.

50. E.g., BDC/SSO Hans-Georg Kaulard (b. 23.5.10), UAb Koblenz, to Kaulard, 6.5.1937; and SDdRFSS, OAb Süd-West, correspondence re Dr. Schinnerer, StA Ludwigsburg, K110/19a.

51. 1937 reports on candidate V-men in T-175/501/9364869–5028.

52. File card, headed Rassenpolitisches Amt, n.d., GStAnWlt.b.d. KG, Berlin, material from Moscow, 14) 144.

53. Copy of CdSHA, "Befehl! über Behandlung von Parteiangelegenheiten," 8.12.1935; and NSDAP, Stellv.d.F., to all RL and GL, 14.2.1936, T-580/93/457.

54. CdSHA, Befehl, 8.12.1935, T-580/93/457; and RFSSuCdSHA, Stabsführer I/1112, Befehl für den SD Nr. 25/26, re Namensnennung von SD-Angehörigen, 22.6.1936, T-175/240/2730223–24.

55. BDC/SSO and RuSHA, Göttsch; and SSO Horst Böhme (b. 24.8.09), Personal-Bericht, 15.7.36.

56. BDC/SSO and RuSHA, Wolf (b. 25.5.08).

57. BDC/SSO and RuSHA, Böhme.

58. RFSS, CdSHA, No. 123, Lagebericht, Mai/Juni 1934, T-175/408/2932449–520.

59. Heinz Boberach, ed., *Berichte des SD und der Gestapo über Kirchen und Kirchenvolk in Deutschland, 1934–1944* (Mainz: Mathais Grünewald-Verlag, 1971), xxix–xxx.

60. BDC/SSO, Ilges, CdSHA to Personalkanzlei, 24.9.1936; and SSO, S-B, CdSHA to CdPersonalamt, 21.1.1937.

61. BDC/SSO and RuSHA Hartmann (b. 7.6.06); GStA, 90/951/193–202; and Geschäftsverteilungsplan GeStapa, October 1934.

62. BDC, E185/SS-5883; and G II 112, "Bericht über den Umbau der Abteilungen bei II 1," 7.12.1937, T-175/410/2934989.

63. Six, "Die Entwicklung des Amtes II," USHRIA RG-15.007M, 23/295/5.

64. See n. 79. On evolution of Nazi and SS policy on Zionism to 1937,

Francis R. Nicosia, *The Third Reich and the Palestine Question* (Austin: University of Texas Press, 1985), 18–64.

65. BDC/SSO, PK, v. Mildenstein (b.30.11.02); Aronson, *Heydrich,* 203; and Jacob Boas, "A Nazi Travels to Palestine." *History Today* 30(January 1980): 33–38.

66. Leon Poliakov and Josef Wulf, *Das Dritte Reich und die Juden* (Berlin: Arani, 1955), 87–88; and G II 112, "Bericht . . . ," 7.12.1937, 2934988. II 112, "Zurückstellung des SS-Scharf. Schroeder . . . ," 26.3.1936, BA, R-58/1156.

67. Aronson, *Heydrich,* 203; II 112, "Bericht . . . ," 7.12.1937; and II 112, "Bericht über den Stand der Arbeiten der Abtlg. II 112 in der Bekämpfung des Judentums," 28.8.1936, T-175/410/2934988–89, -947. Lagebericht der Abtl. II 112, April–May 1936, 25.6.1936, OA 500/4/48.

68. II 112, "Bericht. . . ," 28.8.1936; and "Ausbau der Arbeit der Abteilung II 112 im Jahr 1937," 18.12.1937, T-175/410/2934947–55.

69. II 112, "Tätigkeitsbericht: 1.10.1936–15.2.1937," 17.2.1937, T-175/410/2934963–66.

70. See II 112, Pressebericht Nr. 18, 21.8.1936; and Presse-Übersicht Nrs. 6 and 7, 30.9. and 15.10.1936, OA 500/4/48.

71. II 112, "Tätigkeitsbericht: 16.2.1937–5.7.1937," 5.7.1937; "Tätigkeitsbericht 6.7.1937–5.10.1937," 5.10.1937; and "Bericht. . . ," 7.12.1937, T-175/410/2934977–89.

72. E.g., StA Ludwigsburg, K110/Bü.19b, for OAb Süd-West; and Bü.34, for Subregion Württemberg. SDHA II 112, "Erfahrungsbericht über Lageberichterstattung," 9.6.1937, BA R58/990/17–18.

73. Aronson, *Heydrich,* developed this theory as a main theses.

74. RFSS, CdSHA, CdSipo, "Gemeinsame Anordnung für den (SDdRFSS) und die (GeStapo), betr. Zusammenarbeit (SDdRFSS u. GeStapo)," 1. 7.1937; Heydrich alluded to territoriality between Gestapo and SD, T-175/504/9369224–34.

75. II 112, "Tätigkeitsbericht: 6.7.1937–5.10.1937," 5.10.1937; "Bericht . . . ," 7.12.1937; and "Tätigkeitsbericht v. 1.7.–31.12.1937," 15.1.1938, T-175/410/2934986, -89–90, -94, -99 -5004; BDC/RuSHA, Flesch (b. 1.8.94).

76. II 112, Tätigkeitsberichte, 5.10.1937; and 15.1.1938, T-175/410/2934984, -95–99. Nicosia, *Palestine Question,* 60–64.

77. Raul Hilberg, *The Destruction of the European Jews,* 2nd. ed. (New York: Holmes & Meier, 1985), 2:396–397.

78. Heinz Höhne, *Der Orden unter dem Totenkopf: Die Geschichte der SS* (Gütersloh: Sigbert Mohn, 1967), 301–303; SD reports, e.g., OAb Süd-West report of 27.5.1936, and UAb Württ.-Hohz., to alle ASt, re "Überwachung von Juden und Freimaurern," 4.12.1936, StA Ludwigsburg, K 110/Bü 34; Karl A. Schleunes, *The Twisted Road to Auschwitz* (Urbana: University of Illinois, 1970).

79. II 112, "Ausbau der Arbeit . . . 1937," 18.12.1936, T-175/410/2934950; Schleunes, *Twisted Road,* 178–203; and Nicosia, *Palestine Question,* 63–66, chapters 8–10. For reference to the endgultige Lösung, Schellenberg personnel proposals, 24.2.1939, T-175/239/2728411.

80. StMdI, PPK By, "Die Zusammenarbeit der stl. Polizeibehörden mit dem SD . . . ," 7.12.1934, T-580/93/457; CdSSHA, "Polizeiliche Massnahmen

durch die SS," 18.9.1936, T-175/219/2757464; Pr.GeStapo, stellv.C, PPKdL, "Regelung der Bezahlung des Lohnausfalles bei der Durchführung stapol. Fahndungsaktionen mit Hilfe von SA- und SS-Männern," 20.3.1936, StA Aurich, Rep.21a/10009; GeStapa, "Erfassung des beschlagnahmten und unerwünchten Schrifttums in einer wissenschaftlichen Zentralbibliothek des SD," 22.1.1936, HStA Düsseldorf, RW36/30/17; (SHA) II 1, "Zusammenarbeit mit den entsprechenden Referenten des GeStapa," 16.6.1937, NA, RG238/NO-5877; RFSS, CdS, CdSHA, "Gemeinsame AO an den SD-RFSS und die GeStapo vom 1.7.37," 8.10.1938, T-175/504/9369235–36; and T-175/504/EAP 173–g-10-12/19, especially frames 9369247–55, -70–72, -79–304, -315–322, -327–330, folder recording relations between SD-UAb Koblenz and SLSt Koblenz, 1937–1938.

81. RFSS, CdSA, "Nahmhaftung von Verwaltungsbeamten," 5.12.1934; HStA Wiesbaden, 483/714; SDdRFSS, OAb Rhein, to Albert, 23.8.1935, ibid., 11282/165–167, internal SD memo on the unsuitable attitude of a recent Gestapo-SD recruit; T-175/3/EAP 172–b-05/11, especially frames 2503913–17, -21–23, -45–48, examples and Daluege's objections to Himmler in 1936; RFSSuCdDPiRMdI, "Politische Beurteilung von Angehörigen der Reichskriminalpolizei durch die Parteidienststellen (GL der NSDAP und SDdRFSS)," 28.1.1942, StA Nürnberg, Abg. 1978/1445.

82. Akten der SSt Würzburg, StA Würzburg, 0.43/14339, Franz Seuss.

83. E.g., CdSuSD, "Gehassige und staatsabträgliche Witze und Gerüchte," 13.3.1941, BA, R58/990/42. See, for example, Beförderungsvorschlag, 28.2.36, BDC/SSO Karl Hönscheit (b. 26.2.03); and 22.2.38, BDC/SSO Erich Rasner (b. 7.3.05) for boasts. See also Gestapo file on SD-man, StA Würzburg, 0.43/2784.

84. Höppner testimony, *Trial of the Major War Criminals before the International Military Tribunal (IMT)* 20:193–194; Lawrence D. Stokes, "Otto Ohlendorf, the Sicherheitsdienst and Public Opinion in Nazi Germany." In *Police Forces in History,* edited by George L. Mosse (London: SAGE, 1975) 231–261; Heinz Boberach, *Meldungen aus dem Reich. Die geheimen Lageberichte des Sicherheitsdienstes des SS, 1938–1945* (Herrsching: Manfred Pawlak, 1984), 13–14 and 19–38; Felix Kersten, *The Kersten Memoirs* (New York: Macmillan, 1957), 206–220; Ohlendorf interrogations, 25 and 29.10.1945 (NA/RG 238); and secret cover letter, RFSS/CdSHA/CdS, 1.7.37, T-175/504/9369224–26.

85. BDC/SSO and PK, Höhn (b. 29.7.04), Lebenslauf und Untersuchungsergebnis Höhn, 20.6.1938.

86. On this movement, Margaret F. Stieg, "The 1926 German Law to Protect Youth against Trash and Dirt: Moral Protectionism in a Democracy." *Central European History (CEH)* 23(March 1990): 22–56; and Klaus Petersen, "The Harmful Publications (Young Persons) Act of 1926. Literary Censorship and the Politics of Morality in the Weimar Republic." *German Studies Review (GSR)* 15(October 1992): 505–23.

87. BDC/SSO and PK, Höhn.

88. Stokes, "Ohlendorf," 235; Ohlendorf testimony, 26.11.1945 (p.m.), 2; Vernehmung Ohlendorf, 23.6.1947 (a.m.), 14, NA/RG-238; Best letter, 2.4.1977; and Gerhard Ritter, "The German Professor in the Third Reich." *Review of Politics,* 8 (April 1946): 242–254, for his impression of SD work in the universities (see especially 252–253).

89. Vernehmung Ohlendorf, 23.6.1947, 14; and Military Government of Germany, Fragebogen, NA/RG-238.

90. RFSS, CdSHA, Stabskanzlei, I/1111, "Sachkartei und Sachakten," 8.12.1936 and attached Richtlinien, HStA Düsseldorf, RW33/1/1–18.

91. StA Bamberg, M34 II: surviving Personenkartei of UAb Byr. Ostmark. Every twentieth card in the file was sampled. See case Nr. 25, for "educational" methods.

92. Communications among 104 001 (II 23), 104 039, and DAF offices in StA Bamberg, M30/779, 782, and 812.

Chapter 9

1. George C. Browder, *The Foundations of the Nazi Police State: The Formation of Sipo and SD* (Lexington: University of Kentucky, 1990). 132–35.

2. Ibid., 172–176.

3. Ibid., 176–181.

4. T-175/405/2928199–204, and 422/2950307, Gestapo and Abwehr directives; StA Bamberg, M30/150, DAF records; M30/812, SD reports of sabotage; StA Ludwigsburg, K110/Bü.34, subregion directives to outposts for counterespionage work.

5. Gerhard L. Weinberg, *The Foreign Policy of Hitler's Germany* (Chicago: University of Chicago, 1970); Heinz Höhne, *Der Orden unter dem Totenkopf: Die Geschichte der SS* (Gütersloh: Sigbert Mohn, 1967), 246–256; Robert L. Koehl, *The Black Corps: The Structure and Power Struggle of the Nazi SS* (Madison: University of Wisconsin, 1983), 141–156, 186–193; and Valdis O. Lumans, *Himmler's Auxiliaries: The Volkdeutsche Mittelstelle and the German Minorities on Europe, 1933–1945* (Chapel Hill: University of North Carolina Press, 1993).

6. E.g., PrGeStapo, GeStapa, re Russische Vertrauensstelle, 7.7.1936, T-175/423/2951216–17.

7. BDC/NS, PK, SSO Schumann (b. 30.8.99); and OA 519/3/4 and 5.

8. Louis de Jong, "The Organization and Efficiency of the German Fifth Column." In *The Third Reich,* edited by Maurice Baumont, et al. (New York: Praeger, 1955) 881–884; Michael Burleigh, *Germany Turns Eastwards: A Study of Ostforschung in the Third Reich* (Cambridge: Cambridge University Press, 1988), 73; and Donald M. McKale, *The Swastika Outside Germany* (Kent, Ohio: Kent State University Press, 1977), 55–58, 97.

9. McKale, *Swastika,* 45–49; de Jong, "Fifth Column," 872–878; and Schellenberg testimony, 7.3.1946, 7–14, NA, RG-238.

10. RdErl.d.RuPrMdI, re Schriftverkehr mit der Auslandsdienststellen der NSDAP, 18.11.1935; and GeStapa, re Hinweis auf wichtige Runderlasse des RuPrMdI, 16.12.1935, T-175/229/2767275–78.

11. GeStapo, Referat I D, re Zusammenarbeit mit dem Rueckwandereramt der AO, 17.11.1936, T-175/423/2951517; de Jong, "Fifth Column," 875–878; Schellenberg testimony, 7.3.1946, 11–18; BDC/SSO and RuSHA, Wermke (b. 9.5.05); and McKale, *Swastika,* 113, 121–122.

12. Robert L. Koehl, *RKFDV: German Resettlement and Population Policy, 1939–1945* (Cambridge: Harvard University, 1957), 36–38; and Lumans, *Himmler's Auxiliaries,* 31–61.

13. Höhn, *Der Orden,* 256–258; Hans-Jürgen Döscher, *Das Auswärtige*

Amt im Dritten Reich (Berlin: Siedler, 1987); Ronald M. Smelser, *The Sudeten Problem, 1933–1938* (Middletown, Conn.: Wesleyan University Press, 1975), 178–179, 181–182; BDC/ SSO, Dr. Hans-Emil Schumburg (b. 14.5.98): RFSS, CdSHA, 17.12.1936; Amtschef IV, 19.7.1944; and Döscher, 119–133.

14. Alwin Ramme, *Der Sicherheitsdienst der SS* (Berlin: Deutsche Militär-verlag, 1970), 57.

15. BDC/SSO, Heinz Jost (b. 9.7.04); Stabsbefehl 3/37; Best to Kahn, 24.11.1974; and Best affidavit, JOS 10, M-895/23/42–45.

16. Naujock's version, Günter Peis, *Man Who Started the War* (London: Odhams, 1960), chapter 3. André Brissaud, *Nazi Secret Service* (New York, W.W. Norton, 1974), chapter 6, equally sensational.

17. Peis, *Man Who Started the War*, chapter 4; and Brissaud, *Nazi Secret Service*, chapter 8.

18. Smelser, *Sudeten Problem*, 169; McKale, *Swastika*, on the AO; and BDC/SSO and RuSHA, Krichbaum (b. 7.5.96)

19. BDC/SSO and RuSHA, Krichbaum.

20. Smelser, *Sudeten Problem*, 169–170.

21. BDC/SSO, v.Lierau (b. 13.8.75); Döscher, *Auswärtige Amt*, 103–105; and Smelser, *Sudeten Problem*, 181–182.

22. BDC/SSO and RuSHA, Preis (b. 19.6.10); ibid., Puchta (b. 22.2.08).

23. BDC/SSO, Brehm (b. 14.2.98); ibid., Liebl (b. 8.12.03); and Smelser, *Sudeten Problem*, 175–176.

24. BDC/SSO, Müller (b. 17.9.93).

25. Smelser, *Sudeten Problem*, 170–171; and T-175/291/EAP 173-b-16-05/156.

26. On ND, BDC/SSO, Ludwig Lenhart (b.15.3.99) and Josef Trittner (b.21.2.07). Peter R. Black, *Ernst Kaltenbrunner: Ideological Soldier of the Third Reich* (Princeton: Princeton University Press, 1984), 80–83; Wolfgang Rosar, *Deutsche Gemeinschaft: Seyss-Inquart und der Anschluss* (Vienna: Europa Verlag, 1971), 91–93, 103–107, on early SD connections in Austria. On Carenthia, Radomir Luza, *Austro-German Relations in the Anschluss Era* (Princeton: Princeton University Press, 1975), 29–30; partially supported by BDC/SSO and RuSHA, Rudolf Thaller (b. 23.12.09).

27. BDC NS, PK, SSO and RuSHA, Butting (b. 22.4.98).

28. BDC/SSO and RuSHA, Hermann Lapper (b. 19.6.10); SSO, Dr. Hans Röhrich (b. 12.10.05); SSO and RuSHA, Wilhelm Waneck (b. 25.11.09); and BDC/SSO Achamer-Pifrader (b. 21.11.00).

29. USHRIA RG-11.001M.01, 16/371, general intelligence reports from 1935; and 15/370, Oka-Berichte, 1936–1937.

30. LdGeStapa, establishing II 1C3, 16.5.1935, T-175/422/2950420; and for Gestapo files, T-175/324/EAP 173-b-16-05/288.

31. BDC/SSO, Dr. Erhard Kröger (b. 24.3.05).

32. BDC/SSO, Dr. Friedrich Buchardt (b. 17.3.09); and NO-4215/NA/RG-238. On Ostforschung, Burleigh, *Germany Turns Eastwards*, 145, 161–163.

33. BDC/RuSHA, Kurt Schneider (b.30.4.04); SSO and RuSHA, Herbert Richter (b. 12.10.06); Übersicht über die SD . . . Abschnitte, 5.12.1935, T-175/250/2742486; and Dienststellen-Verzeichnis, 14.12.1936, T-175/423/2951554.

34. BDC/SSO, Siebert (b. 25.1.04), especially Lebenslauf.

35. PrMdI, "Fernhaltung Unbefugter von der Saarpolitik und vom amt-

lichen Saarnachrichtendienst," 11.9.1933; PrMPräs, GeStapo, same title, 7.3.1934, HStA Düsseldorf, RW18/2 and 1, respectively; BDC/SSO Lürker (b. 28.7.96); Hansjürgen Koehler, *Inside the Gestapo* (London: Pallas, 1940), 67–68; Klaus-Michael Mallmann and Gerhard Paul, *Herrschaft und Alltag* (Bonn: J. H. W. Dietz Nachf., 1991) 180–191, 270.

36. BDC/SSO Lürker, especially Personal-Bericht, 16.9.1936 versus that of 22.2.1938; BDC/RuSHA, Walter Trautwein (b. 21.11.10), Lebenslauf.

37. OA 519/3/31, Wochenberichte der Grenznachrichtenstelle Süd-West der SD RFSS über das Saargebiet, November–December 1934.

38. StA Ludwigsburg K110/Bü.6, foreign press reports, OAb Süd-West.

39. HStA Düsseldorf, RW33/4 and 10: on Ispert, "Erlauterungen zu den Karten A. und B.," 2, 6–7, under cover letter, 19.12. 1936, RW33/4/79, 82–83.

40. Ispert to Dupin, 19.12.1936 with attached "Erläuterungen," HStA Düsseldorf, RW33/4/77–81; and (SD-UAb Aachen) "Aussenarbeit im Westen," n.d. (late 1936 or early 1937), RW33/10/30–38.

41. "Aussenarbeit im Westen," RW33/10/39–51; and Ispert, "Erläuterungen," RW33/4/82–84.

Chapter 10

1. I have identified 639 of about 2,500 recruits for 1935–1936; reviewed 267 personnel files (BDC); for the remainder, data are based on the *Diensalters-liste der SS (DAL)* and a 1944 partial list of SD personnel (T-175/241/EAP 173-b-10-05/40).

2. Appendix C.

3. SS Statistische Jahrbücher, 1937 and 1938, show higher rates of church exit for Catholics, T-175/205/4042235, -280, -345.

4. E.g., BDC/SSO, Bernd Heimer (b. 16.2.03).

5. 83. SS Standarte, 17.4.1936, BDC/SSO, Wilhelm Färber (b. 13.1.94); George C. Browder, "The Numerical Strength of the Sicherheitsdienst des RFSS." *Historical Social Research (HSR)* 28(October 1983):31–32.

6. SD ASt Darmstadt, 6.3.36, HStA Wiesbaden 483/678; SD-Dienststelle Stapo Darmstadt, "Überstellung von Stapoangehörigen zum SD," 4.4.1936, 483/11291; and BDC/RuSHA, Kurt Emmerich (b. 30.3.11), Friedrich Giess (b. 12.8.07), Otto Rittberger (b. 4.4.09), and Georg Weiss (b. 14.7.13). Also, 33.SS-Standarte, "Massnahmen der SD-Stelle beim GeStapa Darmstadt bei Angehörigen des SS-Sturmes 4/33," 16.4.1936, HStA Wiesbaden 483/678.

7. SD-OAb Süd-Ost, Stärkemeldung für Monat April 1936, and SD-OAb Rhein, Stärkemeldung für Monat Januar 1937, HStA Wiesbaden, 483/176; BDC/RuSHA, Paul Pfeiler (b. 26.8.08), P. to CdRuSHA, 9.2.37.

8. Himmler speech to the Nationalpolitischer Lehrgang der Wehrmacht, January 1937, 1992(A)-PS, *Trial of the Major War Criminals before the International Military Tribunal (IMT)* 29:210; cf. *Statistisches Jahrbuch der SS,* 1937, T-175/205/4042245. RFSS, CdRSHA, "Nachweis der arischen Abstammung und Erbgesundtheit," 13.12.1934; FdSD OAb Rhein, same title, 12.3.1935; RFSS, CdRSHA, same title, 18.12.1935, HStA Wiesbaden, 483/11282.

9. CdRuSHA-SS, "Rassische Untersuchung von Angehörigen des SD-RFSS und Neuaufnahmen in den SD," 3.6.1936, T-354/453/Fulda-Werra 118/ 4188242.; and CdSHA, "Neuaufnahmen in den SD," StA Darmstadt, G-12B/ 4/2; SSFiRuSwesen im OAb Fulda-Werra, "Musterung von SD-Angehörigen,"

9.12.1937, T-354/453/4188209–11; and BDC/SSO and RuSHA, Walter Anders (b. 28.3.02).

10. BDC/RuSHA, Otto Gattermann (b. 20.3.98); and personnel records, StA Wolfenbtl., 12A Neu/Nr.16072.

11. Press clipping, "0,60 RM. als einheitliche Gebühr," *Tremonia*, 25.4.1935, HStA Wiesbaden 483/11282; BDC/RuSHA, Kurt Mortstadt (b.15.9.09), correspondence with RuSHA, 15.5.37 and 28.3.38; and RuSHA, Hans Leo van Gülpen.

12. CdSHA, "SS-Aufnahme- und Verpflichtungsscheine im SD," 14.2. 1935, HStA Wiesbaden, 483/173.

13. E.g., BDC/SSO, Dr. Erwin Weinmann (b. 6.7.09).

14. CdSS-HA, SS-Ergänzungsamt, "Regelung der Kommandierungen und Versetzungen von der Allgemeinen-SS zum SD und umgekehrt," 4.4.1936, T-175/159/2690585–86.

15. RFSS, Personalkanzlei, "Beförderung von SS-Angehörigen . . . ," 21.9.1935; RFSS, CdSHA, "Beförderung von SS-Angehörigen . . . ," 15.10.1936, StA Darmstadt, G-12B/4/2; and "Beförderung zum SS-Führer," 14.12.1936, ibid., 4/6. See exchanges of Schellenberg and Best, T-175/239/EAP 173-b-05/2A, 2B and 2J.

16. (SDHA) Stabskanzlei, I/11, "Die Laufbahnen im Sicherheitsdienst/ RFSS," 24.2.1939, T-175/239/2728407; especially EAP 173-b-05/2B and 2J.

17. BDC/SSO, Julius Plaichinger (b. 2.1.92), letter to RFSS, 6.3.1936.

18. RFSS, "Bestimmungen über die Gewärung der Besoldung in der allgemeinen SS," 28.5.1935, T-611/47; no changes for 1936. Gerhard Bry, *Wages in Germany* (Princeton: Princeton University Press, 1960), 457–460, table A-47; Dietmar Petzina, Werner Abelshauser, and Anslem Faust, *Sozialgeschichtliches Arbeitsbuch*, Vol. 3, *Materialien zur Statistik des Deutschen Reiches 1914–1945* (Munich: Verlag C.H. Beck, 1978), p. 106; and Konrad H. Jarausch, *The Unfree Professions: German Lawyers, Teachers, and Engineers, 1900–1950* (New York: Oxford University Press, 1990), 159, 249.

19. RFSS, "Bestimmungen über . . . Besoldung . . ."; and "Jahresurlaub für hauptamtliche Angehörigen SD/RFSS," 1936, T-175/249/2730234.

20. RFSS, CdSHA, "Befreiung von SD-Angehörigen vom Arbeitsdienst," 15.3.1935, HStA Wiesbaden, 483/173; and "Zur Bekanngabe an alle SS- (SD-) Angehörigen des GeStapas und des HA Sipo," 21.1.1937, T-175/423/ 2951621–3.

21. Browder, "Numerical Strength," chart 1, 31.

22. E.g., SDdRFSS, OAb.Rhein, "Nachteile wegen Zugehörigkeit zum SD," 16. and 25.10.1935, HStA Wiesbaden, 483/11289/6–9.

23. Heinrich Orb, *Nationalsozialismus, 13 Jahr Machtrausch* (Otten: Verlag Otto Walter, 1945), 78.

24. For two cases, routinely tried and dismissed: BDC, SSO Hans Diepold (b. 6.8.06); and SSO, RuSHA Kurt Schnell (b. 10.2.06).

25. Bernd Wegner, *The Waffen-SS Organization, Ideology, and Function* (Oxford: Basil Blackwell, 1990) 14–19, 165–176, 190–192; and James J. Weingartner, "Law and Justice in the Nazi SS." *Central European History (CEH)* 16(September 1983): 280–281.

26. Beurteilungen in BDC/SSO files; SS and SD school evaluations, Marcel Zschunke, T-175/240/2730135–39, -165; "Bericht des SS Scharf. Kaulard . . . ," 15.2.1935, LHA Koblenz, 662.6/45/3–13.

27. E.g., Marcel Zschunke, SD personnel file, T-175/240/173-b-10/19.

28. Bericht Kaulard, see n. 26.

29. Ibid., 3, 7–13; and lesson plan, "Systematische Arbeit als Grundbedingung des Erfolges der Arbeit des SD d. RFSS," 11.11.1940, LHA Koblenz, 662.5/546.

30. Bericht Kaulard, 3.

31. Ibid., 4.

32. Ibid., 5, 7; and Befehl für den SD Nr. 25/26, "Namennennung von SD-Angehörigen," 22.6.1936, T-175/240/2730223.

33. E.g., BDC/SSO, Otto Wendland (b. 4.3.00), 88 SS-Standarte, 12.8.1935. On liaison, CdRuSHA, Sonderbefehl, 23.3.1935, NO-3477, NA/RG-238.

34. Gunnar C. Boehnert, "An Analysis of the Age and Education of the SS Führerkorps, 1925–1939." *HSR* 12(October 1979): 11.

35. BDC/SSO, Fritz Friedrich (b. 9.8.04).

36. BDC/SSO and RuSHA, Walter Oehme (b.30.5.12), especially RuSHA Lebenslauf.

37. Thilo Vogelsang, "Der Chef des Ausbildungswesens (Chef AW)." *Gutachten des Instituts für Zeitgeschichte* 2: 146–156.

38. BDC files on Christoph Gentart (b. 17.1.08), August Kerber (b. 7.6.12), Erich Naumann (b. 29.4.05), and Fritz Stöder (b. 10.5.99); BDC/SSO, Dr. Karl Gengenbach (b. 9.11.11), Lebenslauf, 9.2.35, and Personal-Berichte; and Erich Ehrlinger (b. 14.10.10), Lebenslauf, 1.4.35, and Personal-Bericht, 1.3.38.

39. SDdRFSS, SD-OAb Rhein, "Meldung von SS-Angehörigen bestimmter Berufsgruppen," 20. and 25.2.1936, HStA Wiesbaden, 483/613/29–43.

40. BDC/SSO Fritz Kranefuss (b. 19.10.00) and Dr. Wilhelm Voss (b. 1.7.96); and Reinhard Vogelsang, *Der Freundeskreis Himmler* (Göttingen: Musterschmidt, 1972), 157–158 and 168.

41. Dennis Anderson, *The Academy for German Law, 1933–1934* (New York: Garland, 1987), 192–195, 214–219; and George C. Browder, *The Foundations of the Nazi Police State: The Formation of Sipo and SD* (Lexington: University Press of Kentucky, 1990), especially chapter 14.

42. BDC/SSO, Dr. Wilhelm Spengler (b. 19.3.07), Lebenslauf, 13.7.1936; Shlomo Aronson, *Reinhard Heydrich und die Frühgeschichte von Gestapo and SD* (Stuttgart: Deutsche Verlags-Anstalt, 1971), 162–163; and Six report, chapter 8, see n. 24.

43. Max Weinreich, *Hitler's Professors* (New York: YIVO, 1946); Gerhard Müller, *Ernst Krieck und die nationalsozialistische Wissenschaftsreform: Motive und Tendenzen einer Wissenschaftslehre und Hochschulreform im Dritten Reich* (Weinheim & Basel: Beltz, 1978); Reese C. Kelly, "German Professorate and Nazism: A Failure of Totalitarian Aspirations." *Higher Education Quarterly* 25(3):261–280, especially notes 1 and 4; and Helmut Heiber, *Universitäten unterm Hakenkreuz*, 2 vols. (Munich: K.G. Saur, 1991–1992). Also Gerhard Ritter's apology, "The German Professor in the Third Reich." *Review of Politics* 8(April 1946): 242–254.

44. E.g., "Lage der Pädagogik an der Universität Bonn," n.d. (circa 1936); and fragment of similar report, HStA Düsseldorf, RW33/3/1–5; Müller, *Krieck,* especially 118–139; Heiber, *Universität,* especially 2: 450–481; and BDC Krieck (b. 6.7.82).

45. See chapter 6, n. 45, and works of Arminger, Faust, Giles, Jaraush, Kater, Stachura, and Steinberg.

46. BDC/SSO, Scheel (b.22.11.07); and Erich Stockhorst, *Fünftausend Köpfe. Wer war was im Dritten Reich* (Bruchsal/Baden: Blick u. Bild, 1967), 376.

47. BDC/SSO, Scheel; Geoffrey J. Giles, *Students and National Socialism in Germany* (Princeton: Princeton University Press, 1985), 166–167, 193, n. 144, 196–199, 200–204, 325.

48. Scheel affidavit, M-985/24/118–20; and Giles, *Students,* 242–244, 248–250.

49. Scheel affidavit; Bericht Kaulard (see. n. 28); and Giles, *Students,* 269–273, 291, 315 (for quotation), 325.

50. BDC/SSO and RuSHA, Sandberger (b. 17.8.11); and Scheel affidavit.

51. Scheel affidavit.

52. BDC/SSO, Sandberger, correspondence in 1937 as Gebietsauftragten Südwest d.RSF; and Sandberger affidavit, 23.4.1947, M-895/9/923–29 (NO-3246).

53. Scheel affidavit; and Heinrich Bernhard affidavit, M-895/23/202 (SAN 32).

54. *Trials of the War Criminals (TWC)* 4: 532, 535, 536; affidavit, 23.4.1947.

55. Michael H. Kater, "The Reich Vocational Contest of Higher Education in Nazi Germany." *CEH* 7(September 1974): 230; and Giles, *Students,* 205, 254–258.

56. BDC/SSO, Six; and *TWC* 4: 521–523. Cf. Aronson, *Heydrich,* 207–208; Alwin Ramme, *Der Sicherheitsdienst der SS* (Berlin: Deutsche Militärverlag, 1970), 272; and Julius Mader, "Eichmanns Chef ist Bonner 'Gesandter z. WV.'" *Deutschen Aussenpolitik* 8(5):405–409.

57. See Gerhard Müller's analysis of Ernst Krieck's initial synthesis within this context, and of Six's writings defining the SD posture, *Krieck,* 120–124, and n. 519.

58. Lawrence D. Stokes, "Otto Ohlendorf, the Sicherheitsdienst and Public Opinion in Nazi Germany." In *Police Forces in History,* edited by George L. Mosse (London: SAGE, 1975), 231–261; Hanno Sowade, "Otto Ohlendorf—Nonkonformist, SS-Führer und Wissenschaftsfunktionär." In *Die Braune Elite: 22 biographische Skizzen,* edited by Ronald Smelser and Rainer Zittleman (Darmstadt: Wissenschaftliche Buchgesellschaft, 1989); his BDC files; and war crimes trials interrogations, NA Microfilms M-1019 and M-895 (NA/RG-238).

59. On Jessen, Heiber, *Universität,* 1: 197–208.

60. SD-HA Stabsbefehl 3/37, 10; Ohlendorf testimony, 3.12.1945 (p.m), 8; and Stokes, "Ohlendorf," 235–238.

61. Walter Schellenberg, *Memoiren* (Cologne: Verlag für Politik und Wirtschaft, 1959), 25–27; Schellenberg testimony, *TWC,* 12: 1228–30; BDC/SSO, Schellenberg (b. 16.1.10); Miscellaneous personal records, T-175/R572/EAP 173-b-20-18/10, -18/15.

62. Schellenberg testimony, *TWC,* 12:1230; and personal records, T-175/R572/9449719.

63. George C. Browder, "The SD: Significance of Organization and Image." In *Police Forces in History,* edited by George L. Mosse (London: SAGE, 1975), 223–224; Vernehmung von August Finke, 19.2.48, NA Microfilm M-1019/17.

64. Louis P. Lochner (trans.), "A Dissident Nazi: Hans-Jörg Maurer's Diary." *Wisconsin Magazine of History* 50(summer 1967): 347–391.

65. Ibid., 358–360.

66. E.g., BDC, SSO August Beirau (b. 28.11.82).

67. Daniel Lerner, *Sykewar: Psychological Warfare against Germany* (New York: George W. Stewart, 1949), 294–296; A.L. Unger, "The Public Opinion Reports of the Nazi Party." *Public Opinion Quarterly* 29(1965/66): 572, 578; Donald D. Wall, "The Reports of the Sicherheitsdienst on the Church and Religious Affairs in Germany, 1933–1944." *Church History* 40(1971): 439–440; Stokes, "Ohlendorf," 259–261; and Heinz Boberach, *Meldungen, aus dem Reich* (Herrsching: Manfred Pawlak, 1984), 1: 18–38.

68. BDC/SSO Gregor Schwartz-Bostunitsch (b.1.12.83); and Aronson, *Heydrich*, pp. 208, 303–304, n. 61a. BDC/SSO and RuSHA, Friedrich Polte (b. 20.1.11), Lebensläufe.

69. Affidavit of Gustav-Adolf Scheel, NA Microfilm M-895/24/118–20; Interrogation of Justus Beyer, 30.4.1947, OCCWE, NA RG-238; and Interrogation of Dr. Hans Ehlich, 16.11.1946, ibid.

70. Beyer interrogation, OCCWE, NA RG-238.

71. Scheel affidavit; and Eidesstattliche Erklarung von August Finke, 14.1.48, NA Microfilm M-1019/17.

72. Robert L. Koehl, "Toward an SS Typology: Social Engineers." *American Journal of Economics and Sociology* 18 (January 1959): 113–126.

73. Justus Beyer (n. 70).

Notes to Conclusion

1. Klaus-Michael Mallmann and Gerhard Paul, "Omniscient, Omnipotent, Omnipresent? Gestapo, Society and Resistance." In *Nazism and German Society, 1933–1945*, edited by David F. Crew (London: Routledge, 1994), 166–196; Robert Gellately, *The Gestapo in German Society: Enforcing Racial Policy, 1933–1945* (Oxford: Oxford University Press, 1990); and cf. *Terror, Herrschaft und Alltag*, edited by Brigitte Berlekamp and Werner Röhr (Munster: Westfälisches Dampfboot, 1995).

2. Detlav Peukert, *Inside Nazi Germany: Conformity, Opposition, and Racism in Everyday Life* (New Haven: Yale University Press, 1987), 247–248.

3. George C. Browder, *The Foundations of the Nazi Police State: The Formation of Sipo and SD* (Lexington: University Press of Kentucky, 1990).

4. Reinhard Heydrich, *Wandlungen unseres Kampfes* (Munich-Berlin: Eher Verlag, 1935), 3–6, 17–20; idem., "Die Bekämpfung der Staatsfeinde." *Deutsches Recht* 6 (April 1936): 121–123; T-175/239/2728158,-161–62, -175, and 276/5486074; Hoeppner testimony, *(IMT) Trial of the Major War Criminals before the International Military Tribunal* 20:195; and Werner Best, "Die Geheime Staatspolizei." *Deutsches Recht* 6 (April 1936): 126.

5. Stephen Schafer, "The Concept of the Political Criminal." *Journal of Criminal Law, Criminology, and Police Science (JCL,C&PS)* 62(1971): 380–387.

6. Fred Weinstein, *The Dynamics of Nazism* (New York: Academic Press, 1980).

7. Martin Broszat, "Plädoyer für eine Historisierung des Nationalsozialismus." *Merkur* 39(1985): 373–385; cf. Ian Kershaw, " 'Normality' and Genocide: The Problem of 'Historicization'." In *Reevaluating the Third Reich,* edited

by Thomas Childers and Jane Caplan (New York: Holmes & Meier, 1993), 20–41, with whose conclusions I concur.

8. Browder, *Foundations*, 141–143.

9. Heinrich Orb, *Nationalsozialismus 13 Jahr Machtrausch* (Olten: Verlag Otto Walter, 1945), 65–66; BDC/SSO Hugo Linhard (b. 4.3.96); and Mrugowski, Interrogation, 19.7.1946, M-1019/47.

10. Vernehmung von August Finke, vom 19.2.1948, M-1019/17.

11. Browning, *The Final Solution and the German Foreign Office* (New York: Holmes Meier Publishers, Inc., 1978), 1–2.

12. Deutsche Hochschule für Politik Übungszeugnis, Theo Gahrmann, "Welche völkerrechtlichen Regeln stehen einem sogenannten totelen Krieg entgegen?" Winter 1937/38, BDC/SSO Theo Gahrmann (b. 14.3.10), quote from 2.

13. Charles Sydnor argues that Heydrich was signaling such a trend by 1939, and offering plans by January 1941, in "Executive Instinct: Reinhard Heydrich and the Planning for the Final Solution" (Paper presented at the Inaugural Conference of the Holocaust Research Institute of the U.S. Holocaust Museum, Washington, D.C., December 6, 1993). This complements Richard Breitman, *The Architect of Genocide: Himmler and the Final Solution* (New York: Knopf, 1990), and idem., "Plans for the Final Solution in Early 1941." *German Studies Review (GSR)* 17(October 1994): 483–493.

14. Testimonies of Franz Six and Dr. Martin Sandberger, *Trials of the War Criminals (TWC)* 4: 523 and 535; and Affidavit of Gustav Scheel, M-895/23/118–20, on Sandberger. 3rd U.S. Army Interrogation Report No. 20, 12, on prosecution of Erich Rasner, NA/RG-238; and BDC/SSO Paul Kern (b. 9.1.02), results of trial, 7.4.42.

15. On unsuitability of Kurt Emmerich and others, February and March 1936, HStA Wiesbaden 483/678; BDC/SSO Martin Kurtz (b. 1.11.05) and Erich Rasner (b. 7.3.05).

16. Heinz Boberach, *Meldungen aus dem Reich* (Herrsching: Manfred Pawlak, 1984), 27–30; and for Ohlendorf's version, NA/RG238/testimony, 29.10.1945, 2–4 and 7–8. Michael Gayer, "National Socialist Germany: The Politics of Information." In *Knowing One's Enemies: Intelligence Assessment before the Two World Wars*, edited by Ernest R. May (Princeton: Princeton University, 1984), 310–346, argues that Nazi leadership "used" intelligence rather than being influenced by it.

17. Omer Bartov, *The Eastern Front, 1941–1945* (New York: St. Martin's, 1986); and Bartov, "The Missing Years: German Workers, German Soldiers." *German History* 8 (1): 46–65 (1990).

18. Ibid., 54.

19. Ibid., 56.

20. Compare with Konrad H. Jarausch's conclusions about *The Unfree Professions: German Lawyers, Teachers, and Engineers, 1900–1950* (New York: Oxford University Press, 1990), especially 196 and 223.

Selected Bibliography

Research and Reference Materials

Bibliographies, Historiographies, Catalogs, and Guides

Ash, Mitchell G., and Ulrich Geyer. "The Current Situation in the Archives of the New German State." *German Studies Association Newsletter* 17(Spring 1992): 20–31.

Berlin Document Center. *The Holdings of the Berlin Document Center: A Guide to the Collections.* Berlin: The Berlin Document Center, 1994.

Boeninger, Hildegard R. *The Hoover Library Collection on Germany.* Stanford: Stanford University Press, 1955.

Brachmann, Botho. "Akten betreffe des Geheimen Staatspolizeiamts zur Widerstandbewegung der deutschen Arbeiterklasse 1933–1939. " *Archivmitteilungen* 11(1961): 74–80.

Browder, George C. "Captured German and Other Nations' Documents in the Osoby (Special) Archive, Moscow." *Central European History* 24(4): 424–445 (1991).

———. "Update on the Captured Documents in the Former Osoby Archive, Moscow." *Central European History* 26(3): 335–342 (1993).

Cline, Marjorie W., Carla E. Christiansen, and Judith Fontaine, eds. *Scholar's Guide to Intelligence Literature.* Frederick, Md.: University Publications of America, 1983.

Frohn, Axel. "Archives in the New German *Länder*." *German Historical Institute Bulletin* Spring 1992: 13–21.

Gellately, Robert. "Rethinking the Nazi Terror System: A Historiographical Analysis." *German Studies Review.* 14(1): 23–38 (1991).

———. "Situating the 'SS-State' in a Socio-Historical Context: Recent Histories of the SS, the Police, and the Courts in the Third Reich." *Journal of Modern History* 64(1992): 338–365.

Giles, Geoffrey J. "The Stasi Archive in the Freienwalder Strasse, East Berlin." *German Studies Association Newsletter* 16(Winter 1991): 34–38.

Gilmore, William J. *Psychohistorical Inquiry: A Comprehensive Research Bibliography.* New York: Garland, 1984.

Granier, Gerhard, Josef Henke, and Klaus Oldenhage. *Das Bundesarchiv und seine Bestände.* Boppard am Rhein: Boldt, 1977.

Gugenhäuser, Max. *Geschichte des geheimes Nachrichtendienstes: Literaturbericht und Bibliographie.* Frankfurt: Verlag für Wehrwessen, 1968.

Heinz, Grete, and Agnes F. Peterson. *NSDAP Hauptarchiv: Guide to the Hoover Institute Microfilm Collection.* Stanford: Hoover Institution, 1964.

Hülke, Hans-Heinrich. *Verbrechen, Polizei, Prozessse. EineVerzeichnis von Büchern und kleineren Schriften in deutscher Sprache.* Wiesbaden: Bundeskriminalamt, 1963.

International Police Association. *International Bibliography of Selected Police Literature.* London: M&W Publications, 1968.

Marczewski, Jerzy. "Polish Research on the Role and Activity of the S.S." *Polish Western Affairs* 1982: 110–121.

Mensch, Terry G. "Psychohistory of the Third Reich: A Library Pathfinder and Tropical [sic] Bibliography of English Language Publications." *The Journal of Psychohistory* 7(1979/1980): 331–354.

U.S. Department of State, Historical Office. *A Catalog of Files and Microfilms of the German Foreign Ministry Archives, 1920–1945.* 3 vols. Stanford: Hoover Institution, 1962, 1964, 1966.

U.S. National Archives and Record Administration. "Captured German and Related Records in the National Archives. "Washington, D.C., revised February 1993.

———. *Guides to German Records Microfilmed at Alexandria, VA.* Washington, D.C., 1958–.

———. Pamphlets describing *Records of the United States Nürnberg War Crimes Trials.* Washington, D.C.: 1973–.

Verein deutscher Archivare. *Archive in der Bundesrepublik Deutschland, Österreich und der Schweiz.* Münster: Ardey-Verlag, 1995.

Whitehouse, Jack E. *A Police Bibliography.* New York: AMS Press, 1980.

Biographical, Statistical, and Other References

Bailey, William G., ed. *The Encyclopedia of Police Science.* New York: Garland Press, 1989.

Das deutsche Führerlexicon. Berlin: Otto Stollberg, 1934.

Germany, Statistischesreichsamt. *Statistisches Jahrbuch für das deutsche Reich.* Berlin: Verlag von Reimar Hobbing, 1930, 1931, 1938.

National Council of the National Front of Democratic Germany. *Brown Book: War and Nazi Criminals in West Germany.* Dresden: Verlag Zeit im Bild, n.d.

Noelle, Elisabeth, and Erich Neumann, eds. *The Germans: Public Opinion Polls, 1947–1966.* Westport, Conn.: Greenwood Press, 1981.

Petzina, Dietmar, Werner Abelshauser, and Anselm Faust, eds. *Statistische Arbeitsbücher zur neueren deutschen Geschichte.* Vol. 3, *Sozialgeschichtliches Arbeitsbuch. Materialien zur Statistik des Deutschen Reiches 1914–1945.* Munich: Verlag C.H. Beck, 1978.

Roeske, Ulrich. "Das amtliche Quellenwerk der deutschen Reichsstatistik. Eine Übersicht über die veröffentlichungsreihe 'Statistik des Deutschen Reichs' 1873 bis 1944." *Jahrbuch für Wirtschaftsgeschichte* 1985: 213–243.

Smelser, Ronald, and Rainer Zittelmann. *Die Braune Elite: 22 biographische Skizzen.* Darmstadt: Wissenschaftliche Buchgesellschaft, 1989.
Stockhorst, Erich. *Fünftausend Köpfe: Wer war was im Dritten Reich.* Bruchsal/Baden: Blick u. Bild, 1967.

Documents

Readers might consult my comments on problems of locating and using the surviving documentary evidence about Sipo and SD to be found in the bibliographical essay in *The Foundations of the Nazi Police State.* More material now comes from several additional archives holding records of the former Länder, the recently opened Osoby (Secret) Archive in Moscow, which holds most of the German records captured by Soviet forces in Germany, and the microfilmed RSHA archives captured by the Poles. Cross-references to guides are given in parentheses. Archival abbreviations are in brackets.

The Archives of Former Reich Agencies

The Bundesarchiv Koblenz (see Granier) [BA]

NS-1	Der Reichsschatzmeister, NSDAP
NS-6	Der Stellvertreter des Führers
NS-10	Persönliche Adjutantur des Führers und Reichskanzler
NS-19	Personalstab des Reichsführer SS
NS-26	NSDAP Hauptarchiv (see Heinz and microfilm)
R-18	Reichsministerium des Innern
R-43	Reichskanzlei
R-58	Reichssicherheitshauptamt, its subordinate agencies: Geheime Staatspolizei, Reichskriminalpolizei, Sicherheitsdienst des Reichsführers SS and predecessors (microfilm T-175) Subsequently divided into R-134, Sicherheitspolizei und politische Nachrichtendienste
Schu	Schumacher Sammlung, a miscellaneous collection taken from the holdings of the Berlin Document Center (microfilm T-580 and T-611)

Bundesarchiv-Militärarchiv-Freiburg [BA-MA]

RH-1	Oberbefehlshaber des Heeres-Adjutantur
RW-4	Oberkommando der Wehrmacht/Wehrmachtführungsstab
RW-5	OKW-Amt Auslandsnachrichten und Abwehr (microfilm T-77)
RW-6	Allgemeines Wehrmachtamt, Abtl.-Ausland (microfilm T-77)
OKW-901	Reichsministerium, Wehrmachtabteilung, Geheime-Akten über persönlicher, politischer Schriftwechsel

Bundesarchiv Aussenstelle Berlin-Zehlendorf (see U.S. Document Center Berlin)

Archives of the Former Länder

Baden:

Generallandesarchiv Karlsruhe [GLA Karlsruhe]

Abt.233	Staatsministerium
Abt.234	Justizministerium
Abt.235	Kultus-Ministerium
Abt.236	Innenministerium
Abt.237	Finanzministerium
Abt.345	Badisches Bezirksamt Buchen
Bst.465c	NSDAP, Verbände und Polizei in Mannheim
Bst.465d	NSDAP, Verbände und Polizei

Staatsarchiv Freiburg [StA Freiburg]

Aus	US-Gewahrsam zuruckgegebenes Schriftgut der NS-Zeit
LRA	Landratsamt Konstanz, Kriminalpolizei Singen
Rep.LKK	Landeskommissär Konstanz, Polizei

Bavaria: (see Heinz and Hauptarchiv microfilm)

Subsequent to my research, in 1977, the Hauptstaatsarchiv underwent reorganization, with all relevant holdings consolidated into Abteilung II.

Bayerisches Hauptstaatsarchiv, Munich, Abteilung I [ByHStA]

Bayerisches Innen Ministerium

Bayerisches Hauptstaatsarchiv, Munich, Abteilung II

Reichsstatthalter Epp
Gesamtstaatsministerium, MA-99
Akten des byr. Ministerpräsident Siebert, MA-106

Staatsarchiv, Bamberg [StA Bamberg]

K-3	Regierung von Oberfranken
K-5	Bezirksamt Bamberg
K-100	Oberlandesgericht
M-30	NSDAP, Gau Byr. Ostmark
M-32	Former Sammlung Schumacher
M-33	Kreisleitung der NSDAP im Gau Byr. Ostmark
M-34	Sicherheitsdienst des Reichsführers SS

Bayerisches Staatsarchiv, Munich [ByStA Munich]
Polizeidirektion Munich

Staatsarchiv Nürnberg [StA Nürnberg]

Rep.218   Polizeidirektion Nürnberg-Furth
Rep.270^{IV} Regierung von Mittelfranken, Kammern des Innern,
             Abg. 1968
             Abg. 1970
Rep.503   SD (U.S. Nürnberg Material)

Staatsarchiv Würzburg [StA Würzburg]

Rep.III.8.0.1 NSDAP, Gau Mainfranken
Rep.III.8.0.2 SD-Hauptaussenstelle Würzburg
Akten der Gestapo-Stelle Würzburg, 0.4.3

Bremen:

Staatsarchiv Bremen [StA Bremen]

3-P.1.a.   Senatsregistratur, Polizeisachen im allge.
4,13-P.1.c.   Sicherheitspolizei, Kriminalpolizei, Geheime Staatspolizei
4,65   Polizeidirektion Bremen, Nachrichtenstelle

Senat des Inneres holds selected folders from the above.

Braunschweig (Brunswick):

Niedersächsisches Staatsarchiv, Wolfenbüttel [StA Wolfbtl]

112 A Neu   Braunschweigisches Staatsministerium
133 Neu   Polizeidirektion Braunschweig

Hesse:

Hessisches Staatsarchiv Darmstadt [StA Darmstadt]

G-12   Akten des Sicherheitsdienstes und der Geheimen Staatspolizei
             Darmstadt
G-12(A)   Landespolizeiamt Darmstadt
G-21   Hessisches Justizministerium
N-1   NSDAP Akten
R-1   Ersatzdokumentation über die Tätigkeit des hess. Innen Minis-
             terium bezw. des Reichsstatthalter in Hessen, Ministerial-
             ausschreiben dieser Behörde von 1907–1944 aus Landrats-
             ämter, usw.

Lippe:

Staatsarchiv Detmold [StA Detmold]

L-76   Reichsstatthalter und Staatsminister
L80 Ie   Lipp. Regierung, Abtl. des Innern, Polizeiangelegenheiten,
             1924–1949

L-80 IeP   Der Landespolizeidirektor und der Führer der Landespolizei
L-133   NSDAP, Kreisleitung Detmold und Lemgo

Oldenburg:

Niedersächsisches Staatsarchiv Oldenburg [StA Oldenburg]

136   Oldenburgisches Staatsministerium des Innern

Preussen (Prussia):

Geheimes Staatsarchiv Berlin-Dahlem (Hauptarchiv Berlin, successor to
the Prussian State Archive) [GStA]

77   Preussiches Ministerium des Innern
90   Preussisches Staatsministerium (90, Abtl.P, holds the most relevant
         materials)
219   Landes Kriminalpolizeiamt Berlin
240   NSDAP—Gauarchiv Ostpreussen from StA Königsberg

Hessisches Hauptstaatsarchiv Wiesbaden

Abtl.483   NSDAP Hessen-Nassau containing records of SD Gruppe
               West, later OAb Rhein, and Stapostelle Frankfurt a.M.

Niedersächsisches Hauptstaatsarchiv Hannover [HStA Hannover]

Hann.112a   Oberpräsident der Provinz Hannover
Hann.310I   NSDAP, Gau Südhannover-Braunschweig and Gau Osthan-
               nover

Niedersächsisches Staatsarchiv Aurich [StA Aurich]

Rep.21a   Regierung Aurich
Acc.22/89   Dezernat 201, Dezernat 207
Acc.7/1978I Dezernat 201

Niedersächsiches Staatsarchiv Stade [StA Stade]

Rep.80P   Polizei
Rep.274   Landkreis Stade

Nordrhein-Westfälisches Hauptstaatsarchiv Düsseldorf [HStA Düsseldorf]

NSDAP, Gauleitung Düsseldorf, Köln
Regierung Aachen, Düsseldorf, Köln
SD-Abschnitt Aachen, Köln, West
Staatspolizeistelle Aachen, Düsseldorf, Köln, and subordinate posts
Polizeibehörden vor 1945

Nordrhein-Westfälisches Staatsarchiv Münster [StA Münster]

Oberpräsidium Münster
Regierung Arnsberg, Münster
Polizeipräsidium Bochum, Dortmund, Hagen
Politische Polizei "Drittes Reich"
NSDAP, Gauleitung Westfalen-Nord, Westfalen Süd, Kreis und Ortsgruppenleitungen

Rheinland-Pfalz Landeshauptarchiv Koblenz [LHA Koblenz]

Best.441	Regierung Koblenz
Best.442	Bezirksregierung Trier
Abtl.517,1	Polizeidirektion Koblenz
Abtl.662,3	NSDAP Trier-West-Land
Abtl.662,5	Documents returned from U.S. National Archives relating to Gestapo and Kriminalpolizei posts
Abtl.662,6	Sicherheitsdienst Koblenz

Schaumburg-Lippe:

Niedersächsiches Staatsarchiv Bückeburg [StA Bückbrg.]

L4   Lfd. Reierungsregistratur-Rep. IV-

Württemberg:

Hauptstaatsarchiv Stuttgart [HStA Stuttgart]

E-130 b II	Staatsministerium
E-130 IV	Staatsministerium
E-140	Reichsstatthalter in Württemberg—Personalakten
E-151a	Ministerium des Innern, Abtl.I, Kanzleidirektion
E-151b	———, Abtl.II, Recht und Verfassung
E-151c	———, Abtl.III, Polizeiwessen

Staatsarchiv Ludwigsburg [StA Ludwigsbrg.]

E 188c	Landespolizeidirektion Nordwürttemberg—Personalakten
K 100	Staatspolizeistelle Stuttgart, 1933–1945
K 110	SD-Dienststellen in Württemberg und Hohenzollern, 1933–1945

Other Archives

Generalstaatsanwaltschaft bei dem Kammergericht Berlin
[GStAnWlt.b.d.KG, Berlin]

Materials assembled for the prosecution of NS criminals

Institute für Zeitgeschichte, Munich [IfZ]

Miscellaneous collection of literature and documents

Polizei-Führungsakademie Hiltrup

Collection of literature, manuscripts and miscellaneous documents

Russian Center for the Preservation of Historical Documentary Collections, former Osoby (Secret) Archive, Moscow (see Browder) [OA]
See also U.S. Holocaust Research Institute Archives.

500	Reichssicherheitshauptamt
501	Geheime Staatspolizei
503	Stapostelle Stettin
505	Polizeipräsidium Berlin
519	NSDAP
1148	Stapostelle Köslin
1163	Stapostelle Weimar
1185	Stapostelle Erfurt
1240	SD Abschnitt Stettin
1241	SD Abschnitt Erfurt and Weimar
1323	German Police Agencies in Germany and Occupied Territories (1841–1945)

U.S. Document Center, Berlin (see Browder) [BDC]
Now the Bundesarchiv Aussenstelle Berlin-Zehlendorf.

Files on individuals, used for political and judicial purposes, the most important relevant to Sipo and SD:

NS	Party Membership Files
PK	Party Correspondence
SSO	SS Officers Files
RuSHA	Rasse und Siedlungs Hauptamt files on SS personnel

U.S. Holocaust Research Institute Archive, Washington, D.C. [USHRIA]
Holds among other things selectively microfilmed documents from European and Israeli archives:

RG-11.001M former Osoby Archive, Moscow (phase I filming):
 01 Reichssicherheitshauptamt
 07 NSDAP
 10 Reichsministerium des Innern

RG-15 Poland

 007M   Reichssicherheitshauptamt. Archival repositories of the RSHA captured by Polish forces and held by the Central Commission for Investigation of Crimes against the Polish Nation, Warsaw.

U.S. Library of Congress, Washington, D.C. [LC]

Manuscript Division

The Deutsches Auslands-Institut Collection
The Himmler Files
The Rehse Collection (Hauptarchiv der NSDAP)

U.S. National Archives, Washington D.C. (see National Archives) [NA]

Most relevant holdings have now been microfilmed. Citations to documents researched prior to microfilming are listed as

RG 238   Collection of World War II War Crimes Records
RG 242   Collection of Foreign Records Seized, holds the microfilmed documents listed below.

Microfilmed Documents

Captured German Documents Microfilmed at Berlin for the American Historical Association. T-580.
Captured German Documents Filmed at Berlin for the Hoover Institution (Hauptarchiv der NSDAP). HA.
Captured German Documents Filmed at Berlin (University of Nebraska). T-611.
Miscellaneous SS Records: Einwandererzentralstelle, Waffen-SS, and SS-Oberabschnitte. National Archives Microfilm Publications. T-354.
Records of the National Socialist German Labor Party (NSDAP) and the Deutsches Ausland-Institut, Stuttgart. National Archives Microfilm Publications. T-81.
Records of the Reichsführer SS and Chief of the German Police. National Archives Microfilm Publications. T-175.
Records of the United States Nurnberg War Crimes Trials: Interrogations, 1946–1949. National Archives Microfilm Publications. M1019.
———. *USA v Otto Ohlendorf et al. Case IX.* National Archives Microfilm Publications. M895.

Published Documents

Boberach, Heinz, ed. *Berichte des SD und der Gestapo über Kirchen und Kirchenvolk in Deutschland, 1934–1944.* Mainz: Mathias Grünewald-Verlag, 1971.
———. *Meldungen aus dem Reich. Die geheimen Lageberichte des Sicherheitsdienstes der SS, 1938–1945.* 17 vols. Herrsching: Manfred Pawlak Verlagsgesellschaft, 1984.
Breitman, Richard, and Shlomo Aronson. "Eine unbekannte Himmler-Rede vom Januar 1943." *Vierteljahrshefte für Zeitgeschichte* 38 (April 1990): 343.
Brommer, Peter, ed. *Die Partei hört mit. Lageberichte und andere Meldungen des Sicherheitsdienstes der SS aus dem Grossraum Koblenz, 1937–1941.* Koblenz: Verlag der Landesarchivverwaltung Rheinland-Pfalz, 1988.
Broszat, Martin, Elke Fröhlich, and Falk Wiesemann, eds. *Bayern in der NS-*

Zeit. Soziale Lage und politisches Verhalten der Bevölkerung im Spiegel vertraulicher Berichte. Munich: R. Oldenburg Verlag, 1977.

Browder, George C. "Die Anfänge des SD: Dokumente aus der Organisationsgeschichte des Sicherheitsdienstes des Reichsführers SS." *Vierteljahrshefte für Zeitgeschichte* 27(1979): 299–324.

Diamant, Adolf, ed. *Gestapo Frankfurt a.M. Zur Geschichte einer verbrecherischen Organisation in den Jahren 1933–1945.* Frankfurt aM: W. Steinmann & Borschen, 1988.

———. *Gestapo Leipzig. Zur Geschichte einer verbrecherischen Organisation in den Jahren 1933–1945.* Frankfurt aM: Graphica-Druck, 1990.

International Military Tribunal. *Trial of the Major War Criminals before the International Military Tribunal.* 42 vols. Nuremberg: Secretariat of the Military Tribunal, 1947–1949.

Klein, Thomas, ed. *Die Lageberichte der Geheimen Staatspolizei über die Provinz Hessen-Nassau 1933–1936.* 2 vols. Cologne: Böhlau, 1986.

von Lang, Jochem, ed. *Eichmann Interrogated.* New York: Random House, 1984.

Maurer, Ilse, and Udo Wengst, eds. *Staat und NSDAP, 1930–1932. Quellen zur Ära Brüning.* Düsseldorf: Droste Verlag, 1977.

Mlynek, Klaus, ed. *Gestapo Hannover meldet . . . Polizei und Regierungsberichte für das mittlere und südliche Niedersachsen zwischen 1933 und 1937.* Hildesheim: August Lax, 1986.

Plum, Günter. "Staatspolizei und innere Verwaltung, 1934–1936." *Vierteljahrshefte für Zeitgeschichte* 13(April): 191–224.

Poliakov, Leon, and Josef Wulf, eds. *Das Dritte Reich und seine Denker.* Berlin: Arani, 1959.

———. *Das Dritte Reich und die Juden.* Berlin: Arani, 1955.

Rürup, Reinhard, ed. *Topography of Terror. Gestapo, SS and Reichssicherheitshauptamt on the "Prinz-Albrecht-Terrain:" A Documentation.* Berlin: Willmuth Arenhövel, 1989.

Schadt, Jörg, ed. *Verfolgung und Widerstand unter dem Nationalsozialismus in Baden: Die Lageberichte der Gestapo und des Generalstaatsanwalts Karlsruhe, 1933–1940.* Stuttgart: Verlag W. Kohlhammer, 1976.

Schumann, Heinz, and Gerhard Nitzsche. "Gestapoberichte über den antifaschistischen Kampf der KPD im früheren Regierungsbezirk Aachen, 1934–1936." *Zeitschrift für Geschichtswissenschaft* 7(1959): 118–130.

Thevoz, Robert, et al., eds. *Die Geheime Staatspolizei in den preussischen Ostprovenzen, 1934–36: Pommern, 1934/35.* 2 vols. Cologne: Grote, 1974.

Timpke, Henning, ed. *Dokumente zur Gleichschaltung des Landes Hamburgs, 1933.* Frankfurt A.M.: Europaische Verlagsanstalt, 1964.

U.S. Government Printing Office. *Trials of the Major War Criminals.* 15 vols. Washington: Government Printing Office, 1946–1949.

Vollmer, Bernhard. *Volksopposition im Polizeistaat: Gestapo- und Regierungsberichte 1934–1936.* Stuttgart: Deutsche Verlags-Anstalt, 1957.

Contemporary Literature and Publications

Alquen, Gunter d'. *Die SS, Geschichte, Aufgabe und Organisation der Schutzstaffeln der NSDAP.* Berlin: Junker und Dunnhaupt Verlag, 1939.

Anonymous. *Volk und Schupo.* Cologne: Gilde Verlag, 1929.

Barck, Lothar. *Die Organisation des staatlichen Sicherheitsdienstes in Baden.* 1931.

Best, Werner. *Die Deutsche Polizei.* Darmstadt: L.C. Wittich Verlag, 1941.

———. "Die Geheime Staatspolizei." *Deutsches Recht* 6(April 1936): 125–128.

———. "Neubegrundung des Polizeirechts." *Sonderdruck aus Jahrbuch der Akademie für Deutsches Recht* 1937: 132–138.

Cantor, Nathaniel. "Recent Tendencies in Criminological Research in Germany." *Journal of Criminal Law and Criminology* 27(March 1937): 782–793.

Daluege, Kurt. *Nationalsozialistischen Kampf gegen des Verbrechertum.* Munich: F. Eher Verlag, 1936.

Frank, Hans, et al. *Grundfragen des Deutschen Polizei. Arbeitsbericht des Akademie für Deutsches Recht.* Hamburg: 1937.

———. "Rede des Reichsjustizkommissare Staatsminister Dr. Frank bei der Gründungskundgebung der Deutschen Rechtsfront in Hamburg." *Deutsches Recht* 2(July 1933): 33–36.

Gay, Willy. *Die preussische Landeskriminalpolizei.* Berlin: Kameradschaft Verlagsgesellschaft, 1928.

Gritzbach, Erich. *Hermann Göring, Werk und Mensch.* Munich: 1938. Translated by Gerald Griffen. *Hermann Goering, the Man and His Work.* London: Hurst & Blackett, 1939.

Hartenstein, Wilhelm. *Der Kampfeinsatz der Schutzpolizei bei inneren Unruhen.* Berlin-Charlottenberg: Offene Worte, 1926.

Henning (Polizeirat). "Das Wesen und die Entwicklung der politischen Polizei in Berlins." *Mitteilungen des Vereins für die Geschichte Berlins* 43(1925): 88–92.

Heydrich, Reinhard [Dieter Schwarz, pseud.] *Die Freimaurerei, Weltanschauung, Organisation und Politik.* Berlin: Eher, 1938.

———. "Die bekämpfung der Staatsfeinde." *Deutsches Recht* 6(April 1936): 121–123.

———. *Wandlungen unseres Kampfes.* Munich-Berlin: Eher Verlag, 1935.

Höhn, Reinhard. "Die Wandlung im Polizeirecht." *Deutsche Rechtswissenschaft* 1(1936): 100–123.

———. *Die Wandlung in staatsrechtlichen Denken.* Hamburg: Hanseatische Verlagsanstalt, 1934.

Honig, Fredrich. "Recent Changes in German Criminal Law." *Journal of Criminal Law and Criminology* 26(January 1936): 857–861.

Kampffmeyer, Paul. "Die politische Polizei." *Sozialistische Monatshefte* 35(1929): 23–29.

[Korrod, Walter?] *Ich kann nicht schweigen.* Zurich: Europa-Verlag, 1936.

Koschorke, Helmut, ed. *Die Polizei—einmal anders!* Mit einem Gleitwort des Reichsführers SS . . . Geschrieben von der deutschen Presse zum "Tag der deutschen Polizei." Munich: Zentralverlag der NSDAP, 1937.

———. "Von der 'Knuppelgarde' zur Volkspolizei." *Jahrbuch der Deutschen Polizei—Leipzig,* 1936.

Landecker, Werner S. "Criminology in Germany." *Journal of Criminal Law and Criminology* 31(January 1941): 551–575.

Nationalsozialistische Jahrbuch. Munich: 1934.

Plascowe, Morris. "The Organization for the Enforcement of the Criminal Law in France, Germany and England" [sic; should read Italy]. *Journal of Criminal Law and Criminology* 27(September 1936): 305–327.

Preuss, Lawrence. "Punishment by Analogy in National-Socialist Penal Law." *Journal of Criminal Law and Criminology* 26(January 1936): 847–856.

Prussia, Ministerium des Innern. *"Landeskriminalpolizei." Vorschriften für die staatliche Polizei Preussens.* Berlin: Kameradschaft Verlagsgesellschaft, 1927.

Schlierbach, Helmut. *Die politische Polizei in Preussen.* Emsdetten: H&J Lechte, 1938.

Schoenfelder, Roland. *Vom Werdern der deutschen Polizei: Ein Volksbuch.* Leipzig: Breitkopf & Härtel, 1937.

Schultze, Fiete. *Fiete Schultz—Briefe und Aufzeichnungen aus dem Gestapo-Gefängnis in Hamburg.* Berlin: Dietz, 1959.

Schuster, V.J., ed. *"Die Deutsche Polizei." Herausgabe im Auftrage des RFSSuCdDPiRMdI.* Berlin-Schöneberg: Verlag Deutsche Kultur-Wacht, 1937.

Schweder, Alfred. *Politische Polizei: Wesen und Begriff der politischen Polizei im Meternichschen System, in der Weimarer Republik und im nationalsozialistischen Staate.* Berlin: Carl Heymanns Verlag, 1937.

Sonderegger, Rene, ed. *Mördzentrale X. Enthüllungen und Dokumente über die Auslandstätigkeit der deutschen Gestapo.* Zurich: Reso-Verlag, 1936.

Stephen, Otto (Polizeirat). "Polizei und Wehrmacht." *Die Polizei* 19(July 20, 1922): 143–146.

Numerous other articles from *Die Polizei* and other police journals, articles and clippings from *Völkische Beobachter, Schwartze Korps* and other contemporary newspapers will be found in the endnotes.

Memoirs, Apologia, Inside Exposés

Best, Werner. *Dänemark in Hitlers Hand. Der Bericht des Reichs bevollmächtigten Werner Best über seine Besatzungspolitik in Dänemark mit Studien über Hitler, Göring, Himmler, Heydrich, Ribbentrop, Canaris u.a.* Edited by Siegfried Matlok. Husum: Husum Verlag, 1988.

Diels, Rudolf. *Lucifer ante Portas. Es spricht der erste Chef der Gestapo.* Zurich: Interverlag, 1950(?) (Also a Stuttgart edition, 1950).

Dodd, Martha. *Through Embassy Eyes.* New York: Harcourt Brace, 1939.

Dodd, William E., Jr., and Martha Dodd, eds. *Ambassador Dodd's Diary, 1933–1938.* New York: Harcourt Brace, 1941.

Friedensburg, Ferdinand. *Die Weimarer Republik.* Berlin: C. Habel, 1946.

Gisevius, Hans B. *Bis zum Bittern Ende.* 2 vols. Hamburg: Classen & Goverts, 1947. Translated as *To the Bitter End.* London: Alden, 1948.

———. *Wo ist Nebe? Erinnerungen an Hitlers Kriminaldirektor.* Zurich: Drömer, 1966.

Goebbels, Josef. *Die Tagebücher von Josef Goebbels. Sämtliche Fragement.* Edited by Elke Fröhlich. 4 vols. Munich: K.G. Sauer, 1987.

Grezesinski, Albert C. *Inside Germany.* Translated by Alexander S. Lipschitz. New York: E.P. Dutton, 1939.

Heydrich, Lina. *Leben mit einem Kriegsverbrecher* Pfaffenhofen: W. Ludwig, 1976.

Hoettl, Wilhelm. *The Secret Front: The Story of Nazi Political Espionage.* Translated by R.H. Stevens. New York: Praeger, 1954.

Kersten, Felix. *The Kersten Memoirs, 1940–1945.* New York: Macmillan, 1957.

Koehler, Hansjürgen [pseud.]. *Inside the Gestapo.* London: Pallas, 1940.

——. *Inside Information.* London: Pallas Publishing, 1940.

Orb, Heinrich [pseud.]. *Nationalsozialismus. 13 Jahr Machtrausch.* Olten: Otto Walter, 1945.

Papen, Franz von. *Memoirs.* Translated by Brian Connell. New York: Dutton, 1953.

Peis, Günter. *The Man Who Started the War.* London: Odhams, 1960.

Schäfer, Karl. *20 Jahre im Polizeidienst (1925–1945).* Frankfurt aM: Decker & Wilhelm, 1977.

Schellenberg, Walter. *The Schellenberg Memoirs.* Edited and translated by Louis Hagen. London: Andre Deutsch, 1956.

——. *Memoiren.* Cologne: Verlag für Politik und Wirtschaft, 1959.

Severing, Karl. *Mein Lebensweg.* 2 vols. Cologne: Greven Verlag, 1950.

Personal Correspondence and Unpublished Materials by Participants

d'Alquen, Gunter. Letters to the author, 14 June and 24 July 1978.

Best, Werner. Materials made available through Shlomo Aronson: Beantwortung des Fragebogens (Aronson); Beantwortung der Fragen in (Aronson) Schreiben von 3.12.1964.

——. Letters to the author, 2 April, 28 May, 1977, 21 July 1978, 10 August 1980.

Hoettl, Wilhelm. Material made available through Peter Black: Protokoll eines Interviews mit Herrn Dr. Wilhelm Hoettl, am 14. und 15. April 1977; Letter, 8 November 1977.

Leffler, Paul. "Auszug aus dem Bericht des Dipl.-Ing. Paul Leffler über des SD." Made available by Best through Aronson.

Mehlhorn, Herbert. "Antwort—Dr. Mehlhorn auf Fragebogen vom 20. November 1965." Made available by Aronson.

Molke, Freya von. Letters to author, January 25 and February 5, 1990.

Neumann, Hans-Henrick. Letter to author, 9 December 1986.

Subsequent Literature

Unpublished Materials

Banach, Jens. "Das Führerkorps der Sicherheitspolizei und des SD 1936–1945. Vorstellung erster Ergebnisse." Paper presented at the Gestapo-Tagung, October 4–7, 1995, Salzau bei Kiel.

Browder, George C. "SIPO und SD, 1931–1940: The Formation of an Instrument of Power." Ph.D. diss., University of Wisconsin, Madison, 1968.

Fricke, Peter. "Anfänge und Organisation der Nachrichtenstelle bei der Polizeidirektion Bremen." Dienstlicher Bericht im Rahmen der Laufbahnprüfung für den gehobenen Archivdienst des Landes Bremen, 1966.

McGee, James H. "The Political Police in Bavaria, 1919–1936." Ph.D. diss., University of Florida, 1980.

Sengatta, Hans-Jürgen. "Der Reichsstatthalter in Lippe 1933–1936." Wissenschaftliche Hausarbeit zur Erlangung der Befähigung für des Lehramt an Gymnasium, Technische Universität Hannover, n.d.

Stokes, Lawrence D. "The Sicherheitsdienst (SD) of the Reichsführer SS and German Public Opinion." Ph.D. diss., Johns Hopkins University, 1972.

Sydnor, Charles W. "Executive Instinct: Reinhard Heydrich and the Planning for the Final Solution." Paper presented at the Inaugural Conference of the Holocaust Research Foundation of the U.S. Holocaust Memorial Museum, Washington, D.C., December 6, 1993.

Ziegler, Herbert F. "The SS Führer Korps: An Analysis of Its Socioeconomic and Demographic Structure, 1925–1939." Ph.D. diss., Emory University, 1980.

Books and Articles

Arnau, Frank [Heinrich Schmitt]. *Das Auge des Gesetzes. Macht und Ohnmacht der Kriminalpolizei.* Düsseldorf and Vienna: Econ Verlag, 1962.

Aronson, Shlomo. *The Beginnings of the Gestapo System: The Bavarian Model in 1933.* Jerusalem: Israel University Press, 1969.

———. *Reinhard Heydrich und die Frühgeschichte von Gestapo und SD.* Stuttgart: Deutsche Verlags-Anstalt, 1971.

Augstein, Rudolf, et al. "Das Spiel ist aus—Arthur Nebe." *Der Spiegel* 3, 4(1949–1950).

Beamten der Geheimen Staatspolizei, Die. Denkschrift des Bundes Deutscher Polizeibeamter e.V. Kassel, 1953.

Beneke, Paul. "Die Rolle der 'Gestapo'." *Weg* (Buenos Aires) 10(1956): 353–358, 476–480.

Berlekamp, Brigitte, and Werner Röhr, eds. *Terror, Herrschaft und Alltag im Nationalsozialismus: Probleme einer Sozialgeschichte des deutschen Faschismus.* Münster: Westfälisches Dampfboot, 1995.

Bessel, Richard. "Policing, Professionalism and Politics in Weimar Germany." In *Policing Western Europe,* edited by Clive Emsley and Barbara Weinberger. New York: Greenwood Press, 1991.

Black, Peter R. *Ernst Kaltenbrunner: Ideological Soldier of the Third Reich.* Princeton: Princeton University, 1984.

Blaudau, Kuno. *Gestapo-Geheim! Widerstand und Verfolgung in Duisberg 1933–1945.* Bonn: Verlag Neue Gesellschaft, 1973.

Boas, Jacob. "A Nazi Travels to Palestine." *History Today* 30(January 1980): 33–38.

Boehnert, Gunnar C. "An Analysis of the Age and Education of the SS Führerkorps, 1925–1939." *Historical Social Research* 12 (October 1979): 4–17.

———. "Jurists in the SS-Führerkorps, 1925–1939." In *Der Führerstaat, Mythos und Realität: Studien zur Struktur und Politik des Dritten Reiches,* edited by Gerhard Hirschfeld and Lothar Kettenacher. Stuttgart: Kett-Cotta, 1981.

Bowlby, Chris. "Blutmai 1929: Police, Parties and Proletarians in a Berlin Confrontation." *The Historical Journal* 29(1): 137–158 (1986).

Bracher, Karl D., Wolfgang Sauer, and Gerhard Schulz. *Die natio-*

nalsozialistische Machtergreifung: Studien zur Errichtung des totalitaren Heerschaftssystem in Deutschland 1933/34. Cologne: Westdeutsche Verlag, 1960.

Bramstedt, Ernst K. *Dictatorship and Political Police.* London: Kegan Paul, 1945.

Breitman, Richard. *The Architect of Genocide: Himmler and the Final Solution.* New York: Knopf, 1990.

Brissaud, André. *The Nazi Secret Service.* New York: W.W. Norton & Company, 1974.

Broszat, Martin. "Politische Denunziationen in der NS-Zeit." *Archivalische Zeitschrift* 73(1977): 221–238.

Browder, George C. *Foundations of the Nazi Police State: The Formation of Sipo and SD.* Lexington: University Press of Kentucky, 1990.

———. "The Numerical Strength of the Sicherheitsdienst des RFSS." *Historical Social Research* 28(October 1983): 30–41.

———. "The SD: The Significance of Organization and Image," in *Police Forces in History,* edited by George L. Mosse. London: SAGE Publications, 1975.

Buchheim, Hans, Martin Broszat, Hans-Adolf Jacobsen, and Helmut Krausnick. *Anatomie des SS-Staates.* 2 Vols. Olten und Freiburg: Walter-Verlag, 1965. Translated as *Anatomy of the SS State.* New York: Walker and Company, 1968.

Bühler, Karlheinz. "Landespolizei Mecklenburg-Schweren und Mecklenburg-Strelitz, 1919–1935." *Zeitschrift für Heereskunde* 51 (330): 49–52 (1987).

Calic, Edouard. *Reinhard Heydrich: The Chilling Story of the Man Who Masterminded the Nazi Death Camps.* New York: William Morrow, 1985.

Crankshaw, Edward. *Gestapo: Instrument of Tyranny.* New York: Dell Publishing, 1965.

Danner, Lother. *Ordnungspolizei Hamburg: Betrachtung zu ihrer Geschichte, 1918 bis 1933.* Hamburg: Verlag Deutsche Polizei, 1958.

Delarue, Jacques. *The Gestapo: A History of Horror.* New York: Dell Publishing, 1965.

Deschner, Günther. *Reinhard Heydrich: Statthalter der totalen Macht.* Esslingen: Bechtle, 1977. Translated as *Reinhard Heydrich: A Biography.* New York: Stein and Day, 1981.

Desroches, Alain. *La Gestapo: Atrocités et secrets de l'inquistion Nazie.* Paris: Ed. de Vecchi, 1972.

Dicks, Henry V. *Licensed Mass Murder: A Socio-Psychological Study of Some SS Killers.* New York: Basic Books, 1972.

Domröse, Ortwin. *Der NS-Staat in Bayern von der Machtergreifung bis zum Röhm-Putsch.* Munich: R. Wölfle, 1974.

Döscher, Hans-Jürgen. "Geheime Staatspolizei und allgemeine Verwaltung im Regierungsbezirk Stade." *Stader Jahrbuch* 42(1972): 70–90.

Emsley, Clive, and Barbara Weinberger, eds. *Policing Western Europe: Politics, Professionalism and Public Order, 1850–1940.* New York: Greenwood Press, 1991.

Fairchild, Erika S. "Women Police in Weimar: Professionalism, Politics and Innovation in Police Organization." *Law and Society Review* 21(3): 375–402 (1987).

Gayer, Michael. "National Socialist Germany: The Politics of Information." In *Knowing One's Enemies: Intelligence Assessment before the Two World Wars*, edited by Ernest R. May. Princeton: Princeton University, 1984.

Gellately, Robert. *The Gestapo in German Society: Enforcing Racial Policy, 1933–1945*. Oxford: Oxford University, 1990.

Gordon, Harold J. "Police Careers in the Weimar Republic." In *Proceedings of the Citadel Symposium on Hitler and the National Socialist Era*, edited by Michael B. Barrett, 160–169. Charleston, S.C.: Citadel Development Foundation, 1982.

Graf, Christoph. *Politische Polizei zwischen Demokratie und Diktatur: Die Entwicklung der preussischen Politischen Polizei vom Staatsschutzorgan der Weimarer Republik zum Geheimen Staatspolizeiamt des Dritten Reiches*. Berlin: Colloquium, 1983.

Harnischmacher, Robert, and Arved Semerek. *Deutsche Polizeigeschichte*. Stuttgart: W. Kohlhammer, 1986.

Hey, Bernd. "Zur Geschichte der westfälischen Staatspolizeistellen und der Gestapo." *Westfälische Forschungen* 37(1987): 58–90.

Höhne, Heinz. *Der Orden unter dem Totenkopf: Die Geschichte der SS*. Gütersloh: Sigbert Mohn, 1967.

Hunold, Tanis. *Polizei in der Reform*. Düsseldorf/Vienna: Econ Verlag, 1968.

Irving, David. *Das Reich hört mit. Görings "Forschungsamt": Der geheimste Nachrichtendienst des Dritten Reich*. Kiel: Arndt, 1989.

Jellonnek, Burkhard. *Homosexuelle unter dem Hakenkreuz: Die Verfolgung von Homosexuellen im Dritten Reich*. Paderborn: Ferdinand Schöningh, 1990.

Johnson, Eric A. "German Women and Nazi Justice: Their Role in the Process from Denunciation to Death." *Historical Social Research* 20(1995):33–69.

Kaestl, Claus. "Reich und Länderpolizei in der Weimarer Republik." *Die Polizei* 53(October 1962): 302–305.

Kammler, Jörg. "Nationalsozialistische Machtergreifung und Gestapo: Am Beispiel der Staatspolizeistelle für Regierungsbezirk Kassel" In *Hessen unterm Hakenkreutz: Studien zur Durchsetzung der NSDAP in Hessen*, edited by Eike Henning. Frankfurt aM: Insel, 1983.

Koch, Horst-Adelbert. "Zur Orgaisationsgeschichte der Deutschen Polizei, 1927–1939." *Feldgrau* 5, 6(1957, 1958).

Koehl, Robert L. *The Black Corps: The Structure and Power Struggles of the Nazi SS*. Madison: University of Wisconsin, 1983.

———. "Was There an SS Officer Corps?" *Proceedings of the Citadel Symposium on Hitler and the National Socialist Era, 24–25 April 1980*, edited by Michael B. Barrett. Charleston, S.C.: The Citadel Development Foundation, 1982.

Kohler, Eric D. "The Crisis of the Prussian Schutzpolizei, 1920–1932." In *Police Forces in History*, edited by George L. Mosse, 131–150. London: SAGE Publications, 1975.

Kotze, Hildegard von. "Hitlers Sicherheitsdienst im Ausland: Belege zur Zeitgeschichte II." *Die Politische Meinung* 8 (1963): 75–80.

Kren, George, and Leon Rappaport. "SS Atrocities: A Psychological Perspective." *History of Childhood Quarterly* 3(1975): 130–137.

Kurz, Thomas. "Arbeiter Mörder und Putschisten. Der Berliner 'Blutmai' von 1929 als Kristallistionspunkt des Verhältnisses von KPD und SPD vor der

Katastrophe." *Internationale Wissenschaftliche Korrespondenz zur Geschichte der Deutschen Arbeiterbewegung* 22(3): 297–317 (1986).

Lang, Jochen von. *Die Gestapo. Instrument des Terrors.* Hamburg: Rasch und Röhring Verlag, 1990.

Levine, Herbert S. "A Jewish Collaborator in Nazi Germany: The Strange Career of Georg Kareski, 1933–37." *Central European History* 8(September 1975): 251–281.

Liang, Hsi-Huey. *The Berlin Police Force in the Weimar Republic.* Berkeley: University of California, 1970.

———. *The Rise of Modern Police and the European State System from Metternich to the Second World War.* Cambridge: Cambridge University Press, 1992.

Mader, Julius. "Eichmanns Chef ist Bonner 'Gesandter z. WV'." *Deutsche Aussenpolitik.* 8(5): 405–409 (1963).

Mallmann, Klaus-Michael, and Gerhard Paul, eds. *Gestapo: Mythos und Realität.* Darmstadt: Wissenschaftliche-Buchgesellschaft, 1995.

———. *Herrschaft und Alltag: Ein Industrierevier im Dritten Reich.* Bonn: J.H.W. Dietz Nachf., 1991.

———. "Omniscient, Omnipotent, Omnipresent? Gestapo, Society and Resistance." In *Nazism and German Society, 1933–1945,* edited by David F. Crew. London: Routledge, 1994.

Mann, Reinhard. *Protest und Controlle im Dritten Reich: Nationalsozialistische Herrschaft im alltag einer rheinischen Grossstadt.* Frankfurt: Campus Verlag, 1987.

Marssolek, Inge, and Rene Ott. *Bremen im Dritten Reich: Anpassung—Widerstand—Verfolgung.* Bremen: Schünemann Verlag, 1986.

Mayer, Milton. *The Thought They Were Free: The Germans, 1933–45.* Chicago: University of Chicago Press, 1955.

Neusüss-Hunkel, Erminhild. *Die SS.* Marburg: Norddeutsche, 1956.

Nippert, Erwin. *Prinz-Albrecht-Strasse 8.* Berlin: Militärverlag der DDR, 1988.

Prinz, Arthur. "The Role of the Gestapo in Obstructing and Promoting Jewish Emigration." *Yad Vashem Studies on the European Jewish Catastrophe and Resistance* (1958): 205–218.

Raible, Eugene. *Geschichte der Polizei.* Stuttgart: Richard Boorberg Verlag, 1963.

Ramme, Alwin. *Der Sicherheitsdienst der SS. Seine Stellung in der faschistischen Diktatur unter besonderer Berücksichtigung seiner Besatzungspolitischen Funktionen im sogenannten Generalgouvernement Polen.* Berlin: Deutsche Militärverlag, 1970.

Reeifner, Udo, and Bernd-Rüdeger Sonnen, eds. *Strafjustiz und Polizei im Dritten Reich.* Frankfurt: Campus Verlag, 1984.

Reitlinger, Gerald. *The SS, Alibi of a Nation, 1922–1945.* New York: Viking Press, 1957.

Richardi, Hans-Günther. *Schule der Gewalt. Die Anfänge des Konzentrationslager Dachau 1933–1934.* Munich: Verlag C.H. Beck, 1983.

Richardson, James F. "Berlin Police in the Weimar Republic: A Comparison with Police Forces in Cities of the United States." In *Police Forces in History,* edited by George L. Mosse, 79–93. London: SAGE Publications, 1975.

Ritter, Gerhard. "The German Professor in the Third Reich." *Review of Politics* 8(April 1946): 242–254.

Rubehn. "Der Dienst in der Geheimen Staatspolizei." *Zeitschrift für Beamtenrecht und Beamtenpolitik* 6(1958): 270–276.

Safrian, Hans. *Die Eichmann-Männer.* Vienna and Zurich: Europaverlag, 1993.

Schilde, Kurt, and Johannes Tuchel. *Columbia-Haus: Berliner Konzentrationslager 1933–1936.* Berlin: Hentritch, 1990.

Schleunes, Karl A. *The Twisted Road to Auschwitz: Nazi Policy toward the Jews, 1933–1939.* Urbana: University of Illinois Press, 1970.

Schwarze, Johannes. *Die bayerisches Polizei und ihre historische Funktion bei der Aufrechterhaltung der öffentlichen Sicherheit in Bayern von 1919–1933.* Munich: Kommissionbuchhandlung R. Wölfle, 1977.

Schwarzwälder, Herbert. *Die Machtergreifung der NSDAP in Bremen 1933.* Bremen: Schünemann, 1966.

Sereny, Gitta. *Into that Darkness: An Examination of Conscience.* New York: Random House, 1974.

Siggemann, Jürgen. *Die kasernierte Polizei und das Problem der inneren Sicherheit in der Weimarer Republik: Eine Studie zum Auf- und Ausbau der innerstaatlichen Sicherheitssystems in Deutschland, 1918/19–1933.* Frankfurt aM: R.G. Fischer Verlag, 1980.

Smith, Arthur L., Jr. "Life in Wartime Germany: Colonel Ohlendorf's Opinion Service." *Public Opinion Quarterly* 1(Spring 1972): 1–7.

Sowade, Hanno. "Otto Ohlendorf—Nonkonformist, SS-Führer und Wissenschaftsfunktionär." In *Die Braune Elite: 22 biographische Skizzen,* edited by Ronald Smelser and Rainer Zittleman, 188–200. Darmstadt: Wissenschaftliche Buchgesellschaft, 1989.

Steiner, John M. *Power Politics and Social Change in National Socialist Germany: A Process of Escalation into Mass Destruction.* Atlantic Highlands, N.J.: Humanities Press, 1976.

———. "The SS Yesterday and Today: A Sociopsychological View." In *Survivors, Victims, and Perpetrators: Essays on the Nazi Holocaust,* edited by Joel E. Dimsdale. Washington: Hemisphere, 1980.

Stokes, Lawrence D. "Otto Ohlendorf, the Sicherheitsdienst and Public Opinion in Nazi Germany." In *Police Forces in History,* edited by George L. Mosse, 231–261. London: SAGE, 1975.

Terhorst, Leo. *Polizeiliche planmässige Überwachung und polizeiliche Vorbeugungshaft im Dritten Reich.* Heidelberg: C.F. Müller Juristischer Verlag, 1985.

Teufel, Manfred. "Die geschichtliche Entwicklung der Kriminalpolizei—unter besondere Berucksichtigung der Verhältnisse in Baden-Württemberg." *Das Polizeiblatt* 34(June/July 1971): 87–106.

Tuchel, Johannes. *Konzentrationslager. Organisationsgeschichte und Funktion der "Inspektion der Konzentrationslager" 1934–1938.* Boppard a.R.: Harald Boldt Verlag, 1991.

——— and Reinhold Schattenfroh. *Zentrale des Terrors. Prinz-Albrecht-Strasse 8: Hauptquartier der Gestapo.* Berlin: Siedler, 1987.

Ullrich, Wolfgang. *Verbrechensbekämpfung. Geschichte, Organisation, Rechtsprechung.* Berlin, Luchterhand, 1961.

Unger, A. L. "The Public Opinion Reports of the Nazi Party." *Public Opinion Quarterly* 29(1965/66): 565–582.

Wall, Donald D. "The Reports of the Sicherheitsdienst on the Church and Religious Affairs in Germany, 1933–1944." *Church History* 40(1971): 437–456.

Wehner, Bernd. *Dem Täter auf der Spur: Die Geschichte der deutschen Kriminalpolizei.* Bergisch Gladbach: Gustav Lübbe Verlag, 1983.

Weyrauch, Walter O. "Gestapo Informants: Facts and Theory of Undercover Operations." *Columbia Journal of Transnational Law* 24(1986): 554–596.

———. *Gestapo V-Leute: Tatsachen und Theorie des Geheimdienstes; Untersuchungen zur Geheimen Staatspolizei während der nationalsozialistischen Herrschaft.* Frankfurt a.M.: Fischer Taschenbuch, 1992.

Wighton, Charles. *Heydrich, Hitler's Most Evil Henchman.* London: Odhams Press, 1962.

Wilde, Harry. "Rudolf Diels—Porträt einer verkannten Mannes." *Politische Studien* 9(1959): 475–481.

Zaika, Siegfried. *Polizeigeschichte. Die Exekutive im Lichte der historischen Konflikforschung.* Lübeck: Schmidt Römhild, 1979.

Ziegler, Herbert F. *Nazi Germany's New Aristocracy: The SS Leadership, 1925–1939.* Princeton: Princeton University, 1989.

Zipfel, Friedrich. "Gestapo und SD in Berlin." *Jahrbuch für die Geschichte Mittel und Ostdeutschlands* 10(1961): 263–292.

———. *Gestapo und Sicherheitsdienst.* Berlin-Grunewald: Arani Verlag, 1960.

Index